IRRATIONALITY

 Francisco Goya, *The Sleep of Reason Engenders Monsters* (1799).

IRRATIONALITY

A HISTORY OF THE
DARK SIDE OF REASON

JUSTIN E. H. SMITH

PRINCETON UNIVERSITY PRESS
PRINCETON AND OXFORD

Requests for permission to reproduce material from this work
should be sent to permissions@press.princeton.edu

Published by Princeton University Press
41 William Street, Princeton, New Jersey 08540
6 Oxford Street, Woodstock, Oxfordshire OX20 1TR

press.princeton.edu

Library of Congress Control Number: 2018953426
ISBN 978-0-691-17867-7

British Library Cataloging-in-Publication Data is available

Editorial: Rob Tempio, Matt Rohal
Production Editorial: Lauren Lepow
Text Design: Leslie Flis
Jacket Design: Amanda Weiss
Production: Jacqueline Poirier
Publicity: Julia Haav, Katie Lewis

This book has been composed in Arno with DIN Pro and
DIN 1451 Engschrift display

Printed on acid-free paper. ∞

Printed in the United States of America

10 9 8 7 6 5 4 3 2 1

This book is dedicated to the memory of
Kenneth Von Smith (1940–2016)

For to every philosophy there are certain rear parts, very important parts, and these, like the rear of one's head, are best seen by reflection.

—HERMAN MELVILLE, *The Confidence-Man* (1857)

CONTENTS

➤➤➤➤➤

IRRATIONALITY

A Mathematician's Murder

➤➤➤➤➤

THE GULF OF TARANTO, FIFTH CENTURY BCE. They held his head under the sea until the life-breath ebbed out of him. The four of them had been chosen by the leader himself, from among the least learned of the sect, brawny men whose lack of comprehension in mathematics was compensated by their zeal for enforcing loyalty. They were instructed to wait for their poor victim to go to the side of the boat to pull up the nets, and to not let up until his limbs had ceased to twitch. He never saw what was coming, passed straight from eager thoughts of the pickerel and mullet about to appear as he heaved the wet ropes onboard, to horrid vision of death.

One does not betray the secrets of the sect, least of all when these secrets undermine the foundations upon which the sect is built. But this is what Hippasus had done. Word got out, among those who do not wear the robes, among those who laugh at the Pythagoreans, about a little problem with the way things, so to speak, add up. The world cannot be built up from numbers, from proportions, from ratio—from reason—because, they had begun to say, mathematics is rotten at its core. If the world is built up from numbers, then it must be as irrational as they are. This is what the sect had lately discovered from the diagonal of a square: it is incommensurable with the square's side. If you try to calculate it, you will end up with a decimal series that has no natural end. How can that be? If there is no determinate fact about what that number is, how can it possibly be the number that characterizes a particular thing in the world? No, this is wrong. It is irrational. Whoever leaks it must surely die.

>>>>>

It is from Iamblichus that we initially learn a version of this legend: the drowning of Hippasus of Metapontum, a Pythagorean philosopher who flourished, for a while, a century or so before Socrates. The first recorder of this legend, writing seven centuries later, tells us that Hippasus was thrown into the sea not by his fellow sect members, but by the gods, and he seems to believe that it was not for the crime of divulging the nature of irrationality, but rather for teaching to non–sect members the less controversial art of inscribing a dodecahedron in a sphere.[1] Centuries after Iamblichus, Pappus of Alexandria, in the fourth century CE, seems to be the one who first suggests, almost a millennium after the fact, that Hippasus was intentionally killed for revealing the mystery of the diagonal of the square.[2] It almost certainly never happened, but like any good legend it does not need to have happened in fact in order to convey its profound lesson.

The mythological parallels for this story are many, but it is hard not to think of it as a sort of philosophical analogue to the opening scene of Stanley Kubrick's 1969 film *2001: A Space Odyssey*, the moment when a protohuman creature discovers its own power to use a bone as a weapon, first to kill a lowly tapir, and then to dominate or kill its fellow hominid rivals. Scientific discoveries, technological innovations, cognitive breakthroughs: all mark a step forward for human rationality, even if as a rule they also serve as an engine of new violence, providing the means for new forms of it that the world had not previously known. Rationality and brutality, then, are the twin poles of human history, and each new innovation—weapons from bones, the control of fire, writing, gunpowder, the internet—adds to the stockpiles of each. In both of the essentially fictional cases we have evoked, that of the hominids and that of the Greeks, something in the protagonist clicks, and then he is, or we are, doomed. This clicking is sometimes represented in myth, as in the case of Pandora, as an opening of an external box, but it would be more accurate to imagine it as an internal event, an epiphany, a breaking-through, after which nothing is the same.

New power carries with it new danger, and new occasions for violence. Such examples could easily be multiplied from the history of science and technology, of marvelous theoretical discoveries that are at the same time the beginnings of new chapters of human destructiveness. This is the tragic arc of science, discerned by James Merrill in his 1982 poem *The Changing Light at Sandover*, when he writes of the "powers at the heart of matter" that we "have hacked through thorns to kiss awake," and that

> Will open baleful, sweeping eyes, draw breath
> And speak new formulae of megadeath.[3]

This last term, which would inspire the name of a well-known thrash-metal band, is in fact a unit of measurement, designating one million human deaths by nuclear explosion. The possibility of doing real reckoning with such units, Merrill understands, cannot be separated from our desire to probe into nature and to understand, by reason, its workings. Tool use, geometry, theoretical physics: all seem to be alike in that they have brought out the best and the worst in us. Correlatively, a sober assessment of human history suggests neither progress nor degeneration, but an eternally fixed balance of problem solving and problem creating. Occasions for the employment of the most exalted faculties of the human mind have also been occasions for the flexing of muscle and, when this is not enough, the raining down of blows.

The case of Hippasus, on Pappus's telling, is in some respects just another in this long and repetitive history, yet there is also something special about it that sets it apart. The discoveries that gave us nuclear weapons did not reveal anything irrational about how the world works; we already knew that the world consists of many things that are too hot or too cold, too corrosive or cutting, to be compatible with human life. These discoveries only afforded us more opportunities to be vicious to one another, and at a greater scale. The discovery of irrational numbers is more poignant, as it involves a group of people, the Pythagoreans, dedicated to a sort of worship of rationality as exemplified in mathematics, who study mathematics precisely as an expression of this worship, and who unwittingly uncover the irrationality at the heart of

the very thing they took as their object of worship, unleashing irrational violence on one of their own as a result. This sequence of steps
takes us out of the history of science and technology narrowly conceived, and into a social and political history whose chapters are often
characterized by just this sort of dialectical motion: from commitment
to an ideal, to the discovery within the movement of an ineradicable
strain of something antithetical to that ideal, to, finally, descent into
that opposite thing.

This is the history of rationality, and therefore also of the irrationality that twins it: exaltation of reason, and a desire to eradicate its opposite; the inevitable endurance of irrationality in human life, even,
and perhaps especially—or at least especially troublingly—in the
movements that set themselves up to eliminate irrationality; and, finally, the descent into irrational self-immolation of the very currents
of thought and of social organization that had set themselves up as
bulwarks against irrationality. At the individual level irrationality
manifests itself as dreams, emotion, passion, desire, affect, enhanced
by drugs, alcohol, meditation; at the social level it is expressed as religion, mysticism, storytelling, conspiracy theory, sports fandom, riot-
ing, rhetoric, mass demonstrations, sexuality when it bursts out of its
prescribed roles, music when it breaks away from the notes on the sheet
and takes on a life of its own. It encompasses the greater part of human
life and has probably governed most periods of human history. Perhaps
it has always reigned, while the historical periods in which human
beings convince themselves that they are successfully keeping it at bay
are few and far between.

Introduction

>>>>>

Reason's Twin

For the past few millennia, many human beings have placed their hopes for rising out of the mess we have been born into—the mess of war and violence, the pain of unfulfilled passions or of passions fulfilled to excess, the degradation of living like brutes—in a single faculty, rumored to be had by all and only members of the human species. We call this faculty "rationality," or "reason." It is often said to have been discovered in ancient Greece, and was elevated to an almost divine status at the beginning of the modern period in Europe. Perhaps no greater emblem of this modern cult can be found than the "Temples of Reason" that were briefly set up in confiscated Catholic churches in the wake of the French Revolution of 1789. This repurposing of the august medieval houses of worship, at the same time, shows what may well be an ineliminable contradiction in the human effort to live our lives in accordance with reason, and to model society on rational principles. There is something absurd, indeed irrational, about giving reason its own temples. What is one supposed to do in them? Pray? Bow down? But aren't these the very same prostrations that worshippers had previously performed in the churches, from which we were supposed to be liberated?

Any triumph of reason, we might be expected to understand these days, is temporary and reversible. Any utopian effort to permanently set things in order, to banish extremism and to secure comfortable quiet lives for all within a society constructed on rational principles, is doomed from the start. The problem is, again, evidently of a dialectical nature, where the thing desired contains its opposite, where every earnest stab at rationally building up society crosses over sooner or later, as if by some natural law, into an eruption of irrational violence. The harder we struggle for reason, it seems, the more we lapse into unreason. The desire to impose rationality, to make people or society more rational, mutates, as a rule, into spectacular outbursts of irrationality. It either triggers romantic irrationalism as a reaction, or it induces in its most ardent promoters the incoherent idea that rationality is something that may be imposed by force or by the rule of the enlightened few over the benighted masses.

This book proceeds through an abundance of illustrations and what are hoped to be instructive ornamentations, but the argument at its core is simple: that it is irrational to seek to eliminate irrationality, both in society and in our own exercise of our mental faculties. When elimination is attempted, the result is what the French historian Paul Hazard memorably called *la Raison aggressive*, "aggressive Reason."[1]

Enlightenment into Myth

The continuous movement between the two poles of rationality and irrationality—the aggressive turn that reason takes, transforming into its opposite—is described in compelling detail by Theodor Adorno and Max Horkheimer in their monumental 1944 work *Dialectic of Enlightenment*.[2] Composed in Californian exile as the war unleashed by the Nazi regime was raging in their home country and largely destroying the civilization that had formed them, theirs is an account that need not be repeated, and that cannot be bettered. The German authors are particularly interested in how "enlightenment reverts to mythology," that is, how a social philosophy based upon the perfection and application of reason for the solution of society's problems, for the benefit of all, may transform or harden into fascism: a political ideology that involves no real exercise of reason at all, but only the application of brute force, and manipulation of the majority for the benefit of a few.

Quite a lot has happened since 1944. Adorno and Horkheimer were prescient, and remain relevant, but there is much that they could not anticipate. Marxism remains a valuable analytical tool for scholars to understand the course of global history. Revolutionary movements aiming at radical economic redistribution also continue to exercise their attraction for many people throughout the world, even as the first great attempt to establish socialism through revolution collapsed before the end of the twentieth century. In the early twenty-first century, we are still struggling to understand the new phenomenon of Trumpism-Putinism, which seems unprecedented in its ideological nebulousness, but which also seems to be a clear announcement of the end, or at least the life-threatening crisis, of liberal democracy, which had until this most recent era had its stronghold, as an aspiration and an ideal, in the United States.

Adorno and Horkheimer are credited with predicting that the iteration of liberal political ideology—which on their view only pretends to be an absence of ideology—that reigned in the mid-twentieth century had an arc that naturally bent toward fascism. Recently some have similarly argued that the current global surge of populism, locally inflected in the United States with the rise of Donald Trump, is simply the inevitable conclusion of a process. Liberal democracy molts its skin, and what emerges is variously identified as either the slick serpent of fascism or the common garden snake of populist nationalism: in either case an emergence that had been predicted decades earlier by a pair of insightful German Marxists in strange sun-kissed exile. Trump is pretending to be a successor to Washington, Jefferson, and Lincoln, but he does not care about the same things they did. The imperative to "make America great again" is grounded in a mythology of what America once was that is fundamentally incompatible with Enlightenment, with knowing who we are and where we in fact came from. Adorno and Horkheimer's formula has come true, then: Enlightenment has reverted to mythology. The German authors took this to be a problem with Enlightenment itself, though other explanations, as we will see in the chapters that follow, also present themselves.

It is not at all clear, in any case, that Trump himself is an anti-Enlightenment ideologue. He does not appear to have the requisite clarity or maturity for such a well-defined commitment. He has, however, been surrounded by such ideologues. He benefits from their support, and so has become if not an irrational agent of anti-Enlightenment, then at least a subrational vector of it. His rise coincides historically with the appearance in the intellectual landscape of many authors and personalities who are articulating coherent critiques of the core commitments of Enlightenment philosophy. We may summarize these commitments as follows: first, that each of us is endowed with the faculty of reason, capable of knowing ourselves and our place in the natural and social worlds; second, that the best organization of society is the one that enables us to freely use our reason in order both to thrive as individuals and to contribute in our own way to the good of society. We may wish to make some more fine-grained revisions to this rough-and-ready definition of Enlightenment, but it will be good enough for now. It will be good enough, in particular, for understanding what it is that is now under attack, by Trump and Vladimir Putin and their epigones; by the nouveaux riches of Silicon Valley who are fostering a culture of post-Enlightenment, postdemocratic values, sometimes consciously, sometimes unconsciously; and by the various thinkers who, for now, manage to position themselves within our intellectual landscape as "edgy" by rejecting such long-cherished desiderata for society as equality and democratic participation.

The dialectic of enlightenment—here I mean not the book, but the process—has been well studied, and not just by Marxists. Even the neoconservative French thinker Pascal Bruckner argued already in 1995 that individualism has tribalism as its ultimate logical terminus, since in a society based on individual freedom the individual "may have gained freedom, but he has lost security."[3] Thus the now-familiar transformation of the likes of the young computer hacker and the old cattle rancher who, circa 2008, thought of themselves as libertarians, but by 2016 were ready to sign up for a sort of statist-nationalist personality cult.

It was the liberal philosopher Isaiah Berlin who popularized the term "counter-Enlightenment" in English in a 1973 article. As Zeev Sternhell notes, the term first appears in German, as *Gegen-Aufklärung*, in Friedrich Nietzsche, and is widespread in Germany in the early twentieth century. Sternhell himself, a liberal historian of ideas, published his important study *The Anti-Enlightenment Tradition* in 2006;

there he details the significance of the work of such figures as Edmund Burke and J. G. Herder for the history of modern political thought. According to Sternhell, the two tendencies are born together in the eighteenth century, a period that "marks not only the birth of rationalist modernity, but also its antithesis."[4] To identify the thesis and antithesis as appearing together both historically and conceptually is to see counter-Enlightenment less as Enlightenment's opposite than as its twin, and to see unreason less as reason's opposite than as the dark side of a unified and indivisible whole.

As Sternhell notes, the counter-Enlightenment, as a movement and a sensibility, existed long before it was given a name. He sees the early eighteenth-century Neapolitan thinker Giambattista Vico as the first to articulate a vision of the world that values that which is irreducibly individual, as opposed to what would soon become the Enlightenment's emphasis on the importance of the universal. Sternhell's taxonomy, of who belongs to which side of the split between Enlightenment and anti-Enlightenment, is sometimes idiosyncratic, as indeed any attempt at such a taxonomy must be. For example, he identifies Jean-Jacques Rousseau as a central figure of the French Enlightenment. More recently, Pankaj Mishra, in his popular *Age of Anger: A History of the Present*, contrasts the paradigmatic Enlightenment thought of Voltaire with Rousseauian particularism as its opposite. Emblematic of their respective stances, Mishra thinks, are the positions these thinkers took up regarding the question of Poland's right to national self-determination. Voltaire, in the service and pay of Empress Catherine of Russia, believed that the Poles were a hopelessly backward and benighted people, and that this condition helped to justify a prospective military conquest of Poland by the Russian Empire. They must be brought Enlightenment by force, Voltaire thought.

Rousseau, by contrast, in his *Considerations on the Government of Poland*, written in the early 1770s, argued that Poland should maintain its own national customs and not allow itself to be absorbed into any homogenized, pan-European culture. If this sort of cultural resistance is achieved, Rousseau thinks, then even under political domination by a foreign power, a nation cannot be fully subdued or annihilated. "See to it that no Pole can ever become a Russian," he writes, and "I guarantee that Russia will not subjugate Poland."[5] Mishra takes the respective positions of these two thinkers to stand at the beginning of two very different lineages of modern thought. Voltaire's zeal for spreading Enlightenment by force, and his belief that there is, in effect, only one way to do things right, a universal standard for how society should be organized, would have as its latter-day descendants such failed adventures as the 2003 neoconservative-led invasion of Iraq. Rousseau, in turn, is the ancestor of those counterhegemonic forces that resist universalist imperialism and globalism in the twentieth and twenty-first centuries, such as Islamic fundamentalism, and such as the varieties of populism that resulted in Brexit and the election of Donald Trump.

The Enlightenment has come back into broad public attention in the United States in the past few years, promoted and celebrated by thinkers and pundits who are susceptible neither to the siren call of right-wing populism nor to indignant identitarianism, the withdrawal into identity groups and the corresponding preoccupation with hierarchies of privilege that has emerged on the left, and that has in particular captured the spirits of many American university students. Some thinkers who reject both of these poles see them as enantiomorphic expressions of the same illiberal rejection of individual reason and autonomy, and have insisted in turn on what is now sometimes described as "radical centrism." The psychologist Steven Pinker, notably, has to his credit sensed that at the present historical moment, in which there is widespread and generally unreflective dismissal on both the right and the left of the legacy of the Enlightenment, it is time to reevaluate and to defend its real contributions to human progress. Pinker's 2018 book *Enlightenment Now: The Case for Reason, Science, Humanism, and Progress* makes the case that there is much that is defensible.[6] Yet he has been rightly criticized for conflating Enlightenment philosophy with scientific rationality, whereas the historical record plainly shows that the great majority of canonical Enlightenment philosophers placed great value on the role of the sentiments and passions in guiding the conduct of our lives, and warned of the many dangers of subordinating ourselves to the supreme authority of the faculty of reason.

"Is Minsky the opposite of rationality"
What begins as rational already plants
the seeds of its future whateverths —
Introduction • 11

A less common but no less serious criticism that may be leveled at Pinker's work has to do with his apparent lack of sensibility to what we have been calling the dialectic of Enlightenment. Pinker scarcely mentions Adorno and Horkheimer, which is not necessarily a fault in itself. What is faulty, however, is the ungrounded presumption that the way in which Enlightenment entails its opposite is not worthy of serious attention in a book devoted to recovering that era's philosophical and political legacies for today's world. Failure to take this entailment seriously means not only that there is no serious reckoning with the sort of mutation, from liberalism into fascism, that interested Adorno and Horkheimer most from their perch on the left. It also leaves the Enlightenment-defender unable to account for the evident hypocrisy and limitations innate in Enlightenment discourse—the refusal, for example, of the defenders of the 1791 *Universal Declaration of the Rights of Man* to accept Olympe de Gouge's feminist riposte, the *Universal Declaration of the Rights of Woman and of the Female Citizen*; or the refusal of many French revolutionaries to accept that the values inspiring them might also quicken the slaves of Saint Domingue into revolt. There are serious arguments to the effect that these are not just glitches in a basically well-worked-out program; rather, the ways in which Enlightenment contradicts and undermines itself have been intrinsic to the project all along. Even if one rejects these arguments, they are not coming from the fringe, and they deserve to be addressed.

Much further downstream from the Enlightenment we have Jordan B. Peterson, who has appeared lately on the North American cultural scene almost as if to illustrate Adorno and Horkheimer's thesis especially for us. Peterson has claimed to be a "classic liberal," and yet the following he has garnered for himself might better be understood as the spontaneous congealing of an identitarianism for young, disaffected men. This identitarianism vividly mirrors the one being promoted on what is now sometimes called the "intersectional" left, or in the corners of the internet that are said to be "woke," that is, roughly, attuned, perhaps hyperattuned, to the ways in which racism, sexism, and other forms of oppression structure everyday social reality and define the range of every person's experiences, whether consciously aware of this or not. Peterson's fans have been effectively excluded from these woke circles (unless prepared to take on the prostrate and unctuous role of "allies"), and they flock to him seething with resentment and a newfound identitarian consciousness of their own. He is perhaps not to blame for the crowd he attracts, but, even on its own merits, his claim to be a successor to the Enlightenment fails to make much sense of what the Enlightenment in fact was, and of the many complicated branchings of its legacy. One of his enduring preoccupations is with the ravages wrought by twentieth-century state communism. Unlike Adorno and Horkheimer, who take fascism alone to be the dialectically entailed opposite of Enlightenment, Peterson takes left authoritarianism to be the opposite simply and straightforwardly, which is to say nondialectically, of the political and social philosophy he claims to prefer. What this misses, obviously, is that the various twentieth-century revolutions of workers and peasants, from the Bolsheviks in 1917 to the genocidal Cambodian regime in the late 1970s, have a real genealogical link to the philosophy articulated in the 1791 *Universal Declaration*, which may be seen as a distillation of the philosophical spirit of the Enlightenment. This is not to condemn the Enlightenment for giving us the Khmer Rouge, but only to acknowledge what should be obvious, that no one should be taken seriously in his claim to be the Enlightenment's heir who does not in turn acknowledge all the other wayward heirs, however estranged from them he may be. The Enlightenment may indeed be worth defending, but it is at least "problematic" enough, as the illiberal left has taken to saying, to obligate its serious defenders to face up to, and to attempt to account for, all of its *dérives*, all the ways it has failed to live up to its own vision of human potential.

The Present Moment

This is a book and not a social-media post, and for that reason it is perhaps unwise to engage overmuch with figures who may well have lapsed back into obscurity—from which they had briefly emerged by the power of clicks alone—in the months between final submission of the manuscript and its appearance in print. So let us try to hew close to those sources that by now appear safely canonical. However our canonical authors divide things up, and whatever the political orientation informing their historiography, Adorno and Horkheimer, Berlin, Sternhell, Mishra, and other authors agree, and compellingly show, that there has been a basic tension in the history of modern thought, between universalism and particularism: between those who think that humanity has a single destiny in virtue of a nature that is shared equally by all peoples, and those who think that each group has a *Sonderweg*—a particular path that makes what is right or fitting for it untranslatable into other contexts, and impossible to place within a hierarchical scheme that compares or ranks the attainments of one group relative to those of another. It is not my intention to recite, again, this very familiar story, even if it is inevitable that our concerns significantly intersect with the concerns of all those who have recited it so well. Historians of Enlightenment and counter-Enlightenment have typically been interested primarily in theories as to what constitutes the best ideals and values around which to organize a society. They have been, obviously, aware that reason is a value associated with the Enlightenment, while the counter-Enlightenment, if not always celebrating unreason, has at least been wary of setting its opposite up as the supreme principle of social organization. Significantly less attention has been paid by these authors, for the most part, to reason as it is conceptualized in modern philosophy, as a particular faculty of the human mind, and, in turn, to the respects in which the political philosophy of the Enlightenment—to invoke the central insight of Plato's *Republic*—is in the end a philosophy of the human soul writ large. Or, as Germaine de Staël put it in the early nineteenth century, "Maintenance of the principles that constitute the basis of the social order cannot be contrary to philosophy, since these principles are in agreement with reason."[7]

Whether or not we are justified in moving between these two scales, the soul and the city, the individual and the state, it is important to understand that as a matter of fact our contemporaries do move back

As Indexing already sowed its seed in future irrationality.

from Bogle to ETFs ⟶

and forth freely, just as Plato did, and seldom pause to ask whether the individual really is such a microcosm of society, whether what we learn of the one applies at the same time to the other. Thus, to cite a recent example from the press on the now-common theme of the effect of social media on our cognitive functioning and on social order, Paul Lewis writes in a *Guardian* article in late 2017, "If Apple, Facebook, Google, Twitter, Instagram and Snapchat are gradually chipping away at our ability to control our own minds, could there come a point, I ask, at which democracy no longer functions?"[8] Is democracy, then, the sum total of the workings of individuals who exercise control over their own minds? Is the loss of such control, which is precisely a loss of what we often call rationality, necessarily a loss, as well, of the best arrangement of society?

The history of reflection on the mental faculty of reason, on which the social philosophy of Enlightenment is supposed to be built, of course far precedes the beginning of the modern period, even if it is only in the modern period that it came to be broadly mythologized, in Adorno and Horkheimer's sense, turned retroactively into the basis of a civilization dating back to antiquity (or perhaps only retroactively dated back to antiquity), "the West," even if in its early incarnations in ancient Greece it was sooner a sort of fetish of strange cults, like the Pythagoreans, than it was a widely shared civic virtue.

Many believe that the zone we call "the West," and the values of the people in it, occupy a unique place in world history, yielding up achievements and monuments unlike those of what is sometimes disparagingly, and rhymingly, dismissed as "the rest." It is not my direct purpose here to refute this view, but perhaps a few words in that direction will be useful. At the time of the first European encounter with the Americas, Europe was a relatively insignificant—relatively unproductive, relatively unaccomplished—peninsula of Eurasia. The great centers of activity were not France, Holland, England, Germany, but rather the Mediterranean, the Middle East, central and East Asia. Europe began to become what we think of it as being, the center of the world, at the moment it entered into extremely intensive economic coexistence with the broader Atlantic region. From this moment on, moreover, Europe took it as its mission and destiny to engulf the rest of the world within its fold. There is no "West" without a non-West outside of it that is seen to be ever in need of Westernization. Europe is nothing by itself. No region of the world ever has been, or ever could be. This is not, then, a slight against Europe and its extensions, but only a matter of basic geographical and historical literacy. This is something that the most recent incarnations of extreme, identitarian politics quite manifestly lack, and it is part of my purpose here to disrupt this lazy ignorance.

This ignorance has grown worse of late. Just when it might have seemed that an era of true cosmopolitanism was at hand, societies around the world have retreated into crude nationalism, and have invented or revived infantile mythopoetical explanations for their own exceptional status among the world's peoples—that the ancient Indians invented airplanes, for example, and that you can read about these in the Vedas: their own divinely or biologically ordained *Sonderweg*. Some Americans of principally or apparently European heritage have embraced a form of identitarianism that makes a fetish out of something as flimsy and as little understood as a haplotype. They have been spotted celebrating milk, of all things, as a symbol of white supremacy, both because it is itself white, and also because they vaguely understand that there was a genetic mutation among their European ancestors, some thousands of years ago, that led to a relative predominance of lactose tolerance, which in turn is thought to have conferred certain survival advantages.[9] This may in fact be how things happened in the Paleolithic, yet it is a strange source of cultural pride in the present moment, and one cannot help but seek to understand the forces that are driving it.

It is undeniable that the internet has done much to facilitate this most recent explosion of irrationalism in public life. White-supremacist dairy parties are but one of countless manifestations of what seems to be a moment of cultural frenzy, of unsustainable intensity, marking a transition to a new and still unforeseeable landscape of customs and mores, underlain by new political norms and new institutional structures. And it is those on the margins, people with nothing to lose, who are best positioned to benefit from these transformations. Anyone can get on the internet and make some noise. Anyone can troll, and change the world for the worse; and it is not hard to hope, when trolling from the margins, that out of this worsened condition new opportunities will emerge to accrue power or at least to thrive in a small-scale way. Thus the internet is the great vehicle of what has been called "accelerationism," whereby those with nothing to lose intentionally make things worse, in order that they may get better sooner, in ways that cannot be foreseen, while those who have something to lose at present also have reason to fear. This is only one of the respects in which the internet is a revolutionary tool.

Just as the internet has made possible the disruption or in some cases destruction of journalism, academia, commerce, the movie and publishing industries as we knew them, and the like, so too has it made possible a circumvention of the establishment checks determining what had previously been considered acceptable political discourse. The internet is the new transformation of the apparatus that confines, catalyzes, and accelerates the passions of the *bête humaine*, as Émile Zola characterized humanity in its new relation to the railroad in an 1890 novel of that name: a human creation that speeds up and intensifies human social life, and plows through so much of what we had previously valued, even if its initial promise was only to give us improved access to what we valued.

Only a short decade or so ago, it could still plausibly be hoped that this new forum might serve as the "public sphere" in Jürgen Habermas's sense, the locus in which deliberative democracy happens, and the best decisions are made through collective deliberation. Now it appears a far darker place, where the normal and predictable response to reasonable statements is, if it is coming from strangers, sheer abuse, and often concerted and massive campaigns of abuse; if it is coming from friends, then it is generally vacuous supportiveness, sheer boosterism with no critical engagement or respectful dissent. And unless we are dealing with people whose flesh-and-blood existence we have been able to confirm, on the internet we often do not know whether our abuse is coming from a real person at all, or only from a bot, or some sock puppet laboring away at a Russian troll farm, working to insinuate some new falsehood into public consciousness. And to make it all worse, distinctions between friend and foe have become largely a matter of algorithms working on and reinforcing our innate—but, until recently, surmountable—tendency to carve up social reality according to a binary us/them dichotomy.

Most recently, moreover, the ignorant, paranoid, and hateful spirit of unmoderated comments sections has managed to spill out into political reality, congealed in the very person of the president of the United States. The causes of this fall and this failure are numerous. In part it may be that mass participation in internet discourse, a discourse we for far too long thought of as fundamentally text-based (even though our actual practices on the internet mark a radical break in the history of textual communication), has unwittingly shifted our attention to the sort of information that is not, and cannot be, conveyed in reasoned arguments, but rather only in suggestions, images, insinuations, jokes.

Very few internet users are prepared to justify, or are at all interested in justifying, their political commitments by means of reasoned arguments. Instead, memes proliferate that associate or juxtapose ideas— Hillary Clinton is sickly; Bernie Sanders is a charmed old man with the power to attract birds to his podium when he speaks; Donald Trump would look good adorned with an imperial crown and staff—in ways that alter our perception of political reality without the occurrence of any real process of reflection. What we far too long took to be the transition of political debate into a new medium has in fact degenerated into an exchange of tropes we know from storybooks, of crones and wizards and naked emperors. These figures are so familiar and meaningful to us that we are able to forget that, as folktales, these units of culture, these memes, fulfill a human need very different from the one that political participation has been thought, at its best, to fulfill.

These units of culture satisfy the imagination, momentarily, but leave the world unimproved. They are a consolation for those who are disenfranchised from politics, not a suitable vehicle of political participation itself. When in 2016 politics became largely a matter of meme warfare, we were thrust into a situation in which, not only could we no longer pretend we were living in a deliberative democracy, but we had now abandoned even the aspiration to this, in favor of a pursuit of politics at a purely cultural level. This "politics," with memetic myths and tall folktales, has ancient roots in the free play of the imagination among people who had no hope of participating in the political life of their societies. Imagination is a powerful tool, but—as the faculty of which no one, not even the most disenfranchised and underinformed, can be deprived—it is also often deployed in desperation. The narrator of Virginia Woolf's 1929 short story "The Lady in the Looking Glass: A Reflection" describes the method available to us when we are confronted with the silent and enigmatic character of Isabella: "It was absurd, it was monstrous. If she concealed so much and knew so much one must prize her open with the first tool that came to hand—the imagination."[10] Imagination prizes things open, and we resort to it, particularly, in the absence of knowledge. Imagination is like a bright-colored dye infused into a cell on a microscope slide: it makes the invisible visible, even as it distorts and perhaps endangers the thing we had wanted to see, to know, by means of it.

To some extent, of course, politics has always played out, even in the most enlightened times, through visuals and suggestions, through hints and insinuations, and has always gone to work on us at an affective level. But new tools for carrying this work out, tools that combine both creative imagination and technical expertise, have ceded an outsized responsibility for our political destiny to the technologically literate but argumentatively subliterate, to the meme-makers, to online subcultural insiders. It should not be altogether surprising that these sectors of society were not necessarily prepared to wield their new, tremendous power in a responsible way.

We are living through a moment of extreme irrationality, of fervency and ebullience, of destabilization and fear. An important part of the story of how we arrived here seems to be the collapse of traditional safeguards for the preservation of rational procedures and deliberation, and the unwitting injection of so much colored dye into public debate as to obscure altogether the objects these colors were initially intended to bring into clearer view. Again, there are many people who

WE Define first then see ?...

Lippmann

evidently welcome this turn. It is rather those who value caution and
reserve who feel suddenly as if they belong to another era, and have
woken up to find their concerns, their habits—in short, their world—
simply gone. It is those who have a weakness for legitimation from a
crumbling establishment, from what will soon be the ancien régime,
who have the most to lose, those who seek to preserve the old way of
doing things: maintaining subscriptions to print media, publishing
books, getting humanities degrees, supporting mainstream candidates
in mainstream political parties, listening to well-reasoned arguments.
These are the people who likely feel the sharpest disappointment at
the seizure of the internet by the forces of aggression and chaos, at a
moment when we can still hear echoing, from the most recent past, the
grandest claims about its power to serve us as an engine for the rational
ordering of human life in society.

We are, then, not so far from where Hippasus found himself millennia ago. The Greeks discovered the irrationality at the heart of geometry; we have most recently discovered the irrationality at the heart
of the algorithm, or at least the impossibility of applying algorithms
to human life while avoiding their weaponization by the forces of
irrationality. If we were not possessed of such a strong will to believe
that our technological discoveries and our conceptual progress might
have the power to chase irrationality, uncertainty, and disorder from
our lives—if, that is, we could learn to be more philosophical about
our human situation—then we would likely be far better positioned to
avoid the violent recoil that always seems to follow upon our greatest
innovations, upon bagging the great hunting trophies of our reason.

Irrationality: A Road Map

In chapter 1 we consider logic, along with its limits, its abuses and
distortions. We look at the ways in which it has often been set up in
contrast to rhetoric throughout history, even if in fact it has often been
co-opted for similar ends. In this connection we consider the peculiar
and understudied phenomenon of claims or arguments that are

perfectly true from a logical point of view, but that are summoned for purposes that can only be described as dishonest—thus the phenomenon of truths that "have the operation of falsity." We go on to consider the preoccupation with fallacies and sophisms in the history of logic, and the way in which these were sometimes deployed to produce what might be considered a distorted mirror image of the science of reason, now deformed into a science of unreason. From an initial investigation of logic in a narrow sense, we move on to the adjacent domain of rational-choice theory; we investigate the many muted presuppositions about human agency and rationality this theory involves— presuppositions that patently fail to capture what is often at work in actual human decisions. We turn next to what in some senses appears as the exact opposite of logic—claims of mystical experience, in which by definition the subject is unable to formulate in shareable propositions the experience in question, and thus unable to submit claims about it to logical scrutiny. At the same time, historically speaking, mystical experience, and the way it is mobilized socially for the founding of new religious sects, has much in common with the paradox-mongering of some philosophical sects. In fact, while we think of cults as devoted to dogmas that are inscrutable or immediately false to outsiders, in fact they are also able, if not just as likely, to form around a shared interest in critical thinking or reason. Thus we see an illustration of the problem at the heart of our investigation, where devotion to reason as a supreme principle all too easily collapses into unreason.

In chapter 2 we turn to what may be called the **"no-brainer"** problem. Throughout history, there has been a certain ambiguity in the way the term "rational" is applied. It is often applied to machines, to nature as a whole, to abstract processes or systems, and (rather less commonly), to animals, where any of these things are able to function in a proper or suitable way without going haywire or breaking down. At other times, though, "rational" is reserved for human beings, and perhaps also for God and the angels, to the extent that these beings not only function properly, but also make conscious decisions. Human beings, using their brains, follow a course of deliberation to arrive at a conscious decision; this decision may turn out to be either wrong or right. Some have argued that this deliberation, and this tendency to get things wrong, make us less rational, not more, than all those things that lack brains and do not deliberate, but simply do what they do automatically in accordance with their nature. That which is considered least rational by some, then, such as a mere animal, may be considered most rational by others; and human beings, from a certain point of view, may be said to be not exemplars of reason, but faulty approximations of it. In this connection, we look in particular at some recent work on rationality as an evolved superpower, one that is flawed like many evolutionary adaptations, but still remarkable and rare in the order of nature. We turn next to some concrete illustrations of the failure of reason in human life (and in the author's life), failures that seem to be illustrations of the status of reason as a mere adaptation, one that does what it can to enable us to survive, but has its limits, and sometimes causes unexpected problems.

In chapter 3 we take on **dreams**, or, more precisely, the curious and troubling fact that about one-third of a typical human life is spent in the grip of delirious hallucinations. These often defy all of what we think we know about the rational order of the world; most troublingly of all, when we are in their grip the fact that our reason has absconded does not seem to bother us. This ineliminable feature of human life has been dealt with in different ways in different places and times, and the differences reveal much about the particular value of rationality in a given society. Aristotle remained cautiously open to the idea that dreams are prophetic. In the early modern period, Native North Americans planned their lives and structured their group decisions around dreams, which seemed illogical and even terrifying to the Europeans who encountered them. The emerging, and sharply contrasting, sensibility within Europe itself by now held that dreams were something best moved on from at the moment of awakening, while waking, in turn, now needed rigorous philosophical arguments to prove that it was not in fact dreaming. At the same time, of course, dreams would never be fully suppressed even if philosophy sought to minimize their importance. They would continue to permeate culture more broadly, and by the end of the nineteenth century they would roar back onto the scene with psychoanalysis and the purported discovery of the unconscious as the real locus of our individual identities. Throughout the previous three centuries or so, much discussion had centered on dreams, not only in the narrow sense of what we experience in sleep proper, but also any phantasm of the mind, any images produced that cannot be precisely matched to the external world, any voices heard with no speaker outside of us to be found. How to deal with these manifestations of the irrational, and where to draw the boundary between productive imagination and delusional phantasm, defined much of the discussion of rationality in modern Europe, and was central to the emergence of the cluster of ideas, or rather conceits, about modern Europe's singular place in world history.

In chapter 4 it is **art** that holds our attention, though this is not much of a departure from the concerns of the previous chapter, since the creation of artworks has often been conceptualized as the materialization of the sort of phantasms that occur inwardly in dreams. Over the course of the modern period, as dreams were pushed out of science, politics, and other domains, they were allowed to continue in the creative disciplines. In classicism art had typically, or in its best instances, been seen as a reflection of the proportions and the order that govern the natural world, and thus as part of the same mode of engagement with the world as occurs in science; in romanticism and related movements, however, there opened a gap separating creativity from understanding, and inspiration from love of order. Nowhere is this clearer than in the modern cult of the genius. While ingenium was once understood as a natural disposition to learn, perhaps not equally distributed but also not exceptionally rare, by the late nineteenth century genius came to be seen as something exceedingly rare, a capacity that goes beyond all learning. It is that ability to do things for which no rule can be given, with the resulting work seen not as a failure, but as a new form of success. Against this, there are other competing conceptions of art that are never fully suppressed, such as the archaic view that places art in the same general sphere of activity as ritual (a view with which I acknowledge considerable sympathy), and the conception of art as a vehicle for moral uplift or social progress, as is common in totalitarian societies where the creation of art becomes co-opted for the purposes of propaganda (for which, by contrast, I avow a proportional antipathy).

In chapter 5 we turn to **pseudoscience**, and so also necessarily to science, as the so-called problem of demarcation between the two domains imposes itself in any attempt to determine what exactly is to count as a spurious, or perverted, or dishonest attempt to present or pursue a given body of knowledge. Here we proceed through case studies, looking particularly at creation "science," at flat-earth theory, and at the antivaccination movement (consciously leaving out, though only for lack of space, other no less flagrant cases, including, alas, climate-change denialism). This chapter begins, like the introduction, with a discussion of Adorno, in particular his criticism of newspaper horoscopes in 1950s Los Angeles. We also consider Paul Feyerabend's well-known argument for a maximal permissiveness, promiscuity even, in our understanding of what programs of inquiry and what practices might in principle contribute to the advancement of science. We go on to explore the ways in which both of these analyses fail to capture the rather fine-grained diversity of reasons different groups of people pursue different varieties of inquiry on the margins of, or indeed in straightforward opposition to, establishment science. When we consider this diversity of reasons, we see that some pseudosciences are motivated by substantive differences between the theoretical commitments of their defenders and those of mainstream science, while others in fact have very little to do with defending any particular theory of how the natural world works at all, and are indeed little more than cover for conspiracy theories about how the social world works. Once these distinctions are made, neither Adorno's austerity nor Feyerabend's flexibility seems adequate for dealing with the challenges of pseudoscience.

In chapter 6 we take on **the Enlightenment**. Even as I write, there are armies of young people on social media vigorously debating whether this nebulous historical phenomenon was good, or rather bad. Many of them have never read a book about it, drawing what they know out of the strange and distorting filter of "weird political Twitter" and similar social-media subcultures, where ironic and jarring juxtapositions of text and image are far more persuasive than argumentation and similar online communities, but their strong opinions show at least that it continues to matter today, in a way that it perhaps has not for some time. It matters because its legacy is at a critical juncture and may well not survive. In this chapter we revisit the historical sources, at the moment and in the context of their first articulation, in order to more clearly understand what we have already identified, if cautiously, as the dialectical relationship between Enlightenment and counter-Enlightenment. We engage substantively with the critical perspective according to which, from its inception, the Enlightenment has been a parochial project that falsely proclaims its own universal legitimacy, and thus has been hypocritical or at least unforthcoming about the question of who stands to benefit from it, and what a society or an individual must give up in exchange. Of interest to us also is the way in which Enlightenment contrasts with, but also, as Adorno and Horkheimer warned, degenerates into, myth. We must consider carefully what exactly myth is, and whether it is by definition an obstacle to progress, to equality, and to the rational ordering of society. Here, in particular, Giambatista Vico's investigation of the relationship among myth, history, and poetry is particularly useful. Finally we turn to the ways in which Enlightenment values, notably free speech, can be, and in fact have been, perverted and repurposed for decidedly counter-Enlightenment ends. Knowing that this is possible, that this may even be the general tendency of such ideas, we are compelled to consider the legacy of the Enlightenment in a far more cautious way than the usual presentation of the binary options, to accept or reject, would dictate.

In chapter 7 we turn at last to **the internet**, which has been haunting us from the beginning. How, we will seek to determine, has the rise of this new form of communication distorted public debate, and what role does it have in the degeneration of the norms of rational discourse? How, moreover, has its early utopian promise evaporated so quickly, and how could commentators have been so incautious about the extent of the transformations it would bring about? We begin with a historical excursus on what may be called the prehistory of the internet, in mid-nineteenth-century telecommunications inventions both real and fraudulent, in order to show that, to some extent, the hopes that have been placed in the internet in recent years are not in fact so new, and in order to show that from the beginning the enterprise of connecting the world has been tainted by a certain propensity to deceit and manipulation. We move on to look at some vivid instances of the degeneration of online discourse, particularly in the way in which social media are structurally determined to exacerbate extremisms and to generate stalemates between opposed camps. We devote some considerable time to the ongoing online discussion of the question of the nature of gender identity, as an illustration of the severity of the problem. Mobbing, stalemates, information bubbles, and craven like-seeking are not just local or occasional weaknesses of online discussion; they are built into it, and this brings us to a new and almost paradoxical situation in which the seemingly rational inclination to engage in public debate by sharing ideas and working through arguments can in fact only further contribute to an intrinsically irrational system, can only help feed this new angry beast we have conjured into life.

In chapter 8 we again encounter what only looks like a thorough change of subject, when we turn to **jokes and lies**. The internet threatens to put authors out of work, but also comedians and humorists, as there is a practically infinite supply online of anonymous, spontaneously generated humor that is basically edgier and quicker than most of what is produced by professionals. But this new overabundance is also accompanied by breakneck transformations in political norms, and in ideas about which forms of humor are effective satire, and which ones go too far or warrant that now-common label, both vacuous and vicious at once, "problematic." In order to motivate this discussion, we go back a few years to 2015, when the work of a group of satirists in Paris was responded to with extrajudicial assassination. The reactions to this event quickly expanded to include the question of the nature of satire: whether one may engage with the world in a special satirical mode characterized by moral and political commitments that differ from those that obtain in the declarative mode. The debate expanded also to include the question of the hypocrisy of Enlightenment values and the limits of free speech. I describe my initial full-throated defense of the satirists in question in the Paris attack; I then describe how the US presidential election the following year compelled me to rethink the arguments I had previously deployed in defense of the existence of a special satirical mode. This leads to a consideration of the barely existent subdomain of philosophy that might be called "gelastics," or the philosophy of humor, in which we pay particular attention to Kant's attempt to define the joke as a "sudden transformation of a strained expectation into nothing." So defined, jokes bear a peculiar relationship to logical arguments: they are, so to speak, perverted or curdled syllogisms, where the purpose is not to draw a true conclusion from premises, but to distort our conception of truth by subverting our expectations. They are often dishonest, and yet they continue to bear a special relationship to the truth. This discussion, in turn, leads us to the broader discussion of lies: in particular, the extent to which lying may be deemed irrational, apart from any consideration of its immorality, and also the extent to which the understanding of being honest as consistently making only true claims is adequate. That is, does the difference between the liar and the honest person only come down to the truth-value of their respective statements? This discussion is developed, by now unsurprisingly, against the background of, and with examples drawn from, recent political history.

In chapter 9, we begin to prepare to **die**, with a reflection on what I, inspired by Lev Tolstoy, have dubbed "the impossible syllogism": the one that leads to a full comprehension of our own mortality. We consider those forms of irrationality that seem to consist, in some way or other, in the denial of our own individual future deaths; we also consider the ways in which this denial at the same time shapes human life and imbues our social existence with value.

CHAPTER ONE

The Self-Devouring Octopus;
or, Logic

➤➤➤➤➤

The Operation of Falsity

"Reason" is the English translation of the Latin *ratio*, which in turn renders the Greek *logos*. The Greek term features in what is perhaps the best-known verse of the Bible—"In the beginning was the *logos*" (John 1:1)—and it provides the suffix in the names of countless fields of scientific study, from mineralogy to epidemiology to psychology. It also gives us the name of a field in which the Greek term figures not as the suffix, but as the root: *logic*. Logic has for much of history been conceived as, so to speak, the science of reason.

Philosophers today might balk at this characterization, as it is generally held now that logic is the study rather of validity, which is a property of arguments, and not a faculty of human minds. But this is a recent turn of events, and it occurs at a moment when most philosophers have forgotten that reason itself, as will be discussed in chapter 2, was not always held to be confined to human minds; rather, it was understood to permeate and give shape to the entire order of nature. So let us not be too faithful to the sensitivities of the present moment. Instead, let us consider the broad sweep of the history of logic, of reasoned argument, and the many ways in which reason's endeavors have proved self-subverting.

One of the key elements of philosophy's myth of origins is that it was born at the moment debaters came to value truth, rather than victory, as the goal of debate. This was, legend has it, the moment of separation of the philosophers from the sophists: the splitting off of two distinct ancestral lines. At the moment of this split, the role of the philosopher had already been distinct for some time from that of another person-age: the seer. That is, in Greek antiquity already, ordinarily, a philoso-pher did not tell you of his visions in dreams or other ecstasies; he did not tell you, ordinarily, what had been dictated to him by God or by some personal muse, without necessarily understanding it himself. Philosophers do not take dictation but always come to their views on their own. Nor do they make arguments simply for their own sake, or simply in order to win a debate. Yet both sorts of activity, that of the seers and that of the sophists, contribute amply to the ancestral DNA of modern philosophers.[1]

Today philosophers are much more likely to recognize their shared genetic link with the sophists than with the seers (though the method of intuition, beloved to many philosophers, may appear, upon scru-tiny, to be little more than a secularized form of "seeing"). Lawyers, rhetoricians, and debate-club members share common ancestors with logicians, metaphysicians, and ethicists, though since antiquity they have evolved in a different niche, with an overarching purpose that is not just different from, but in many respects counter to, the aims of philosophy. Cicero, the first-century BCE Roman statesman and lawyer, is a sort of patron saint for those who follow in the same pro-fession, or at least for the ones who have learned a few things about their profession and its history. Thomas Cromwell's law education in the sixteenth century consisted in memorizing large portions of the Roman author's oeuvre.[2] And Cicero is also held in high esteem by academic philosophers, even if most cannot tell you much about him.

Socrates for his part was falsely, and outrageously, accused by his peers at Athens of making the weaker argument the stronger, among other crimes, for it was precisely this practice that Socrates had spent his public life disavowing. He did not want anything so vain as to win a debate. He wanted the truth, if this was to be had, even if it was fur-nished not by him, but by one of his interlocutors. Yet still today over-achieving high school students are encouraged to make the weaker argument the stronger when they are assigned, by lot and as teams, one side or the other of a debate topic: that capital punishment is justifi-able, perhaps, or that capital punishment is unjustifiable. It is generally hoped or expected that these students will go on to law school, and will someday take on clients, whom they will successfully defend, regardless of what they might themselves believe about their clients' guilt or innocence. And many of them, between high school debate teams and postgraduate study of law, will undertake a program of undergraduate study in philosophy, which they will be encouraged to think of as "prelaw." Yet philosophy cannot in fact be preparatory to lawyering; the search after truth and the search after winning arguments can come together only when reality itself permits this. In practice, however, the two ends are often intertwined, and likely the more venal the society in which philosophy struggles to hang on to some modest institutional standing, the more it will have to present itself as useful for the practical aims of making the weaker argument the stronger.

There are of course other uses of the rhetorical art than lawyerly power plays. To the extent that it is an *art*, those who practice it may sometimes aspire to the creation of beauty. Upon his professorial appointment in Paris in 1551 at what would later become the Collège de France, the great French humanist Petrus Ramus (Pierre de la Ramée) took the title of "Regius Professor of Philosophy and Eloquence," effectively institutionalizing the vision of learning he had spelled out in his *Address on Combining Philosophy and Eloquence* of 1546.[3] We may not be startled by this conjunction today, but what Ramus sought to do in putting these two terms together was to combine two great—and, by the time of the Renaissance, sharply opposed—traditions: Scholasticism on the one hand, which gives us logical arguments concerned most of all with form; and humanism on the other, which gives us the arts and letters, all of what today might be called "content." It is the latter that makes it worthwhile to know anything at all and that gives us something to which we might apply, though preferably not obsessively or superciliously, the rules of logic that we have mastered. Ramus encouraged his students to learn from syllogism and poetry alike, and in so doing caused tremendous controversy. An anonymous anti-Ramist pamphleteer accused him of "following no particular route but merely barking at theoretical odds and ends."[4] In the sixteenth century as today, there was a generally unspoken rule that philosophy is not to become too eloquent, and to the extent that it encompasses poetry and oratory within its purview, it is abandoning its assigned post.

Today philosophers hardly speak of eloquence, either for or against, though a term that covers much of the same territory, "erudition," occurs with surprising frequency. It seems, often, among academic philosophers, to function as a backhanded compliment: the erudite philosopher is one who knows many facts, but has not synthesized them into a rigorous or systematic account of anything important. When it occurs outside of academic philosophy, in turn, "erudite," like "brilliant," is a word ideally suited for Twitter, hastily summing up, in a single flat-footed adjective, hard-earned knowledge of things that are not now considered worthy of hashtags, that are not currently trending. Erudition is either a compensation for rigor, then, or it is an incomprehensible and moderately impressive quirk. Like eloquence, of which it is a direct descendant, it is suspect, not least in its very human eclecticism. We are reminded by Ramus's *Address* of the long history of philosophy's effort to safely cordon off this other sort of knowing.

The best argument in favor of this cordoning, perhaps, is that poetry and oratory can be deployed to work upon people's passions, while syllogism, valid inference, deduction, work only on the reason. And these two magisteria, to invoke Stephen Jay Gould's account of the relationship between science and faith, must never overlap.[5] Yet the best and most eloquent rhetoricians have always known that such a sharp separation gives logic an undeserved pass. Cicero had mastered logic, but was sharply aware of its potential for, so to speak, weaponization. He understood that the rules of valid inference might be deployed for questionable ends, and indeed that arguments that check out logically might still be wrong to the extent that they have been deployed for nefarious reasons, as tools in a maneuver for power. Lawyers might dazzle their adversaries with rhetorical flourishes having only a semblance of truth, but Cicero himself knew that one can also dazzle, and subdue, and vanquish a conversational partner using logical arguments that involve no legerdemain at all, that are perfectly true, yet perfectly petty and manipulative. It is just such a prospect, of being true and spurious at once, that Herman Melville's eponymous character in *The Confidence-Man* invokes, attributing it, somewhat peculiarly, to the work of the Roman author of *Germania*: "Even were there truth in Tacitus," he writes, "such truth would have the operation of falsity, and so still be poison, moral poison."[6]

How can the truth ever be "moral poison"? What is it to be true, but to have "the operation of falsity"? One long-standing problem in the history of the teaching and transmission of logic, has been this: in order to be able to skillfully discern sound and valid arguments, one must also become skilled in identifying spurious ones. Thus a significant portion of logic has consisted in the study of sophisms, to the point that it has seemed impossible, for some, to see logic as anything more than the science of sophism. Like police detectives who go undercover and become too attached to the trappings of the criminal underworld to ever return from it, so too are logicians drawn in by sophisms. Thus Cicero complains of logicians whose whole endeavor is "to make contorted conclusions, to speak filthily, to use petty little arguments."[7] We see much the same complaint in the second-century CE satirist Lucian of Samosata, who insists that logicians "have nothing other than miserable little words and measly interrogations, . . . with which they feed their minds."[8] And the fourth-century CE Byzantine rhetorician Themistius expresses a similar view when he complains that logicians waste their time on "rude and troublesome sophisms, difficult to understand and useless to know."[9] Or the second-century CE Gellius, author of *Attic Nights*, who warns that to spend too much time in "those mazes and meanders of logic" can only result in a sort of "second childhood," a mental infantilism unbefitting any wise or even competent adult.[10] To return again to Cicero, the Roman author finds it fitting to cite Plutarch's description of "the octopus [who] sits through the winter devouring himself," as a suitable metaphor for the self-defeating activity of the logicians.[11] Logic, these authors worry, is nothing but an inane, self-destructive, shameful distraction: the science of truth, corrupted by the operation of falsity.

Explosions

Likely no philosopher has ever been more committed to the promise of rationality than Gottfried Wilhelm Leibniz, writing mostly from Germany at the end of the seventeenth century and the beginning of the eighteenth. He believed, evidently sincerely, that if we simply succeed in devising an adequate artificial language, with all of our terms rigorously defined and all of the rules of inference clearly spelled out, there will be no more conflict, from small family squabbles to wars between empires. We will simply be able, whenever the first signs of conflict begin to appear, to declare, "Let us calculate!" (or, translated differently, "Let us compute!"). In this way we will see, "without any ceremony, . . . who is right."[12] The problem, of course, as many of Leibniz's contemporaries already saw, is that many of us are simply too attached to the ceremony that Leibniz's method dispenses with. We like "drama," as is often said today; we do not want our positions in disputes to be formalized and clarified. We want, rather, to press our case with the help of our passions, our imaginations, and whatever other smokescreen we have at our disposal to deploy against our enemies, to stun them and confuse them. We do not want the magisteria of rhetoric and logic to overlap in any way that must be explicitly acknowledged, but this does not mean that those in the magisterium of logic will not wish to show their mastery of a foreign tongue when it proves useful. Such magisterial overlap between these two "languages," between straightforward argumentation and manipulative rhetoric, is particularly common in the case of international conflict and high-level diplomacy, of the sort, in fact, in which Leibniz himself was implicated as a career courtier and privy councillor to dukes and emperors. When indeed is the case for war ever pressed, by those who wish to launch into it, on the basis of a consideration of the objective evidence for its justice or for an overall greater utilitarian good as its expected outcome? When did any state ever change its mind about going to war on the basis of a Leibnizian calculation that yields up a conclusion in favor of the antiwar faction, that shows that it is not reasonable, that the truth of things prohibits it? When opposed diplomats press their cases to one another, do their claims not always give evidence, even when true, of what Melville calls "the operation of falsity"?

The seventeenth-century French philosopher Pierre Gassendi, for his part, explains Plutarch's image of the self-devouring octopus as an expression of the idea that logic can only "be fed on its own discoveries." For Gassendi, "there is no use for its precepts beyond itself, and therefore it were necessary that whatever is born within its limits be consumed within them."[13] Many other philosophers, ancient and modern, have further noted the deep problem, to which I have already alluded, that the logical arguments that we dismiss as "sophisms" are often perfectly valid and sound, and yet also are plainly distractions at best, and, at worst, dangerous rhetorical tools. Take the famous sophism of the horns: "You have whatever you have not lost; but you've never lost your horns; therefore, you have horns" (this is an ancestor, in turn, to the comedy routine in which an innocent man struggles to answer the question "When did you stop beating your wife?"). Or this one, a variation on the so-called fallacy of composition from the early eighteenth-century African philosopher Anton Wilhelm Amo, who had a long career in Germany, in his 1738 work, the *Treatise on the Art of Accurately and Soberly Philosophizing*:

> This goat is yours.
> This goat is a mother.
> Therefore, this goat is your mother.[14]

If these examples look something like jokes, it is with good reason: the formal structure of a joke may be understood as something like a satire of logical inference. Immanuel Kant would define jokes as "the sudden transformation of a strained expectation into nothing."[15] This is the reverse of what happens in a proper, nonsatirical logical inference, where the conclusion is the final confirmation that a burgeoning expectation is indeed something.

Sophisms, we might say, are the soured, curdled form of arguments. They are of course also great fun, and highly seductive. The fact that logicians have often amused themselves by exploring the commonalities of these forms of inference, and attempting to construct inferences that displayed features of both the logical argument and the joke at once, should not be surprising. That falsehood opened up the door to a universe of imaginative possibilities, as hilarious as they are irresponsible, was even enshrined as a rule within logic itself, delightfully known as the "Principle of Explosion": *Ex falso sequitur quodlibet* (From a falsehood anything follows). Once you've allowed even the tiniest untruth into your argument, well, from there, as the song has it, anything goes.

We have seen two principal complaints about logic: that it too easily degenerates into sophistical distractions, and that it is like an octopus that "devours its own cups," that is, that it has only itself to feed upon. Plutarch's complaint, cited by Cicero, is not unrelated to the common observation over the centuries, for example by Ludwig Wittgenstein in his 1921 *Tractatus Logico-Philosophicus*, that logic cannot tell us anything about the world, but can only clarify what we already know about the world through nonlogical means.[16] In his 1925–26 lectures published as *Logic: The Question of Truth*, Martin Heidegger would observe around the same time, somewhat more disparagingly, that Scholastic logic, or the art of syllogism, "is a form of sloth tailor-made for instructors, ... a fraud perpetrated on the students."[17] From their very different perspectives, Cicero, Wittgenstein, and Heidegger are all concerned that logic is empty, and that to revere it too much by treating it as if it were in itself valuable is at best a waste of intellectual effort. Gassendi, for his part, perceives a connection between two objectionable practices: the habit of taking logic as an end in itself, on the one hand, and, on the other, the misappropriation of logic for "logomachy," for doing battle for power over others by means of logical arguments. Thus he complains of "those ancients who passed their lives contriving the mazes and meanders of sophisms, and brawling over those things that are taught in logic, and clinging to these things as if they were not the path, but the destination towards which we are hurrying."[18]

Not even logic, in short, is safe from human unreason, from pettiness, distraction, passion, insult, and bickering. In fact, if the philosophers I have selected to cite here are correct, logic—which has often been expected to serve as our great bulwark against unreason—is not only not safe from corruption; it is *particularly* prone to corruption by human passions and self-interest. There might be ways to train it so as to serve toward human and individual improvement, but what is clear is that it is not going to train *us*, as we are always training it upon our adversaries and for our own ends. These ends are often naked maneuvers for power, and they are also often, as in the various sophisms we have surveyed, simply mischievous fun. Not infrequently the line between these two sorts of deviation is blurred: as we will see in chapter 8, one of the basic functions of jokes is to gain power over others by taking them down a notch, by exposing their inferiority. Sophisms and jokes alike, then, often function as little explosions, smoke bombs we set off to confuse or to stun as we advance our own interests. These strategies, moreover, are not somehow opposite to the art of logical argumentation; they are often virtuosic instances of it.

Kaspar Hauser and the Limits of Rational Choice

Contemporary academic philosophy is not generally interested, as Cicero, Gassendi, Wittgenstein, and Heidegger were, in the way in which even a mastery of reason can be turned toward the exercise of unreason in human life. It mostly limits itself, rather, to attempts at precise definitions of what reason is, and to the production of possible counterexamples to these attempts. Thus for example in causal decision theory—a branch of philosophy with significant relevance to the work of economists and political scientists—there has been abundant discussion over recent decades of what is called "Newcomb's problem."[19] You are presented with two boxes, one that is transparent, and one that is not transparent and whose contents you do not know. The transparent one contains one thousand dollars. The opaque one contains either one million dollars, or nothing. You are told that you are permitted to take either one box, or both boxes. The hitch is this: whether the opaque box has one million dollars in it or not is determined by another party involved, the so-called reliable predictor, who reliably predicts in advance which choice you will make, and determines to put nothing in the opaque box in the event that you take both boxes. You are aware of this factor at the time of the choice. You want to maximize your wealth. So here is the problem: Do you take one box, or two? Some people reason that whatever is in the opaque box cannot be changed at the moment the choice is made, so you may as well take both. Others reason that you had better take only the opaque box on the expectation that it will indeed contain one million dollars.

A tremendous proliferation of variations on this problem has kept alive a small scholarly subdiscipline for some decades, and it has yielded valuable results in its own terms. But the situations this literature addresses are fairly remote from those that are of interest to us: those situations, for example, in which rational inferences are weaponized for irrational or transgressive ends; or those situations in which agents seem to be rationally choosing to behave irrationally; or those situations in which agents seem to simply be acting independently of any concern to be, or to appear, rational—and in so doing do not seem to be failing at exemplifying what it is to be distinctively human; rather, for better or worse, they seem to be excelling at it. For example, when people say that nuclear brinksmanship between the United States and North Korea is "irrational," or when we say that a streak of irrationalism pervades postwar French philosophy or characterizes the work of the alt-right meme-mongers who wanted Trump to get elected just for the payoff this would bring in "lulz," we do not mean that the parties involved here were behaving like a Newcomb one-boxer, or, if you are yourself a one-boxer, like a two-boxer.

One might take an interest in rationality and irrationality without wishing to solve the canonical problems of rational choice. The aim might be, rather, to understand the conditions under which agents decline to engage with these problems—in which they reject, for example, the expectation or the demand that they must wish to maximize their wealth, or that they must seek to give the answer the experts are expecting. Imagine, for example, a Franciscan monk in the early thirteenth century, who has sworn never to possess more earthly wealth than he is able to beg in a day and then to dispense or consume again within the same day. If a monk is caught hoarding, Francis himself might come and unleash his wrath, just as Christ did when the traders undertook their commerce in the temple. What use would it be for this monk to wager correctly in some experiment devised by rational-choice theorists to measure his rationality? Everything in a medieval Franciscan's conception of the value in life is grounded in his avoidance of all that is of monetary value, not least money.[20] Rational-choice theory has landed upon a default measure of rationality as profit seeking, but its practitioners are not generally aware of this. The same broad homogenizing force also construes every individual as at least an aspiring voter, an aspiring homeowner, an aspiring member of a thriving nuclear family; it does not hold open the possibility of opting out of all this, of withdrawal, asceticism, or monasticism. Consider by way of contrast the old idea, as in traditional Hindu faith,[21] that one may choose either the path of the householder or the path of the ascetic, as a way of expressing one's devotion to a society's shared values. This notion is all but absent in contemporary philosophy's reasoning both about rationality and, in the realm of values, about what we may call "the good life." Today it is taken for granted that we all wish to be householders, and, therefore, that we all will need to make our mortgage payment each month, and, therefore, that we all could use that extra money that would come as a result of getting the rational-choice theorist's experimental question right.

Some might argue that if we wish to extricate ourselves from the financial calculus preferred in the standard approaches to such thought experiments as Newcomb's problem, we could simply replace monetary rewards with spiritual rewards of some sort. But such a substitution may not be so simple, for it seems to imply that spiritual rewards are the sort of thing that can be easily exchanged, as if on a currency market. Some who live their lives spiritually are not necessarily for that reason seeking spiritual "payoff." They may well be seeking degradation, confirmation of their individual nothingness before God, which comes through the performance of humble acts that, if performed successfully, will go unrecognized. The reward is in the absence of a payoff, and if the doer is thinking in terms of payoff, then ipso facto he or she is no longer deserving of the reward. It is difficult to imagine what sort of promissory note could be substituted for such a person into the opaque box in which others might hope to discover one million dollars.

The way we respond to thought experiments that purport to test our rationality has much to do with the things we value, and with who we are. We may recall the vivid scene in Werner Herzog's 1974 film *The Enigma of Kaspar Hauser* about a *Naturkind*, a purportedly feral child of the sort that had been of interest to philosophy since Jean-Jacques Rousseau.[22] A young man, Kaspar Hauser, is discovered after having apparently spent his childhood alone, or perhaps in intimate community with animals, in the state of nature. He is barely able to communicate, but little by little learns some of the language and customs of nineteenth-century Germany. After two years, a professor is called in to determine whether Kaspar is capable of thinking logically. The professor presents him with a sort of riddle. There is a village in which all the inhabitants tell only the truth. There is another village inhabited by habitual liars. Two paths lead to these villages from where you are standing, and you are at the crossroads. A man comes down one of the paths, and you ask him whether he comes from the village of the truth-tellers or the village of the liars. You are allowed to ask him only one question, in the aim of determining which village is which. What is the question?

Kaspar is silent, and the proud and self-serious professor eventually divulges the answer to him: "If you came from the other village, would you answer 'no' if I were to ask you whether you came from the liars' village?" That's logic, the professor says, at which point Kaspar finally speaks up, saying he knows another question that would do the trick: ask the man whether he is a tree frog. This would indeed reveal which village is which, but the professor does not accept it; he is only irritated, since it "is not a proper question." What the professor means is that it reveals nothing about Kaspar's ability to respect the rules of logic in his thinking. If Kaspar had been presented with Newcomb's problem instead of the professor's provincial puzzle, he surely would have said that he did not want the money, or would have come up with a comparably inappropriate question for the reliable predictor, and the expert would have been infuriated that his subject had refused to follow the rules.

We need not be on Kaspar's side to recognize the importance of what is at stake in the misunderstanding between Kaspar and the professor, between the expert who believes that logic rules all, and the outsider or dissenter who adheres to a form of thinking that he finds more direct, or "authentic," or adequate to lived experience. The mandarin professor here is in some respects, in spite of his self-image, not unlike the sly lawyer who is consciously making the weaker argument the stronger. In the professor's monopoly of the truth, there is a certain operation of falsity, and Kaspar Hauser, as they say these days, calls it out. But in other respects the professor and the rhetorician are dissimilar. The rhetorically adept advocate is operating from a position of only partial power. He needs to convince the judge and jury of his argument's truth, and he is looking for argumentative tools, logically valid or not, to accomplish this. The professor for his part is operating from a position of total power over Kaspar (at least until the forest-boy makes a mockery of his logic test and provokes a titter from the housemaid), and he lacks a certain self-knowledge that the sophist lawyer probably has: he takes himself to be a simple vehicle of the necessary truth of logic, rather than an agent who is asserting his own power by means of this truth. The sophist's argument is his own creation, while the professor's logic, at least as he understands it, is something external to him. In a sense he is merely taking dictation (though he would never see it that way). But this difference may only be a measure of the relative degree of power the professor possesses. He does not need to convince anyone of anything, as Kaspar is a nobody, a feral child. In any case the kind of truth the professor deals with, in contrast to the lawyer's as he stands before the judge, is true whether his audience is convinced or not.

Kaspar, anyhow, is not convinced. He is, of course, only a fictional character. But he is one who has played an important role in real history, as an iteration of a stock figure of many Enlightenment-era philosophical thought experiments. Nor has he left the stage. There is quite a bit of him, in fact, in Werner Herzog himself. There are plenty of people who think the Herr Professor, along with others like him, is laughable, and do not want to listen to him. Their existence needs to be accounted for.

Carrying On about the Ineffable

The spontaneous insights of children said to be raised by wolves withstand efforts at logical treatment, but there are many other expressions of human life that put up resistance too. Among these are the deeply held beliefs of religious communities. Since the seventeenth century, the largest and most protracted battle between the forces of rationality and irrationality has been played out around the place of religion in modern society. That religion is marked as "irrational" and secularism as "rational" is a contingent fact about our society and our recent history. In other historical contexts it has been the unbelievers who are the raving, unhinged, and marginal characters, while religion in turn has enjoyed the full support and buttressing of the best logical arguments emerging from the most elite institutions of learning. For religion to be marked in this way in one era and not in another, one suspects, is yet another instance of the phenomenon we will consider in chapter 8, whereby the political left is seen to be effervescent in one era, and sober in another. Like the magnetic polarity of the earth, the moral character we associate with one of the two poles of social life—the left or the right, the religious or the secular—can switch all of a sudden, for reasons the scientists, social as well as natural, still do not fully understand.

But what is secularism? Beginning already in the Renaissance, the idea began to emerge that while religion is necessary for individuals, society itself is best organized as a truly neutral public space, independent of the church. In the following centuries the call for a separation of these two components of society, the church and the public space, often hardened into a demand for the thorough suppression, or at least restriction, of the power of the former. Thus, as mentioned in the introduction, in the Reign of Terror in France in the early 1790s, we see the conversion of Catholic churches into Temples of Reason, and in the Soviet Union under Stalin propaganda posters proliferated declaring that "Religion Is Poison," borrowing the iconography of pagan witchcraft in order to tarnish the Orthodox Christian Church.

Until very recently, the public role of religion in modern Western societies seemed to be declining. The German philosopher Jürgen Habermas, also invoked in the introduction, has lived long enough to see the thorough disconfirmation of the thesis for which he had spent his decades-long career arguing: that the modern world was destined to fully achieve the goal that had begun to be articulated in the Renaissance, and had only been growing in appeal since then, of a neutral public space, where rational arguments prevail over the affective commitments of the particular communities making up a given society. This view is simply no longer tenable: from Islamic jihad to the display of the Ten Commandments in Alabama courthouses, religious commitment has flooded into political life with a vengeance in the late twentieth and early twenty-first centuries.

This sudden and surprising resurgence has stimulated a serious rethinking of the limits of the widespread presumption of a link between modernity and rationality. For centuries, it had been supposed that the increasing rationality of society could be measured by the retreat of religion, which had become equivalent to superstition, belief in false and nonexistent things. But the evident staying power of religion has now forced many—even Habermas in his later work—to ask whether, like art and the passions, religion might not be here to stay. Indeed we must ask whether philosophy, following several centuries of estrangement, might not do best to reconcile with it.

But what exactly must we come to terms with? And have modern secular philosophers perhaps been fundamentally mistaken about the nature of the thing they were hoping humanity would have the strength and clarity to overcome?

Much religious discourse is organized around what are taken to be the core "mysteries" of faith, the claims that cannot be made to cohere perfectly with our ordinary use of language, or even with the other claims of the religion itself. The mysteries, moreover, are shared by all members of a religious community, contemplated, discussed, debated, quite apart from the question whether anyone really understands them or not.Beyond enigmatic mysteries, which are the common patrimony of the members of a religion, there is mystical experience, which is had, or purportedly had, by only a small number of people within the community. Mystical experience is often characterized by the fact that it cannot be formulated in natural-language propositions—thus the mocking definition of the mystic as a person who has learned something ineffable and won't shut up about it. Ordinarily, mysticism lies strictly beyond the bounds of philosophy. Where meaningful propositions leave off is where the tradition of rational debate descending from Socrates leaves off and a very different variety of human experience begins.

Yet philosophy has often sought to go right up to this boundary, and to get some notion of what might be on the other side, by feeling out the contours of the boundary itself. The early Wittgenstein thought that one could indicate something about the nature of the mystical, not by saying it—which would involve a performative contradiction, since the mystical is unsayable—but by showing it. Kant sought to apprehend at least something of unknowable ideas, such as the idea of God, by aiming not to understand them as positive objects of knowledge, but rather to appreciate the way they regulate our understanding without themselves being understood.

Aristotle for his part moved up to the very limit of meaningful language at only one point in his entire body of work, when he described God's activity as "a thinking of thinking."[23] What on earth could such thinking be like? Aristotle cannot know, for all we mortal embodied human beings are ever able to think about is this or that particular object of thought, not thought itself. Even if we attempt to think about thinking, we are actually still focused on a given object of thought, and are not thinking simply and purely. Epistemology does not immediately guarantee transcendence to the person who takes it up. Aristotle moves up to the limit of the unsayable, ventures a single incomprehensible proposition (that God's thinking is the thinking of thinking), surely in part because he feels a need to incorporate this one entity, God, which we cannot understand, into his systematic account of everything we are capable of understanding. God lies outside of nature, and so lies outside of Aristotle's scope, but God still needs to be accounted for in order for nature itself to be understood as a unified and comprehensive whole. And so he goes up to the boundary, but does not linger there for long.

Other philosophers have shown themselves to be rather more addicted to the jolt that flirting with this boundary can carry, like cattle perpetually trying an electric fence. Thus according to Plotinus's disciple Porphyry, the third-century CE Neoplatonist philosopher achieved ecstatic union with God, not once, but "four times, during the period I passed with him, . . . by no mere latent fitness but by the ineffable Act."[24] Porphyry claims that he himself achieved the same thing only once.[25] We may wonder what the intervals between Plotinus's repeated unions were like, whether, say, after the third of them he began to find some resources within himself to give an accurate account of the experience, to say whether its basic pattern or unfolding started to feel routine, or whether rather it remained just as ineffable as after the first time. It seems strange, almost comical, to number mystical experiences in this way, since even counting gives a kind of structure and recognizability to something that is supposed by definition to remain entirely beyond all description.

As the experience is beyond all description, the person who has it is also beyond accountability, and this status can obviously be useful to one in pursuit of charisma within a religious movement—useful, that is, unless the winds change, and those who were previously impressed come to take the mystic for a fraud, come to see his claim to divine afflatus as just so much hot air.

To the extent that philosophers have claimed to have ineffable experiences of their own, they are generally seen to be leaving the community of philosophers narrowly understood. More frequently we find philosophers trading in mysteries, of the expressible but still perplexing sort. Such tools of the trade are in fact very common among practitioners of what we might call "Paris irrationality": the academic mandarins of the French university system in the late twentieth century, most notably Jacques Derrida, who spoke as successors to the tradition of philosophy even as they claimed to be "overcoming" this tradition. They did everything they could, in the name of this "overcoming," to lead those who were willing to listen to them down false paths, to make statements that could not possibly be understood, and to dissimulate and pretend that the fault for the lack of understanding lay not with them, but with their followers (who were often gullible monolingual Americans).[26] This "overcoming" has generally been understood as a breaking free of tradition by casting off ever more of its articles of faith, but this endeavor may just as easily be seen as a purifying or distilling of that tradition. It has seldom involved an openness to the discovery of other traditions, which in turn would make possible the rediscovery of one's own as something neither to be overcome nor to be zealously defended.

But such an irenic and simple path could never be taken by the overcomers of tradition; that would be too easy. And so their preferred strategy is to riff on tradition, to play upon it like improvising musicians, without being called to express any overt loyalty to it. Even if some value may be extracted from their work, we must nonetheless agree with Perry Anderson that "the most striking feature of the human sciences and philosophy that counted in this period [in France] was the extent to which they came to be written increasingly as virtuoso exercises of style, drawing on the resources and licences of artistic rather than academic forms."[27] We may still turn to them for their "oracular gestures" and "eclectic coquetries," but there is no particular reason to limit ourselves to the creative works of the twentieth century that packaged themselves, rather deceptively, as "philosophy" or "theory," when in fact there remain vastly greater resources to draw on from the same period in arts and literature.

Many Paris irrationalists themselves borrow liberally from arts and culture, as well as from canonical philosophers, in order to concoct a strange new brew of their own, whose mixed ingredients can no longer be discerned or savored. Thus Alain Badiou intuitively throws together secret recipes of theory from the combination of Platonism, communism, set theory, the New Testament, and adds a special sauce of piquant allusions to twentieth-century dictators. For example, he attempts to develop an axiomatic system borrowed from Cantorian transfinite set theory in order to elucidate what he takes to be some salient differences between Stalin and Mao. Has he just affirmed his support for some horrible thing? one wonders in listening to him. The elements are too jumbled, and their recombinations too dazzling and quick, to enable a listener or reader to say what counts as an assertion and what is only virtuosic play.[28] The overall effect of his work is something like a pop song that relies on the technology of sampling to drop in elements of other songs, from other genres, in a spirit of ironic recombination; or like a meme that features hammers and sickles or Red Army tanks together with a clever slogan and some other visual cue borrowed from Hollywood, say: all of which together yields up something that appears not so much an affirmation as a flirtation.

Badiou is not a terribly funny thinker or author, and it is to the credit of the Slovene philosopher Slavoj Žižek, in important respects Badiou's successor, that the latter has understood, or intuited, that the genre in which he is working is, in the end, comedy. Where Badiou gives us pure mystifications, Žižek delivers generally well-timed punch lines. These are as if designed to illustrate the so-called incongruity theory of humor, according to which comedic effect is attained by the juxtaposition of incongruous elements, like set theory and Stalinism, for the unfunny Badiou, or like Jacques Lacan's theory of the *objet petit a* as illustrated in some horrible Hollywood rom-com, for the quicker-witted Slovene. Žižek has got tremendous mileage in his career out of a sort of self-Orientalizing schtick, the shame of which lies more with his admirers who buy into it than with him who performs it, in which he plays up his persona as a stock character from somewhere or other in the Eastern Bloc. This enables him to play at undermining the pieties of liberal democratic or bourgeois society, as he comes from a place where, the prejudice has it, these pieties have no hope of taking root in the inhospitable soil. The difference between being the son of a Slovenian economist in Tito's Yugoslavia, and being, say, a victim of dekulakization in the USSR under Stalin, is all too easily obscured in his performances before American or British publics: he comes, it is supposed, from that part of the world that can be ruled only with an iron fist, and that was never so delicate as we in the West have become about man's brutality to man. And so, when he holds forth on such subjects as the power of ideology to structure our fantasies, he is speaking with special insight; and when he speaks of the contradictions and hollowness of Western capitalism, he does so with the blunt truthfulness of which only a foreigner is capable. This is a variety of political commentary that was already perfected in Montesquieu's invention of the characters of Usbek and Rica for his 1721 epistolary novel *The Persian Letters*: the exotic *naïfs* who reveal to us what the Parisians are really up to, behind their various conceits and self-delusions. It is also the basic template of *The Beverly Hillbillies*. In this genre, truth telling is always cut with a good amount of joke telling. Because one of Žižek's primary points of access to "the West" happens to have been Lacanian psychoanalysis, it is inevitable that the truth-telling component of his contribution to this genre should turn out rather small, and that in the end—and I do not mean this in an entirely dismissive way—his entire oeuvre will in all likelihood be remembered as an unusually compendious joke book.

Far more common than mystery or ineffable mystical experience in the history of philosophy is what we may call paradox-mongering. This to some extent overlaps with the sophism-mongering we have already explored, but it focuses not so much on arguments that give the appearance of truth, even though they are plainly spurious, as on arguments that seem to compel our condemning them as false, even though we cannot find any grounds for doing so. Paradox-mongering is the perverse celebration of statements that must be true, but cannot be true. Whoever stumbles upon a new paradox—such as Zeno the Eleatic, who proved that motion and change are impossible—has got something with the charge of a mystery in his possession. He will claim that he is just following out reason itself, wherever it leads him, down the paths of rational inference. But the discovery can easily induce in the follower the suspicion, again, that the world is itself irrational, and the consequent feeling that the philosophical leader who, or movement that, touts this paradox is in a unique position, also perhaps paradoxically, to provide protection from the cruelty and uncertainty of an irrational world.

Zeno is persuasive not just because his reasoning is seemingly incontrovertible (though some fairly compelling resolutions of the paradox have been put forth over the millennia), but also because his conclusions are absurd. His "race course paradox," for example, tells us that in order to complete a race course, we must first cross it halfway, but in order to do that we must first traverse a quarter of the field, but in order to go that distance, we must first go across an eighth of the field, but before that, a sixteenth, and so on to infinity. Thus, in order to travel any distance whatsoever, we must undertake an infinite number of preliminary voyages before even getting started. And therefore, no motion is possible. We are led to this conclusion by reason, even though it flatly denies what in some sense we know to be our daily experience.

Philosophers may feel as though their love of philosophical paradox is superior to the sort of religious belief motivated by absurdity alone, with no reverence at all for reason, but the two might not be so different in the end. We are not required, after all, to think about paradoxes if we choose not to, and even if we do think about Zeno's paradox, and find ourselves convinced by it, there is nothing about this conviction that prevents us from going on moving about in our daily lives, from completing race courses as often as we please. Thus, in an admonition that would later be cherished by Jorge Luis Borges, Leibniz wrote to Simon Foucher in 1692, "Ne craignez point, monsieur, la tortuë" (Sir, do not fear the tortoise).[29] The philosopher is referring to another version of Zeno's paradox, which articulates the same problem of the impossibility of motion through a continuum, but does so through the fable of Achilles's race against a tortoise. There is no need to worry, Leibniz wishes to say. We can still beat the tortoise, no matter what the paradox seems to tell us.

Or let us consider a more recent case, in which the setting up of reason as an exalted goal leads to another sort of paralysis. A corporation called NXIVM, founded by Keith Raniere, uses its founder's "patent-pending technology" in its "Executive Success Programs" for improving our faculty of reason. The Rational Inquiry website announces that this "technology" is "more than a philosophy." It is, rather, "a tool to create or examine philosophy—a process of philosophical development," which can "assist individuals to maximize their potential, gain a deeper understanding of ethics, develop critical thinking skills and the use of logic, and develop a deep and compassionate understanding of humanity." The website invokes unnamed sources, who have lauded Rational Inquiry as a "discovery of historical proportions." Could these be our modern-day Pythagoreans? Just as Hippasus of Metapontum was thrown out of a boat by fellow Pythagoreans for having divulged the secret of irrational numbers to outsiders, so NXIVM has harshly punished its "traitors." In a *New York Times* article of October 17, 2017,[30] it was reported that NXIVM had requested nude images of its women members, to be uploaded to a Dropbox account, and had threatened to release them publicly if the women who had submitted them ever betrayed the organization's secrets. The report also reveals that initiates were instructed by a company official, Lauren Salzman, to request of their "master" (i.e., their recruiter), "Master, please brand me, it would be an honor," at which point they received a painful, cauterized brand displaying the initials of the founder, "KR."

Is this where rational inquiry leads? I myself move within a social milieu that more or less ensures that I will not hear of an operation such as NXIVM until its scandals reach the *New York Times*; when they do, members of my world are conditioned to scoff and shake our heads. We believe we are the ones who are honestly engaged in rational inquiry, and that what Keith Raniere calls Rational Inquiry is nothing but a fraud. The confirmation of this belief comes with the journalistic exposés and the complaints filed with state medical regulators. But we are missing an opportunity to understand ourselves better if we presume too quickly that our own enterprise is purely legitimate and therefore exists across a great divide from Raniere's. For one thing, there is considerably more money in the strange hybrid world where entrepreneurship meets self-help and spirituality, and where major corporations are able to pay for workshops and retreats for their employees, than there is in the budgets of many academic philosophy departments.

And where there are entrepreneurs with money, there is always the possibility of maneuvering into legitimate institutions and endeavors. This is why wealthy people with no experience or competence often find themselves elected to political office, while people of modest financial means, who also have no experience or competence, never are. NXIVM for its part was able to host a visit to the United States by the Dalai Lama, whose own peculiar brand features a mixture of entrepreneurialism and rather obvious self-help advice for getting one's life in order. The Dalai Lama's aura of profound spirituality seems to derive from the vague idea his Western audiences have about the Buddhist metaphysics of the incarnation of the bodhisattva: he is said to have supernatural origins, and so his advice to be honest and kind is taken to have particular weight to it. And thus the Dalai Lama is at least in some contexts a legitimate figure to invoke in academic philosophy in a way that, say, Keith Raniere is not. We have all heard of the former, probably respect him to some extent, will likely accept undergraduate papers that cite him, and will happily share in the financial largesse of the Mind & Life Institute that he cofounded, if it helps us to pursue our careers.

So the divide between NXIVM and your favorite university philosophy department is not total. What this case compels us to consider, moreover, is a clear illustration of the uncomfortable fact that cults and cult-like organizations need not declare their devotion to irrationalism, need not announce that in signing up with them you are leaving critical thinking behind in favor of some more profound or primordial experience of consciousness or emotion. It is just as easy to found a cult that explicitly announces the opposite, that it is there to do nothing more sinister than to help you develop your critical thinking skills, and that these skills are the best thing our conscious minds have to offer. No mystical union with the godhead, no voyages to the astral plane. Just reliably valid inferences and a sharpening of your fallacy-detection abilities. And a brand of the leader's initials beneath your hip.

The uses of language, in mystery, myth, incantation, reverie, sweet song, never fully went away, even if, over the past few thousand years humankind has come to aspire to a standard of thinking and of speaking that we call, often without fully understanding what we ourselves mean, by the name of "reason." But the very methods and practices that were supposed to have been set up to counter the damaging effects of the human mind's propensity to unreason ended up, soon enough, mired in the very problems they were meant to solve. Logical arguments mutated into mysterious paradoxes, or degenerated into sophisms that could be deployed in order to violently cow one's adversaries. And lovers of reason allowed the object of their love to be idolatrized in Temples of Reason and profaned in perverted cults of critical thinking. Not only has logic not led us away from unreason. It has not even managed to purge deceit, tricksterism, power plays, and legerdemain from its own quarters.

CHAPTER TWO

"No-Brainers"; or, Reason in Nature

➤➤➤➤➤

An Ordered Whole

Logic might be, metaphorically, an octopus, as Cicero said. But the octopus, literally, is no logician, even if, significantly, between 2008 and 2010 an octopus named Paul was hailed as possessing the power to divine the outcomes of football matches. Widespread public openness to cephalopod intelligence helped to create the appearance that something more than simple divination was occurring—as one might believe in trying to predict the future from the course of motion of an ant or a goldfish: something more like a true prophetic intelligence. But of course few would confess to being truly convinced by the appearance, as reason, on the most widespread view today, belongs to human beings alone (and even human beings cannot predict the outcome of unfixed future sporting matches). Everything else in nature, in turn, from bears and sharks to cyanobacteria, rain clouds, and comets, is a great force of unreason, a primordial, violent chaos that allows us to exist within it, for a while, always subject to its arbitrary whims.

This view sets us up, as human beings, starkly against, or at least outside of, nature. And this is the view that has been held by the majority of philosophers throughout history. Most of them have understood this outsider status to be a result of our possession of some sort of nonnatural essence that makes us what we are, such as an immortal soul, endowed from a transcendent source and ultimately unsusceptible to erosion, corrosion, and other natural effects. For philosophers of a more naturalistic bent, who have dominated philosophy only in the most recent era, human reason is not ontologically distinct from vision or echolocation or any of the other powers evolution has come up with, enabling different kinds of organism to move through the world. It is part of something vastly larger—namely, nature, and all the evolved adaptations that it permits favoring the survival of organisms by myriad pathways—but that vastly larger thing itself still has no share in reason.

This feature of the currently prevalent, naturalistic understanding of reason—namely, that it is found within the human being exclusively, even if it is just as natural as echolocation or photosynthesis—is more indebted to the Cartesian tradition than is usually acknowledged. Descartes grounded his human exceptionalism in dualism, taking the soul as something nonnatural and ontologically discontinuous with the human body, which for its part was on the same side of the great ontological divide as animal bodies, oceans, volcanoes, and stars. But naturalism has been effective at finding ways to preserve human exceptionalism while at the same time collapsing the ontological divide posited by dualism. The most prevalent view today is that reason is something uniquely human, which we deploy in a world that is variously conceived as either nonrational or positively irrational. In this, modern thought sharply departs from certain basic presuppositions of the ancient world. On the most common ancient understanding of the human being as the rational animal, it was taken for granted that human beings were sharing in something, reason, that did not simply exist immanently within them, but rather had its own independent existence. Human beings were, among animals, the only ones that possessed reason as a mental faculty that they could bring to bear in their choices and actions, but this did not mean that the rest of nature had no share of reason at all. Rather, the world itself was a rationally ordered whole: it was permeated by, was characterized by, was an expression of, reason.

It is true that in the history of analytic philosophy we find a prominent view that is fairly similar to the ancient one. Thus in Gottlob Frege and the early Wittgenstein, the structure of facts in the world is the same as the structure of propositions in human-generated arguments: the real and the intelligible are one. In more recent years John McDowell has pushed an even bolder account of the identity of mind and world, to the point that some critics have accused him—as if it were prima facie evident that this is a bad thing—of absolute idealism.[1] But for the most part the presumption has been that, as Gassendi put it in the seventeenth century, logic is the art of ordering our thoughts, and not the force that makes the world itself an ordered whole rather than a dark chaos.

The widespread ancient sense of rationality is perhaps what also lies behind the curious expression in contemporary American English, in which we describe a decision that is particularly easy to make as a "no-brainer." The implication here is that one could take the pre-scribed path even if one did not have a brain—the organ standing in here metonymically for its function—simply in virtue of the fact that its rightness is inscribed in the order of things. Not having a brain, or any consciousness at all, yet doing the correct thing anyway, this pe-culiar phrase reminds us, might be the ultimate expression of reason.[2]

This is the vision of the world, and of humanity's place in it, im-parted in the Australian poet Les Murray's lines:

> Everything except language
> knows the meaning of existence.
> Trees, planets, rivers, time
> know nothing else. They express it
> moment by moment as the universe.[3]

The world itself is, on this view, what bears meaning. Our own lan-guage, and our efforts to portray the world in it, far from being what is meaningful, are only feeble and inadequate echoes of this world, cut-ting us off from it. It does not connect us to the world; still less does it make us the world's masters. This is also something like the metaphysi-cal and cosmological vision, if we dare to call it that, at the heart of the Gospels. When John writes, "In the beginning was the Word," he is describing the condition of the world independently of human reflec-tion on it, and the term he finds to best characterize that condition is *logos*. In St. Jerome's Latin Bible this term will be rendered not as *ratio*, but rather as *verbum*, not as "reason," but as "word." But the historical and conceptual link to reason is clear. The world is an ordered whole, with each part where it should be, thanks to *logos*. This *logos* has often been assimilated to Christ, or seen as the abstract conceptual principle underlying the concrete natural world, and whose human counterpart, or whose embodiment, is Christ. Conceptualizing Christ in this way was central to the early articulation of a philosophically rich Christian theology, one that made it palatable to the Greeks. Thus, for example, Origen, the third-century CE church father writing in Alexandria, articulated an account of Christ as that being whose soul is most perfectly assimilated to the *logos*, and in turn took the *logos* to be nothing other than the rational order of nature. As Carlos Fraenkel remarks, someone who thinks in this way "will hardly concede that the doctrine at the heart of Christianity is not accessible to reason."[4]

These associations might seem too specific to Christian theology to be of much use for our understanding of the history of the concept of reason. But we might also understand them, from the opposite direction, as the result of an effort among Christian thinkers to render philosophical concepts so as to anchor them in the holy texts, and thus, perhaps, give them safe passage in a civilization increasingly narrowly devoted to its scripture as the exclusive authority in human life. In philosophical schools from antiquity to the modern period, Christ is conceptualized abstractly as the principle pervading the world and making it an ordered whole. Such a view is particularly prominent in early modern rationalism. In the seventeenth century, the Jewish philosopher Baruch Spinoza explicitly states his sympathy for a version of Christianity in which Christ is rendered abstractly in just this way, as the rational principle of the world. In his *Ethics*, published in 1676, as well as in his *Theological-Political Treatise* of 1670, Spinoza explicitly identifies the "Spirit of Christ" as nothing other than "the idea of God."[5] On this alone, he explains in the later work, "it depends that man should be free, and desire for other men the good he desires for himself." Here Christianity, into which centuries earlier Origen had worked to incorporate philosophy, has now itself been converted into the articulation of a bold rationalist egalitarianism. The Cambridge Platonist philosopher Anne Conway, a near contemporary of Spinoza, gives a similar philosophical interpretation of Christ—she comes to this view via the burgeoning Quaker movement, which had syncretistically incorporated many influences from Jewish Kabbalistic thought. In seventeenth-century Europe, Judaism and Christianity were in some spots converging to produce new articulations of reason grounded in ancient traditions of faith.

For Leibniz—who was born in Leipzig as a Lutheran but would arrive by the end of his life at a maximally liberal variety of nondenominational Christianity—the persons of the Trinity for the most part do not figure into the treatment of the world's rationality. This rationality for him seems rather to be inspired in no small measure by the ancient Stoic vision of the cosmos as a harmony, in which everything "breathes together" or "conspires." But the Stoic vision and the Christian vision, in turn, are both variations on a more general idea: that reason is not just "in our heads," and if it is in there, this is only because the human mind, with its faculty of reason, is a reflection of the rational order of the world.

To hold that the world is itself rational is generally to hold that it is composed in a rational way, that all of its parts make up an ordered and unified whole—that it, to cite the Greek term that translates the Hebrew Bible's "formless and empty," is not a "chaos" ("Now the earth was formless and empty, darkness was over the surface of the deep, and the Spirit of God was hovering over the waters" [Genesis 1:2]). On the most common understanding of divine creation in the Abrahamic religious traditions, God does not make the world out of nothing, but rather imposes order on something that is already there, namely, that which had previously been formless and empty, "chaotic." It is only when the order is there that it deserves to be called a "world" at all, or, alternatively, a "cosmos." Both of these terms are connected etymologically with the ideas of decoration and adornment. The latter term shares a common ancestor with "cosmetics": what you apply to your face in the hope of transforming it from a chaotic mess into an ordered whole.

Thinking of reason as the principle of order in a composite whole brings us closer to the other primary meaning of the Latin term *ratio*. It is not just the equivalent of our "reason," from which we also get "rationality"; "ratio," in the mathematical sense, is the relation between the numerator and denominator of a fraction. The two senses are not as far apart as they might as first seem. Think, for example, of the traditional study of musical harmonies. In Pythagorean tuning there are "pure" and "impure" ratios between intervals. Knowing what the ratios are is what enables us to play a scale on a musical instrument, picking out notes that agree with one another and that sound pleasant together. This pleasant sound is a sensual sign of the world being constituted out of ratios, or, to put it another way, of the world's rationality (bracketing, for now, problems such as the diagonal of the square that caused Hippasus such grief).

The Stoic philosophers, such as Epictetus, would hold that the well-orderedness of the cosmos qualifies it as a living being in the literal sense, with its own organic body like an animal or plant. This view would be rejected by the majority of subsequent philosophers, in part because it seemed to threaten to bring with it the corollary view that God is the soul whose body is the world. It would be the worst sort of heresy, in the Abrahamic traditions, to conceive of God as immanent in the world rather than as transcendent. Spinoza, famously, courted precisely that heresy with the view that "God" and "nature" afford two different ways of saying exactly the same thing. The Stoics for their part had not held this view, but instead defended the doctrine of a "world soul," distinct from any transcendent creator God.

Some, such as Leibniz, who rejected the view that the world is ordered by a unifying soul principle, would nonetheless take the world to be in itself rational in the sense that its order is a reflection of the rationality of its creator. The world is for him rational, not in that it consciously makes inferences or carries out proofs, but rather in the more limited sense that it reflects, in the totality of individuals that exist within it and in the degrees of perfection that these individuals realize, the existence of reason. Where does this reason exist, if not as a faculty of the rationally ordered world? Most often it is attributed to the creator God, outside of the world, of whose reason the world is a sort of mirror or testimony. All of nature would thus be rational somewhat as a pocket watch with intricate interworking parts is rational. It is not itself *reflecting on* the concept of time, but it is nonetheless *reflecting* this concept, as a sort of monument to, and congelation of, some external agent's rational mastery of it.

Brute Beasts

Natural beings are, we might say, on the account articulated in the previous section, embodiments of reason, but not possessors of reason. They are themselves no-brainers, in the sense just described. This view, in turn, offers a new insight into the question whether there are any beings in nature besides humans who may be considered rational. Excluding angels, which are arguably not natural (though this has also been much debated in the history of philosophy), the nonhuman candidates for rationality that have most frequently presented themselves are animals, often denoted by the somewhat more derogatory name of "beasts" (Latin, *bestia*), to which is frequently added the pejorative "brute" (Latin, *bruta*).

The majority view has been that human beings are rational, and animals are not, because human beings are capable of entertaining propositions, and making inferences based on them. Animal cognition has typically been held to be based on knowledge of concrete individual things alone, rather than of the universals under which these individual things are subsumed. Such a degree of cognition has generally been held to be something of which a being endowed only with a sensitive soul, as opposed to a rational soul, is capable. It is difficult to know how exactly such cognition might work, and philosophers have long debated whether the theory is even coherent. A dog is supposed to be able to recognize its master, but not to be able to subsume its master under the universal concept of "human." What is involved in the recognition, then? Is there no awareness that the master is in some respects more like other human beings, including even strangers, than he is like, say, a cat? And how can this awareness occur if it does not involve some sort of mastery of the universal concept in question?

In more recent times, following the demise of belief in animal souls (a belief that had previously been a matter of the straightforward meaning of the term involved: an animal is just that which is endowed with an *anima*, the Latin word for "soul"), we have tended to account for animal cognition in terms of "instinct" and "stimulus"—though it is worth asking how much of this new account is really new, and how much it simply involves updated vocabulary that preserves a much more deeply rooted theory. Somehow we have managed, from the era of animal souls to the era of animal instincts, to adhere to some sort of hierarchy of higher and lower, with humans and nonhuman animals occupying exactly the same positions as before.

Consider, again, the octopus. In recent years, this animal has been elevated from its previous lowly rank of self-destructive autocannibal to being, as the media reports have tended to put it, the alien among us, our invertebrate equals, the minds in the sea, and so on. In his remarkable 2016 book *Other Minds: The Octopus, the Sea, and the Deep Origins of Consciousness*,[6] a work based on both rigorous philosophical inquiry and deep knowledge of the relevant empirical facts, Peter Godfrey-Smith explores the cephalopod's evolution of mind in a process quite distinct from our own evolution. We would have to go back six hundred million years to find a common ancestor, and what we see in the octopus today is a system for instantiating mind quite unlike our own. The neurons responsible for what we take to be conscious activity in it, for one thing, are distributed throughout its entire body, not least throughout the arms that Plutarch believed he had observed being devoured by their owners (he may in fact have been observing the detached male hectocotylus, an adapted arm with genital power, that remains lodged in the female after mating).[7] Octopus intelligence, distributed as it is throughout the body, might well serve as an emblem of what we have called the "no-brainer", though now in a very literal sense: reason realized in nature otherwise than through the activity of an outsized neocortex.

The octopus, Godfrey-Smith suggests, "lives outside the usual body/brain divide."[8] Because it has evolved along such a different path from us, and its mental capacities seem to be organized so differently from ours, it seems misguided to seek to assess its intelligence according to a scale that sets up humans as the standard. None of the evidence adduced in *Other Minds* for the octopus's curiosity and resourcefulness suggests, however, that in its mental life the octopus is, say, racked by doubt, that it is ever blocked in the course of its actions by deliberation, or that it worries about what lies beyond the sphere of its own knowledge; that it wonders about the ontology of negative numbers, or the social construction of gender. It also evidently lacks episodic memory of the sort that would enable it to reminisce about its own early life, as well as lacking the mental projective capacity to reflect on its future or to worry about its finitude. Insofar as it lives in an eternal present, there is no compelling argument for attributing any great moral status to the octopus, any inherent right to life or to not being a prized commodity in Mediterranean cuisine. To this extent, even in one of the most forceful cases for the richness of another animal's mental life, the basic divide between human beings and all the others is kept in place.

The octopus, we presume, makes fairly clever choices, but does so without deliberating, hesitating, or doubting. In this respect we are generally prepared to attribute to it only a semblance of rationality, for true rationality, many have thought, requires the power to entertain alternatives and to decide between them. There has, however, been a minority view throughout history, which has held that animals, precisely to the extent that they do *not* make inferences, and therefore do not deliberate, are for this very reason not only rational, but still more rational than human beings. This is the view expressed in Girolamo Rorario's sixteenth-century treatise *Quod animalia bruta ratione utantur melius homine*, that is, *That Brute Animals Make Better Use of Reason than Men.*[9] Animals do not deliberate; they simply cut, as the saying goes, right to the chase. They act, rather than thinking about acting, and they are never, ever, wrong. This is not to say that they are never foiled in their actions, that they never turn the wrong way in fleeing from a predator only to find themselves cornered. It is simply to say that their actions are, so to speak, one with the flow of natural events in the world, unhesitating.

It is human hesitation, deliberation, reasoning things through before acting, that has often been thought to cause a sort of ontological rupture between us and nature. Many philosophers have held this rupture up as what makes us distinctive and special, and as what makes us the only beings in nature that are not entirely *of* nature. But it has always been a great problem that it is precisely this rupture—which is, on the one hand, the thing that makes us relatively impressive among natural beings, the thing that connects us to the angels—that is also, on the other hand, the very thing that cuts us off from nature; it makes our movement through the natural world often feel more like groping and grasping than like real mastery. For some philosophers, such as Descartes, this problem is expressed in terms of the proneness of our faculty of reason to make mistakes. It is a flawed faculty because our will is infinite, while our understanding is finite.[10] If we were simply not to will ourselves to draw conclusions about what our understanding does not yet know, then we would never be in error. Brute beasts, to the extent that they have no free will, for the same reason are incapable of error.

Many later philosophers would in turn come to see this power not as something that might give us a sense of security or power in relation to the external world, but indeed as the source of a deep unease. The twentieth-century French existential philosopher Jean-Paul Sartre described the human being, or the "for-itself" character of human existence, as a "hole of being at the heart of being."[11] Hardly a comforting thought. Animals, by contrast, have generally been seen as beings of nature in the fullest sense, not as holes in being but rather as, so to speak, that which fills being up. This does not mean that they are less than us, but rather that they do not share in our peculiar existential plight, of being immersed in nature while also set apart from it: set apart, that is, by our deliberations and our long, labored processes of decision making within the space of application of our reason. According to Heidegger, animals are "poor-in-world": you look at a squirrel, and you can be confident there is just not that much going on in there. But being poor-in-world means that animals are more solidly *of* the world than we are, not cut off from it, but moving through it in a way that they do not themselves experience as problematic or complicated.

Rorario's work, while composed in the first half of the sixteenth century, would become far better known only with its several reeditions beginning in 1642, and would inspire an extensive and influential article, entitled "Rorarius," in the French freethinker Pierre Bayle's *Historical and Critical Dictionary*, first published in 1697.[12] Bayle's article, ostensibly on his Italian predecessor, reads like a strange experiment, the work of an early modern David Foster Wallace, as roughly 90 percent of it consists of long footnotes in which he gives himself over to free reflections on the problem of animal souls. He notes that Rorario's own work is hardly a philosophical treatise, but more a compendium of "singular facts on the industry of animals and the malice of men."[13] The Italian author, who at the time of writing was serving as the papal nuncio to the king of Hungary, had believed that if these singular facts were simply acknowledged, it would be impossible to deny to animals the use of reason; the only remaining criterion for distinguishing human beings from animals would be not on the basis of reason, but rather on the basis of free will.

These two capacities have generally been run together: to be able to make free choices, to do this rather than that, presupposes the power to deliberate about the options, to make inferences, right or wrong, from known facts, as to the best course of action. Vice versa, to be able to deliberate has been supposed to involve the power to take one course of action rather than another as a result of this deliberation. But there is nothing essential about this connection. Rorario seems to think that it is enough for reason to be manifested in a creature's actions, whether these actions be freely chosen or no, in order for that creature to be deemed rational. Bayle for his part asserts that the facts cataloged by Rorario should "be an embarrassment both to the sectaries of Descartes and to those of Aristotle."[14] As Dennis Des Chene has noted, this is a strange thing for Bayle to say.[15] After all, the Scholastic philosophers, followers of Aristotle in the late Middle Ages and into the early modern period, had a perfectly coherent way, or so they thought (and so, evidently, does Des Chene think) of accounting for what appears to be learning and judgment in animals. For the sixteenth-century Scholastic philosopher Francisco Suárez, when the sheep flees the wolf, it is exercising a certain *vis aestimativa* or estimative power, which does not involve reason, indeed "does not exceed the grade of the sensitive [powers]."[16] The sheep is able to recognize the wolf as a wolf, and as an enemy, but without having to subsume the wolf under any universal concepts. As Des Chene explains, it does not place the wolf "under a concept of badness, it simply *recognizes* the wolf as bad."[17]

Again, whether such conceptless recognition is possible has been the source of long debate in the history of philosophy, and the debate continues today, though in updated terms, in discussions of animal cognition. Descartes would for his part find a way of accounting for the sheep's ability to perceive the wolf and to flee it without appealing to any cognitive function in the sheep at all. He and the Scholastics were certainly aware of the remarkable industry of animals. But then as now, a priori commitments about what sort of being an animal is generally prove powerful enough to account for anything an animal is shown to be able to do. If you are committed on such a priori grounds to the view that no nonhuman is capable of higher cognitive function, you will always be able to account for any complex behavior in animals without having to revise your views.

What much of this discussion seems to miss, however, is that the attribution of reason to animals might not require any proof of higher cognitive function in them at all, for it may be that their "industry" itself is rational—just as the pocket watch is rational as a congelation of the reason that structures the world, as a "no-brainer." We may extend this conception of rationality far further than animals. Emanuele Coccia argues, in a recent book calling upon philosophers to take plants seriously, that "it was not necessary to wait for the appearance of human beings, nor of the higher animals, for the technical force of shaping matter to become an individual faculty."[18] He asserts that there is a "cerebrality" innate in the vegetal seed, as "the operations of which the seed is capable cannot be explained except by presupposing that it is equipped with a form of knowing, a program for action, a pattern that does not exist in the manner of consciousness, but that permits it to accomplish everything it does without error."[19]

This might seem like loose analogy, or equivocation on the meaning of "knowing," and it might seem question begging to assume at the outset that whatever possesses a "program" must therefore possess knowledge. However, if we are in fact prepared to go with Rorario's conception of animal reason, as grounded in what animals *do* rather than in what they think, then there can in fact be no reason to withhold reason from those natural beings, such as plants, that have seldom been suspected of having any knowing, in the sense of cognition, at all. This is the understanding of knowing or thinking that is also at work in Eduardo Kohn's recent, bold account of "how forests think."[20] For him, setting out from a theory of signs elaborated by the American pragmatist philosopher C. S. Peirce in the nineteenth century, any system, such as a rain forest, may be interpreted as a system of signs, quite apart from the question whether any individual vectors within this system are beings capable of interpreting these signs. There are, Kohn argues, nonrepresentational signs too; once we acknowledge this, we are able to see thought spread abundantly throughout nature, rather than being limited to only a few "higher" creatures with particularly big brains.

A similar sort of uncertainty as to whether reason is an internal state of a thinking being, or rather the external execution of the right motions by a being that may or may not be thinking at all, seems to be the cause of an equivocation at the heart of much, if not most, discussion of the specter of artificial intelligence—particularly among people in the technology industry and in tech journalism with little patience for philosophical distinctions. Are the machines going to "surpass" us, as many AI commentators often say, at the moment they start doing, better than we do, things we now consider to be fundamentally human? Or are they going to surpass us when they begin to *consciously* deliberate about what they are doing, and when they develop the power to do one thing rather than another for no other reason than that that is their entirely arbitrary whim? Is it enough that they accomplish what they do without error? Is this too a form of knowing? If it is good enough for plants, then why should it not be good enough for machines?

The fact that these questions have never really been worked out to general satisfaction, for animals, plants, machines, extraterrestrials, and the physical universe, reveals that we really do not know what intelligence is, and so we cannot possibly know what we are looking for when we are seeking to identify instances of artificial intelligence or nonhuman intelligence. The same problems plague the discussion of reason. A sober assessment of the way the term "rationality" is in fact used would lead us to conclude, with Hartry Field, that it functions as little more than "an approval-term."[21] There is no settled fact of the matter as to what rationality is, whether it is something that can characterize unthinking natural or artificial systems, or whether it is the thinking itself, with which only a few beings are endowed, and in virtue of which these few beings stand to some extent outside of these systems. There is, however, an important asymmetry between rationality and irrationality here: what Rorario and Coccia emphasize about animals and plants is, in effect, that they always get things right. The absence of deliberation means that they do what they do without error—even if, again, sometimes there are other powers or beings in nature preventing them from arriving at their natural end. Even if rationality extends beyond human beings, or beings with higher cognition and the capacity for abstract representation, irrationality still seems to be limited to the narrower case of beings that have higher cognition and that fail to deploy their abstract representations in the correct way, beings that, as holes in being at the heart of being, just keep screwing up.

For Rorario, animals are more rational than human beings because, lacking higher cognition, they can *only* be rational. Higher cognition gives us, on this line of thinking, not rationality, but only irrationality. This might be cause to despair, but it is also an interesting reversal of a familiar old formula. On this new inverted account, rationality is widely distributed, and all too common. What makes us human beings unique is our irrationality. We are the irrational animal.

An Imperfect Superpower

The prevailing view in philosophy remains the opposite of the one defended by Rorario. It holds, rather, that we are the rational animal. This definition is occasionally lengthened to include other apparently universal properties—thus, for example, the late-antique Spanish polymath Isidore of Seville writes that a human being "is an animal, rational, mortal, land-dwelling, bipedal, capable of laughter"[22]—but rationality and animality are the only members of this list that have consistently made the cut. This remains the case even though the notion of rationality is no longer one in which human beings share in some otherworldly or transcendent reality from which other beings are excluded. Rather, rationality is generally understood today as an adaptive trait common to all and only human beings, and comparable to any other trait we might find throughout nature, even if its origins and function are harder to account for, and even if it remains a great mystery why it is not more widespread in nature.

In their 2017 book *The Enigma of Reason*,[23] which represents, at the time of this writing, a cutting-edge synthesis and novel interpretation of experimental and theoretical research on rationality, Hugo Mercier and Dan Sperber portray human rationality as comparable to echolocation in bats: a sort of superpower, which must have emerged as a result of selective pressures, but which is also perplexingly rare in the animal world. Mercier and Sperber, like nearly all researchers in their field, are thoroughgoing naturalists, but also human exceptionalists. They are trying to find a satisfying naturalistic account of what it is that makes human beings so special; they take it as more or less settled that human beings *are* special, and that human reason is not simply our own inflection of something that is spread much more widely throughout nature.

Reason is for them a special kind of inferential ability, which is acquired over the course of our early lives, rather than being instinctive. It is, further, something of which we are conscious when we are deploying it; it involves intuition rather than being a faculty, as many other thinkers have supposed, distinct from intuition. Reason is, for them, a variety of intuition that involves the representation not of things and events, but rather the representation of representations. In other words, it is intuition about abstract ideas, "a mechanism for intuitive inferences about one kind of representations, namely, reasons."[24] Mercier and Sperber take reason to be an "enigma" in a double sense:

both because it is such a rare and exceptional superpower, and also, more relevantly for our purposes, because it is evidently so severely flawed, so apt to lead us astray. We continually find ourselves in situations in which we disagree with our fellow human beings as to what qualifies as a rational conclusion with respect to logical and social questions. And we are plagued by rampant confirmation bias: the systematic error of noticing, preferring, and selecting new information that reinforces what we already believe. Mercier and Sperber cite Descartes's attempted explanation of how such flaws are possible: "The diversity of our opinions," Descartes writes, "arises not from the fact that some of us are more reasonable than others, but solely that we have different ways of directing our thoughts, and do not take into account the same things . . . The greatest minds are capable of the greatest vices as well as the greatest virtues."[25]

Mercier and Sperber protest that this does not provide a solution to the enigma of our flawed reason but simply restates it. Their answer to the enigma proceeds from their naturalism, where reason is in the end a "modest module," existing alongside other intuitive inference models, and selected in the course of human evolution in view of the work it does for us in producing and evaluating "justifications and arguments in dialogue with others."[26] This is what they call the "interactionist" approach, which they contrast with the "intellectualist" approach, according to which the function of reason "is to reach better beliefs and make better decisions on one's own."[27] On this latter, more traditional view, reason is expected to deliver to us the truth, and so we find it problematic when it fails to do so. On the new, interactionist approach, by contrast, reason is simply an adaptation that helps us, to some extent, in our interactions with others. It made no promise to be a deliverer of truth, and so if we are disappointed in it for leading us astray, our disappointment is misplaced. Mercier and Sperber locate the reason for reason's imperfection in nature. Reason is imperfect because it is a product of natural evolution, which simply does the best it can with available materials within given environmental conditions. This account conforms well with the experience many of us have of our own faculty of reason, as akin to the experience of pain in the spinal column that holds up our bad backs: an arrangement that is doing the best it can, but that seems always on the verge of giving out.

One may view online ample footage of pitiable tourists, unable to continue along glass walkways over deep canyons. Some of them collapse, cling to the side, and moan with terror. It does no good to tell them that the glass building materials are structurally as sound as steel, and that the simple fact that we cannot see through steel, as we can see through glass, changes nothing as to the actual danger involved.

I myself am terrified of flying. This is not a terror of the unknown: I do it all the time, and each time I am thrust anew into indescribable dread. I feel forsaken, left to the cruel and indifferent whim of the sublime forces of the sky, where no human being was ever meant to penetrate. The last thing I wish to hear when I confess this very personal fact about myself is a recitation of statistics concerning the relative safety of air travel. Trust me, I want to reply, I *know* the statistics. I have memorized them. For any airline, I can tell you the year, the place, the causes, and the number of fatalities of all of its major disasters. I know that this all adds up to a small fraction of the comparable fatalities in car accidents, but it makes no difference. I am not afraid of cars; I am afraid of airplanes. I assume this has something to do with the continuity of highway travel with the sort of experiences my hominid ancestors may have had. Simply running down a hill or floating in rapids is experientially somewhat like riding in a car, while none of these is anything like flying several miles above the earth, over the ocean, over the clouds.

Nor do I enjoy discovering bats flying around my home, as happened some years ago, even if I know that they occupy an important ecological niche, that no blood-sucking bat species inhabit my continent, and so forth. Here, too, I feel as though there has been a change of subject, and as though I'm being scolded or lectured at—batsplained, as it were—as if my displeasure had something to do with a lack of education or awareness of the relevant scientific facts.

One more example of this sort suggests itself, though one removed from my own personal experience. I have largely overcome ethnocentrism and xenophobia in my own life, having worked toward a vision of the kind of life I decided I wanted to lead, early on, in which other-ness was held to be high-status and desirable, rather than low-status and in need of avoidance. And yet it is fairly clear that this approach to human social reality functions as an inversion of the normal approach to diversity throughout human history and across human cultures, which has been, by default, based on at least an implicit presumption of one's own group's superiority. Research has shown, in fact, that the folk science of human difference tends to involve an implicit essential-ism about the differences between groups, that is, a folk theory of dif-ference that is expressed in the modern world as racism.[28]

We may presume that this has at least something to do with the fact that interacting with strangers really does involve risks that interaction with familiars does not. A certain wariness of other groups makes good sense—when it is, for example, perfectly likely that they are intending to raid your cattle under cover of night. It should not be at all surprising to find that this wariness has been underlain throughout human his-tory by a propensity to essentialize, or to take as not merely superficial, but rather as deeply and irreversibly real, the differences that divide one human cultural group from another.

Racism is bad, in part because it is false. It is scientifically un-grounded: the differences we perceive as essential and salient are al-ways ultimately trivial. Yet it is also, from the long perspective of human evolutionary history, perfectly rational. As Edouard Machery and Luc Faucher have written, sometimes bad folk science can be good epistemology: the way we divide the world up makes good sense for many purposes, even if science can make no use of it once we begin to articulate the underlying principles.[29] This fact, in turn, can easily make the deployment of scientific information in argument against racist ideology seem futile, in much the same way that it is futile to tell me about airline safety statistics or the harmlessness of insectivorous bats. In all of these cases we are dealing with phobias, and it is only the most inadequate understanding of how phobias work that would take them to be curable by a supplement of information.

As we will consider in detail further on in this book, there is an ad-ditional problem, in the case of race if not in the case of airline safety.

This problem arises from the concerted effort among many who suffer from the relevant phobia—that is, racists—to lapse into severe confirmation bias and to conjure up alternative information of their own. As a result, not only does correct information sent their way about the science of human diversity not have the desired effect, but it is shot down, before it can be processed, by the various half-truths and errors that the racist has weaponized in his defense. This effort on the racist's part is roughly comparable to the unlikely scenario in which an aviophobe constructs for herself an alternative set of facts, a novel interpretation of the available statistics, say, in which travel by air turns out, for those who know the "real" facts, to be far more dangerous than travel by car.

Why does such an effort seem unlikely? Why is it that aviophobes usually just own up to the fact that they are "being irrational," whereas racists build up such a thick carapace of protective pseudofacts? I may be underestimating my fellow aviophobes, or have not yet discovered that particular corner of the internet, but it seems likely that the difference lies in the fact that we suffer our way through in-flight turbulence alone, deeply alone, whereas racists turn their suffering, at the thought of the equal existence of others who do not appear to be like them, into joy and solidarity within a community of people who do so appear. This is easier to do with some phobias than with others, for reasons having to do with the nature of the phenomena or things or people triggering them. All of the phobias we have considered here seem to be, like back pain in vertebrates only recently converted to bipedalism, a consequence of the fact that reason is an evolved faculty, which does the best it can under real-world, and perpetually changing, circumstances. We can massage these phobias, and organize society so as to minimize their damage, but they are not going to go away.

Small Pain Points

Or are we just giving up too easily? Might there be some way to improve our thinking so as to truly overcome fear of flying, fear of bats, fear of ethnic others, fear of glass-bottom bridges? Perhaps the most prominent para-academic community of rationalists is the internet-based group known as LessWrong, founded in 2009 as an online forum and blog by Eliezer Yudkowsky. This group is devoted to applying Bayes's theorem, borrowed from probability theory, in their own daily lives, in order to make decisions conducive to greater happiness and thriving. Its members are focused on studying how cognitive biases influence our unexamined reasoning processes, and thence on how to eliminate them. LessWrong is not a group of logicians in a narrow sense, but if we understand "logic" in the broad Gassendian sense of the art of ordering our thoughts, then it would include most of the core interests of LessWrong's members. Yudkowsky has spelled out many of his theoretical views on these topics and on artificial intelligence, not in a doctoral dissertation or in academic or even popular nonfiction books, but in *Harry Potter* fan fiction, which he posts online at the LessWrong website. LessWrong is linked to the Center for Applied Rationality (CFAR), and to the Machine Intelligence Research Institute (MIRI), both based in Berkeley, and both thoroughly immersed in the world of Silicon Valley libertarianism.[30]

Tellingly, Yudkowsky is hailed, like many in this subculture, as a high school dropout, whose intelligence must therefore be something not inculcated by a methodical tradition of pedagogy, but rather a sort of innate spark of something called "genius" (to which we will turn our attention in chapter 4). Such a life course is valued throughout Silicon Valley, and not just at LessWrong. Thus a fellowship program run by Peter Thiel—the billionaire founder of PayPal and (at least initially) a supporter of Trump's presidency, who as early as 2009 declared that he no longer believed in the compatibility of freedom and democracy[31]—offers $100,000 to selected young people who are willing to drop out of university to pursue a project of invention or innovation. Another project funded by Thiel, Imitatio, was "conceived as a force to press forward the consequences of [the French theorist] René Girard's remarkable insights into human behavior and culture."[32] Imitatio's website tells us of its executive director Jimmy Kaltreider that he is "Principal at Thiel Capital," and, moreover, that he "studied

History at Stanford, where he almost graduated."[33] Kaltreider's bio perhaps reveals an ambivalence that is less evident among the more radical techno-capitalists: there is no better-credentialed academic than René Girard. He received his prerequisite diplomas—a first one in medieval history from the prestigious École des Chartes in 1947, and then a PhD in history from Indiana University—and went on to a comfortable teaching and writing career at Stanford. Kaltreider is caught in between Girard's mandarin legitimacy and Thiel's maverick outsiderhood: wishing to promote the significant body of work of a canonical academic thinker, he also wishes to share in the free spirit that funders like Thiel are aggressively promoting, part of which involves the idea that educational institutions, with their slowly accrued curricula and traditions, with their hoops to be jumped through, are nothing but an impediment to the full expression of individual genius. So while Yudkowsky dropped out of high school, Kaltreider "almost graduated" from Stanford. The age at which one jumps ship is also a measure of the depth, the hardcoreness, of commitment to the romantic ideal of the go-it-alone great man.

CFAR offers rationality workshops at which one can, for several thousand dollars, learn such things as "the science behind the body's stress reactions, and skills to make it easier to ask experts for knowledge, clients for business, or investors for capital."[34] The Thiel Foundation has contributed over 1.5 million dollars to MIRI. We will return to the political dimensions of recent Silicon Valley ideology later on. What is important here is to note a curious development within the LessWrong community that seems to confirm the worries of Cicero, Gassendi, and so many others throughout history. In April 2017 the LessWrong community planned an event called, for reasons unclear to outsiders, a "Hufflepuff Unconference," which seems to have been provoked by the realization that "many people in rationality communities feel lonely," and that "there are lots of small pain points in the community."[35] The organizers determined it would therefore be necessary for the members of the community to get together to talk about their feelings. "The emotional vibe of the community," it was explained, "is preventing people from feeling happy and connected, and a swath of skillsets that are essential for *group* intelligence and ambition to flourish are undersupplied."[36]

One might wonder, particularly as an outsider: wasn't this project of the emendation of the faculty of reason supposed to be the ticket to happiness? Wasn't this, mutatis mutandis, the promise made by the Stoics and by Spinoza, that if you will just set about ordering your thoughts in the right way, and making the right inferences from what you know, then your thoughts will be harmonized with reality and you will therefore protect yourself from the disappointments that arise from disharmony with it? Is it not this disharmony that leads to the dominance of reason by the passions? The emphasis in the LessWrong announcement is on the fact that troubles arise when we move from individual rationality to group intelligence. (Hell is other people, Sartre wrote.)[37] But long ago the Stoics, at least, posited that any individual is capable, by his own means, of ordering his thoughts in such a way as to be unperturbed by the various ways others disappoint and undermine us.

What has gone wrong? There seems to be an acknowledgment in the announcement for the Unconference that the negative emotional vibe is not simply incidental to the core activity of the group, but is somehow being generated by this activity. And one wonders, here, whether we are not seeing the limits of autodidacticism, of a go-it-alone approach whose pitfalls might have been avoided if Plutarch and Cicero had occupied a somewhat more prominent role in this movement's canon, and Harry Potter a somewhat less prominent one. To attempt to work through these great problems, of rationality and happiness, to attempt to ameliorate self and society, without attention to history, is irrational if anything is.

CHAPTER THREE

The Sleep of Reason; or, Dreams

➤➤➤➤➤

Upon Awakening

NEW FRANCE, 1671. The reverend father had grown accustomed to beaver meat and squash, and even to the cakes made from maize flour chewed up and spit out by elder women before baking. These were considered a delicacy, though the first time he was made to eat one, he could not keep himself from retching. He had grown accustomed to the sight of prisoners of war, captured and taunted, who seemed to fall into delirious ecstasy as they burned, as the bones of their feet and hands were broken one by one. Could a man train himself to endure such an ordeal with defiant joy, not only tolerating but even relishing the pain? He knew that many of the tribe's men had been through it. They had not been born to the tribe at all, but were adopted after being taken in war and subjected to long torture. They had been given new names, and then incorporated into families as if nothing could be more natural, and seemed now, though scarred and hobbled, perfectly at home. A man can get used to many things, but one thing that would never leave the priest fully at ease was the way these men reacted to their dreams.

He had come to New France to spread the gospel and to baptize the Iroquois into the Roman Catholic Church, and often he had the impression that he was making a persuasive case to the generous men who had allowed him to come live with them, to hunt with them, and to eat with them. At moments it became clear to him that no matter how persuasive he took his case for conversion to be, in the end whether the natives consented to baptism depended not at all on his gift of persuasion, on logical arguments or even imaginative descriptions of the tortures of hell. They were swayed, rather, only by the dreams they had had, which, they believed, gave them visions of the world beyond this world, from which spirits dictated to them their course of action in waking life.

For the first several months he refused to answer when the men asked him, upon awakening, what he himself had dreamed. He shrugged off their questioning and told them it did not matter. But after a time it became clear to him that the report of a dream worked far better than an argument for winning a person over to one's own side. These men take their dreams for God himself, he began to think. Dreams are the only God of this country. But the only spirit that comes to them in dreams is the devil, and if one night a dream reveals to them the truth of our faith, the very next night that revelation may be reversed.

The chief had even given his consent to be baptized, and had nodded his head approvingly when he was instructed in the principal mysteries of the faith. But one morning soon after, upon awakening, he called for the reverend father and informed him somberly that these doctrines were nothing but a great deceit, "that he had seen himself in a dream, in Heaven, where the French had received him with howls, as it is their custom to do at the arrival of prisoners of war, and that when he had escaped from them, they had already taken red-hot pokers in their hands with which to burn him."[1] The Jesuit had thought himself successful in portraying Christian salvation as the opposite of the world of suffering and misery that, he believed, was all that the Iroquois knew. And now he saw that this effort had been in vain; heaven looked no different from the fate of a prisoner of war after he had been captured. He worried that the chief might decide to kill him, on the basis of nothing more than a dream: something that just comes to us, passively, a string of pell-mell impressions, not anything attained through active reasoning.

The archaeologist and historian Bruce Trigger wrote a generation ago of early modern Jesuit encounters with the Iroquois's neighbors and frequent enemies, that "in terms of their beliefs about the supernatural forces that were at work in the world, Jesuit and Huron shared considerably more in common with each other than either does with twentieth century man."[2] Trigger might have been working with an idealized version of what "twentieth century man" was really like, but beyond this—however much both the French Jesuit and the Native American worldviews were in the seventeenth century populated by supernatural beings and forces—on the question of epistemic access to these beings and forces, the French and the Americans could not have been more different. This difference marks out a crucial feature of the emerging identity of the modern West.

Our Jesuit is writing, from what would later be Quebec, to his superior in France. This was thirty years after the publication of Descartes's *Meditations on First Philosophy*, a work all of the following generation of French Jesuits knew well, even if it was subject to their frequent criticism. In this work, not only does Descartes reject the impressions that come to us in dreams as unreliable reports of how the world really is. More crucially, one of his principal concerns is to demonstrate that the knowledge we have of reality is not merely dreamed, but instead comes from actually existing external things, and that, with the help of philosophical reason, we are able to clearly and certainly distinguish between waking and sleeping. Descartes's authoritative source of knowledge was nothing other than his own mind. He believed this mind to be endowed with the faculty of reason; it was also, for better or worse, endowed with some lesser faculties, such as imagination and sensation, that arose from the fact that the mind, during this life, is intimately wrapped up with, though ontologically distinct from, the body.

It may be that there is no better measure of an era's relationship to the faculty of reason than its willingness or unwillingness to pay attention to dreams. By the time of the first contact with Native Americans, European travelers would find the reliance of indigenous peoples on oneiromancy—decisions about future actions made on the basis of dream interpretation—foreign and "savage" in the extreme, characteristic of a distant early stage of human history. The modern European mentality that accompanied the travelers to the Americas was the one most clearly formulated by Descartes, who in his *Meditations* effectively seeks to provide a convincing argument that life is not but a dream, that we may be absolutely certain of the difference between our waking lives and the hallucinations that come to us in sleep. These hallucinations, for Descartes, are nothing more than a regrettable error, to be regretfully acknowledged and then relegated to their proper corner of human experience.

Even for those who are not canonical defenders of rationalist philosophy, in the modern world there is something at least mildly shameful about sleep. Marcel Proust's narrator in *In Search of Lost Time*, published in seven volumes between 1913 and 1927, tells of the family maid, the blushing Françoise, who would deploy the most implausible euphemisms to avoid openly acknowledging the fact that she had fallen asleep—that she had not only shut her eyes but, in so doing, slipped into another cognitive state in which her usual decorum and faithfulness to rules could no longer be expected to hold. And at around the same time this provincial French maid was slipping into dreams in which she found herself not quite herself, and yet somehow more herself than ever, in which her usual guard was let down and all decorum suspended, a Viennese psychiatrist was developing the idea that it is in dreams that the deepest level of the self comes out. This self, the psychiatrist imagined, is a bubbling cauldron of irrational desires, and the rationality of waking life is but a thin wrapping placed around these desires in the vain hope of keeping them contained. Over the course of the twentieth century, it would become fashionable in many quarters to acknowledge, and even to celebrate, this irrationality, to excuse one's self-destructive behavior on the grounds that it was only the unconscious at work, and nothing could be done to stop it.

We might say that modern philosophy is born in the seventeenth century at the moment Descartes proves, or claims to prove, that he knows with certainty that our waking experiences are not mere illusions, are not a dream. There follow a couple of centuries in which waking life is the only life that counts, at least for grown men. And then dreams come back with a vengeance, with what their great advocate at the end of the nineteenth century would call "the return of the repressed." In Sigmund Freud's psychoanalysis, dreams are not an aberration, not a sequence of mistakes to which we are regrettably subjected each night. They are, rather, the key to understanding who we really are. Freud's purportedly scientific work would have vast repercussions in nearly all domains of arts and culture throughout the early to mid-twentieth century. In this respect, he ushered in an age of irrationality, one that has been resisted, of course, by sundry species of prudes and squares. But it would pass its electric charge down from the various Dadaists and surrealists and other avant-gardes of the First World War, through to the cultural revolutionaries of the 1960s—and, one might contend, on to the internet trolls of today—sowing discord, disrupting the business-as-usual of rule-governed civil discourse, wreaking havoc, having fun, letting imagination and unreason run wild.

But let us not get ahead of ourselves. There were of course dream interpreters lurking around Paris, Amsterdam, and London when Descartes wrote his treatise as well. Kings and other highly placed people were known to consult them. But by the mid-seventeenth century such consultations were either motivated by a sort of ostentatious irrationalism, when undertaken by the elite, or carried out in semisecrecy, in the back alleys of the city, with a stigma not far from that of prostitution. In fact this hierarchical distinction between waking and sleeping as sources of knowledge begins to be elaborated long before Descartes. In his short treatise *On Prophecy in Sleep*, Aristotle had acknowledged of dream divination that "it is not an easy matter either to despise it or to believe in it," and asserted that it has at least "some show of reason."[3] The Greek philosopher would ultimately reduce whatever visionary capacity there might be in sleep, however, either to coincidence, or to the sort of physiological rumblings of a coming illness that might first be felt in sleep even if they are still subperceptible to the waking mind.

Aristotle found it dubious, however, that "the sender of such dreams should be God," given that "those to whom he sends them are not the best and wisest, but merely commonplace persons."[4] Certainly, among the Iroquois and the Hurons, not just anyone's visionary dream would carry significant weight. Rather there were people occupying a special role, shamans or seers, who were not merely commonplace people. Jesuit missionaries often noticed the ways in which the significance of dreams was emphasized or downplayed, depending on the practical exigencies of waking life. It was as if the seer was drawing on visions from sleep, but doing so with a full understanding that it was up to him to freely select which parts of which dreams might be invoked as relevant for waking life, and that it is only in waking life that the actions based on our choices have real consequences. But the fact remains that there was no one among the Native Americans attempting to demonstrate, as Descartes was, that what we think of as reality is not just a dream. For the most part they unproblematically included dreams within a unified vision of reality; they understood dreams to be instructive and meaningful as guides to what happens in waking life, and perhaps even connected together with waking life within the same causal web. Dreams mattered and were not to be explained away, or quickly brushed aside and forgotten, once we awaken and turn our attention to the real problems of sober-minded, rational, adult human life.

In Europe dreams would remain unseemly and worthy of repression in the centuries following Descartes, indeed up to the present day, notwithstanding Freud's earnest attempts beginning in fin-de-siècle Vienna to bring them out into the open, to create a sort of science of them, and to make them part of our rational public discussion. Freud had an impact on culture, particularly in the arts, but even at the height of psychoanalysis's popularity in the English-speaking world in the mid-twentieth century, it was generally a grave social error to, say, tell your boss about the dream you had last night. Your boss does not want to know about your dreams; your boss wants to know about your "solutions," and if these came to you in a dream, it were best to leave that part out. This is just part of what it means to be a competent person within our rationally functioning society. Oneiromancy is, for us, countercultural, counterproductive, and alien to a well-ordered life. It goes on, of course, but mostly in milieus that are as obscure as sleep itself.

A number of Descartes's contemporaries wrote works that they themselves described as "dreams," not because they were sincerely reporting their own dreams, but because they wished to permit themselves, in their writing, to appeal to the imagination rather more than would be possible in a straightforward philosophical text. Thus in 1608 Johannes Kepler wrote his *Somnium*,[5] in order to relate a number of bold ideas concerning lunar astronomy, in the course of an outlandish science-fiction story of witchcraft, out-of-body travel, and strange lunar beings. In 1692 the Mexican nun Sor Juana Inés de la Cruz published *El Sueño*, a philosophical poem in which the soul takes a voyage through a vivid symbolic landscape in its search for true knowledge of God.[6] Descartes's own *Meditations* themselves play on the dream genre in philosophical and confessional writing. The work is, among many other things, a flight of the imagination, but rather than embedding this flight in a dream, he presents it as a reflection, in waking life, that may be proved to not be a dream.

In the following century, in 1769, the materialist philosopher Denis Diderot plays with the dream genre in order to present his own philosophical views, in *Le rêve de D'Alembert* (*D'Alembert's Dream*).[7] And in 1799 we have one of the most iconic representations of a dream in modern history, not in literature but in figurative art: Francisco Goya's drawing *El sueño de la razón produce monstruos* (*The Sleep of Reason Engenders Monsters*). A man has fallen asleep, and owls and bats and other unidentifiable nocturnal creatures flutter out from his head. This is the vision of dreaming that motivates Descartes's concern to prove that we are not dreaming, or at least not always; for Descartes dreaming is a shutting down of reason, and the productions of the mind, when reason is shut down, are dangerous and dark. Yet a countertradition continues throughout modern philosophy, which recognizes the paradoxical result of the suppression of dreams. "In focusing upon one type of experience," the iconoclastic French philosopher Gaston Bachelard wrote in 1948, "the philosopher makes himself unresponsive to other types of experience. Sometimes very lucid minds become enclosed in their lucidity and deny the many glimmers given off from more shadowy psychic zones."[8] A theory of knowledge of the real world, he concludes, "which is disinterested in oneiric values, severs itself from certain of the interests that push us toward knowledge."[9]

Breaking the Law

What is it about dreams that makes them irrational, apart from the fact that they are not of reality, that they are, in effect, hallucinated? Geometry, on one influential understanding, is not of reality either, since its objects, triangles and circles and so on, are ideal entities and not physical objects in the world. Geometry, then, is about entities that are "in the head" no less than dreams are. Yet geometry is often taken to be the field in which rationality finds its purest and most perfect expression, while dreams are the field where unreason runs rampant. Thus whatever rationality is, it cannot be a matter of correct or accurate correspondence to the "real" world. That might be what *truth* is, but rationality, we may say as a first stab, has to do rather with making the correct inferences involving what we know, and we can indeed know quite a few things about imaginary or ideal entities. We can know, to trot out an example familiar to philosophers, that a unicorn is one-horned. This is not a fact that would need to be checked out through an empirical survey of real unicorns, as its truth does not depend on the existence of unicorns at all. It depends only on what is packed into the concept of a unicorn, and it is an existence-independent fact about unicorns that if you add another horn or two, then they cease to be unicorns altogether.

Dreams are not like geometrical proofs involving triangles, nor are they, generally, like our waking reflections upon unicorns. The descriptions we give are highly culturally specific, and what we remember of them is determined in no small measure by our personalities and by what we value. A medieval knight might have a dream of parhelia, and wake up believing it was an omen of an impending battle's outcome; I tend to have dreams saturated with animated images borrowed from Looney Tunes and antique video games, and when I wake up I think only about how strange it is that my dreams are historically conditioned in this way. I will not attempt a phenomenology of dreams valid for everyone, but it will suffice to say here that everyone's dreams are, well, weird. One way of fleshing out this strong judgment is to say that in dreams we commit constant and flagrant violations of the law of the excluded middle. This law, many Western philosophers have thought, is the very foundation of human reason. It holds that everything either is or is not the case, that either *A* or not-*A* must be true, but not neither or both. Yet in dreams this law typically does not hold: one and the same being, for example, can both be and not be a unicorn. Not only might it sprout an extra horn; it might take on the outer form of a pig, or of our ex-landlord (to cite an example from comedian Mitch Hedberg), or it might be dematerialized into pure, shimmering light. Such metamorphoses do not typically trouble us in dreams. We seem somehow able to track deeper truths about the stable identity of the beings that appear there, truths that are not captured by our waking attempts at essential definitions, of the sort "Unicorns are one-horned, hooved animals," "Landlords are residential-property-owning bipeds," and the like.

Now, in order for something to both be and not be a horse—let us take an actually existent animal, not a unicorn, in order to simplify the example—we must reject or suspend a deep-rooted metaphysics of natural kinds. Extending back most importantly to Aristotle, this metaphysics has it that in order for a given being to exist from one moment to another, it must be a being that remains of the same kind from one moment to another. For Bucephalus the horse—to invoke a beloved mascot of medieval Latin logic—to cease to be a horse is for Bucephalus the horse to cease to be altogether. There are some noteworthy natural phenomena that have sometimes been taken to problematize this law, notably the metamorphosis of insects, but such phenomena have generally been held to be marvelous and exceptional precisely because they threaten our general account of how things in nature are supposed to work. For the most part, an individual being can be only the sort of being it is, and if it becomes another sort of being, then it ceases to be the same individual it was before.

The discreteness of kinds and the law of the excluded middle, as two pillars of our conception of rationality, are erected already in the philosophy of Aristotle, for whom, again, to be is always to be a being of a certain sort and not some other. Violation of these rules would of course continue after Aristotle, not only in dreams, but in works of literary imagination too. Ovid's *Metamorphoses* would celebrate a picture of the world in which individual beings regularly migrate across natural boundaries, and come to belong to kinds to which they did not previously belong, while still remaining fundamentally the same individual beings. The Latin poet's work is now canonical, and is not perceived as dangerous or threatening. But its safety is won for it by the presumption that it is a product of the poetic imagination and does not purport, in sharp contrast with Aristotle, to tell us how the world really is. (In chapter 4, however, we will see that this distinction is not always enough to guarantee safety for fantastical flights of the imagination.)

Other, later works in the European tradition have dealt with metamorphosis while playing at the boundary between poetry and literalism. In the twelfth century, the Danish Christian chronicler Saxo Grammaticus wrote in scolding condemnation of the Scandinavian pagan legends that celebrated creaturely transformations, in which, for example, a certain Hardgrep, who wishes to seduce her own foster son, "mutably change[s her]self like wax into strange aspects."[10] The size of her superhuman body is "unwieldy for the embraces of a mortal," and so she transforms herself, as she puts it, "at my own sweet will."[11] Saxo does not himself believe that such a thing ever happened, yet elsewhere in the same work he casually mentions that the earliest Danish kings are descended from bears. He is writing at a time and place in which the elements of what we think of as "rationality"—such as adherence to the law of the excluded middle and to the metaphysics of fixed substances belonging to natural kinds—are undergoing consolidation, and are strongly associated with the cultural-political project of Christianization.

This process is also inseparable from the expansion of textual literacy—Saxo Grammaticus's very name may be translated, roughly, as "the Literate Dane," as if it were a great novelty that these two features should be combined in the same person. But they were, as literacy was an intrinsic feature of the expansion of Christian (i.e., Mediterranean) civilization into the more distant regions of Europe over the course of the Middle Ages. The anthropologist Jack Goody has compellingly argued that it was the technology of writing itself that made it possible to conceptualize the world in terms of logical oppositions, the most basic of which is Aristotle's law of noncontradiction.[12] Goody's argument would bring us far beyond our central concerns here, but it is worth noting that even if much writing—Ovid, notably—engages in fantastical imaginings that violate the laws of logic, still we might venture that such violations come to be perceived as such, as "fantasy" rather than "truth," only in cultures that anchor their understanding of how the world is in authoritative written texts.

Saxo is witness to the shift of an outlying region of Europe from one sort of culture to the other. Violations of logic would appear over the next several centuries in fantastical legends and fairy tales throughout Europe; they would play an important role in the political project of romantic nationalism in the nineteenth century, when the Brothers Grimm in Germany,[13] Aleksandr Afanasyev in Russia,[14] and Elias Lönnrot in Finland[15] would gather the very un-Aristotelian lore of their countries' folk traditions, and would present it as evidence of authentic national culture and as grounds of national pride. From Greece and Rome and France, these countries imported their logic, science, and technology. From within, in turn, they were discovering their spells for warding off bears, their tales of witches who aim to roast children in their ovens and of the children who outsmart them, their talking animals and forest sprites. These defiantly irrational, phantasmagorical expressions of culture were to mark out what was unique and irreducible about particular European nations, while their rational heritage was held in common with at least all of their neighbors in the broader region, and, it was to be hoped, would someday be shared with humanity as a whole. This nineteenth-century partition—between the cherished irrational expressions of one's own culture and the imported, universal benefits of rationality—was deeply connected both with irrationalist tendencies in philosophy and with the irruption of irrationalism as a political force in Europe in the twentieth century.

But for now our concern is with dreams, and with the question why, beyond the fact that they are the product of hallucination, we have come to be so wary of them. And a large part of the answer seems to be that they are, so to speak, metaphysically incorrect: that they perpetually violate the fixity and order that, we have managed to convince ourselves, reigns in waking reality.

Spirits, Vapors, Winds

"The land of shadows is the paradise of dreamers," Immanuel Kant writes in the preface to *The Dreams of a Spirit-Seer* (1766). "Here they find an unlimited country where they may build their houses as they please. Hypochondriac vapors, nursery tales, and monastic miracles provide them with ample building materials."[16] The German philosopher's target in this work, the "spirit-seer," is the Swedish mystic Emmanuel Swedenborg, who claimed that a revelation had given him the power to visit heaven and hell at will, and to communicate with angels and other supernatural beings. Kant begins his work with an epigram from Horace: *Velut aegri somnia, vanae finguntur species* (Like a sick man's dream, creating vain phantasms).[17] Swedenborg's writings, in other words, for Kant, are the product of febrile delirium.

In this peculiar and very atypical work of the young Kant, his main target may not really be Swedenborg at all, for whom he seems in fact to have an enduring affection in spite of the apparent scorn. Rather, what Kant wishes to show is that the metaphysicians are in no position to criticize the spirit-seer. Here Kant is using the label "metaphysician" to designate respectable academic philosophers, in contrast with the unhinged speculators and rhapsodists like Swedenborg. The metaphysicians and the seers are equally guilty, Kant believes, of holding forth on topics about which they know, and can know, strictly nothing. Kant is articulating this view of metaphysics at the beginning of a long process that would, by the late nineteenth century, give us the positivist philosophers, who went so far as to denounce "metaphysics" as a bad word, along with colorful characters such as the Theosophist Helena Blavatsky, who were quite happy to see their esoteric projects described by this label. By the end of the twentieth century, a typical nonacademic bookstore would feature works by Shirley MacLaine, on her many past lives, in the "Metaphysics" section. The academic philosophers would by now have nothing to say about this, and if pressed would likely shrug off the classificatory scheme in play at the mall bookstore as lying outside of their realm of governance.

The term had moved centrifugally out into the margins as those at the center of the practice of philosophy grew increasingly uncomfortable with it. At the beginning of this centuries-long flight from the center, when Kant was writing, the source of the discomfort lay in the fact that metaphysics, since Aristotle, had been by definition an exploration beyond the scope of scientific observation and experiment, into the first causes of scientifically observable phenomena. After the seventeenth century, only the unhinged, the Swedenborgs and the Blavatskys, could claim innocently to have undertaken such explorations, while meanwhile the serious, the cautious, as it were the hinged, felt compelled to back up their claims of knowledge gathering beyond the realm of experience by some sort of account of how such an undertaking could be possible.

Our principal concern for the moment is not with metaphysics, but with dreams. Kant's move is to indict metaphysics, as it is being pursued in his time, by characterizing it as little more than the phantasm produced in a sick man's dream. Recall, now, Aristotle's view that a genuinely predictive dream is likely going to be one in which the first symptoms of an illness are initially felt in sleep. A person dreams of an illness to come because it has in fact already come, even if it remains for now subperceptible during waking life. Vivid dreams, typically, were held to be symptomatic of many illnesses, and any ancient reader would have taken for granted Horace's identification of the dreams of a sick man with "vain phantasms." The spirit-seer, Kant thinks, is like such a person even when he is awake. His phantasms are constructed out of "vapors," a literal manifestation of which would traditionally have been implicated in the images produced in the mind of a vivid dreamer. But here Kant uses the term metaphorically: the life of a spirit-seer is in a sense a waking dream, to the extent that he allows the dark shadows of his imagination to play a role in his explanation of reality. He mistakes the phantasms of his imagination for concepts of reason.

Certain English translations of Kant's work have shied away from a literal rendering of the philosopher's concluding observation in the third chapter of part 1. Emmanuel F. Goerwitz prefers to allude vaguely to a "disordered stomach," and then to give the original German in a note, which, he says, is "hardly bearable" in English. But the English is no more scandalous than the German, and what Kant in fact says is this: "If a hypochondriac wind clamors in the gut, it all comes down to the direction it takes: if it goes downward, it becomes a fart, but if it goes upwards, it is an apparition or a holy inspiration."[18] If we think Kant is reaching here for humorous effect, we should note that the German term *Eingebung*, here translated as "inspiration," has traditionally been rendered as "afflatus," as in "divine afflatus." The conceptual connection in Western thought, between spirit as something exalted and holy, on the one hand, and on the other as mere "wind," is very deep. The connection exists in popular expressions in many Indo-European languages, and the possibility of a confusion between the two registers of spirit has been a staple of comedy since Greek antiquity. For example, the character of Socrates in Aristophanes's *Clouds* mocks the gods by suggesting that thunder, far from being a sign of the superhuman might of these beings, is really nothing more than the atmospheric equivalence of intestinal upset. Such comedy often plays on the misperception that a given character has of the importance of his own words: he takes them to be "spiritual," in the sense of "lofty" or "important," while his listeners take them to be spirituous in the sense of just so much "wind." This is what it is to be a "windbag," to emit *flatus vocis* as if they were profound observations. Kant is of course aware of, and playing on, this deep association.

The philosopher also underlines in this chapter the conceptual association not just between "spirit" and "wind," but between both of these and "vapors." He is certainly aware, in turn, of the hard effort that Descartes had made before him to eliminate any thought of vapors from the effort to understand mental activity, or indeed minds or souls. Vapors, Descartes had insisted, are not some sort of intermediate principle between the body and the soul, partaking of the properties of both of these ontological regions and moving back and forth freely between them. Rather, for the dualist philosopher, every entity is either mind or body, and because vapor is extended and consists in material particles, however fine or spread out they may be, it simply cannot be considered spirit in any rigorous sense of the term. To conceive of spirit as if it were a wind, gas, or vapor is to allow the imagination to get in the way of rational inquiry into a problem of philosophy where no imagination is necessary or useful: there is nothing to form an image of, nothing to "imaginate."

"Vapors," of course, or more correctly "the vapors," is also the name of a well-known medical condition, one from which upper-class women in particular were long thought to suffer. Upper-class women and those preoccupied with them found "the vapors" useful as an explanation of social behavior such as dramatic swooning or a disinclination to get out of bed. The socially constructed character of this condition was a fairly common theme already in the seventeenth century. Thus in 1676 Leibniz notes that "there is a sort of sickness in Paris of which the women habitually complain, and which they call 'vapors' ... These blind them as if some thick cloud came and darkened their vision and their mind." Leibniz observes skeptically that the common comparison of the human head to an alembic, as used in chemical experiments, in which gases rise upward through a narrow passage, is nothing more than a metaphor, an aid to the imagination that captures something about the way we feel when we are light-headed, but that does not properly identify the agents that are in fact responsible.

Vapors are what the British anthropologist Mary Douglas would call a "natural symbol."[20] Fog, mist, candle smoke, and other such liminal entities seem, evidently across all human cultures, to connect earthly reality with some other reality generally more difficult of access. With the dawn of modern philosophy in the seventeenth century, there is a consistent effort, continuing up through the work of Kant, to expose this liminal connection as mere seeming, as simply a bit of folk wisdom that has no place in the rigorous project of clarifying and analyzing concepts, such as those of mind and body. To see vapors or otherwise believe oneself to be affected by vapors is to rush too quickly to a purported explanation of one's lapse into irrationality, while in fact what is irrational, from the point of view of modern philosophy, is to suppose that vapors are playing a role in one's mental activity at all.

Of course, sometimes vapors really do affect the mind, notably in the form of inhaled smoke of tobacco, or of opium, the use of which by the Turks was of great interest to the young Leibniz: "The Turks are in the habit of using opium in order to bring about cheerfulness," he writes in 1671, "they believe that it . . . revives a man's soul."[21] The fact that there are such substances, by which people can revive or otherwise transfigure the soul simply by inhaling or ingesting them, speaks strongly in favor of the folk view that the philosophers were arguing against: that the soul itself partakes of the nature of such fine or aery substances. Beyond this, moreover, the very existence of narcotics, of stupefacients and hallucinogens, is itself the source of a number of philosophical questions that did not escape attention in the early modern period, and that are centrally connected to the question of dreams. In Kepler's *Somnium* the transit to the moon is brought about by the ingestion of certain unspecified herbal potions, of which, we may presume, Kepler's own mother Katharina, née Guldenmann, in fact had knowledge. She was, at the time the astronomer wrote this treatise, in a prison in Stuttgart awaiting trial on suspicion of witchcraft.

Is it from her that Kepler got the idea of taking a drug that would send a person to the moon, figuratively speaking? Whether or no, it is significant that Kepler understands a drug-induced quest as a variety of "dream." A dream or *somnium* in this expanded sense is not necessarily what one experiences in sleep, but rather what one experiences alone, in one's mind, even as one's body stays put in bed, or in a chair, or simply stoned and staring at the wall.

Hearing Voices

We have already seen that a philosopher is not a seer. A philosopher is not, or should not be, a magician, an enthusiast, or a feverish vapor-headed visionary, even if these social roles are all part of the lineage of philosophy, and thus ones that can only be grown out of, rather than dismissed as the eternal opposite of philosophy. This is what Virginia Woolf understood when she asked: "And what is knowledge? What are our learned men save the descendants of witches and hermits who crouched in caves and in woods brewing herbs, interrogating shrew-mice and writing down the language of the stars?"[22] A philosopher does not divine, or invoke, or simply take dictation from a higher source, real or imagined, but rather thinks through things, step by step, for himself. But things have not always been this way.

According to the bold and influential thesis of Julian Jaynes, the transition from seers to philosophers is one that tracks transforma-tions experienced by humanity as a whole in the relatively recent past. In his 1976 book *The Origin of Consciousness in the Breakdown of the Bicameral Mind*, the psychologist argues that until somewhere between three and five millennia ago, human beings "heard voices" pervasively and continually; they thus had waking "dreams" in the expanded sense we have already considered, in the way that today a relatively small number of people classified as mentally ill do. They lived their lives attuned to their inner voices, and it is only when, by some as yet poorly understood evolutionary leap, the bicameral mind breaks down that we begin to engage in individual conscious deliberation.

What is the bicameral mind? Jaynes explains that in it "volition, planning, initiative is organized with no consciousness whatever, and then 'told' to the individual in his familiar language, sometimes with the visual aura of a familiar friend or authority figure or 'god', or some-times as a voice alone. The individual obeyed these hallucinated voices because he could not 'see' what to do by himself."[23] Jaynes believes that we can turn to written history, to texts, as evidence for this thesis, and that in particular in the earliest prose writing we see little evidence of individual consciousness. He takes the work of Homer, presumably composed around 800 BCE, as exemplary in this regard. "Who . . . were these gods that pushed men about like robots and sang epics through their lips?" Jaynes asks. "They were voices whose speech and directions could be as distinctly heard by the Iliadic heroes as voices are heard by certain epileptic and schizophrenic patients."[24]

But what can we really conclude from the strangeness of the world Homer describes? Jaynes looks to texts for evidence of a fundamental difference between the minds of early Greeks and our own; ironically, anthropologists such as Jack Goody and historians of science such as G.E.R. Lloyd have compellingly argued that it was the production of texts themselves, the elaboration of ideas in lists, tabulations, and so on, that gradually led to a closer attention to the possible forms of argument, and to the emergence of explicit accounts of what we now think of as reason. But writing, while it makes this emergence possible, is good at doing a number of other things too, among them capturing the experience of reveries, ecstasies, and other apparent signs of the inner working of "voices."

Does the earliest writing really reveal a mentality different from our own?[25] Or does it simply reveal a writing different from ours? Even in the space of just a handful of centuries that divides our own era's vivid novels from medieval knights-errant tales, we see a vastly different approach to human interiority. We take our own era's works to be "superior" in this regard: Proust and Woolf, we suppose, probe more deeply into the human soul, are greater "psychologists"—as Nietzsche said of Stendhal—than, say, the authors of *Piers Plowman* or of the Norse sagas. Does this mean that there has been yet another evolutionary leap in human history since the Middle Ages? Or does it mean that our expectations as to what sort of things might best be done with a particular technology and a particular creative tradition—namely, writing and literature—have changed? Are we even correct about the greater depth of works of literature closer in time to us, or are we simply more responsive to these works *because* they are closer to us?

If we suppose that the work of Homer is a sort of transitional fossil between different evolutionary stages of human cognition, should we, moreover, suppose that the genetic mutation that caused the unification of the bicameral mind happened first in the eastern Mediterranean? Other literary traditions with many of the same features (e.g., psychologically flat characters with no apparent interior states, capable only of automatic action) emerge considerably later in other parts of the world; are we then to suppose that the evolutionary leap Jaynes dates to the period of the Mycenaean bards who gradually generated the *Iliad* happened only centuries later in Scandinavia? Oral poetic traditions that preserve these same features continue to enjoy some vitality today in Serbia, in Yakutia, and elsewhere. Do these cultural survivals mean that the people who practice them are at a lower stage of evolution than other human groups?

Jaynes was a bold thinker, but the legacy of his thesis is severely compromised by his hasty hermeneutical method: he presumed that cultural practices, such as those that left written traces of archaic story-telling, might reveal something to us about intrinsic features of the individual minds implicated in these practices, rather than simply re-vealing something to us about the cultures these individual minds inhabited. In the West, certainly, there was a significant shift over the past three millennia from revelation to deliberation, from seers to phi-losophers; indeed the very idea of what we take to be the West is cen-trally wrapped up with this shift. But to take this as a natural, evolu-tionary phenomenon, rather than as the product of particular cultural practices—as, for example, Lloyd has done[26]—is an expression of pure parochialism. Jaynes's approach is in principle promising: we should not be afraid to look back to textual history as part of our effort to understand the natural history of humanity, back to philology as a part of the full naturalistic account of what it is to be human. But if we are going to use cultural traces to help make sense of the natural, we must be sure that what we take to be natural is not itself in truth a cultural trace.

It may be that we are no more justified in asking why Homer did not seem interested in personal identity or in logical inference, in the way that many of his fellow Greeks would be just a few centuries later, than we would be in asking why James Joyce does not devote any time to the quantum superposition problem, or why Barbra Streisand does not sing about the Anthropocene. It may be that they are unaware of the great conceptual innovations going on during or near the time at which they are creating their work, but it also may be that that's just not the kind of work they are doing. Homer, like countless Siberian, Balkan, or Australian bards over the past fifty thousand years, is concerned not with originality, but with intonation and delivery: such bards are perfectly attuned to the circumstances of the day, and to the mood and expectations of their listeners. But the work of art is not an improvisation; it is performed from a score, so to speak, one that exists only in intergenerational memory and in the instances of its performance.

The words of the poet himself, as opposed to the scribes who later wrote these words down, could in no way have been anchored in visible signs, in text. And in this the first Homer—the oral Homer who preceded the written Homer by some centuries—shared in the experience of poetry and recitation that is much more common in the history of humanity than the experience of reading from written texts. For the vast majority of the time that human beings have been on Earth, words have had no worldly reality other than the sound made when they are spoken. As the theorist Walter J. Ong pointed out in his 1982 book *Orality and Literacy: The Technologizing of the Word*, it is difficult, perhaps even impossible, now to imagine how differently language would have been experienced in a culture of "primary orality."[27] There would be nowhere to "look up a word," no authoritative source telling us the shape the word "actually" takes. There would be no way to affirm the word's existence at all except by speaking it—and this necessary condition of survival is important for understanding the relatively repetitive nature of epic poetry. Say it over and over again, or it will slip away. In the absence of fixed, textual anchors for words, there would be a sharp sense that language is charged with power, magic: the idea that words, when spoken, can bring about new states of affairs in the world. They do not so much describe, as invoke.

Literacy, then, brings with it a suite of conceptual transformations that ought to be of interest to philosophers and to cognitive historians such as Jaynes. For it may well be that we can explain the apparent brain mutations of the Neolithic not as internal events in the history of hominid evolution, but rather as the consequence of new practices emerging around new technologies of knowledge storage and transmission. Logic, in particular—insistence on making the right inferences about how the world really is, rather than offering poetic invocations of how the world could be—could be simply a side effect of writing. Homer's epic poetry, which originates in the same oral epic traditions as those of the Balkans or of West Africa, was written down, frozen, fixed, and from this it became "literature." There are no arguments in the *Iliad*: much of what is said arises from metrical exigencies, the need to fill in a line with the right number of syllables, or from epithets whose function is largely mnemonic (and thus unnecessary when transferred into writing). Yet Homer would become an authority for early philosophers nonetheless: revealing truths about humanity not by argument or debate, but by declamation, now frozen into text.

Plato would express extreme concern about the role, if any, that poets should play in society. But he was not talking about poets as we think of them: he had in mind reciters, bards who incite emotions with living performances, invocations and channelings of absent persons and beings. It is not orality that philosophy rejects, necessarily. Socrates himself rejected writing, identifying instead with a form of oral culture. Plato would also ensure the philosophical canonization of his own mentor by writing down (how faithfully, we do not know with precision) what Socrates would have preferred to merely say, and so would have preferred to have lost to the wind. Arguably, it is in virtue of Plato's recording that we might say, today, that Socrates was a philosopher. Plato and Aristotle both were willing to learn from Homer, once he had been written down. And Socrates for his part was already engaged in a sort of activity very different from poetic recitation. This was dialectic: the structured working-through of a question toward an end that has not been predetermined—even if this practice emerged indirectly from forms of reasoning actualized only with the advent of writing. The freezing in text of dialectical reasoning, with a heavy admixture (however impure or problematic) of poetry, aphorism, and myth, became the model for what, in the European tradition, was thought of as "philosophy" for the next few millennia. The place of poetry, aphorism, and myth has often been disputed, and these are frequently cast out of philosophy strictly conceived. But, as Horace said of the nature we ever seek to shut out, they all just keep roaring back.

The emergence of reason as an ideal, and the discovery of the individual self as the locus of reasoning, required no genetic mutation, no internal transformation in the brain causing the voices to go silent and a new, more ordered and logical regime to take over. It required only a change of practices. James C. Scott has compellingly described writing, as it emerged in the early Mesopotamian state, as a "a new form of control,"[28] and we may understand this in the dual sense with which we are already familiar from Plato's *Republic*: it permits the control of society through administrative record keeping, and it permits the control of the individual mind as a prosthetic to memory and reasoning.

Bitter Little Embryos

E. R. Dodds, in his groundbreaking 1951 book *The Greeks and the Irrational*, notes that uneasy contemporary scholars have been inclined to dismiss the role of dreams in Homer as so much "poetic convention" or "epic machinery," rather than revealing to us something important about the place of dreams in early Greek society. For him it is significant that the Greeks speak always of "seeing" a dream, rather than "having" one: the dreamer "is the passive recipient of an objective vision."[29] For the Greeks, "as for other ancient peoples,"[30] there was a crucial distinction between significant and insignificant dreams.[31] Among significant dreams, there are, as Dodds explains, following Macrobius, three subcategories. First, there are the symbolic ones, which "dress up in metaphors, like a sort of riddles, a meaning which cannot be understood without interpretation."[32] Others fall into the category of the *horama*, or "vision," "a straightforward preënactment of a future event."[33] And finally there are the *chrematismos*, or "oracle" dreams, "when in sleep the dreamer's parent, or some other respected or impressive personage, perhaps a priest, or even a god, reveals without symbolism what will or will not happen, or should or should not be done."[34]

Modern psychoanalysts, one might note, would accept only the first sort of significant dream, the one that requires interpretation; if a dreamer were to encounter a straightforward vision or oracle, they would assume that it only appeared as such, but did not in fact mean what it said. It is easier to assume of the two latter sorts of dreams, as many Greeks did, that they were sent by a god or by some higher source. Dodds notes that such "divine dreams" are common in Assyrian, Hittite, and Egyptian sources, and that they are also well attested among "primitive" people today.[35] The Greeks often "incubated" such dreams, by fasting, self-injury, and other harsh techniques to induce an atypical state of mind.

In dreams, Aristotle notes, "the element of judgment is absent."[36] Yet it is in what Freud called the "secondary elaboration" of the dream, in waking, that it becomes incorporated into what Dodds describes as a "culture-pattern." This is a meaningful cultural nexus where the strangeness of the dream is sloughed off, and what remains is only an eminently meaningful core, ready to be incorporated into pragmatic social action. There is, Dodds explains, a "pattern of belief which is accepted not only by the dreamer but usually by everyone in his environment."[37] The form of the experience of a dream "is determined by the belief, and in turn confirms it; hence they become increasingly stylised."[38] The Victorian anthropologist Edward Tylor saw this as a "vicious circle": "What the dreamer believes he therefore sees, and what he sees he therefore believes."[39] Dodds sees it rather as a variety of what we might call, following W.V.O. Quine, "meaning holism":[40] the dream is received into a web of significations determined in advance by society, and in which it loses its individual character and takes on a social life. It is in the absence of any shared social understanding of what dream images mean that they seem to us so irreducibly strange, so untranslatable.

Freud, for his part, was hardly able to offer a key for the translation of dreams that might have made dreams part of shared social space rather than remaining our own private baggage—baggage that we carry throughout the day and cautiously keep to ourselves. In his 1899 *The Interpretation of Dreams*, he aims to lay out a "psychological technique by which dreams may be interpreted," and moreover to establish "that upon the application of this method every dream will show itself to be a senseful psychological structure which may be introduced into an assignable place in the psychic activity of the waking state."[41] His framework for understanding dreams is largely based upon the idea that we are all living to a greater or lesser degree with neuroses, and that these manifest themselves symbolically in our sleep.

Thus, for example, one of Freud's female patients dreams that "a man with a light beard and a peculiar glittering eye is pointing to a sign board attached to a tree which reads: uclamparia—wet."[42] We can leave out some of the details in order to zero in on some elements that are exemplary of Freud's method. He determines that "wet" contrasts with "dry," and that "Dry" had been the name of the man the woman was going to marry, had he not been an alcoholic. It is also connected etymologically to *drei*, or "three," which reveals an unconscious thought of the monastery of the Three Fountains, where she had once drunk an elixir, made from eucalyptus, that was given to her by a monk. The neurosis for which she is consulting Freud had initially been diagnosed as malaria, and the nonsense dream word is in fact a portmanteau of "eucalyptus" and "malaria." "The condensation 'uclamparia—wet' is therefore," Freud explains, "the point of junction for the dream as well as for the neurosis."[43]

Now this may be more or less satisfying as an explanation, likely depending on one's prior investment in believing in Freudian theory. But it is important to note that it hardly places the patient within a community of publicly accepted and shared dream meanings, as had been the case, say, for the Iroquois. Rather, she shares her private story with the expert, and gets a private account of its real significance, and then, most likely, she keeps this significance strictly to herself, while the analyst keeps her money.

Vladimir Nabokov would level, in spectacular fashion, the complaint that psychoanalysis is in the end only "oneiromancy and mythogeny," that Freud's world is "vulgar, shabby, fundamentally medieval," with its "crankish quest for sexual symbols."[44] He denounced Freud's patients, like the one whose dream we've just considered, as "bitter little embryos spying . . . upon the love life of their parents."[45] What

Nabokov could not abide is the idea that we might be mysteries to ourselves, that we might not be fully in command of our own lives, but rather are all driven by strange tics and hang-ups that we must turn to someone else, a purported expert, to discern. What is interesting to us here is the accusation that Freud's work advances not at all beyond the divinatory practices of what is often held to be a more benighted age. But Freud is in an important sense less ambitious than the soothsayers. He does not want to have statesmen making decisions on the basis of dream symbolism. At most he would want to help statesmen, or at least the Viennese *haute bourgeoisie*, to gain sufficient psychological well-being to make sound and adequately reasoned decisions.

In any case Freud did not by and large succeed, and dreams remain for the most part on the margins of our society. In most countries psychoanalysis is relatively less successful today than more focused psychotherapies. The latter seek to train people to overcome concrete aspects of their behavior with which they are unhappy, rather than attempting in some way to reveal the truth about the causes of these behaviors and thereby to enable them to better know themselves. Psychological therapy today in most parts of the world is less philosophical, and far more effective, than psychoanalysis.

Even if Freudianism had proved more enduring than cognitive behavioral therapy and similar approaches, dreams would not have been part of our shared public life, but only part of our psychoanalysts' confidential files on us. There is no shared culture-pattern in Dodds's sense enabling us to incorporate them. Thinkers from Descartes to Tylor did their best to keep dreams excluded. In spite of Freud's labor, for the most part the keys to their interpretation will be found not in the psychology section of the bookstore, but on the shelves labeled "occult" (or again, which is often the same thing, "metaphysics"). Here, we may wonder whether this approach is in fact the most rational. Or is the society—such as the Iroquois or the Greek—with an established process for receiving its members' dreams into shared waking experience in fact the one that is better at managing a human experience that is, in any case, irrepressible and ineradicable?

Postscriptum Fabulosum

The reverend father awakens at dawn and sees a few remaining embers glowing in the campfire. The Huron men are still asleep around him; a few of them are twitching and muttering. Just a moment earlier he had been in Rouen, or so he thought, stroking an orange cat in an alleyway between his boarding school and the home of the old maid with the wandering eye. The cat looked at him and communicated, somehow, without speaking, the message that God does not exist. Then it suddenly darted away, as if in fear. The alleyway smelled like asparagus. He woke up. He knew right away his comrades would soon be asking him, as they always did upon awakening, if he'd had any significant dreams. What could he possibly tell them? Who can know what signifies what in that mad storm of phantasms? If it means anything at all, then the meaning comes only from the order we impose upon the dream after we wake. In itself it is just madness. Cats do not hold forth on theological matters. And in any case God *does* exist. There are incontrovertible proofs of this, and any man who has the use of his faculty of reason can study them and convince himself that they are true. There is, moreover, no asparagus in America, the Jesuit thinks. To smell it on this side of the sea is to conjure a sensation directly out of one's own desire. There is power in the madness of dreams, he thinks. Altogether too much power.

CHAPTER FOUR

Dreams into Things; or, Art

➤➤➤➤➤

Many Worlds

On May 15, 1648, the Peace of Westphalia was signed, bringing about an end to the Thirty Years' War, a conflict that had, by most estimates, claimed the lives of eight million people, military and civilian, throughout Europe. There had been seemingly no end of atrocities, men tortured and hung up in iron cages, severed heads on spikes placed outside the gates of cities as a warning and a threat. There was no sense in the era that the warring parties were all, in view of their shared Christianity, ultimately on the same side. Catholicism and Protestantism appeared as distant from one another, and irreconcilable, as Islam and Christianity do today from the point of view of the most ideologically intransigent jihadist or the most Islamophobic European.

The 1648 peace treaty contained the seeds of the modern global order based on the sovereignty of nation-states. Two years after it was signed, the great rationalist philosopher René Descartes died. At the core of his philosophical project, as we began to see in the previous chapter, was a quest for certainty that he was not dreaming or hallucinating, but that the world as he experienced it, and even his own consciousness, were real. The philosopher himself had served in the army of Maximilian of Bavaria and was present at the Battle of White Mountain near Prague in 1620. It is at least conceivable that he witnessed significant death and injury, and soldiers who had lost arms and legs but continued to feel pain in them. Years later he would write of the problem of phantom limbs, of the challenge they pose for our understanding of the distinct concepts of body and mind. Descartes's successor in the rationalist tradition, Leibniz, was born in 1646, and spent his early life in the fragile but hopeful new postwar reality of Protestant Saxony. Leibniz's career, both as a diplomat and as a philosopher, would be devoted to reconciliation of opposed camps—Protestants and Catholics, Cartesians and Aristotelians, any two parties that believe themselves to be in fundamental disagreement. For Leibniz, as we have already briefly seen, such belief is always based on an illusion, for in fact all human minds, as reflections of the same divinely created rational order, believe, deep down, fundamentally the same thing. The task of philosophy then, for Leibniz, is to clarify our terms to the point where we are all able to see that we in fact agree. Of course Leibniz's vision seems wildly optimistic to us today, as we tend to suppose that the reasons politicians give for going to war are only ad hoc pretexts for grabs at power and territory in which the consideration of who is *in fact* right or wrong is something close to a category mistake. But Leibniz's vision shows just how much stock was placed in reason at the beginning of the modern period.

Another rationalist philosopher, Spinoza, was so hopeful about the power of reason to solve human problems that he wrote a work on ethics modeled after the rigorous deductive style of Euclid's work on geometry. Spinoza's conclusions do indeed follow from his axioms and propositions. He refused to acknowledge, however, that in matters of ethics, unlike geometry, the first principles to which one commits oneself have a great deal to do with one's cultural values, one's contingent attachments, and are far from self-evident truths. Spinoza, like other rationalist philosophers, was also very nearly phobic about the faculty of the imagination, which, as was usual in the era, he understood, as the word suggests, in part as the power of the mind to generate images. The faculty of reason deals with pure concepts, but the imagination falls back on visions, phantasms, hallucinations of sorts, when reason proves too weak to go forth on its own without crutches. It is, to return to our own metaphor, the bright-colored dye that makes the invisible visible, even as it distorts the creature's true nature and threatens to destroy it altogether. It is the imagination, Spinoza suggests, that is at the root of all superstition, and therefore of all suffering.

But while the philosophers were busy designing ways of escaping from madness and illusion, and suppressing the faculty of imagination that served as a gateway to these, the storytellers, the novelists, and the artists were contriving delirious new forms of them. No one provides a sharper contrast with Descartes than his near contemporary, the Spanish novelist Miguel de Cervantes, whose character Don Quixote seems to assure us that all our pursuits in life may be a dream, that we may in fact never be able to determine whether we are mad or not, and that in the end this is simply the human condition—and indeed a basic existential fact in which we may take delight. Over the course of the following century, the genres of fantasy and science fiction would enjoy a boom, with authors such as Savinien de Cyrano de Bergerac and Margaret Cavendish allowing their imaginations to roam freely in those directions that rationalist philosophy had sought to limit.

Dreams, fictions, and artistic creation in general are species of the same genus, as all involve submission to the sort of fantasies to which the mind is naturally inclined, and which reason compels us to keep always at bay. Both take us off to other worlds, to other possibilities, while reason tells us that there is only one world. To live according to reason is to live in that one world, which is shared and common, while to lapse into unreason, whether waking or sleeping, is to drift off into a private and unshareable world.

Bleeding Out

Novels, and not only those in the "romance" genre narrowly defined, are capable of evoking passions in the reader, largely as a result of the way in which they play on the imagination. In an older and by now mostly forgotten meaning of the term, "passion" was understood simply as the opposite of "action," where an "agent" is one who acts, a "patient" one who undergoes the consequences of an action. We can see how the old sense led to the new one: we say that people who have "fallen" in love are "swept off their feet" or "bowled over"; the common French expression for falling in love at first sight, *un coup de foudre*, invokes a lightning strike. To fall in love, or to be overcome with anger, or jealousy, or joy, is to lose self-control, to come under the control of external forces, working on us through the body.

Such loss of self-control has generally been understood as an expression of irrationality. And yet we find ourselves in bodies—there is nothing to be done about it, at least not as long as we are alive—and so we must somehow come to terms with the fact that we are going to be, to some extent, determined in the course of our human affairs by the fluctuations of our passions. Even Descartes, who believed that the soul, the true locus of our individual selfhood, is entirely immaterial and only contingently wrapped up with the body, nonetheless wrote an entire treatise, the 1649 *Passions of the Soul*, accounting for the ways in which our bodily, passionate existence defines who we are. Descartes knew we could not fight the passions but must rather modulate them to the extent possible so as to make them work in accordance with reason. A century later David Hume would reverse this approach, maintaining that "reason is, and ought only to be a slave to the passions."[1] The Scottish empiricist is not arguing here that we should all abandon ourselves to unreason, but rather that the body is naturally outfitted and disposed to operate in a rational way, and we are only complicating things if we attempt to find a priori rules of conduct that the mind would haughtily dictate to the body in advance of any experience.

The history of philosophy does not so much resolve as mirror some of the most common tensions of human social life: whether one should listen to "the head or the heart," whether one should trust one's gut feelings or reason things through. These are clichés, but their very existence and endurance provides an important illustration of the depth of our attachment to something other than reason as the source of meaning in human life.

Visual art, too, and not only literary fiction, works through the body, at least to the extent that it sends us visual images, or indeed sonic waves, which move through our eyes or ears, and, eventually, affect our mind or soul for better or for worse. This basic condition of the experience of art has been seen as both a threat and an opportunity throughout the history of Western thought, not least in philosophy. In his 1794 *Letters on the Aesthetic Education of Man* Friedrich Schiller described in detail how art might be employed to cultivate the feelings of a developing psyche, eventually yielding a grown human being who is a slave neither to reason nor to sensual impulse. But typically any hope that is placed in certain exemplary works of art, or in certain genres, comes at the expense of others, and the history of promotion of art's edifying value is inseparable from the history of censorship and of the chauvinistic hierarchization of taste.

In the *Republic* Plato had been particularly wary of music, as an art form that works directly on the body, without any role for the rational soul. What is music about? Unlike literature, and unlike most visual art, music generally refuses to say, and only entrances us with its otherworldly call. The Greek philosopher had been mostly concerned about particular chords, while in the twentieth century most calls for the censorship of music—at least those that did not focus on lyrics, the nonmusical element of a subset of musical works—have been concerned with certain types of rhythm, particularly those that American bigots of the 1950s associated with the "jungle." In the seventeenth century it was the dances that accompanied the music of southern Italy that caused consternation throughout Europe, such as the tarantella, held to be directly descended from ancient Bacchanalian rites, and to carry with it the danger of not being able to stop dancing once one has started: like the fear of rock and roll, this too was a fear of irreparable loss. Again and again, we see the same fear returning, that music's siren song will pull our loved ones, especially our children, away from us, into the domain of unreason, a vaguely sensed parallel world, where bodies rule.

The history of censorship, at the same time, reveals to us alternating strategies for dealing with this threat: again, do we simply try to suppress the danger, or do we recognize that it is to some extent ineliminable, and attempt to lasso it and train it toward the allegedly rational ends of society? Authoritarian regimes, typically, are intent on passing off the society they control as the only possible one, as necessary and inevitable. Consequently, the imagining of other possible worlds, even if they are only fictional, is subject to tight control. Even the imagining of *this* world, but through a lens that seems borrowed from another world—a lens that shows the world through officially unrecognized registers or moods—already drifts too far from the version of actuality the regime seeks to enforce.

In the early years of the Soviet Union, Isaak Babel was the great chronicler of the lives of the poor Jews of Odessa, the gangsters, small farmers, clueless rabbis, fat girls in love with cretinous boys, at the time of the Bolshevik Revolution, and for a few years thereafter. In Babel's world, as on the dance floor, bodies rule. He was early on a protégé of Maxim Gorky, who would never fall from grace during Stalin's reign, when socialist realism was set up as official state aesthetic ideology. Babel, by contrast, was arrested by the NKVD (the Soviet secret police, and predecessor to the KGB), and his death sentence was personally signed by Stalin's henchman Lavrenty Beria. He was murdered by firing squad in 1940.

Babel had done his best, under socialist realism, to, as he put it, work in the new literary genre of silence. But his stories from the early 1920s were too memorable not to echo. Their crime, if it must be made explicit, is nothing other than to show the joy and confusion of life, to portray characters who are both good and bad, insightful yet inarticulate, and generally unable to think about their misery or their momentary triumphs through the lens of class consciousness. Sometimes they invoke working-class solidarity, but generally in ways that show they have not really grasped the concept. They often smell bad: odors of milk and flesh emanate from Babel's characters, and right off the pages. Gorky would later, when Babel had fallen into ill repute, complain of his protégé's "Baudelairean predilection for rotting meat."[2] Babel's work is vital, raucous, politically disobedient, and hilarious.

As Mary Douglas reminds us, the essence of humor is to thrust us back into our bodies in social contexts in which these are supposed to be screened out, in which we are supposed to conduct ourselves as if we were pure disembodied intellects. The reason our bodies are so offensive has something to do with the fact that they are always rotting, or threatening to rot, and that we must engage in considerable upkeep to ensure that this not happen. We are mortal and corruptible, in other words. The official philosophy in the context in which Babel was writing was dialectical materialism, which taught among other things that everything that exists is a corruptible body. But this philosophical commitment did not prevent a humorless and oppressive disdain for the living body from finding its way back into arts and culture.

In 1947, after Babel was dead, Stalin's lead censor, Andrei Zhdanov, would give a speech[3] criticizing the literary magazine *Zvezda* for having published a story by Mikhail Zoshchenko entitled "The Adventures of a Monkey."[4] The censor complains that the author had "portray[ed] Soviet people as lazy, unattractive, stupid and crude. He is in no way concerned with their labour, their efforts, their heroism, their high social and moral qualities."[5] Zhdanov says that it is characteristic of "philistine" writers to emphasize the "baseness and pettiness" of people, and he cites Gorky as an authority in support of this view. But Gorky's own protégé had shown a generation earlier that we must fearlessly enter into the baseness and pettiness of people; we must attend to the small conversations at the wedding feast in Odessa and hear of extortion schemes, of petty plans to be buried in the best spot in the cemetery. Only thus may we gain experience through literature of something close to human love: love for imperfect, fallen, desperate souls, an emotion that remains entirely beyond the horizon, in his moralistic elevation of the virtues of solidarity and exemplary heroism, of Zhdanov's limited artistic sensibility.

Babel's fate is in important respects yet another echo of Hippasus's, who was drowned by his fellow mathematical cult members for speaking publicly of irrational numbers. On the surface the two are indeed different: the Pythagorean divulged a new discovery and a well-guarded secret, while the Russian author described what people have already known for as long as they have come together in families and communities—that human beings are obscene, petty, vain, selfish, and loving. But Babel also divulged a discovery of sorts, namely, a literary innovation, in which he discerned how, like few before, to capture these real traits of real people in a lucid, honest, and verisimilar way. His characters were not idealizations; they did not belong to an ideal realm of reason and virtue, but rather revealed the complexities and contradictions that prevail wherever there are real people. And for this he had to die, sacrificed to an ideology whose adherents believed, in spite of all evidence, that the irrational kinks in the relations among human beings would soon be ironed out, by force of political will, and that society would be structured in a rational way unsusceptible to undermining by the vicissitudes and passions of imperfect individuals. Unlike Hippasus's murder, we know that Babel's happened, and we know exactly why it happened. We know that the rubbing out, in the name of rationality, of people who acknowledge the existence of irrationality is not a legend, but part of the regular course of human affairs.

While one would not wish to lend them even a faint hint of support, the censors employed by various regimes throughout history are not entirely wrong to believe that fictional worlds cannot be entirely contained, that in the simple invention and description of them there is some real risk of their seeping out into reality and altering it: that world description is at the same time world making. The very word "poetry," in the broad sense of the creative spinning out of possible alternative realities, is derived from *poiesis*, the primary meaning of which is "making." This sense endures in strange relics of English vocabulary such as the word "playwright," which evokes not the mere writer, but rather the wheelwright or the shipwright, artisans who actually bring some new entity into existence through their labor. Do writers too introduce something into the world, something that was not there before? I have on occasion felt a reaction to powerful literature along these lines: this really should not have been allowed; someone should have censored this. I recall in particular the titular character in Philip Roth's *Sabbath's Theater* inducing such a thought, as well as virtually every line from Louis-Ferdinand Céline. As with the alphabets of Tlön in Borges's famous story, I have sometimes felt in reading that I am seeing "the first intrusion of the fantastical world into the real world,"[6] and it seems dangerous indeed.

Some things that are said have the strange quality of bleeding out from within the quotation marks we use in the vain hope of containing them.[7] Ordinarily philosophers distinguish between the use of a word and its mention: if I say that I heard someone on the metro today saying the word "chien," it does not follow that I have just spoken of *Canis familiaris*. I might not even know, when I give you this report, what the word "chien" means. But if your child tells you that someone at school said the word "fuck," then he cannot resort to the claim that he has not himself just used that word. It bleeds out of the quotation marks; it's powerful enough to override the use/mention distinction. This is something like the experience of powerful literature I have attempted to describe: it is as if Philip Roth has inserted into reality a character as morally rotten as Mickey Sabbath, and it does not seem entirely satisfactory to protest that in effect the entire life of that character occurs between something like quotation marks, between the covers of a book that announces itself as a novel. Fictional worlds are possible worlds not just in the sense that they are nonactual; when we spin them out in writing, they come to seem—if I may deploy a phrase that verges on oxymoron—like real possibilities.

Babel's spinning out of a fictional world (which, again, was really a description of a slice of our real world, seen in a certain mood and register) had real and tragic consequences for him. He was murdered, in the end, because the officials did not want the mood and register he evoked to be part of the reality under their control. The register they preferred was so-called realism, which depicted a world that exists nowhere, full of morally transparent heroes and villains, and simple and straightforward contrasts between right and wrong. The world depicted in socialist-realist literature is an impossible world.

To kill off or imprison those who invent worlds according to their own unauthorized vision of life is of course a great crime. And yet it at least recognizes something that the familiar liberal argument against censorship typically ignores, in its insistence on a dichotomy between the ideal and the real realms, between stories and history. The early modern period witnessed such an intense proliferation of imaginings of possible worlds, such a fruitful hybridity of fiction and philosophy, in large part because it was a period of intense and sustained efforts to rethink the actual world and our place in it. The long-term consequences of this rethinking included upheavals and revolutions in both the political and scientific realms, but they could not have been brought about—or even, likely, begun—without the art of imagination, an art the strict enforcers of reason have repeatedly warned against and sought to control or suppress.

Genies, Genius, and Ingenium

As we have already seen, for some early modern philosophers the mental faculty of imagination was conceived as a sort of waking dream, as it involved the production of images of things that are not, strictly speaking, there. Philosophers were divided in their assessment of it: was it a regrettable tendency to which the human mind is prone, or could it be mastered and channeled in productive and rational ways? Virtually no one thought that the imagination should simply run free. The task of mastering it was generally thought to be a central part of the project of "improvement of the intellect," to cite part of the name of a 1662 treatise by Baruch Spinoza.[8]

Because imagination involves the production of images, it was typically seen as a fundamentally bodily process, or at least as occurring at the point of intersection between the mind and the body. It was generally thought that some mental faculties, such as intellect or understanding, could carry on as usual even if the body with which a mind is associated were to disappear from existence. But imagination involves bodily sensation, and so the body cannot be removed from the use of this faculty, and the proper training of it involves knowing when reliance on it is useful, and when by contrast it is simply a distraction. Thus in the sixth of his *Meditations* Descartes makes the case that in geometry we represent to our minds, or on paper, an image of a polygon; but this is just a representation, pleasing to the imagination, while ultimately unnecessary to a rational mind that is powerful enough to grasp the various properties of a polygon without having to envision it.[9] A great rational mind could do all geometry, even geometrical proofs involving a thousand-sided chiliagon, without ever having to sketch the plane figure in question on paper or imagine it in his head. The imagination is a mark of human weakness, perhaps sometimes a necessary crutch, but always to be kept in check by reason or understanding, to which in turn it always poses a threat. Even at its best, imagination is only the more salutary expression of what can easily degenerate into "feverish imaginings," the upward motion of vapors toward the brain, which causes us to see what is not there. At its worst, imagination is to reason what idolatry is to true religion: a mistaking of the sensual representation for the thing itself.

While an image rendered to the mind with the help of the imagination might be useful, its more or less consistently evil twin, so to speak, is the phantasm, rendered to the mind by means of fantasy. In his *Pensées* of 1670, Blaise Pascal would describe fantasy, along with opinion, as the "mistress of error," and as a "superlative power" (*superbe puissance*) that stands as an "enemy of reason."[10] Fantasy is for him a sort of antireason, fighting it out with its positive counterforce in a perpetual Manichaean struggle. Fantasy works for evil rather than good, Pascal thinks, to the extent that it makes no distinction between the true and the false, but rather represents both what exists and what does not exist with the same faithfulness. Fantasy amounts to a second nature in human beings, seeking ever to dominate and control our reason. It often prevails, since it is better at making us happy, especially when we are not by natural disposition wise. Fantasy "cannot make the mad wise, but it makes them happy, to the envy of reason, which can only make the friends it has miserable."[11] Pascal for his part was certainly no rationalist in the strict sense, with a capital *R*, as were Descartes, Spinoza, and Leibniz, since he believed that faith must lead us to our ultimate commitments, while reason always comes up short in human life. Nonetheless, like the Rationalists, when it is not faith that is opposed to reason, but rather imagination or fantasy, Pascal agrees that these latter faculties are sooner worthy of our suspicion than of being exalted as what makes us distinctly and most excellently human.

In the most recent era we have largely lost this wariness of imagination and fantasy. We no longer associate them with unreason, let alone with madness. On the contrary, the use of the imagination is now a central part of all but the most conservative and backward-looking educational philosophies. Children grow smart by cultivating their imaginations, and imaginations must be cultivated, allowed to grow on their own (even if channeled in this more promising direction rather than that less promising one, by use of clever wooden toys rather than violent video games), rather than being curtailed, domesticated, or dominated. We are aware that some people might get so lost in their imaginations as to become altogether disconnected from reality—might, for example, get so lost in fantasy fiction as to be unable to pay their bills and show up to appointments—and we recognize that this is a problem. But it is not generally thought to be a problem already incipient in any indulgence of the imagination whatsoever. The badness of such disconnection, it is generally thought today, no more makes imagination bad than burned food makes cooking as such bad.

But what changed, exactly? Who are the ancestors from whom John Dewey, Maria Montessori, and other enlightened, pro-imagination pedagogues of the twentieth century descended, if not from Descartes, Spinoza, Leibniz, and Pascal? The short answer is that we are living out the dual legacy today, and have been for a long while now, of rationalism and romanticism. This becomes particularly clear when we chart the transformation, since the seventeenth century, of the concept of "genius."

We sometimes inadequately choose the translation of the Latin *ingenium*, as it occurs in early modern philosophical texts, as "genius." This choice conceals the incredibly complex history of the Latin term. We have already seen it in the title of Spinoza's *Tractatus de emendatione ingenii*. Although the term can be translated as "intellect," a more appropriate rendering would come in the form of a multiword gloss: ingenium is the propensity for learning, or aptitude for discovery, or any number of other, similar, ultimately inadequate variations. For Cicero "ingenium" had designated the "innate seeds of virtue, which, if they are able to grow, by nature itself will lead us to a happy life."[12] Writing in French in the *Discourse on Method* of 1637, Descartes uses the term *bon sens*—not quite what he would have intended by *ingenium* were he writing in Latin, but also not part of a completely different semantic cluster—in order to mockingly suggest that people believe falsely of themselves that they possess all of it that they might need, indeed all that any human being might hope to possess: "Good sense is the best distributed thing in the world," he writes, "for everyone thinks himself so well endowed with it that even those who are the hardest to please in everything else do not usually desire more of it than they possess. In this it is unlikely that everyone is mistaken."[13] It is unlikely that *everyone* is mistaken, but likely, Descartes implies, that *most* people are.

For Descartes as for Cicero before him, while ingenium may be held by all, it is more acutely developed in some than in others. Moreover, this acuity is likely a natural endowment rather than something that can be inculcated by instruction: even though a textbook full of rules, such as Descartes's 1628 *Regulae ad directionem ingenii* (variously translated as *Rules for the Direction of the Mind* or, in a rather more cumbersome fashion, *Rules for the Direction of the Natural Intelligence*), can help a person to direct her ingenium, the sharpness or strength of the ingenium in question may well be a fixed quantity throughout that person's life. The fact that ingenium is something not fully teachable therefore means that those of "greater ingenium" may cultivate it simply by attention to nature. Thus Descartes writes in the *Rules*, describing his own proposed method of learning, "Since the utility of this method is so great that, without it, the pursuit of learning would seem to be more harmful than helpful, I am easily persuaded that those of greater ingenium have already seen it in some manner—even under the guidance of nature alone."[14]

The folkloric, but also very deep-seated, figure of the genius as a supernatural spirit, associated with but not identical to an individual human being, would become a common fixture of eighteenth-century treatments of the faculty that had been called, from Cicero to Descartes, ingenium. Thus Kant writes in the 1790 *Critique of the Faculty of Judgment* that "it is probable that the word *Genie* is derived from *genius*, that peculiar guiding and guardian spirit given to a man at his birth, from whose suggestion these original ideas proceed."[15] At the beginning of Kant's century, in the first French translation of *A Thousand and One Nights*, brought out in stages between 1704 and 1717, the Arabic *al-jinnī* had been rendered by Antoine Galland as *le génie*.[16] This of course will soon become the familiar "genie," that early example of cultural appropriation, who comes out of a lamp, as a vaporous puff, and grants wishes. The shared etymology is, however, spurious: the spiritual creature of Islamic folklore shares no common origin with the genius, whose name ultimately shares the same root with such things as genes, genera, and generation. But in the early eighteenth century the terms "genius" and "génie" were unstable, teetering between signifying some particular mental capacity of an individual human being, and denoting a supernatural being that guides or intervenes in human life somewhat in the manner of an Arabic *jinnī*. Thus in the *Theodicy* of 1709 Leibniz would insist that "there is an inconceivable number of genies [*génies*]" inhabiting the heavenly spheres, too great in magnitude to enter into our field of perception.

In the *Critique of the Faculty of Judgment*, Kant identifies "genius" as "the innate mental disposition (*ingenium*) through which nature gives the rule to art."[17] The parenthetical Latin is Kant's own: for him, ingenium is an innate mental disposition, but it is elevated into genius properly speaking only when it involves the rare power of nature to "give the rule to art." That is to say, for Kant the genius artist is the person who has received a gift from nature that becomes manifest in the artist's creations. This creates for Kant a sort of hierarchical distinction between the respective values or powers of scientists on the one hand, and of artists on the other: "In science," he writes, "the greatest discoverer only differs in degree from his laborious imitator and pupil; but he differs specifically from him whom nature has gifted for beautiful art."[18]

This distinction, in turn, would be the beginning of a celebration of "genius" in the new and unprecedented sense in which it would be understood in German romanticism: the exceptional gift of certain individuals that enables them to have creative breakthroughs, to innovate artistically, to see the world in a new way and to make new works of art in accordance with this new way of seeing. For the rationalists, reason had been the highest faculty of the human mind, and was shared equally by all human beings simply in virtue of their humanity—even if, to be sure, many human beings do not train it in the right way and never really excel as the rational beings they were, in some sense, created to be. Genius, by contrast, in the early romantic understanding of it, is a scarce resource, and there is not necessarily any reliable method of drawing it out of any individual person. You either have it or you don't, and no instruction book could ever possibly be written to explain to you how to get it. "If you have to ask, you'll never know," as Louis Armstrong said of the meaning of "swing."

Descartes had wanted to provide a method to as many people as possible, with whatever rudiments of *bon sens* they may have been born, to master bodies of knowledge, as well as the right rules of inference concerning these bodies of knowledge. He did not have much concern about art as an autonomous domain of human existence that might be well suited to bring human excellence into evidence. With Kant, and all the more with the German romantic movement that will develop over the half century or so that follows his work (and often in conscious opposition to important elements of this work), art will by contrast be propelled into the center of attention. Art, moreover, will be sharply distinguished from craft or craftsmanship: that which any person with rudimentary potential could in principle be trained to produce. Art, rather, will come to have "fine art" as its exemplary, even as its sole legitimate, instance: the sort of art that only the ingenious may hope to produce, not by learning rules and following them, but rather by learning rules, and, eventually, breaking them as only a genius can. And at this point, genius, which had initially been conceived as a natural disposition to learning any rule-bound skill or science, including logic, is now set up in stark opposition to logic and identified with deep and incommunicable inner feeling. Thus in 1901, in Montana, the nineteen-year-old genius Mary MacLane will write: "If I were not so unceasingly engrossed with my sense of misery and loneliness my mind would produce beautiful, wondrous logic. I am a genius—a genius—a genius. Even after all this you may not realize that I am a genius. It is a hard thing to show. But, for myself, I feel it."[19]

To master science, to learn the rules as Descartes hoped to bring people with good sense to do, is to conduct oneself with integrity, to do what is right in the right circumstances, which includes making the right inferences from the right knowledge, constructing one's

BSK

machines in the right way, and so on. But this conception of human excellence, and of the human good, is at odds with the human particularism that rationalist thinkers such as Descartes also stress; it makes the well-trained human being, the one who has mastered the rules, little different from the predictable egret or lizard, who moves now this way and now that, depending on what is happening around it, what its body needs, and so on. Descartes expresses on a number of occasions the common observation of animals that "the high degree of perfection displayed in some of their actions makes us suspect that [they] do not have free will."[20] For Descartes, an animal can have integrity but cannot have idiosyncrasy; it can achieve the excellence of the sort of being it is, only to the extent that it continues to do what we expect it to do. If it does something unexpected, this is probably because it is enraged, or dying, and even then we expect it to undergo these changes in patterned and species-specific ways. But surely there is something more that human beings might hope for, and that sets them apart? There is: idiosyncrasy, doing now this and now that, for no other reason than that it suits our exceptional individual natures. And the idiosyncrasy of the exceptional few, who do now this and now that for reasons we cannot understand, but with results we recognize as valuable, is nothing other than genius.

The shift in philosophical interest from ingenium to genius, in the sense just described, from teachable and collective science to individual accomplishments of art, from reason to inscrutable inspiration, came at a great cost: it could not pretend to offer us a general account of how human beings are and of what their potential might be. It was of necessity preoccupied with rare birds among men. Moreover, in abandoning any expectation of an explicit account of what makes great art great, or exceptional artists exceptional, abandoning any hope that the rules of great art may be stated, set down, and then followed by others, it acknowledges that what matters most in human life is something for which the reasons cannot be given. Art is, to this extent, irrational, as is the society that sets art up as a supreme good, without any expectation of understanding why it is so—the society, for example, in which a local museum jockeys and petitions for the acquisition of a Jeff Koons sculpture, which Koons himself did not make with his own hands, but which is believed nonetheless to carry, by a series of certifiable transmissions, the authentic trace of his inscrutable genius.

What Is Art?

Much of the tradition of Western "fine art," prior to and in some cases parallel to romanticism and later movements such as expressionism and surrealism, has been devoted to tempering and dominating irrationality, to converting wild dreams into things, into physical objects and commodities. Even if the rules of these objects' production cannot be given, they can still be rationalized to some extent as commodities with a certain monetary value, and any other sort of value can be debated by critics and viewers with greater or lesser degrees of futility.

E. R. Dodds begins *The Greeks and the Irrational*, to which we have already been introduced, by relating an encounter in a museum that occurred not long before the book's publication in 1951.[21] He meets a young man by chance who tells him that he has no taste for Greek art or culture because, the young man says, the Greeks had been too preoccupied with reason. At the time Dodds was writing, museums, striving for austerity, were filled with monochrome canvases and ready-made industrial products (which were not strictly speaking created by the artist to whom they are attributed, but rather, to speak with Arthur Danto, were "transfigured" by the artist).[22] The museums also favored "primitive" sculptures inspired by the artistic traditions of non-European cultures—traditions that Kant would have insisted do not rise to the level of true art, "fine art," but rather should be kept cordoned off in the lesser category of decoration or craft. The *air du temps* for the midcentury urban Westerner, the young man presumably felt, was preoccupied with the return of the repressed, with everything that cannot be confined within a pristine rational order.

Dodds took this encounter as the starting point for his own groundbreaking investigation of Greek culture. Is it *really* so easy to sum up what Greek life had been about by calling it "rational"? And has there ever, moreover, been a culture that deserves this appellation unambiguously or unqualifiedly? Or is it rather something that is of service only as a stereotype deployed at a great distance, either in space or in time, or perhaps as a conceit that one might use within a given culture by screening out everything that does not conform to it? "To a generation whose sensibilities have been trained on African and Aztec art," Dodds writes, "and on the work of such men as Modigliani and Henry Moore, the art of the Greeks, and Greek culture in general, is apt to appear lacking in the awareness of mystery and in the ability to penetrate to the deeper, less conscious levels of human experience."[23]

An important role is played, in engaging these deeper levels, by repetition. The poet Les Murray, quoted earlier, has compellingly described religion as poetry to the extent that its rituals are enacted "in loving repetition." Or, as the German choreographer Pina Bausch has articulated her own use of repetition as the vehicle of her artistic creation: "Repetition is not repetition. The same action makes you feel something completely different by the end."[24] Here we may also recall the multiple mystical visions of Plotinus, discussed in chapter 1. Could these repetitions have failed to structure his purportedly ineffable experiences, to give them sense and form, like a choreographed dance? And is there perhaps something in the notion of repetition that can provide for us a bridge between the seemingly separate realms of art, on the one hand, and religion and ritual on the other?

When I was thirteen, I was baptized in the Catholic church. I had been the only unbaptized student in a Catholic elementary school, and it was judged at some point that I might fit in better if I were to become a member of the flock. I acquiesced, happily, and for a year or so I muttered the rosary with deep inward yearning: in loving repetition. This experience overlaps in my memory with a period of intense, ridiculous, adolescent Beatlemania. I knew all the band members' birthdays, all their parents' birthdays, the precise layouts of the streets of Liverpool, of Hamburg. I knew, most of all, the precise aural contours of every available recording of every Beatles song, whether canonical or bootleg. I do not remember whether the Beatles came before, or after, the

Catholicism. What I remember is that they blended perfectly into one another in my fantasy life.

Now the recordings, though I played them back in loving repetition, were not, strictly speaking, repeated. They were each performed only once, in a studio, at some point in the 1960s, before I was born. Perhaps these singular performances involved tracks, and so multiple recordings of different elements, but in any case the whole production of the authoritative version was completed in a finite, no doubt very short, series of steps. What was produced was what Nelson Goodman would call an "allographic" artwork: a work that can be fully experienced even if the thing itself remains remote, even if the thing itself is in its essence unlocatable.[25] My copy of the *White Album*, scooped up at a San Francisco garage sale from some kindly hippie, repairing his Volkswagen bus, circa 1985, cannot in any sense be said to be *the* work of art itself, and yet I have experienced the *White Album* as fully as anyone has, simply by bringing this copy home and putting it on the record player and listening to it: in loving repetition. The recording of that album fixed and eternalized a number of contingencies, a number of things that could just as well not have happened, some words muttered, George Harrison's fingers staying on the strings a microsecond too long and generating that superfluous but not unpleasant string noise for which there is surely a term. These contingencies become canonical. They are awaited lovingly by the knowing listener. They arrive as expected, and they reconfirm the aesthetic order of the world.

We know that a number of the world's most glorious works of epic poetry, including Homeric epic, began as traditions of oral recitation, presumably involving some degree of rhythmic articulation, and perhaps also inflections of the voice's pitch and timber. In this respect, literature and music are really only different trajectories of the same deeper aesthetic activity: a repetition that reconfirms, or reestablishes, or perhaps re-creates, the order of the world. To be invested in this repetition aesthetically, following Murray, is nothing other than love itself. The Yakut heroic epos, the *Olonkho*, is considered to be the urtext of pre-Islamic Turkic mythology, preserved across the centuries in the oral tradition of northeastern Siberia. It speaks of snow, and reindeer, and human beings, and ancestors, and the transcendent cause of all of this. When reading it, I envision an expert raconteur, someone who relates the *Olonkho* with a degree of mastery comparable to the mastery we recognize as involved in conducting the Ring Cycle or playing Othello. What one would particularly relish, it is easy to imagine, experiencing the recitation directly, and intimately, would be the variety of deviations, and the way the master raconteur controls the deviations for such-and-such desired effect. "Here comes that part where he's going to make a bear-grunt noise!" the Yakut adolescent might think to herself. And then it comes, and it is slightly different from the last time, yet perfectly, satisfyingly different. The repetitions are irreducibly social, variable yet constant (unlike the recording of George's fingers on the string, they are a little bit different each time, and yet the same), and mediated through a figure who in turn mediates between the human and the transhuman spheres of existence.

It is an unusual experience when the repetition can be experienced, as I experienced the Beatles' music, both in a way that is not directly social, at home with headphones on in front of a record player, and in a way that involves total invariability from one "performance" to the next. My experience of the Catholic faith was also somewhat unusual: it consisted almost entirely in private mutterings of memorized prayers, in a way that remained almost completely oblivious to the existence of the church, the coming together of two or more people that in turn calls God to presence as well. But these obsessive compulsions, like the socially mediated recitation of epic, or like technologically mediated communion with godlike pop stars through recorded tokens of their canonical creations, are all, as already suggested, the work of love, or at least of some passion that feels a lot like love when it is being experienced. Let us just call it love. This love seems to send a person straight outside of himself. But since this cannot really happen, since we all in fact stay right where we are, the sweet irrational ecstasy arrives in the next best way possible: through a cycling back, again and again, to the syllables and sounds that order the world, and that may give some hint of its true cause and nature.

The essence of much art lies in repetition of the sort I have just described, and to this extent it is at least a close relative of ritual. Yet for more than a century now art has been principally preoccupied not with the eternal cycling back of the same, but with the perpetual, forward-marching innovation of the new. The irrational, as expressed in modern art, has been not only about mystery and the unconscious, but also about transgression, so much so that critics have often written as if transgression is an essential feature of modern art. Kieran Cashell describes the pressure on critics to conform to this view: "Either support transgression unconditionally or condemn the tendency and risk obsolescence amid suspicions of critical conservatism."[26] A small but significant portion of the transgressive artworks of the past several decades have incorporated violence, not an exploration of the theme of violence, but actual violence, enacted by the artist either against him- or herself, or against animals, or, in some rare cases, against unwitting spectators. Perhaps nothing signals transgression in art quite so easily as splattered blood, even if some who have used it, such as the Vienna actionist artist Hermann Nitsch, insist that they are attempting to return to something ritualistic and archaic, rather than aspiring to the singular and cutting-edge.[27]

What, in the end, are such ritualized displays of transgression getting at? I spent a good part of my youth, within a few years of the remission of my Beatlemania, attending the concerts of bands considerably harder than the Beatles at their hardest, bands that made "Helter Skelter" sound like a lullaby. To thrash about under the spell of such music, we ordinarily assume, and I certainly assumed while in flagrant delectation, is the very opposite of submission to authority, to top-down diktats from the state, the church, the military, or the family as to how we ought to be conducting ourselves. But the opposition is not so clear: the revelry, while anarchic, is occurring in front of, and usually somewhat beneath, a band. The revelers are not bowing down to or worshipping the band, but nor is what they are doing an entirely different species of activity from a church service or a mass rally.

How exactly the one sort of social phenomenon morphs into the other, how individuals move from an ebullient expression of their individuality to an ecstatic transcendence of the self in a supercharged collectivity, is both complicated and crucially important for our understanding of the social manifestations of irrationality. We know that many young people who have enjoyed freaking out and dancing alone under the influence of psychedelic drugs and music have not long after found themselves under the influence of enigmatic and psychopathic cult leaders. Roughly half of the anarchist punks I knew in my adolescence, who listened to bands with names like Social Distortion and the Dead Kennedys—and, with seething irony, one that was called Reagan Youth—are now sincere, utterly unironic Trump supporters. It is but one small step from free-spirited anarchy into a statist-nationalist cult of personality. The last few centuries reveal that individual transcendence cannot exist for long without being followed by a reabsorption into the collectivity, that the two mutually imply each other. The middle of the twentieth century, in particular, seems to have witnessed an intense acceleration of the alternations between the two. The most anarchic and individualistic expressions of avant-garde art in Weimar Germany or in the early Soviet Union quickly gave way to a wave of conformism in which the aims of art were subordinated to the aims of mass politics. Many avant-garde artists themselves, such as the Italian futurists, were eager to sign up for mass movements that submerged their own individuality and that subordinated them to ironfisted rulers.

In the seventeenth century Descartes had sought to banish dreams, to assure himself that the hallucinations of sleep play no part in who he really is, that they are inevitable, but must also be contained and, to the extent possible, forgotten. Freud, by contrast, would maintain that our logical reasoning and clear and distinct perceptions are just a fragile wrapping around the true self that is always bubbling and fermenting underneath, and that is made up, precisely, of dreams, of largely forgotten memories and passions. The Jesuit missionary in New France had worried, recall, that the Iroquois chief's access to his own unconscious, his penchant for taking the content of his dreams as instructions for action, would lead him to act out violently against his missionary guest, perhaps to kill him. The unconscious is not subject to the sort of moral regulation that governs our conscious life. In our society we often suppose that morality consists precisely in keeping a check on the forms of transgression that our unconscious enables us or compels us to imagine. In this regard it would seem natural to suppose that a society in which action is based on the translation of dreams into reality could not possibly be rational or moral: it would involve constant, chaotic transgression. In societies such as those of the twentieth-century West, mystery and the deeper levels of human experience are allowed to seep into public life in the form of sculpture and painting and music, but ordinarily not in the form of direct enactment of the sorts of moral transgression that might be depicted or described in art. This may seem like a healthy compromise, an effective way of deploying a release valve for the unconscious, to return to this common metaphor, without making too great a mess of things.

But this would almost certainly amount to hasty self-congratulation. The fact that violence is strictly morally prohibited in civilian life within our society—that it is monopolized by the state and relegated to the fantasy lives of the state's subjects—does not seem conclusively to mean that there is less overall real violence in our society than in those, such as the Iroquois, in which violence is more fluidly integrated and processed through ritual. Increasingly, the work of war is being transferred to an ever smaller number of people, responsible for ever more powerful war machines. It is science that has kissed awake the new powers of these machines, and this over the course of the same period of history in which the enduring violence of our dreams has been ever more effectively cordoned off from the sphere of real action: restrained within the safe spaces of museums, or, in its lower-brow iterations, packaged as the harmless entertainments of the big and small screens, entertainments that until recently were often said to have been made in "dream factories." The violence sometimes leaps off the screens—it bleeds out, like obscenity out of quotation marks, into the real world—but for the most part we find that the arrangement works fairly well: science and technology monopolize real violence, congealed into missiles and drones that are held to be more effective the less often they are used; while art has unfettered access to fantasy violence, and may do with it whatever it wishes, as long as no one (or no human) gets hurt.

To the extent possible, we try to see these, too, as nonoverlapping magisteria. We try not to think at all about the unimaginable violence hanging over our heads at all times; and we try to see the imaginative violence on our screens and in our art museums as belonging to an entirely different metaphysical and moral order: the one that is possible but not actual, the one that is just for fun. The safe space of unreason.

The Two Magisteria

In his 1759 poem "Jubilate Agno," Christopher Smart, locked away in a mental asylum with his cat Jeoffry, would write of this faithful companion:

> For by stroking him I have found out electricity.
> For I perceived God's light about him both wax and fire.
> For the Electrical fire is the spiritual substance, which God sends from heaven to sustain the bodies of man and beast.[28]

What is electricity? For many, in the years before it was harnessed and transformed into a central part of our everyday lives, it was a spirituous substance and a sign of God's power. More than a century after Smart, in his 1885 "Dissertation on Monads," the Canadian Métis resistance fighter and mystic Louis Riel, evidently recalling the lessons on Leibniz's philosophy he must have had decades earlier while at the Sulpician college of Montreal, would write from his Saskatchewan jail cell, awaiting execution: "A monad is an electricity [*sic*]."[29] Over the course of the twentieth century, in turn, electricity would be taken away from the raving visionaries, and transformed into something for the use of which we receive a burdensome bill each month. It would be normalized, deprived, so to speak, of its charge of strangeness, and of all the interest it had previously had for those who position themselves outside the mainstream.

It is generally clear only in hindsight where the line in fact lies between science and its embarrassing cousin pseudoscience. Karl Popper had believed in the mid-twentieth century that the two could be sharply bounded off from one another by the criterion of falsifiability: if a proposition cannot in principle be falsified, then it is not a scientific proposition.[30] But it is often impossible to know in advance how to class different propositions according to this criterion, and for this reason other prominent philosophers of science, notably Larry Laudan, have argued that the demarcation question "is both uninteresting and, judging by its checkered past, intractable."[31] More recently, Massimo Pigliucci has compellingly argued, in turn, that Laudan's eulogy was premature. As Pigliucci notes, most of us think we know pseudoscience when we see it. It is perhaps only inevitable that we should continue to try to find a rigorous definition of it, even if none is forthcoming.[32] We will return to explore pseudoscience in more detail in the next chapter. For the moment what interests us is the way in which natural forces, such as electricity, can themselves move, from one moment of history to another, across the demarcation line between the supernatural and the natural. This is a motion that often maps on, at least partially, to the transition from the realm of the creative and imaginative arts to the realm of sober science.

In the seventeenth century many who denied the reality of action at a distance or other varieties of sympathetic power were seeking to advance a clockwork model of nature, with every motion of a body explainable by the fact that some other body has directly imparted its motion to it, just as a gear in a clock moves only because it is pushed along in its rotation by another gear. Naturally, on such a model, miracles and wonders, God's delivery of anything as a sign or as a gift, also had no place. But many who sought to deny miracles did so not because they wished to deny God's infinite power, as it might have seemed to a medieval theologian some centuries earlier, but because, as they argued, it would in fact serve to diminish this power if one were to maintain that God had created a natural order in need of periodic interruptions. How much more worthy of exaltation would be a God who had set up the order of nature so perfectly at the beginning that any subsequent interventions could only cast into doubt nature's status as a monument to his perfection. Yet however sincere the theological motivations behind this new theological noninterventionism may have been, it brought with it the threat of the *Deus absconditus*: a God who is no longer needed, whose entire responsibility is wrapped up in the Creation, and who, once he has established the initial conditions of things, along with the unchanging laws of nature, is free to simply abscond.

To some extent, this is a problem that reaches back to antiquity: in order to properly exalt God, many theologically oriented philosophers found it fitting to push him out of the ordinary affairs of the world. Some ancient thinkers, including Aristotle, supposed that God must be so great as to not be at all dependent on the existence of the world, and that if he were even so much as to think about the world at all, then this would already amount to a sort of dependence. But in the modern period, with the long legacy of Christianity, it was no longer nearly so easy as it had been for Aristotle and other Greek philosophers to imagine God as indifferent to the human world: after all, the Christian God is supposed to have created this world for human beings, and, however complicated the relationship has been, to love them as well. No modern Christian philosopher, no matter how radical, could simply deny that God has a relationship to the world at all. For this reason it would prove far more difficult than it had been for the Greeks to strike the delicate balance between exaltation of God and his elimination.

Nor was sincerity in one's faith necessarily enough to avoid contributing to the emergence of a naturalistic model of the world in which God would ultimately prove otiose and superfluous. No one was more adamant than Robert Boyle, the English experimental philosopher of the late seventeenth century, that nature may be exhaustively explained as a clockwork. Boyle also insisted that there is no form of life more in keeping with Christian piety than the one devoted to conducting the sort of experiments that reveal how what appears miraculous in nature may in fact be explained in terms of previously undiscerned regularities and undiscovered laws of nature. Boyle is in this respect a world away from a libertine thinker such as Pierre Gassendi, who wishes to account for eclipses, for example, in terms of the ordinary and predictable orbits of celestial bodies, and who takes the possibility of their naturalistic explanation as evidence for the superstitiousness of religious belief in general. For Gassendi, naturalism is a weapon against faith, while for Boyle it is the means to arrive at a more worthy faith.

According to the French historian Paul Hazard, invoked in the introduction, it is in the period between 1680 and 1715 that what we might call "Boyle's program"—the attempt to harness the rational explanation of nature's regularity in the service of religious faith—will prove impossible to sustain.[33] Increasingly over the next centuries, such rational explanation will be seen, by its defenders and detractors alike, as overtly hostile to faith, and faith in turn will retreat, often, into irrationalism, where it either denies the legitimacy of science or attempts unconvincingly to beat science at its own game. By the late nineteenth century in Europe, the rift will have become so pronounced as to obscure from view earlier attempts to hold these domains together. This will be the era in which science, as embodied by the figure of the scientist, becomes the autonomous and authoritative domain of culture, as we continue to understand it, more or less, today. William Whewell would coin the term "scientist," on analogy to "artist," only as recently as 1834,[34] prior to which the preferred term for a person who does what a scientist does would have been "philosopher" or "natural philosopher" or "naturalist." It is only in the mid-1860s that the term begins to be used with any significant frequency.

In the 1880s, the Eiffel Tower was built in Paris, not, as many now groundlessly imagine, as a monument to all that is sensual and seductive, but rather as a feat of engineering in celebration of the French men of science who had contributed to the glory of the Third Republic, and whose names are inscribed in enormous letters around the base of the structure.[35] This is just one of many such triumphalist erections that were appearing throughout the world's capital cities around the same time, and that by no means celebrated romance. Rather, the romantic vision of the world was positively screened out and ignored in the engineers' and the architects' pursuit of a solid, steel-framed future. There was by now nothing "poetic" about such projects, in the sense of *poiesis* invoked earlier. By now *poiesis* has been relegated to the second-tier status of mere writers, creators of merely possible worlds; while the work of the wrighter, so to speak, of the builder or maker, was the creation of a new reality here in our actual world. At the top of his structure Gustave Eiffel included a meteorological observatory and a laboratory for the study of radio waves and other physical phenomena. This elevated station doubled as his apartments, where he would also receive Thomas Edison during the American inventor's visits to Paris. Not long before, Jules Verne was writing a new sort of science fiction, including the 1865 novel *From the Earth to the Moon*,[36] in which he not only envisions a lunar transit, a stock feature of literature since Lucian of Samosata wrote the *True History* in the first century CE, but also attempts to give a plausible account of how such a transit might actually take place in the near future. Verne is, in his way, drawing the stars down to earth, claiming the fiction of the possible—which had previously been under the chaotic reign of the faculty of the imagination—for the faculty of reason.

In Verne's and Eiffel's lifetime the ideal personage of the scientist was taking shape, and only then was philosophy, for its part, forced to split into two camps. There were those who found this new figure of the scientist impressive and longed to share in his new cultural cachet. Others, by contrast, found his purview—that of building on, improving upon, and channeling the forces of the natural world, hacking through nature's thorns to kiss awake new powers, in James Merrill's words—inadequate for the central task of philosophy as it had been understood by one prominent strain of thinkers since antiquity: that of understanding ourselves, our interiority, and the gap between what we experience in our inner lives and what the natural world will permit to be actualized or known.

This was not a strict bifurcation, not every philosopher felt compelled to take sides, and it is not always easy to determine in retrospect on what side of the divide a given thinker fell. Yet there are some for whom there can be no question: for example, Nietzsche, who writes

ecstatically in *The Gay Science* of 1882 that "the wildly beautiful irrationality of poetry refutes you, you utilitarians!"[37] The German thinker
absolutely rejected the vision of the philosopher as sharing a common
cause with the scientist, who, again, at the time Nietzsche was writing
had been around in his present incarnation for only a few decades.
Contemporary poets, meanwhile, whom Nietzsche praised for their
wildly beautiful irrationality, increasingly touted the power and virtue
of madness, childlikeness, and dream states in the creation of their art.
Charles Baudelaire explicitly described the poem as a form of thought
that occurs "musically and pictorially, without quibbling, without
syllogisms, without deduction."[38] Thus for him poetry is a rejection of
philosophy as it had been traditionally understood, and if a philosopher wishes to share in the generative force of the poet's unreason, he
must by the same token reject the recognized tools of his discipline.

These distinctions, again, are not always clear, nor are they distinctions that the figures involved would necessarily have recognized as
pertaining to themselves. One particularly important movement that
had its greatest prominence in the eighteenth century, but that also
weaves in complex ways in and out of the work of nineteenth-century
figures, including that of Nietzsche, is Hellenism: a variety of neoclassicism, resistant to definition, but which may at least be said to not
place poetry and reason in stark opposition to one another. Hellenism,
as the English poet and critic Matthew Arnold understood it,[39] is
opposed to the strict subordination of individuals to rules that cramp
and stunt the free expression of the spirit. As such it is a movement that
is based on spontaneity, but this is conceived quite differently from
anarchy or behaving in any disordered way whatsoever. Rather, the
product of spontaneous action, when issuing from the spirit of true
artistic talent, is one that is in harmony with the natural and transcendental order. It is not chaotic or satanic, which would be rather closer
to what Baudelaire was after, but nor is it rule bound and pious.

Nietzsche's work comes late in the history of modern Hellenism,
and may be said both to mark its crisis and also to offer its swan song.
He was by training a philologist, raised up to be a dusty scholar seques-
tered in a dimly lit library, doing the hard work of reconstructing our

civilization's origins from the textual traces of a long past world. This sort of work was in the nineteenth century the very ideal of scholarship, the very reason for being of a humanistic education, and, very much unlike today, it was a central part of what went on in universities. But what Nietzsche drew from his reading of the Greeks was not at all a continuity of civilizations, and not even a history of decline. It was, rather, something closer to an absolute rupture, whereby the things the Greeks valued can mostly no longer be detected by us—even if we learn their language and believe we are familiar with their world—for these things have simply become too strange and foreign. And these things are not, as the more conservative Hellenists had believed, the gifts of reason, order, geometry, and so on; they are expressions of extreme unreason, of the sort that in the following century E. R. Dodds would more thoroughly excavate: Dionysianism, ecstasies, transgressions without guilt. Nietzsche remained rooted in the Greek world, but did not at all see that world as extending to us a torch to illuminate the pursuit of our shared values of order, perfection, and invention.

A half century before Nietzsche, Johann Wolfgang von Goethe was busy forging the modern German literary spirit, drawing on the neoclassicism that was at its apex during his lifetime, but also cultivating a model of the modern intellectual as one who is at home in the realm of the sensual, and who sees no strong opposition between sensuality and reason, or between imagination and understanding, or romanticism and science. For Goethe, however, acknowledgment of the ineliminability of sensuality, even in domains of human experience that are held to be primarily cognitive, does not at all amount to a compromise with romanticism. In fact he believes that it is only in the modern period that sense and reason have been artificially separated, and that classicism gives us everything we need to bring them back together. Thus his judgment of the two prevailing intellectual currents in his era is clear and decisive: "What is classical is healthy," he writes, "what is romantic is sick."[40]

Goethe's own contributions in science, particularly in botany and in the study of color perception, reveal a path not taken, which had its moment in the early decades of the nineteenth century, just before the

first appearance of Whewell's "scientist," and the congealing over the
remainder of the century of the ideal type of the scientific practitioner:
a cold, detached, and unfeeling experimenter, an ultimate authority to
turn to for answers to questions that the common run of people, too
attached to their passions, are unable to come by on their own. This
type would prevail until the late twentieth century, only to be in turn
replaced by the latest iteration of the figure of the scientist: the more
or less unreflective technician, able to fulfill all of his or her job duties
without appeal to abstract concepts of any sort, and principally accomplished in the art of winning grant money for his or her home
institution.

Goethe envisioned a practice of science that would not exclude the
role of the emotions in the discernment of basic truths about the natural world. In the domains of natural science that interested him most,
botany and optics, qualitative description is ineliminable. In his monumental work of epic poetry, *Faust*, composed in drafts over several
years at the end of the eighteenth century, Goethe also remained aware
of the deep, mythical association of scientific discovery with natural
magic: with probing into the forces we would do best to ignore, and
unleashing them into the world, against our better inclinations, and
against piety. Goethe did not himself see scientific discovery in this
way, as a pact with the devil, but he did think that this deep-seated
understanding of it was important enough to be taken seriously, to be
reflected on. And he thought that the best alternative model of scientific
inquiry would be one that does not simply sweep the old Mephistoph-
elean view aside, but rather modulates it through a humane, sensual
cultivation of the scientific life as the locus of a new sort of virtue.

Goethean science lost out, of course, to the point that his vision of
what science is or ought to be, just two hundred years or so after the
fact, is barely recognizable to most people. The reason for the dramatic
rupture in the late nineteenth century, between the romantics and the
scientists, between—to speak perhaps overly emblematically—the
absinthe bar and the Eiffel Tower, had much to do with this loss, and
with the sudden sense that one must choose a side: that science is not
about feeling or sensuality, and in turn that poetry is not about insight

into the harmonious or rational order of the external world, but rather about laying bare the dark and disordered depths of one's own internal world. This rupture brought about, among other things, a stark radicalization of tendencies in both science and poetry, which were not exactly new in the mid-nineteenth century, but had not until that point come to dominate so fully as the respective spirits of these two basic human activities. Science was now the home of reason; poetry, and art, and the exercise of the imagination more generally, of unreason. Both of these spheres of human life continue to hobble along today, injured by the violence of their separation.

CHAPTER FIVE

"I believe because it is absurd"; or, Pseudoscience

▶▶▶▶▶

The Stars Down to Earth

In a letter to Louis Bourguet of 1714, Leibniz famously writes, "I despise almost nothing—except judiciary astrology."[1] For him, the advancement of any science or discipline is directly connected not just with discovery and theory, but also with the creation of a proper institutional structure for the facilitation of discovery and the production of theories. Leibniz understood, in his medical and epidemiological writings beginning from the 1690s, that processing data about past epidemics would be a far better tool for anticipating future ones than would be more traditional varieties of fortune-telling: thus, effectively, that *retrodiction* can be, when coupled with evaluation of statistical data, a powerful tool for *prediction*. And he saw, moreover, that this could be done with the help of machines, along with the collective labor of employees of state-sponsored institutions.

In spite of his disdainful remark, what Leibniz envisions might in fact be understood as something closer to an improvement, by a change in its basic techniques, of the art of fortune-telling, including judicial astrology, rather than an abandonment of it for more mature intellectual endeavors altogether. Divination of all varieties, whether astrology, tasseomancy (from tea leaves), or astragalomancy (from dice or knucklebones), may appear from the point of view of science to be the very height of irrationality. In fact, however, divination bears an important genealogical and conceptual relationship to scientific experiment as it develops over the course of the early modern period, and also has an important connection to the history of computing or reckoning.

We may think of mantic practices, such as those imposed upon the feeding schedule of Paul the Octopus, or of divination in the most general sense, as the use of experimental techniques under controlled conditions in order to either predict the future or decide on a particular course of action. Today there is a great variety of machines that purport to tell us, either truthfully or no, about the course our future will take. All of these machines are built, more or less, on the same mechanical principles as Blaise Pascal's eponymous "Pascaline" device or Leibniz's stepped reckoner. Some of them, such as the "love meter" or the online personality quiz, are patently fraudulent, while others, such as the online credit-rating service, somewhat more plausibly purport to be able to determine our future fates, based on the fact of who we are at present, through the accrual of our past actions. We may ask, however, whether an anthropologist external to our culture would, in studying us, be able to make sharp distinctions among the horoscope, the personality quiz, and the credit rating, or indeed whether we ourselves clearly understand how they differ. In some parks in the cities of Eastern Europe you can still find standing scales for weighing yourself, and thus for getting a report on a certain factor of your physical health, standing right next to automated fortune-telling machines. Here the side-by-side positions of the scientific instrument and the mantic apparatus cannot but reveal to us their shared pedigree.

 We may not ever, in fact, have been perfectly clear on the boundary between computation and divination. When Leibniz implored his contemporaries to "Calculate!" or to "Compute!" and suggested by this that he had, or was in the course of getting, some sort of engine that might reveal to them their proper future course, it would not have been out of line to interpret this as at least somewhat akin to a call to look into a crystal ball or to consult a chiromancer. We turn to machines to tell us what to do, and how things are going to be. We want the indications they deliver to us to be well founded, but we also want them to reveal fate to us, to mediate between us and the open future.

Divination, in short, is an ancestor of computation. Both are projections of how the future might be. The latter sort of projections are based on rigorous data crunching that takes into ample consideration how the world has been up until now. The former sort also look at the world in its present state, how things have settled into the present moment—how tea leaves have arranged themselves, how the heavens have turned, whether the birds are taking sudden flight or staying put in the fields. They do so, generally, in a piecemeal and impressionistic way, and read past and present signs from one domain of nature into another, or from nature into human affairs, in a way that strikes us today as unjustified. But the shared ancestry is unmistakable.

Yet just as by the late nineteenth century the unity of science and faith in the programs of such comprehensive thinkers as Boyle or Goethe would be largely forgotten, the common ancestry of divination and computation would also, by around the same time, be more or less occluded from memory. By the twentieth century, science was for serious people, astrology for dupes. Or worse, astrology was for the useful idiots of fascism. While still in exile in Los Angeles in the early postwar years, Theodor Adorno took an interest in the peculiar tradition of American newspapers to include horoscopes for their readers, whereby they ostensibly learn of their near-term fates on the basis of the star sign that governs their date of birth. The result of this interest was *The Stars Down to Earth*, Adorno's study of the horoscope section of the *Los Angeles Times* over the course of several years in the 1950s.[2] He rightly saw these horoscopes as a drastically etiolated version of what would have been available to a practitioner of the art of horoscopy during the historical era in which astrology remained a meaningful, rich, and all-encompassing field of inquiry and explanation. To criticize the horoscopes in the *Los Angeles Times* is one thing; to criticize those of John Dee or any other Renaissance magus, or indeed of Galileo himself, who made a respectable income casting horoscopes alongside his more properly astronomical work, is another very different thing. To gloss over the differences, to take this sort of exercise as timelessly and context-independently irrational, is to overlook the ways in which different valences can come to attach to the same practices in different places and times.

For Adorno, midcentury American horoscopy, as well as the broader incipient New Age culture this heralded, was a subtle expression of a fascist tendency, to the extent that it involved submission to an abstract authority in the search for answers to life's deep questions, rather than any effort to critically reason through one's own life and options. A horoscope is not, for Adorno, what its enthusiasts today so often claim: "harmless fun." Horoscope readers who provide this defense will often claim that they do not necessarily believe what the horoscope says, and, moreover, that one does not have to believe it in order for it to retain its power to amuse and distract. This defense is typically proffered as a way of assuring skeptical friends that it is not really so irrational to read one's horoscope after all, that one can do so while still retaining one's sharp critical sense. But it is even worse, Adorno thinks, to submit to abstract authority one knows to be empty. After all, if we sincerely believed that astrology offers the best, most state-of-the-art explanation of the causal links between celestial bodies and the biological and human world of the terrestrial surface, then the appropriate thing would be not just to read it "for fun," but to read it and then to structure one's life around it. To do so would at least have the virtue of conviction.

One of the remarkable features of the horoscopes in the *Los Angeles Times*, Adorno noted, is that they did virtually nothing to account for these purported causal links. They simply stated, without context, without detail, without any insight into the cosmology of the people who came up with horoscopy in the first place, that if you were born on such and such date, such and such suitably vague things will probably befall you—*Astra inclinant sed non necessitant*, as the old saying went, the stars incline but do not necessitate, and therefore any horoscopic prediction that fails to arrive cannot be subject to empirical disconfirmation. It is thus not enough, as a plea for understanding, for a reader of the *Times* horoscopes to say, "I just enjoy astrology!" For a reader of these horoscopes cannot *really* enjoy astrology, as he lacks the necessary historical curiosity and imaginative resources to do so; he cannot work himself into a position in which the correlation of individual fates with the configuration of the stars and planets might actually mean something, might contribute to a sort of self-actualization, the cultivation of a life praxis, rather than simply signifying submission to the voice of an anonymous authority in an establishment newspaper.

Now, again, quite a bit has changed in the United States since the 1950s. For one thing, no American media consumer has the option of submitting to the abstract authority of the voices emanating from establishment news sources, as there are no such sources, but only media that fit or do not fit with our own preferred media profile, with the much-discussed bubble we each create for ourselves with the help of social media and of the glut of choices offered by cable or satellite television. The *Los Angeles Times* is rapidly downsizing, laying off its core staff, who are for their part taking to Twitter in a desperate struggle to stay relevant. Meanwhile there are now horoscopists who write for a self-styled thoughtful, independent-minded, and skeptical audience (e.g., the syndicated author Rob Brezsny), and others who write for specific, finely focused demographics. And most recently—as if at long last explicitly reuniting the lineages of divination and computation, which we traced back at this chapter's beginning to their original unity— internet users are now able to consult "algorithmic horoscopes." As Amanda Hess has noted, "A.I. and machine learning can churn out predictions at speeds unmatched by flesh-and-blood astrologers."[3]

Interestingly, while in general Republicans are less science-literate than the broader American population, they are somewhat less likely than any other group, and indeed than liberal Democrats, to believe that astrology is "very or sort of scientific," according to a 2012 survey.[4] The most prominent conservative media outlets in the United States, such as Fox News and Breitbart, do not feature astrology. This divide along political lines probably has to do with the perception of astrology as a pagan tradition (though of course it was practiced and promoted by members of the church for many centuries). Yet there are also astrologers out there ready to cater to consumers with a "family values" sensibility, or with a love of free markets. And again, these distinctions are extremely fluid. In recent years we have seen Tea Party demonstrators advocating holistic medicine, including traditional Chinese medicine and other cross-civilizational borrowings, as an inexpensive alternative to modern medical care for the uninsured.[5] In the future there is no reason why self-styled conservatives should not also turn, or turn back, to astrology.

Whatever may be the accuracy of Adorno's analysis of American horoscopy in the 1950s, there does not seem today to be any simple submission to abstract authority in the current "harmless fun" of astrology. There is, rather, conscious and elaborate identity construction, in which the sort of horoscope one reads is just one part of a suite of choices that also includes the clothing one wears and the music one listens to, all of which, together, signal what kind of person one is. In the United States today, such signaling is generally inseparable from the matter of which side of the tribalist culture wars one identifies with. *Pace* Adorno, it seems likely that this fragmentation itself, rather than the role that horoscopes play within it, is the more disconcerting sign of incipient fascism.

We are one step further removed here, than the *Los Angeles Times* was in the 1950s, from the lifeworld of John Dee or Galileo, in which astrology presented itself as something to believe, something that genuinely helped to make sense of the world and of our place in it, rather than making it more difficult to do so. And yet even here there remains a faint but unmistakable link to the deeply human, and even extrahuman, effort to orient in the world by reference to the fixed points of the celestial spheres (dung beetles, too, it turns out, navigate by the Milky Way).[6] We admire the stability and regularity of the heavens, and are prone to imagining that whatever share we have of stability and regularity in our chaotic, terrestrial, mortal lives is somehow borrowed from them. For this same reason, we still take exceptional astronomical events as significant, as momentous in ways that cannot be fully explained by their observable effects.

In 1997, thirty-nine members of the Heaven's Gate cult committed suicide together on the occasion of the approach to earth of Comet Hale-Bopp, which, their leaders claimed, was in fact an extraterrestrial spacecraft. Alan Hale, one of the comet's two discoverers, declared the following year: "The sad part is that I was really not surprised. Comets are lovely objects, but they don't have apocalyptic significance. We have to use our minds, our reason."[7] Twenty years later, in August 2017, a total eclipse of the sun passed across the United States, from west to east. The path it followed matched the arc we might easily have imagined to be traced by an intercontinental missile fired from North Korea: entering American airspace in the Pacific Northwest, and moving from there to the south and east across the heartland. The eclipse coincided with extreme tension over a recent war of words between Donald Trump and North Korean leader Kim Jong-un, resulting from the latter's recent successful test of long-range missiles, and from the accumulating proof that his regime now would be able to deliver a warhead to American soil. Many said it was the closest the world had come to a nuclear confrontation since the Cuban Missile Crisis. Meanwhile, domestically, a neo-Nazi rally occurred in Virginia, and the president utterly failed to distance himself from the ideology of the demonstrators. As a result he was abandoned by many business leaders who had previously attempted to abide and deal with his various flaws. He was again reprimanded by many within his own party, and the speculation that his reign was bottoming out, while this had arisen many, many times before, seemed to be reaching a new, fevered intensity. (It did not, in fact, bottom out.)

It was inevitable that some would make a connection between the celestial and the terrestrial scales of events. It was jokingly said on social media, in countless variations, that the eclipse must somehow be a harbinger of the fall of the Trump regime. Less jocularly, rumors flew that it was a conspiracy, or that it would trigger events on earth leading to the collapse of power grids, or other apocalyptic scenarios. Experts who knew better than to stoke such fears nonetheless warned that human behavior during the eclipse, with millions of people displacing themselves in order to observe it, might have significant consequences for the environment and for civic stability. Whether joking, cautious, or ridiculous, American anticipation of the 2017 eclipse differed very little from what happened in the great eclipse of 1654, when the

materialist and atheist philosopher Pierre Gassendi bemoaned the ignorance of all the doomsayers, and of their learned enablers such as
Robert Fludd (who had died some years earlier, in 1637).

It is not that there is no progress, or that we are not getting closer to
a correct account of how the world works. But we still get vertigo on
glass-bottom bridges, we still fear strangers more than friends, and we
still are surely unsettled when the sky turns black at noon. All of these
expressions of irrationality, moreover, are irrational in the narrow
sense of failure to make the right inferences from what we in fact know.
Nor is it necessarily the case that the chatter and jokes and misin-
formed speculations surrounding the things that frighten us, the im-
poverished borrowings from the venerable astrological tradition, are
all just so much noise. These are all expressions of irrationality, but
they do not seem to be, as Adorno had thought of astrology, straightforward expressions of a desire to submit to abstract authority. They
are the products of active searching, not passive acquiescence.

Let a Hundred Flowers Bloom

One consequence of the partition between art and science, considered
in the previous chapter, has been the persistent proneness of science
to infection and mutation, to meddling in its affairs by people who
really do not know what they are talking about—people who are propelled forward by a moral conviction that this domain of human life,
too, is theirs to play in, that the green lawn of science must not be roped
off, transformed into a space that only the haughty college dons are
permitted to cross.

The geneticist Kathy Niakan, who was the first researcher ever to gain
ethics-board approval to conduct research with human embryonic stem
cells using CRISPR gene-splicing technology, has explicitly compared
the innovations made as a result of this research to those that came with
fire, and with the internet.[8] While we cannot possibly know all of the
future applications of today's innovations and discoveries, we have effectively no choice but to continue. For the moment, the mainstream

research community is unanimous in the view that research for medical applications, such as improvements in assisted-fertility treatment, is salutary and should continue, while any research involving the creation of new immortalized germ lines—that is, cells that give rise to offspring that may then become part of the human species' shared genetic profile—would amount to a Promethean ambition to be decisively rejected by any ethics board.[9] Niakan asserts that the public frequently confuses these two sorts of research, and notes that it is largely as a result of this confusion that opposition to human stem-cell research is so widespread in public opinion. In fact, if it were left up to the public—that is, if it were an issue deemed to be worthy of democratic resolution—then Niakan would not have gained approval to conduct research on human embryos. She relies in her work on the approval of boards of experts, but not fellow citizens, and is grateful that this is the current arrangement where she works (in the United Kingdom).

Of course, the possibilities are not exhausted in the simple dichotomy between "expertocracy," on the one hand, and putting the vote before an ignorant public on the other. Another possibility is informing the public to a point at which it is no longer ignorant, and then turning the decision over to it. But the deepening of the crisis of public ignorance that has come with the rise of the internet, and the simultaneous sharpening of opposed opinions among different camps of the public, makes this alternative unlikely, and scientists such as Niakan are no doubt rational in their presumption that they must protect their work from public oversight. Niakan is hacking through nature's thorns and, like Oppenheimer before her, seems to be aware that her work is kissing awake new powers. The moral stance she adopts seems to take for granted that human beings will do whatever they find they are able to do, and thus that new technologies are unstoppable. The best one can then do as an individual at the vanguard of these technologies is to use them responsibly, to satisfy well-composed boards of ethics, whose members establish their qualifications for membership not principally as ethicists, but rather as knowers of the relevant scientific facts.

There are certainly many issues that should not be put to the vote, often because it is unreasonable to expect that the public could acquire the relevant expertise. But as long as scientific progress depends on antidemocratic institutions, the halls of science will continue to be invaded by gate-crashers: the amateurs despised by the experts, who make up in passion what they lack in knowledge, and who are the closest thing in our era to the Goethean dream of a science that can still make room for sentiment. But if they fail to fully realize this dream, it is in part because our era has made little room for a cultivation of sentiment that is not at the same time a descent into unreason.

Since the nineteenth century, as we saw in the previous chapter, there has been an expectation that science must now keep to itself, as the domain of reason, while unreason is free to romp within the limited spheres of art, poetry, and the expression of personal faith. Now that the violence of their separation has been endured, it has generally been supposed, they may be seen as a sort of divided homeland, which, even if naturally and historically unified, must nevertheless be protected against any invasion of the one side by the other.

Of course, low-level incursions have been a near-constant reality since the original partitioning of the two magisteria. Consider the case of that great oxymoron that has served as a wedge issue in American politics for over a century: creationism, or, as it sometimes styles itself, "creation science." There is no fixed, context-free reason why commitment to the recent extinction of the dinosaurs, within human history, should be a component of a politically conservative activist agenda. The particular political significance of a given belief of this sort is subject to perpetual change. In the early seventeenth century the "conservatives" reacted harshly to Galileo's discovery of sunspots. The sun is a superlunar body, and thus is composed not of diverse elements, but of one element only, for otherwise it would be subject to decomposition, mortal and corruptible, as only sublunar bodies are. But if it has spots, then these could only be a sign of composition from at least two elements. Therefore the idea of sunspots is a heresy and must be condemned. Somehow this issue was resolved fairly quickly, and today no Republican politician in the United States has to pander to an antisunspot constituency, even as some lawmakers continue to pretend, even perhaps to pretend to themselves, that the best evidence does not speak in favor of our descent from a common ancestor with the chimpanzees. Things could have been otherwise. Things will be otherwise, soon enough. Soon enough, public figures will be pretending to believe some completely implausible thing they could not, deep down, really believe, and that we cannot, now, anticipate.

According to the anarchist philosopher of science Paul Feyerabend, the fluidity of the social role played by ideas extends to scientific rationality itself. Scientific rationality is an ideology, for him, and as such it had been a particularly powerful and life-improving one in the seventeenth and eighteenth centuries. But its greatest breakthroughs were made, even then, by drawing on traditions that lay far beyond the field of scientific respectability, not only by our own standards today, but by theirs. Thus, to cite Feyerabend's preferred example, in shifting to a heliocentric model Copernicus did indeed have some historical precedents to draw on, but these came from unhinged numerologists and astrologists such as the fourth-century BCE Pythagorean philosopher Philolaus, and not from defenders of views one would have seen as safe or respectable by the late sixteenth century.[10] Writing in the late twentieth century, Feyerabend concludes that scientific rationality has largely outlived its purpose, and it does better when it exists alongside competing ideologies. He declares that he would like to see more Lysenkos—that is, more people like Trofim Lysenko, the Soviet geneticist whom Stalin favored, for a while, in view of his empirically ungrounded claim that a new "proletarian science" could transform grains to grow in cold environments in ways that a strict Darwinian account of adaptation would not allow.[11] Let Lysenkoism live, Feyerabend thought. And let astrology, holistic medicine, and creationism live too!

As already mentioned, in more recent years holistic medicine has been defended, as an expedient alternative to a national health-care system, by American Republicans intent on repealing Obama's Affordable Care Act. In principle there is no reason why these same people should not also take up the cause of Lysenkoism or astrology, and to do so, moreover, not as side interests, but as a central part of their political program. Stranger things have happened. One is in fact strongly tempted to conclude that there is never any way of deriving or predicting the political uses to which a given scientific doctrine will be put, or the political opposition it will face, by simply studying the content of the doctrine itself.

Consider specifically the Museum of Creation and Earth History, opened in Petersburg, Kentucky, in 2007.[12] It features displays inspired by classical natural history museums, but with a twist: its mission is to bolster, or to bring to life, an alternative account of the origins of the diverse species of the world, including dinosaurs, in terms that are compatible with a more or less literal understanding of the book of Genesis. It is in effect a simulacrum of a museum, an institution that reproduces the look and feel of a museum, but that has no real authority to explain the objects it puts on display.

The museum's founder, Ken Ham, defends "young-earth creationism," a strict version of creationist doctrine on which the scriptural account of creation is literally, rather than allegorically, true, and everything that paleontology, cosmology, and related sciences would account for on a scale of millions or billions of years must somehow be accounted for as being not more than roughly six thousand years old.[13] For example, creation scientists have latched onto the phenomenon of rapid or "flash" fossilization, which does happen on occasion, leaving us the remains of prehistoric life forms that fossilized so quickly as to preserve skin and internal organs along with the bones or shells that are more commonly preserved.[14] This possibility, along with such facts as the occasional discovery of a fossil in a stratum claimed by evolutionists to date from long before that species' presumed existence, has enabled savvy creationists to develop an alternative account of the history of life on earth, according to which all events that mainstream science explains in terms of a geological timescale can in fact be explained on the much smaller scale of human history.

Key to note here is that this approach implicitly accepts that the sort of reasoning and provision of evidence that have come to reign in scientific inquiry over the past centuries should not be abandoned, that the scientific method is worthy of respect. It accepts, in effect, that if you want your claims to be taken as true, you must prove that they are true by a combination of empirical data and valid inferences. The

creationists have accepted the rules of the game as defined by the evolutionists. They have agreed to play their game on the home turf of science, and it is not at all surprising to find them here at their weakest.

Creationism has been gaining ground not only in the United States,
but in many other countries throughout the world with a similarly
strong streak of illiberalism and irrationalism in civic life. An interesting exception is East Asia, where the overall number of people who are
uncomfortable with the idea of sharing a common ancestor with chimpanzees is lower than anywhere else in the world, quite apart from the
nature of the political system or the freedom of the press that reigns in
a given country. Turkey, by contrast, is one of the countries in which
skepticism about evolution is even higher than in the United States.
Some years ago, a charismatic cult leader, Adnan Oktar, also known
as Harun Yahya, decided to take up the battle against Darwin, and
found himself adapting many American Christian evangelical arguments and texts for a Muslim audience. This task was easier than one
might expect, and one is struck by how closely his pamphlets—with
their kitsch and childish illustrations of Noah's Ark and other signal
elements—resemble what we might just as well expect to find in Petersburg, Kentucky. Harun Yahya's masterwork was his *Atlas of Creation*, the first volume of which was published in 2006 (that year I myself was mysteriously sent a complimentary copy, of the original
Turkish edition, to my office in Montreal).[15] In an amusing review of
the work, Richard Dawkins noted that one of the supposed photographs of a caddis fly, meant to prove something about how currently
existing species existed in what evolutionists wrongly take to be the
distant past, was in fact an image of a fishing lure, copy-pasted from
some online catalog for outdoor-sports equipment. One could distinctly see the metal hook coming out of it.[16] This image may be
thought of as the very emblem of the creationist movement: shabby,
hasty, reliant on the assumption that its followers have no real interest
in looking too far into the matter.

And yet the question naturally arises as to why they should go to the
trouble at all of producing their simulacra of scholarly texts and august
institutions, their "atlases" and "museums." It is not as if no other

model for religious faith has been defended since the beginning of the era of modern science. Already in the seventeenth century, Pascal articulated an account of religious faith on which it was its indefensibility in terms borrowed from reason that made it worth one's total commitment. Much earlier, in the third century CE, the Christian apologist Tertullian had justified his commitment to the faith precisely in view of what he took to be its absurdity, leaving us with the stunning motto *Credo quia absurdum*: "I believe because it is absurd."[17] In the nineteenth century, again, the Danish philosopher Søren Kierkegaard articulated a vision of his own Christian faith on which this faith is strictly groundless, and on which its distinctive feature is that we come to our faith not through the persuasion of the intellect by reasons, but by an act of the will. For these thinkers, one does not defend religious faith against scientific reason by making the case that it is not absurd, or that its facts are better founded than the facts defended by science, but rather by embracing its absurdity as proof of its vastly greater importance than what may be comprehended by human reason. To make the case that faith is rational is for them self-defeating, quite apart from whether the case is convincing.

One might reasonably conclude that Tertullian and Kierkegaard have reflected somewhat more deeply on the nature of religious belief than Ken Ham has. The latter appears to take it for granted that assent to the truth of Christianity hangs on such matters as whether dinosaurs can be shown to have lived contemporaneously with human beings. This is somewhat as if one were to conceive of the problem of providing a proof for the existence of God in the way that someone might set out to prove the existence of Bigfoot. God will not leave clumps of hair or footprints; it is simply an inadequate understanding of the issue at hand—as it has developed over the course of the history of theology and philosophy—to take God and Bigfoot as relevantly similar, so as to warrant the same sort of proofs and reasoning regarding their similarly disputed existences.

Now, assent to the truth of Christianity in particular involves more complications than does assent to the existence of God, as critics of Descartes's version of the ontological argument for the existence of

God, for example, have noted: we might be able to prove the reality of some generic Supreme Being, but how this might compel us to accept, say, the Trinity or the truth of the Nicene Creed is not at all clear. Descartes pursued the matter through a priori reasoning, while Ken Ham wants to establish the truth of Christianity by empirical facts about fossils and so on, an approach that appears even more inadequate to the task at hand. Descartes can at least, perhaps, give us a generic Supreme Being by his a priori method. Ken Ham can only give us easily refutable empirical claims about the natural world, claims that cannot possibly be expected to ground transcendental commitments.

Skeptics and atheists, such as Richard Dawkins and other members of the "new atheist movement" (largely fractured and weakened in the era of Trump, when the great divide in our society no longer seems to be between the pious hypocrites and the up-front, morally balanced humanists) often suppose that the faithful are particularly credulous in their assent to belief systems that harbor blatant contradictions or absurdities: that God is both one person and three, for example. What they are missing is that it may well be not *in spite* of these absurdities, but rather *because* of them, that the doctrine is seen as warranting faithful assent. As ventured already in chapter 1, if there were no mystery at the heart of a religious doctrine, then the perfectly comprehensible facts that it lays out would likely grow less compelling over time. It is the mystery, the impossibility that is claimed as true, that keeps believers coming back, believing, not in the way that we believe that 2 + 2 = 4, or that humans and chimpanzees have a common ancestor, or that a clump of hair must have belonged to a Sasquatch, but in a way that is indifferent to the standards of assent involved in these latter sorts of claim.

Alternative Facts, and Alternatives to Facts

The way in which mystery—or, to speak with Tertullian, absurdity—generates a hold on followers of a religion is of course explicable in strictly sociological terms, and does not occur exclusively in social movements that are religious in the narrow sense, that is, in movements that make claims as to the nature of the transcendental realm. I have identified the Museum of Creation as a simulacrum of a museum. Another way to put this might be to say that it is an "alternative museum," or, to deploy the most recent convention, an "alt-museum." To describe it in this way is of course to highlight its illegitimacy. After Kellyanne Conway, Donald Trump's then spokesperson, proposed in early 2017 that there may be "alternative facts," this phrase was widely repeated, but more or less only by people who wished to denounce and to ridicule it.

To be fair to Conway, there *are* alternative facts, at least in one respect. As writers of histories know, the past contains infinitely many events. Every slice of time in fact, in every sliver of the world, contains infinitely many. When we write our histories, then, when we periodize and narrate, we select some facts rather than others as being most pertinent to the account we wish to offer. The facts that we leave out—the infinitely many facts—are in some sense "alternatives": we could have included them if we had chosen to do so, and others might do so in their own history of the same topic. Perhaps one should say that these other facts are "facts in reserve." In any case, Conway was not wrong here, though it was easy to interpret her claim uncharitably, given that she was working for a regime that does habitually promote alternative facts in the stronger and more deplorable sense: facts that are not facts at all, but lies (to which we will turn in chapter 8).[18]

Ken Ham's five-thousand-year-old dinosaur fossils, are not, more properly speaking, alternative facts, but rather alternatives *to* facts. What are people doing, exactly, when they offer up these alternatives? It is difficult to be satisfied here by Harry Frankfurt's famous analysis of "bullshit,"[19] in its technical philosophical sense, as being distinct from a lie, in that the liar is concerned about the truth and hides it, while the bullshitter has lost all concern about the truth as an anchor for his claims, and wishes only to persuade. Alternative scientific claims such as those of Ken Ham are indeed made out of concern for the truth, and they are made with implicit knowledge of the fact that establishment science really does have something close to a monopoly here, really is getting things right in a way that the alternative scenarios do not.

The message of the Museum of Creation, on this reading, is not, then, that dinosaurs and human beings really did roam the earth together, but simply that we, creationists, reject your scientific account of things regardless of whether it gets the facts right, and the reason is that it does not speak to us as a community united by shared values. And yet, unable to fully understand that this is a question of values and not facts—unaware of the legacy in the history of theology, from Tertullian to Kierkegaard, of authors who have dealt profoundly with this distinction and come up with accounts of faith that are boldly independent of any countervailing factual claims—characters such as Ham do their feeble best to operate at the level of facts that they, likely, deep down, do not really believe. This is a species in the genus of irrationality, while bullshitting, however similar it may appear, is simply a moral transgression but not an intellectual failure. The successful bullshitter has not behaved irrationally; he has used what he knows to attain desired ends. The young-earth creationist is by contrast irrational to the extent that he does not fully understand what he is trying to do, what he is trying to defend, and he therefore sets himself up to lose in the long run. There is no plausible scenario on which he will be successful, on which he will achieve his desired ends.

If the attribution of disingenuousness to defenders of creation science seems unwarranted, perhaps it will be helpful to go a bit further afield and to consider an even more extreme strain of rejection of the modern scientific consensus: flat-earth theory. It is likely significant that the social movement made up by adherents of this view, while it has been around for several decades (in a 1968 book, the classicist G.E.R. Lloyd had occasion to say of Aristotle that he "was no flat-earther"),[20] has enjoyed a spike in recruitment since Trump's election. One suspects in fact that in multiple areas of social life, and not only in the political arena narrowly conceived, there has been an upping of the ante, or perhaps a widening of the so-called Overton window—a theory of how the range of acceptable ideas shifts in society over time, developed by the founder of the Mackinac Center for Public Policy,

Joseph P. Overton, in the mid-1990s—with the result that the range of acceptable ideas within the public sphere has been significantly shifted.[21]

Flat-earth theory is far more radical than even young-earth creationism (not to mention old-earth creationism or intelligent-design theory), in part because it makes claims about the present state of the world that one would think could be refuted by straightforward observation, while creationism simply offers an alternative account of how the present state of the world came about, and disputes the claims of evolutionists about past processes that none of us are able to observe directly. Standard flat-earth theory holds, for example, that the outer boundary of the disk of the earth is a great ice wall, and that nobody knows what lies beyond it. This claim alone is enough to signal that the theory is likely most attractive to people who, let us say, are not exactly in control of their own destinies, who might be called "low-will" on analogy to the description that political scientists have deployed of certain voters as "low-information." By contrast a high-will individual who sincerely suspected that the disk of the earth is bounded by an ice wall would surely be able to pull together the resources to make an expedition and to observe the thing. Surely a conspiracy of this size, and a basic cosmological truth of this importance, would warrant staking it all, going into deep debt, mortgaging your home, in order to get to the bottom of things. Someone who could rest content with the ice-wall theory is someone who does not ordinarily think of him- or herself as in a position to solve matters of great importance once and for all. Someone else, somewhere, can do that, the flat-earther must think, just as forces somewhere else have passed off their sinister conspiracy on us.

The theory of the ice wall is one that makes a claim about how the world is at present, though of course flat-eartherism also reaches back, like creationism, into the past. It holds for one thing that NASA images of the earth from outer space are a hoax, and that those who run NASA and similar agencies are part of a global conspiracy to keep the masses in perpetual ignorance. In order to make sense of NASA's dastardly scheme, whereby the commonsense obviousness of a flat earth is denied in favor of the counterintuitive theory of a round earth, one must also suppose that Kepler, Galileo, and even Aristotle were in on it too, since all of them claimed that the earth is round long before NASA came onto the scene. This must be an elaborate scheme indeed, to have been sustained for so long, in contrast with the scheme to convince us that human beings are descended from other animal species, which really came together only in the nineteenth century.

But the primary focus of the flat-earthers is an alternative interpretation of present sensory evidence. Unlike creationists, who tend to suppose that evolutionists are sincerely wrong, rather than being liars, flat-earthers take round-earth theory (as it were) to be a theory that is not really believed by its most active promoters, namely, the perpetrators of the NASA hoax. Moreover, to the extent that it is believed by the masses, this is only because of the manipulations of its elite promoters. Flat-earth theorists tend, in debate, to pass rather quickly from the details of the theory itself—the ice wall, for example, not to mention the epicycles in the orbits of the planets (for flat-earthers there are in fact round planets, but the earth is simply not one of them; it is not in fact a planet at all)—to discussion of the social and political dimensions of the conspiracy. One senses, in fact, that the commitment to the actual content of the theory—that the world is flat—is rather minimal, and that the true nature of the movement is that it is a protest, against elite authorities telling us what we must believe.

Feyerabend's point about Copernicus drawing inspiration from the unscientific Philolaus might also be extended to Newton, whose intellectual character drew him to biblical numerology, among other fields. It may well be that if Newton had not been able to satisfy his curiosity in biblical numerology he would also never have succeeded in making the discoveries that the world would come to value. And likewise it is at least possible that today a young scientist on the cusp of some great breakthrough will be triggered into making it while watching a flat-earther's video on YouTube, infuriated, perhaps, at how deeply wrong it is, and driven to epiphany as a result of this anger. But it also does not seem reasonable to place much hope in such an eventuality; on the contrary it seems very reasonable to seek to limit the proliferation of

such videos, not by prohibition, of course, but by education, the cultivation of a level of scientific literacy in schoolchildren that would leave
such videos without an audience.

One might reasonably expect that the popularity of flat-earth theory would sooner prevent breakthroughs than inspire them. These
could well be breakthroughs that are still far from the cusp of being
made, breakthroughs that *would have* been made, somewhat further
off in the future, had some potential young scientist not been dis-
suaded from beginning to pursue a career in science after watching a
video that convinced her that establishment science is an elite and sinister conspiracy. The greatest danger of flat-earth theory is not that it
will convince a young and easily influenced mind that the earth is flat,
but rather that it will initiate the young mind into a picture of the world
as one that is controlled by dark forces, by powerful actors behind the
scenes, rather than by political factions that we as citizens are in a position to understand and, one hopes, to influence. Flat-earth theory is a
threat not primarily because it gets the physical world wrong, but
rather because it misrepresents the human, social world.

To be indoctrinated into such a theory is to be cut off from an understanding of politics as the working out of differences, through
agreed-upon procedures, in a neutral public space, and to accept instead a vision of politics that is modeled on guerrilla warfare, on
asymmetrical combat between total enemies. This sort of indoctrination, which characterizes flat-earth theory, does not appear to be nearly
as present a risk in other, comparable alternative or antiestablishment
domains, such as traditional holistic therapies, or indeed creationism.
One might well be initiated into an interest in botany from an initial
interest in indigenous herbal medicines, for example. Or one might be
initiated into learning about other cultures and their knowledge of the
living world, and from there begin to read about anthropology and
history. No harm here, certainly, even if one risks being cut off from
the prideful confidence in the superiority of one's own culture's attainments that today infects so many aspects of science education.

It is less plausible, but not out of the question, that one might discover an innate interest in the life sciences during a visit to the

Museum of Creation. Many naturalist thinkers have resisted what they see as Darwinian "orthodoxy." Their results may appear as stubborn and wrongheaded, but not necessarily as spurious or completely without value. Interestingly Vladimir Nabokov, who was on the staff at the Harvard Museum of Zoology for a time, and who discovered and gave his name to a species of butterfly, was as vehemently contemptuous of Darwinism as he was of psychoanalysis. Thus he writes in his memoir, *Speak, Memory*, that natural selection "could not explain the miraculous coincidence of imitative aspect and imitative behavior, nor could one appeal to the theory of 'the struggle for life' when a protective device was carried to a point of mimetic subtlety, exuberance, and luxury far in excess of a predator's power of appreciation."[22]

It is safe to say that Nabokov's concerns here are not the same as Ken Ham's, and, in turn, to assume that there is not, and never will be, a Nabokov of flat-eartherism: someone who plays a comparable role for that extreme pseudoscience to the one the Russian émigré author played for anti-Darwinism. A typical creationist, such as Ham, wants to say that nothing is nature, but all is art, or, more precisely, that nature is the artifice of a certain highly esteemed Artificer. Nabokov by contrast wants to say that art is natural, that our own mimetic activity is not an exception to what nature is doing all the time, but an instance of it. I will not help to lend legitimacy to creationism by agreeing with Nabokov here. Or, at least, I will not affirm his claim as a scientific claim. But if we view it as an opening to a general theory of art, he is perhaps onto something. Romanticism, as we saw in the previous chapter, left us with the dead-end idea that art is the product of an artist's struggle, to get something out, something unique—something that belongs to him, uniquely, as a member of that rare class of creatures, the artists. What comes out, it has been thought, is something unlike anything else in the known universe: an artwork! There is no thought here that the work might be a species of secretion whose genus is not exclusive to a small group of human beings, or even to humanity as a whole. A work of art might be the exuberance of nature, channeled through a human being. The natural mimetics Nabokov observes in coleoptera is not the production of paintings and sculptures, but the very making of the beetle body. Of course we know that insects do not literally make their own bodies, but even the most rigid Darwinists will speak as if the butterfly has taken to donning that pseudo-eye on its wing in order to scare off predators. What a fine job it has done! we think, congratulating the insect as if it were showing not itself, but its work.[23]

This discussion of Nabokov may seem like a digression, yet it is important in that it helps us to gain a view of the variety of motivations and philosophical commitments that might lie behind a rejection of the consensus scientific account of the origins of species and the nature of their diversity. By contrast, again, it seems almost out of the question that flat-earth theory might ever serve as a gateway to serious cosmological reflection, or that it might be underlain by any philosophical commitments worth hearing about.

We are in the course here of developing a sort of provisional classification of different varieties of pseudoscience, with the aim of understanding their political uses and the context of their adoption. This classificatory scheme may be further fleshed out by a consideration of the antivaccination movement, which for its part seems to occupy a social niche somewhat closer to flat-earth theory than to interest in holistic medicine or in questioning the Darwinian orthodoxy. It is considerably more plausible to claim that vaccines cause autism than to claim that the earth is flat, but both positions appear to be motivated not so much by the content of the relevant claims, and the evidence on which these theories are based, as they are by wariness of elite authority. Opposition to vaccination might emerge out of an interest in alternative medicines in general, and traditional or indigenous medicines, for complicated and problematic reasons are in our culture conceived as "alternative." But this opposition has a different political significance, and it is important to pay attention to this significance in assessing the theory itself, rather than simply contrasting establishment science with every species of fringe or antiestablishment science that crops up to challenge it, as Feyerabend sometimes seems to wish to do.

Is there anything that may be said in defense of the antivaccination movement? Is there any approach by which we may gain a sensitive anthropological appreciation of what is at stake for its adherents? We may begin, certainly, by noting that people in general do not appreciate having foreign biological fluids injected into their bloodstreams, and this with good reason: ordinarily, to invite such admixture is to risk disease and death, and our revulsion and avoidance are no doubt evolved survival mechanisms, rational in their own way, as all such adaptations are. Fear of vaccines is in this respect comparable to fear of insectivorous bats or of strangers walking toward us in the night.

Many members of the English working class reacted fiercely to the Compulsory Vaccination Act of 1853, resisting it, according to Nadja Durbach, as a form of political opposition to state control of individual bodies.[24] At the same time, we know that long before the significant innovations of Edward Jenner at the end of the eighteenth century, the Chinese were practicing smallpox inoculation (intentional low-level infection) at least eight centuries earlier, and there is some significant evidence from medical anthropology that similar practices have existed in folk-medical traditions around the world since antiquity. In the modern period, then, going back at least to Victorian England, resistance to the injection of disease agents has not been, or not only been, resistance to something new and unknown and apparently "unnatural," but rather, also, to the top-down imposition of state power. It is, at bottom, the expression of distrust of authority, which is accentuated in periods in which government has failed to convince the masses that the ends it pursues are, as is said, "for their own good." If government agents are in general perceived as crooks, it is not surprising that physicians working on behalf of the government are perceived as quacks.

These considerations are as relevant to the present moment in the United States as they were to nineteenth-century London. In March 2014, when Donald Trump was busy building up his profile as a political troll (having launched this phase of his career in 2011 with his contributions to the "birther" conspiracy theory, denying Barack Obama's birth on US soil), the soon-to-be president of the United States launched the following volley on Twitter: "Healthy young child goes to doctor, gets pumped with massive shot of many vaccines, doesn't feel good and changes—AUTISM. Many such cases!"[25] The tweet is in the style of a folktale, and that is how Trump's audience best absorbs its messages from him. We do not know who this child was; it is a generic child, a moral exemplum who need not have existed in fact in order to serve as a vehicle of some alternative truth.

But why did Trump choose at this point, even as his star was rising with birtherism and other more straightforwardly political conspiracy claims, to reach out to the anti-vaxx constituency and to express common cause with frustrated parents of toddlers showing autism symptoms—with Jenny McCarthy and other spokespeople from trash-celebrity culture who, beyond this rather narrow issue, do not seem to be particularly interested in politics? Part of the answer to this complex question is that vaccination, along with opposition to it, is far more political than it may appear on the surface. It is, to speak with Michel Foucault, a paradigm instance of biopolitics, where policy and power collide with the real, living bodies of political subjects.

According to Alain Fischer, focusing on the antivaccination movement in France over the past thirty years, there are both proximate and distal causes for the rapid decline of faith in medical authority over this time period.[26] There have been too many failures of the medical system to prevent sanitation crises, including, in 1991, the bombshell discovery that the Centre National de Transfusion Sanguine (Natural Center for Blood Transfusion) knowingly allowed HIV-infected blood into its supply. The same year a child fell ill with Creutzfeldt-Jakob syndrome after following a course of growth-hormone treatment. The medical system fails sometimes, and if it fails too much, it loses public confidence. But what counts as "too much" is significantly determined by the way the mass media depict risk, and here, according to Fischer, even establishment French media, such as *Le Monde*, have failed miserably. Over the past decade, moreover, the new social media have helped to significantly weaken trust in the medical system by inviting everyone with an internet connection to fuel whatever doubts might already exist with reckless speculation.

Some features of the modern antivaccination movement are common across borders and languages; others are more culturally specific. As Fischer notes, there has long been fear in France that it is the aluminum used in some vaccination procedures that has been most harmful. The same element has been used in many countries, but mistrust of it, and claims as to its deleterious effects, have been limited almost entirely to France. Unlike the United States, France, notwithstanding occasional crises of contaminated blood, has a dependable national health-care system, and there is virtually no danger for a French citizen or resident of being shut out of that system because of lack of money. By contrast, in the context in which Trump was tweeting in 2014, popular confidence in the health-care system could not but be impacted, in part, by the perception and the reality of its inaccessibility. It is difficult to have confidence in a system that erects barriers to accessing it, and it is unreasonable to expect that citizens who are largely shut out from the health-care system, who have no choice but to not be in it, should then be expected to docilely submit when they are informed that there is one single branch of this system, the one that sees to vaccinations, that by marked contrast they have no choice but to accept. The bond of trust is so eroded by the general rule of exclusion that there is little hope of finding any trust for this single exception to the rule, where the expectation is mandatory inclusion.

The epidemiological rationale of vaccination is crowd immunity. Individuals are protected from infectious diseases not because they themselves are vaccinated, but because the majority of people around them are vaccinated. As long as the majority of the population is vaccinated, contagious diseases will be contained, and will be less likely to strike even those few individuals who are not vaccinated. Thus one's own vaccination status is not the key element in determining whether one falls ill. One's own health is not up to one's own free choices, but rather depends upon the general pattern of choices, or of coercions, within the population. Such a predicament is hard to accept if the reigning political ideology is one of individualism, or at least of a sort of microcommunitarianism that refuses to recognize any common cause with neighbors within the same geographical region who look different, speak a different language, or have different values. But diseases cut across community boundaries, whether we like it or not, and in this way epidemiology reveals the limits of a political arrangement based on every individual, or family, or ethnic group, looking out only for itself. But it is precisely this sort of arrangement that was required in order for the Trump campaign to convince enough voters that he would look out for their interests as against the interests of other kinds of people. Even if Trump had not briefly wandered into anti-vaxx conspiracy-mongering in 2014, his political vision would have continued to follow the same logic as this conspiracy theory, the logic that refuses to acknowledge crowd immunity, or its political equivalent: shared responsibility among all citizens for the well-being of the polis.

Fischer identifies a rapid decline of public trust in expert authority as one of the key causes of the rise of the antivaccination movement over the past few decades. He argues that sectors of the public have retreated into "magical thinking," as against the rational thinking of the scientific establishment. As Tom Nichols similarly observes, the most recent era seems to be characterized by "the death of the ideal of expertise,"[27] and accordingly the rise of opinions on all manner of subjects, forged and valued not in spite of but *because of* their ignorance of and contempt for well-informed analyses of these subjects. It is, Nichols writes, "a Google-fueled, Wikipedia-based, blog-sodden collapse of any division between professionals and laypeople, students and teachers, knowers and wonderers—in other words, between those of any achievement in an area and those with none at all."[28] But even this does not sound the full depth of the problem. For one thing it is certain that Leibniz, Voltaire, and other paragons of rationalism and Enlightenment would have been delighted by Google and Wikipedia.

While the concern about the decline of expertise is in part warranted, it is complicated by certain important lessons of history. Sometimes decline in public trust in expert authority can be salutary; moreover, it can be helpful in replacing magical by rational thinking. This, in particular, is the shortest version of what we call, in shorthand, the "scientific revolution." The expert authorities who occupied positions of power in institutions, and who defended the official view that, say, action at a distance may occur as a result of "sympathies" between bodies, were opposed by those who wanted to explain these actions as only apparently taking place at a distance, but in fact as being mediated by subvisible particles. There were many more details to fill out, of course, and within a few decades the theory of gravity would return, in Newton's 1686 *Principia mathematica*, to restore a sort of action at a distance (it is on these grounds that even by the time of his death in 1716 Leibniz still refused to accept gravitation, considering it a mysterious and occult power). But still, those who around 1640 were rejecting the expert authority of the Aristotelians still clinging to power in universities—and who were conspiring to go and establish their own new institutions, which would become the great scientific societies and academies of the era—are considered from most historiographical frameworks to have been history's heroes.

So clearly it is not rejection of authority that is the problem, but only rejection of authority at the wrong times and for the wrong reasons. But how can we be sure of our ability to make such distinctions? It is not enough to say that the science itself is clear and dictates to us in its own clear voice, rather than in the voice of its human representatives, what is true and what is false. For most of us do not have a handle on the science at all. We have not read even a fraction of the relevant scientific literature, nor could we read it if we tried; far less have we carried out the relevant experiments ourselves.

Like it or not, our acceptance of the official account of how infection works, and of how vaccination helps to prevent it while also not causing other problems such as autism or aluminum poisoning, is in the end a matter of trust, in people who appear to us trustworthy because we accept their claim that they have themselves performed the relevant experiments and understood the relevant literature. And this trust in turn is a commitment that is more likely to be threatened or rendered fragile by changes in the social fabric than by new empirical evidence about the scientific truth of the matter. In this respect, the emerging scientific societies of the seventeenth century might in fact reveal to us significant parallels to the websites of today that promote alternative theories of the causes of autism, or that link certain forms of cancer to the "chemtrails" (i.e., vapor trails) left behind by passing airplanes. Whether or not there are parallels—a question that might be of interest to historians and sociologists of science, and also, one hopes, to the public in general—is something that might be determined quite independently of the content of the respective theories, or of whether in the end they turned out to be true.

It is hardly a promising sign, for contemporary alternative-science movements such as the anti-vaxx constituency, that in spite of their alternative stance they consistently play up whatever modest academic credentials their proponents may have. They exaggerate their institutional clout, and they generally include "PhD" after the names of their authorities (and even the occasional "MD"), in contexts in which those working solidly within the establishment would find it undignified or unnecessary to do so. So the establishment continues to have some considerable attraction after all, and one detects already from this that the antiestablishment stance is underlain more by ressentiment than by any real expectation that the alternative movement might, by force of the truths it possesses, hope someday soon to replace the establishment. Whatever else we might say of Francis Bacon or of Descartes, in their desire to raze the old and to build up new systems of inquiry in new institutions, there is no trace of ressentiment in their work. They believed that they were going to take over the establishment, and they were right. Their difference, then, from the confused and alienated citizens who start up websites linking vaccination to autism, or hypothesizing an ice wall that holds our oceans in, may be established without any need for nonscientist opponents of pseudoscience to carry out, or even to fully understand, the science.

The Paranoid Style in the Twenty-First Century

If we think of flat-earth theory's ascendance in the Trump era as more than a coincidence, as having blown in like an icy gust thanks to the widening of the Overton window, we will notice the way in which it echoes a broad turn to the conspiratorial in public life in America. During the Bush and Obama administrations Rush Limbaugh and Glenn Beck were the media personalities suited to provide the account of political reality that was appreciated as an alternative to the one given in the establishment liberal media preferred by coastal elites. It is the internet radio host Alex Jones (locked out of his media platforms on Facebook, Apple, and YouTube as of August 2018, in response to what the corporate governors of these services deemed to be hate speech in violation of their terms of service) who seems their most obvious descendant in the Trump era.

Unlike Limbaugh and Beck, Jones does not aim to give a coherent alternative account of reality, based on a set of presuppositions about how the world works that he and his followers may be presumed to share with followers of the mainstream media. Jones, rather, wishes to call into question many of our most basic presumptions about how social reality works, much as a flat-earther seeks to do for physical reality. Thus, for example, he has promoted an elaborate alternative account of the 2012 shooting at the Sandy Hook Elementary School in Newtown, Connecticut, according to which it was a "false-flag operation," and the members of the victims' families who make appearances in the media are in fact only paid "crisis actors." This elaborate plot is interpreted as a pretext for coming to take away Americans' guns. Jones pretends, like the flat-earthers in their view of NASA, that there are forces in the world that are not only diabolical enough, but also powerful and clever enough, to make ordinary people believe more or less anything. It is only by crossing over to the alternative, socially stigmatized, low-status but nonetheless titillatingly "alternative" accounts being offered by the self-styled outsiders, Jones or the representatives of the flat-earth movement, that one can see things as they are.

We are caught, in trying to make sense of what has been generically called online "trutherism"—which can include everything from September 11 conspiracy theories, to accounts of Sandy Hook such as that described above, to flat-earth theory—between a cautious historian's concern to not overlook continuities with long-standing historical legacies, on the one hand, and, on the other hand, to face up honestly to the radical transformations that the internet has brought on. The Republican candidate in the 1964 presidential elections, Barry Goldwater, had an enduring interest in UFOs, and in the 1970s began pushing for the US government to release its purported secret files concerning them. It was in reference to Goldwater and his followers that the historian Richard Hofstadter wrote his groundbreaking 1964 essay, "The Paranoid Style in American Politics."[29] Americans did not need the internet in order for conspiracy theories to become a central element of national political debate. Hofstadter himself traces the genealogy of this "style" back to at least the early nineteenth century. The ground that Goldwater and others prepared was already particularly fertile for the thriving of personalities like Alex Jones, now enhanced by the communicative superpower of the unrestricted internet.

For the creationists, the elite authorities are simply the members of the scientific establishment, promoting their own hegemonic vision of the world. For the flat-earthers, the elite authorities are a secret cabal, perhaps wealthy bankers, perhaps the same as are held to be spreading chemtrails in the aim of total global mind control. Though not in itself xenophobic or anti-Semitic, flat-earth theory does deploy tropes familiar from the conspiracy theories associated with these ideologies, and it is not at all surprising when on occasion we find them overlapping with flat-earth theory in the worldview of a single individual. In traditional creationism there was wariness of established institutions and their claims to know the truth, but there was no presumption of the power of these institutions to be able to *hide* the truth. The difference between these two species of alternative social movement may in the end be one of degree, but it plainly tracks the transformations that have taken place elsewhere in political life with the rise of Trump: the near-total disappearance of a shared space of common presuppositions from which we might argue through our differences, and the presumption that one's opponents' views are not so much wrong as diabolical.

If we were to agree with Feyerabend, then the proliferation of theories positioned as alternatives to science must count as an unqualified good, regardless of the content of these theories. Holistic medicine, numerology, proletarian genetics, flat-earth theory, creation science: all of these are more or less on a par with one another as alternatives to the hegemonic version of scientific rationality. Yet, in spite of the fact that Feyerabend himself wishes to abolish the myth of apolitical or nonideological science, he does not fully recognize that these various alternative theories may appear variously more or less propitious in different political contexts. It is not just a matter of letting a hundred flowers bloom; one must also pay attention to which sorts of flower bloom in which soils. I have already suggested that flat-earth theory has surged in the most recent period as a sort of scientific correlate of a much broader global trend of political illiberalism, and of growing suspicion of traditional authority that now regularly crosses over into conspiracy theory. It would be hard to imagine a healthy liberal democracy in which flat-earth theory is a viable contender, among others, against the hegemony of scientific reason. We do not need to fall back on any simplistic conception, of the sort that Feyerabend abhors, of the superiority of one scientific theory over another as consisting in its superior correspondence to the way the world in fact is, in order to be confident not only that round-earth theory is better than flat-earth theory, but also that it would be better off without flat-earth theory as its competitor. Flat-earth theory is unworthy to join this contest, even as an underdog.

Is there anything at all that can be said in its favor? It is, certainly, a significant fact about the phenomenology of human life on earth that we experience it as if it were taking place on a flat surface under a dome-shaped sky. For the great majority of human history, this was not only the phenomenology of human experience, but also the standard folk-cosmological account of our place in the world. Martin Heidegger captured this primordial character of our orientation in the world in his critique of the Cartesian view of the spatiality of the world as something pregiven and obvious, and of objects and indeed our own bodies as simply placed or inserted in this pregiven spatial world. In his 1927 *Being and Time*, the philosopher observes that "there is never a three-dimensional multiplicity of possible positions initially given which is then filled out with objectively present things. This dimensionality of space is still veiled in the spatiality of what is at hand."[30] Thus, he explains by way of illustration, "the 'above' is what is 'on the ceiling', the 'below' is what is 'on the floor', the 'behind' is what is 'at the door'. All these wheres are discovered and circumspectly interpreted on the paths and ways of everyday associations, they are not ascertained and catalogued by the observational measurement of space."[31] Heidegger's language is obscure, but his point is profound: we do not start out with a conception of ourselves, and of our surroundings and ultimately of our planet, as inserted into some pregiven spatial expanse. Rather, we get our very concepts of spatial notions such as "above" and "below" from our deep preconceptual experiences. Above is the sky. Below is the earth. No wonder, then, that flat-earth theory is the default model of the cosmos in human history. It sufficed for the purposes of highly developed civilizations such as ancient China, which included an advanced practice of maritime navigation. Even without knowing of the long and distinguished past of this cosmological model, we have our immediate experience, and it is humanly difficult to be told by experts that our immediate experience is not what we think it is.

We witness this difficulty again and again, across numerous examples of what Margaret Wertheim has called, in the course of her revelatory research on the subject, "outsider physics."[32] Outsider physicists do not want to be told that the basic constituents of reality are some new sort of entity that is not encountered by direct experience and can be detected only through the work of experts with their complicated, and expensive, equipment. And so they reject quarks and bosons in favor of something much more familiar, such as smoke rings. In the case of flat-earth theory, there are no alternative entities to ground the account, but only an insistence on phenomenology rather than empiricism, even if some semblance of empirical evidence in favor of the theory is scraped together ad hoc. In this, flat-earth theory ends up bearing a curious similarity to young-earth creationism, to the extent that it wishes to preserve something that is existentially dear—faith in the case of creationism, phenomenology in the case of flat-earth theory—but is not quite self-aware enough to grasp that it is this existential matter that is at issue, and not some mundane matter of fact. And so, again, it agrees to compete on the home field of science, where the rules are empiricism and valid inference, and therefore where it is fated at the outset to lose at a game for which it has signed up without having learned the rules.

Why would any outsider accept such a contest? To do so is irrational, in a much more profound sense than simply holding the wrong theory to be true. To do so is to not fully understand the nature of the thing to which one is committing oneself, mistaking a question of existential devotion for a question of fact. Here, the judgment of irrationality comes not from a disagreement over facts, but rather from a *turning away* from facts that are already known, or, to anticipate a notion that will be of central importance in chapter 9, facts that are known without being known.

There is, as we have been seeing in this chapter, a historically well-established tendency to reject the conception of truth as fact, in favor of a conception of truth as something internal, something felt, when it is clear that the facts are not in one's favor. This move can have significant political implications. The George W. Bush administration's manipulations are often said to have inaugurated a "post-truth" era. That certain claims may be morally true while empirically false is, however, an idea far older than Bush. It is in play in the lexical distinction in Russian between two different sorts of truth—*pravda*, which in principle must be grounded in fact, and *istina*, which is somehow higher than fact. This distinction was inverted by the Bolsheviks, who with no apparent irony gave the name of *Pravda* to the newspaper that didn't so much report on what was the case as describe what they would have liked to be the case. A similar transcendence of the merely empirical helps to explain the reaction, in sixteenth-century Spain, to the fabrications of the Jesuit historian Jerónimo Román de la Higuera, author of the so-called *Falsos cronicones*, which purported to document the antiquity of the Christian faith in the Iberian Peninsula. When it was discovered that he had made it all up, that there had been no martyrs or miracles in Spain in the first few centuries after Christ, Higuera was not denounced as a fraud; instead the empirical falsity of his chronicles was taken as a sign of their power to convey a deeper truth. He had succeeded—by invention, by writing, by telling a story—in retrojecting Christianity into Spain's distant past, which is surely a far greater accomplishment than simply relating facts.

Famously, Nietzsche called for a "transvaluation of all values." What he had in mind was a coming era in which human beings would stop lying to themselves and one another, would be brave in the face of the truth. What less visionary and less brave followers, indeed myopic and craven followers, have preferred to do with Nietzsche's call is instead to transform him into the prophet of a coming era of inegalitarianism, in which only the strongest survive or thrive, based explicitly on a rejection of liberty and equality, the core rational principles of Enlightenment philosophy. Much of the current disagreement about Trump among American voters has to do with which sort of character the president is: a lowly fraudster or a larger-than-life transvaluer of values. It does not have to do with whether or not he is telling the truth in a narrow empirical or factual sense. And so, frustratingly to many opponents, simply pointing out that he is speaking falsehoods can do nothing to set him back. The only principle he consistently follows is something like, as we saw in chapter 1, what the logicians call the "Principle of Explosion": once you have allowed falsehood into your argument, you can say whatever you want.

One thing that historical perspective shows is that earlier eras have been much more subtle and profound than our own in articulating post-fact views, in particular, post-fact views that are at the same time very much committed to truth, even if it is truth grounded in unreason, such as that of Kierkegaardian faith. Instead, today post-fact irrationalists just make up the flimsiest lies, as that dinosaurs and Jesus Christ walked the earth together, and pretend that they believe this, when we know they do not, and they know we know they do not. Trump says one thing, and then its opposite a few hours later, but otherwise acts as if he has the same theory of truth as everyone else. This is a ratcheting up of irrationalism to levels unprecedented in recent history.

When in 2004 a member of the Bush administration reportedly scoffed at those who continue to live in the "reality-based community," many were alarmed.[33] But this stance did have the virtue of grasping and playing on the real difference between deep commitment to bringing about a world that matches what one most values, and submitting to the world as it is because the facts require us to do so. The administration official who coined this phrase lined up with those many thinkers throughout history who have conceived truth as something that can be willed. This is debatable, of course, and we have been debating it for thousands of years. But it is a world away from the dirty conspiracy-mongering of the flat-earthers, of Alex Jones, and of those they have helped to propel into political power.

CHAPTER SIX

Enlightenment; or, Myth

➤➤➤➤➤

Better the Light

In October 2017, an article in the *Atlantic* compares the vision Senator John McCain has for the Republican Party with that of Donald Trump: "Better to heed the voice," Eliot A. Cohen writes, "of someone who has . . . emerged from great suffering with a great love of his country's ideals and not just its soil, and who, as he faces his own end, celebrates his country's future with the optimism that is natively American. In short, better the light."[1] In contrasting soil and light, one need not necessarily be thinking of the divided legacies of Voltaire and Herder, of Enlightenment and counter-Enlightenment—though Cohen may well have these or similar figures in mind—in order to make immediate sense to the reader. Whether capitalized or not, and whether we reject it or not, enlightenment continues to have considerable purchase, as a metaphor, on the way we make sense of society, history, and politics.[2]

It is difficult to say, precisely, when the era of the Enlightenment, with a capital *E*, begins, or where it begins. The term has often been used as a synonym of "eighteenth century," or perhaps of "the long eighteenth century." Jonathan Israel, in a series of compelling historical works,[3] has sought to show that the most "radical" period of the Enlightenment had already begun by the middle of the seventeenth century, as epitomized in particular by the work of Spinoza, who died in 1677 and whose *Ethics* was published later that year. If we see Enlightenment as centrally involving the project of using one's individual faculty of reason in order to cast "light" upon the surrounding world, then we may see the project as starting considerably earlier. The phrase "natural light of reason" occurs already in Descartes's 1628 *Rules for the Direction of the Mind*.

By the eighteenth century, the high hopes for the power of reason to solve all human problems, which had characterized so much thinking of the previous century, began to show signs of stress. It became increasingly difficult to conceal, from public debate as well as from one's own conscience, the fact that the incredible attainments of modern Europe were the result not just of the ingenious breakthroughs and diligence of individual men, but also of the plundering of the rest of the world, both for resources and for labor. The inhabitants of the rest of the world had often been thought to live their lives for the most part below the threshold of reason, according to nature and instinct. And yet it often happened that European colonists depended on local knowledge—of tropical medicine, for example—for their very survival.

This peculiar dependence charged the eighteenth century with a certain unmistakable paradox. The great victory of reason on the Continent, it was imagined, cast modern Europe as a sort of island afloat in a sea of unreason: the supposed unreason of the non-European peoples on whom Europe depended, as well as the unreason of the violence and domination that underlay this relation of dependence. Perhaps nowhere was the paradox more evident than in the Haitian Revolution of 1791–1804, which had been explicitly modeled by its leaders, particularly François-Dominique Toussaint Louverture, on the French Revolution's promotion of the universality of the ideals of freedom, equality, and brotherhood.[4] Even postrevolutionary France, it turned out, for all its talk of such abstract principles, needed to preserve its power over a slave colony in the faraway Caribbean, thus revealing the inherent limits of its claim to be in possession of universal ideals. In a parallel motion back at the heart of the metropole, in Paris, in 1791 Olympe de Gouges published the *Universal Declaration of the Rights of Woman and the Female Citizen*. She intended this as a natural extension of what had been laid out by the revolutionary authors of the *Universal Declaration of the Rights of Man and of the Citizen*. But the men, who had presumed the gender inclusivity of the occurrence of "man" in the title of their work, took de Gouges's work rather as a parodical affront, and in 1793 she had her head cut off by the Jacobins.

Both the Haitian revolutionary and the Parisian feminist were seeking to test out the limits of the French revolutionaries' insistence upon the universal validity of their claims. Toussaint Louverture "called out," as social-media activists might say today, the French colonial power-holders in the most elegant of ways, by simply making the same demands that they had already made for themselves. At the same time, other Europeans were calling out French claims to be the world's purveyors of reason and enlightenment, by questioning whether these were in fact the best principles on which to base human life. The Enlightenment barely had time to get its bearings, to come into its own as a historical moment, before what is commonly called the "counter-Enlightenment" came to challenge it. This countermovement is most often associated with German thinkers of the Sturm und Drang and of the romantic movement, who insisted in their various ways that it is not reason at all, but feeling and passion that must govern human life, including human political life. For romantic thinkers, society is based not on an abstract idea of the state that brings people together on the basis of universal ideals, but rather on an idea of community to which people are attached at an affective level.

As discussed in the introduction, Pankaj Mishra has recently argued that the counter-Enlightenment reaction begins, in fact, within the French-speaking world, that the first modern Western thinker to construct his intellectual identity upon the bold rejection of the piety of smug universalist rationality was none other than Jean-Jacques Rousseau. We see this most clearly in the bitter disagreement between Rousseau and Voltaire over the best way forward for the nations of eastern Europe. Voltaire had enriched himself as the favored courtier of Catherine the Great of Russia. With his help, Russia became a great luminary pole of the Enlightenment, but it did so in the most top-down way imaginable: by decree of the sovereign. What Catherine achieved, Rousseau could see, was what the French theorist René Girard, briefly mentioned in chapter 2, would later call "appropriative mimicry."[5] Russian Enlightenment was largely formal, an imported style all the rage among the aristocracy in a country whose economy was still based on serfdom. This did nothing to curb Voltaire's enthusiasm for Catherine's project. In fact he believed she would do best to spread Enlightenment further, by force, exhorting Catherine "to teach European enlightenment at gunpoint to the Poles and Turks."[6] For Rousseau, by contrast, such a top-down approach can only be both wrong and futile.

Voltaire, in broad outline, wrote the urtext for the neoconservatives who invaded Iraq; Rousseau anticipated the jihadists who took over amidst the chaos left by the neoconservatives after they failed in their foolish quest to export democracy. Rousseau also anticipated Trump, or at least Trumpism: the idea that America is for Americans, and must be made great again for Americans. Who was right? A wide-scoped historical view can, at least, help us to see how futile it is to take sides here. Voltaire's universalism, when applied, is always a blind and destructive juggernaut; Rousseau's subaltern resistance seems always to grow dark, if it does not start out that way, when it gains in power.

The German counter-Enlightenment would focus on precisely the sorts of knowledge that rationalist philosophy of the seventeenth century had sought to eliminate or suppress. Now imagination was back in fashion, taking precedence over the abstractions of reason. Rather than emphasizing a priori principles, the new spirit of inquiry focused on fieldwork, the study of culture; one of its greatest attainments was, in the nineteenth century, the collection of folklore that we know today as the fairy tales of Jakob and Wilhelm Grimm. These brothers were part of a broad movement that may be called "soft nationalism": the effort to promote the greatness of Germany by revealing what is particular about it, what is irreducible and distinctive, rather than trying to measure it against some sort of absolute standard of reason imposed from outside. This model—the cultivation of national pride through institutional recognition of iconic markers of a national culture imagined as autochthonous—would in turn be duplicated throughout Europe, and to some extent would echo in the nation-building projects of Africa and Asia in the period of decolonization in the late twentieth century.

Reason had been present as an ideal since Greek antiquity, but it turns aggressive, to again invoke Paul Hazard's fortuitous phrase, only toward the end of the seventeenth century, setting off, in this French historian's view, a "crisis of the European conscience" (or "consciousness," as the same word does double duty in French). Between 1680 and 1715, in Hazard's view, Europeans became intent on enthroning a mental faculty "by which we suppose that man is distinguished from the beasts, and in which it is evident that he surpasses them by far." In order to do this, it was necessary, Hazard thought, to

> extend without limits, to audacious extremes, the powers of this higher faculty. Its privilege was to establish clear and veritable principles, in order to arrive at conclusions that are not less clear or less veritable. Its essence was to examine; and its first charge was to take on the mysterious, the unexplained, the obscure, in order to project its light out into the world. The world was full of errors, created by the deceitful powers of the soul, vouchsafed by authorities beyond control, spread by preference for credulity and laziness, accumulated and strengthened through the force of time.[7]

The author, writing in the mid-1930s, has trouble concealing for more than a few sentences his sharp awareness of how utterly this earlier period's optimism would eventually be dashed. Particularly striking is the retreat from that era's universalism, reflected politically in its transnationalism and secularism, toward crass nationalism and religious persecution. "They were French, English, Dutch, German," Hazard writes; "a Jew despised by the ghetto, Spinoza, provided support to them with his genius. How diverse they were! How they came from opposed worlds to arrive at the same goal!"[8]

Descartes is the king of the aggressive rationalists, but his royal stature "is not absolute, since none ever is in such domains of the spirit, and since, even in the most barren and abstract forms of thought, certain national or racial originalities endure and cannot be eradicated."[9] Thus Descartes proves unable to "conquer that part of English intelligence, that part of Italian intelligence, that defends and maintains the specific existence of England, of Italy. But to the extent that thinkers are speculating on the plane of the universal, Descartes reigns."[10] Hazard does not make clear what part of Descartes's intelligence is sufficiently universal as to not betray his own Frenchness, and as to be transmissible to thinkers of other nationalities with no threat to the integrity of their own nationally specific thought. One of the most fundamental challenges of the Enlightenment, in fact, was that one nation's universalism was another nation's imposition of a peculiar foreign way of doing things. In particular, it was generally the French who mistook their own traditions for universality, and it was their neighbors, most vocally the counter-Enlightenment thinkers of Germany, who sought to unmask this purported universality as in fact merely French, and therefore as incompatible, to speak with Hazard, with the "specific existence" of Germany.

It is instructive here to contrast Leibniz's intense interest in absorbing the *novissima sinica*, the latest news from China, and from all around the world, on the one hand, and, on the other, Descartes's near-total silence about the existence of a world beyond Europe's borders.[11] The French philosopher was not particularly interested in the diversity of humanity, because he took the model of the human being that he himself was articulating as universally valid. He neglected the specific existence of other forms of human social life, which in the two centuries or so following his death in 1650 would begin to be articulated and defended under the banner of nationalism. It is in the eighteenth century, to quote the title of a book by Marc Fumaroli, that "Europe spoke French,"[12] that is, that any European could be expected to express in French an idea that was to have more than local or national validity.

The presumption was that French was simply a neutral vehicle of international communication. The very term *lingua franca* is still used to refer to a language shared by many nations, not as a pidgin or an underdeveloped rudimentary language for basic commerce, but a full-fledged language that all speakers strive to perfect in the aim of participating in a flourishing culture. The adjective *franca* means here not "French," which in neo-Latin is usually designated rather as the *lingua francogallica*, but rather "Frankish," a term for western Europeans in general that dates back to the Crusades. In Turkey even today, modern toilets are sometimes described as *a la franga*. The ethnonym *franc* will gradually evolve into a general term to describe a person who is honest—that is, "frank": a straightforward speaker of truth. But to the German counter-Enlightenment, the French language is anything but a *lingua franca* in this sense, and the French have no particular claim to being truth-speakers. The Trojan horse of universalism, some would protest, allows what is specific to the existence of the French to move across borders. Thus J. G. Herder, in his 1768 poem "To the Germans," exhorts his countrymen to "spew out . . . the ugly slime of the Seine / Speak German, O you Germans."[13]

Aggressive reason provokes violent reactions. Herder is often described as a "soft nationalist," defending German sensibility against French reason, and articulating a view of the nation as the locus of community values and of the irreducible particularity of culture, against the blinding glare of uniformity and indifference to community that seemed to radiate from the Enlightenment. And more recently we have seen the blinding glare of Obamacare radiating from Washington, DC, and the Tea Party protesters who come together in sentimental community, and lovingly shade each other from the light.

The World-Soul on Horseback

On October 14, 1806, Napoleon's troops engaged Prussian forces in the Battle of Jena. Just under seven thousand French troops were killed or wounded, and around thirty-eight thousand on the Prussian side.[14] The day before, G.W.F. Hegel had observed the French leader entering his quaint university town on horseback. In a letter to Friedrich Immanuel Niethammer, the philosopher would effuse: "I saw the emperor—this world-soul—riding out of the city on reconnaissance."[15] This single individual, Hegel wrote, while "concentrated here at a single point, astride a horse," nevertheless "reaches out over the world and masters it."[16] What Hegel means by "world-soul" is complex and would draw us considerably off course if we were to attempt to do it justice. In brief, it is something like the philosophical reflection of the course of humanity's development through history. It exists objectively, and not simply as the narrative that we give to history in order to make sense of it. And it encompasses both the emotional and the intellectual realms of human life. The history of the world is the history of the unfolding of this spirit. For it to be embodied or concentrated in a single person is for that person, by accident or by will, to come objectively to hold the destiny of the world in his hands.

That sometimes the weight of the world can fall into one's hands quite by accident is, some have argued, crucial for understanding Hegel's take on Napoleon. This issue has lately been of some importance again in discussions of political leadership in Europe. In an October 2017 interview with the German magazine *Der Spiegel*, President Emmanuel Macron of France went into considerable detail in clarifying his position in relation to Napoleon Bonaparte. The German interviewers had asked him whether he agreed with Hegel that one man, such as the French emperor, can steer history. Macron denied that this is what Hegel said: "He wasn't being nice to Napoleon," Macron explains, "because he of course knows that history can outflank you."[17] Hegel had believed rather that an individual can "embody ... the zeitgeist for a moment," but that "the individual isn't always clear they are doing so."[18] Nonetheless, Macron reveals that he aims to do so himself, and to do so with clarity. "I think it is only possible to move things forward if you have a sense of responsibility. And that is exactly the goal I have set for myself: to try to encourage France and the French people to change and develop further."[19]

Months of speculation about the new president's Napoleonic ambitions could not have been more decisively confirmed. He goes on to declare that what must be restored (and what, presumably, Hegel had seen Napoleon as providing) are, precisely, "grand narratives" of the sort that French postmodernist philosophers of a generation earlier, such as Jean-François Lyotard, had mocked and dismissed. In his 1979 book *The Postmodern Condition*, Lyotard had gone so far as to assert that the grand narratives that had supported the Enlightenment project are inherently unjust.[20] These narratives concerned, first and foremost, the emancipation of the individual rational subject, and, second, the Hegelian vision of history as the unfolding of the universal spirit. Macron rejects Lyotard's view. As he tells *Der Spiegel*: "We need to develop a kind of political heroism. I don't mean that I want to play the hero. But we need to be amenable once again to creating grand narratives. If you like, post-modernism was the worst thing that could have happened to our democracy."[21] Macron's self-positioning relative to French history is nonetheless clear: he would like to reach back to a moment before doubt took over, before the defining trait of his culture was a brooding hyperawareness of the limits of what can be known, and what can be done.

The fact that overcoming this species of unreason must go together with taking up the mantle of the Enlightenment, warming up to the legacy of Napoleonic imperialism, and rejecting many of the bona fides of the French left, in favor instead of promoting American-style market-driven growth, is as fascinating as it is historically complicated. It is by no means clear that all of these elements naturally belong together, and the fact that Macron is defending them all, in the spirit of a new, no-nonsense, proactive politics beyond left and right, may well be a peculiar circumstance of French history—even if, as we will begin to see further in this chapter, the defense of a vision of politics purportedly beyond left and right has, in the most recent era, come to be seen by many around the world as inseparable from the defense of rationality.

Macron's call for political heroism, while vastly more sophisticated, is not entirely different from Trump's call to make America great again. Or, at least, if we find ourselves attracted to Macron's learned invocations of Napoleon, while repulsed by the memes that are circulating of Trump enthroned as some Nero-like emperor, we may do well to reflect on whether the distinction we make between the two is not more a judgment of taste than an informed articulation of our political commitments. Trump has expressed his admiration for French-style military parades and has said he would like to host some of his own in the same style.[22] We are a long way, now, from the Bush-era mockery of the French as "cheese-eating surrender monkeys,"[23] as hopeless ineffectual pacifists, who, of all unspeakably shameful things, also eat cheese.

Macron has for his part found a wavelength for civil and productive communication with Trump. Yet the two are invoking very different mythologies in their respective forms of political heroism. Trump does not appear to know what the Enlightenment is, let alone to be seeking to restore its principal legacies. It is difficult to imagine him taking sides, as between Lyotard and Macron, on the question whether post-modernism was wrong to seek to abandon grand narratives. Trump would almost certainly not wish to institute the emancipation of the individual rational subject as one of his own society's grand narratives, since the more individual rational subjects there are of voting age in American society, the more voters there will be who understand that the call to make America great again is a call not of reason, but of mythology.

There have been few occasions since 1806 on which German phi-losophers have perceived French leaders as the embodiment of world-spirit, and few times when—beyond perceptions, at the level of hard geopolitical facts—France was so well poised to dictate the future course of the Continent. But Napoleon's own place in the legacy of the Enlightenment—a legacy that Lyotard would consciously reject, and that Trump would not be aware he had the option to take up—is com-plicated. Napoleon is neither ubiquitously memorialized today in France nor consistently villainized. It is widely acknowledged that his outsized ambition is what led to his loss, and that France has no busi-ness dominating Europe from Iberia to Russia.

But there are further more nuanced questions as to what Napoleon really represented: in particular, whether his period of imperial expan-sion abroad, and of consolidation of absolute power at home, amounted to a continuation of the aims of the French Revolution, rooted as it was in the pursuit of the Enlightenment values of equality and freedom, or whether rather it was a reversal of these aims. Napoleon himself did not have much to say that would help us to resolve the matter. Accord-ing to Étienne Geoffroy Saint-Hilaire, who accompanied Napoleon as a naturalist during the Egyptian campaign of 1798–1801, the military leader was very fond of science and imagined that the important work left for science to complete was to describe the infinite "world of details," now that Isaac Newton had described the world's universal general laws.[24] But years after that encounter what struck Geoffroy most was Napoleon's resignation to the fact that he had chosen to pursue a different course in life, that he was now a military strategist and had no time for big ideas of any sort.

At the strategic level, it is clear that the Napoleonic expansion began in the need to secure the border areas that posed a threat to the gains of the revolution within France itself. But it would be difficult to make the case that this effort of securing and reinforcing compelled French forces to expand the buffer zone around the newly founded republic all the way to Moscow and Cairo. The justification for such an expansion, if it is to be found, can only be philosophical, and not strategic: that it carries the promises of universal equality and freedom beyond the boundaries of a single republic, because these are the inheritance of all humanity and not of a single nation. Yet by the time the French Revolution made it to Jena, it was not at all clear to many of the locals that these were the values it was in fact exporting. Hegel welcomed him, but Hegel himself was no simple defender of Enlightenment, if we understand this to centrally involve the emancipation of the rational individual.

Canonical Enlightenment philosophers had argued that the state's legitimate function is limited largely to aiding in individual emancipation, and thus tended to defend theories of state power that supported some version of liberal democracy. In Hegel by contrast, particularly by the time of the 1820 *Philosophy of Right*, it is the state itself that is rational, not the individual, and it is the duty of the individual to submit to the state. This view is at the heart of so-called Right Hegelianism, which would be very influential in Germany in the years of restoration following Napoleon's retreat.[25] This path may easily be seen to be a third way, different from both Enlightenment universalism and Herderian communitarianism. More than once in the past two centuries those who have been attracted to the latter, who have been attached to their communities and wary of what lies beyond, have turned over their hope for survival as a community to a strong state, as personified by a seemingly strong leader, who promises to look out for their community interests. This arrangement seldom ends well, neither for the local community that had been promised protection, nor for the peace of the international community, whose very existence the pandering leader either mocks or denies.

Poetic History

We may find the roots of counter-Enlightenment well before Herder. As we saw in the introduction, Zeev Sternhell identifies Giambattista Vico as one of its early harbingers, and if Sternhell is correct in this, it is because, indeed, the Neapolitan polymath had been an early defender of the view—later associated with names such as Herder, and with the late nineteenth-century anthropologist Franz Boas, among others[26]—that the ways in which individual cultures articulate and define their place in the world, in part by reference to a mythical past, are not signs of stupidity or stuntedness at all; rather, they are simply articulations in a different genre or at a different register of expression.

It is remarkable that Vico's *New Science* of 1725,[27] a milestone of the early emergence of history as a scholarly discipline, should offer such a sympathetic take on myth, which has so often been conceived as the opposite of history, as the preference for some imagined dreamtime out of which a people emerged, over cold and well-founded facts. History, as an intellectual endeavor, is often held to begin only once we have made our way out of mythmaking. In Greek antiquity Thucydides, Herodotus, and Polybius had made significant contributions to the advancement of this discipline, but for the most part well into the seventeenth century history remained principally a matter of genealogy, of tracing out family ancestries, and the ultimate such genealogy was the one found in the Bible, in the long list of generations that begat other generations leading, as a sort of culmination, to the birth of Jesus Christ. Most such genealogies were at least partially mythological. As noted in the twelfth century by Saxo Grammaticus, to whom we have already been introduced, the official genealogical records of Danish royalty in the Middle Ages typically featured marriages with bears, and bear-human hybrid offspring, somewhere back in the fog of time past.[28]

Vico believes, and argues at great length, that all the gentile nations are descended from "giants," which is to say both large and robust people, but also people who are, according to the Greek etymology of the Latin *gigantes*, literally "born out of the earth." If this seems credulous on Vico's part, the author himself also devotes much room in the treatise to the analysis of credulity. He is sympathetic to those who appear to believe in outlandish things, as he maintains that such people are simply expressing themselves in poetic terms, and that there is a logic to this sort of expression. What Vico describes as the "poetic metaphysics" of the giants is in fact the various traditional belief systems of non-Christian, or perhaps more broadly nontextual, peoples.

Significantly, however, Vico believes that originally the stories that native peoples, or "the poetic nations," told about themselves were straightforwardly, factually "true narrations," since "the first men of the gentile world had the simplicity of children, who are truthful by nature," and therefore "the first fables could not feign anything false."[29] But these narrations would later become figurative, as "with the further development of the human mind, words were invented, which signified abstract forms or genera comprising their species or relating parts with their wholes."[30] And so began the process of deliteralization of language, which would ultimately issue in myth. Thus for Vico it is not in the childlike stage of humanity that we make up fantastic stories about who we are and where we come from, only growing into factual, historical descriptions later on. Rather it is exactly the other way around. We start out as historians and later develop into mythologists.

By the late nineteenth century a prominent strain of history would become intent on returning to what Vico saw as this primordial state. The school of positivist historiography, as represented by Leopold von Ranke, insisted that the prime imperative of all history writing is that it must stick to telling us, simply, *wie es eigentlich gewesen* (how it actually was).[31] Any other objective, Ranke and his followers thought, would amount to a degeneration of history writing into mythmaking. Of course this sets up an impossible ideal for the historian, as to simply select some facts to relate rather than others is already to fail to tell how it actually was. Yet because, as already established in reference to Kellyanne Conway, there are infinitely many facts about the past, the historian has no other choice than to make such a selection. The criteria for selection are various, and often include the use of the imagination or the pressure of ideology, but it is hard to see how these criteria could ever be dictated exclusively by the facts themselves. And thus the dream of a positivist historiography was, though many would continue to pretend to believe in it, dead on arrival.

Today most professional historians believe that a good historian will cultivate what is called "historical imagination." This is the ability to fill out "how it actually was" with a bit of "how it might have been," and also, inevitably, a bit of "how it should have been." It is, moreover, the ability to think about how the "was," the "might," and the "should" that are incorporated into the writing of history help to shape our sense of the reality of the present and the possibilities of the future. In short, one is today generally more comfortable than Ranke had been in recognizing that the task of history is not totally separate from the task of myth, that both emerge from the same human needs and satisfy the same desire for self-knowledge, whether of individuals or of communities.

It is undeniable that often history writing has been rather too liberal with its admixture of "should have," and too casual in its loyalty to "was," with the result that many accounts of the distant past come across as mere wishful thinking. In the seventeenth century considerable effort was expended, in some circles, to give an account of the unity of all ancient wisdom, to show that all great intellectual and spiritual traditions in fact flow from the same source. This effort was sometimes called *prisca theologia*, or ancient theology, and it often placed the beginnings of all wisdom deep in the past, in figures who straddled the boundary between the historical and the mythical, such as the Egyptian sage Hermes Trismegistus, or even further back still, in the

Egyptian god Thoth.[32] Often the most important task was to show how all advanced or "civilized" peoples could have had their roots in the ancient Near East, and thus been party to the revelations made to Moses and the other prophets. It was, moreover, important to show that supposedly pagan intellectual traditions, such as that of the Greek philosophers, were likewise part of the same unified tradition of revealed wisdom that also includes the prophets, and thus that Greek philosophers may be saved from the First Circle of Hell, where Dante had placed them a few centuries earlier, since they were not ignorant after all of the revealed truths held by the people of the Book. It was speculated, for example, that Plato had disappeared for some time during his youth into the deserts of Sinai, where he had learned directly from Moses, who, himself a prophet, had foreknowledge of the coming of Jesus Christ. Thus Plato could be retroactively made out as a Christian.[33]

Moving further afield, variations on this same approach to wisdom led some, such as Athanasius Kircher, to argue that the Chinese are originally of Middle Eastern origin, and that their writing is a variation on Egyptian hieroglyphics,[34] while others argued that the Native Americans were one of the ancient tribes of Israel that had gone missing long ago, and could now, in the modern era, finally be brought back into the fold.[35] Knowledge is one, and humanity is unified, according to the *prisca theologia*, and all of history leads back to the same source. All wisdom flows forth from the same primordial origin in the deep past; there is one truth, and it is shared by Christians, pagan Greek philosophers, and even the Chinese and the Native Americans. The impulse to unification was strong, and it yielded up, in *prisca theologia*, a new sort of poetic history as a way of molding the past to fit a new vision of the unity of humankind.

When I was little I sincerely believed, somehow, that my maternal grandfather was an avatar of George Washington, that there was some sort of deep identity between the two of them. I saw the silhouetted head of the first president of the United States on the twenty-five-cent coin, and I sincerely believed that this person was my grandfather, even though I also understood that this person was a founder of the country and had lived a considerable time earlier than the living and breathing man who had raised my mother. This sort of simultaneous identity and difference, between living beings and their timeless, or primordial, or transcendent exemplar, is typical of mythical thought, and somehow I managed to come up with it spontaneously, as a child to whom the responsible adults were at the same time trying, as well as they knew how, to give a proper, nonmythological historical education.

Family lore, even when it does not involve such avatars, is inherently mythological. To learn of some great-great-grandparent who crossed the ocean or the frontier to settle in the region of our birth is to learn something that is of vanishingly little importance for world history, but that cannot but seem, when we learn it, to rival the *Odyssey* or the legend of King Arthur, or indeed the Bible, in its power to give meaning and orientation to our own present existence. These are the stories that shape us, that make us who we are, that make us fully human, though they are also, by and large, lies. Every attempt that I have ever made to corroborate my father's tales about ancestors I never met has revealed to me that his version of the story had little relation to historical events. We were religious dissenters kicked out of England by the king himself; we were immigrants with pluck and wit that got us out of all manner of scrapes; we were Cherokees, somewhere back there. Except that we weren't. These stories shape us and make us fully human not because they are true. We may imagine that a child raised by cruel experimenters who was allowed to hear only accurate accounts of well-documented events would probably show some signs of developmental deficiency. Legends shape us and make us fully human because they fire our fantasies, and enable us to root ourselves in a largely imagined past, so as in turn to be able to project ourselves, with a developed idea of who it is that we are, into the future.

The current prevailing division of tasks in our society places the responsibility for such edifying mythmaking within family units. When we move from the home to the broader society, there is a corresponding expectation, at least if we value Enlightenment, that we will move from uncorroborated lore to documented, or documentable, facts. Yet there are many societies that make no such division, societies that are unified rather in the way that we imagine a family should be: by stories. These societies are held together, and are enabled to find meaning and to orient their practices and plans, by invoking events that happened in a timeless, undocumented, mythical past. They do not do this as an abnegation of the responsibility to know the real historical truths about themselves. Rather, they do this because myth has not for them been switched out for history at the suprafamilial level as the preferred mode of reckoning with questions of identity.

When there is a disagreement between Euro-American archaeologists on the one hand and a Native American group on the other as to the origins or the arrival of that group in a given region—the archaeologists generally dating the earliest events back only a number of thousands of years, while the indigenous people cast themselves back into deep time, into an original era in which animals talked, and the regularities of the natural world as we know them today did not hold—most of us are inclined to think that we should defer at least to the extent possible to the account the indigenous people give. And we do not feel as though we are reverting from Enlightenment to mythology when we do this. Rather, we feel as though this deference is required by the principles of intercultural understanding and toleration, which in turn are part of the inheritance of the Enlightenment. This inheritance is compromised only when we come to believe, as sometimes happens among political activists invested in indigenous causes, that the only intercultural understanding that is adequate is the one that accepts at face value the literal truth of the claims made by an indigenous group about its own origins.[36] This is in fact to fall into the very same trap that has also ensnared Ken Ham and other creation-science defenders: to stake the integrity of a culture's values and faith commitments, whether one's own or those of another group to which one is bound by respect, on the answers it comes up with to mundane empirical questions.

In Trumpian dreamtime, in the primordial era in which the regularities of the present world did not hold, everything was "great." This is a multipurpose adjective and it may be understood in various ways. Presumably any past greatness of the United States would have been forged in the revolutionary era of the late eighteenth century, an era that, for many Americans, appears so far back as to be effectively disconnected from our present reality. I myself have learned, largely through my formation as a specialist in seventeenth-century philosophy, to see the late eighteenth century, the era of the American founding fathers, of the Revolution and the Constitution, as not so long ago at all—as, basically, current events. But for many Americans, brought up in a society with a public school system that has abandoned its responsibility to make students into historically well-informed citizens, the deeds of George Washington may as well have been contemporaneous with those of Moses. And as long as the past is jumbled in this way, basic elements from one long-past period easily surface in another. Thus throughout American history there have been rumors of politicians and public figures claiming that the Bible was written in English, or that English should be the official language of the United States on the grounds that it was "good enough for Jesus."[37] Here the distinction between what Washington and Jefferson themselves recognized as "the ancient" and "the modern" falls away, and the eighteenth century may as well be the first century CE, the high Enlightenment assimilated to antiquity. Once this happens, it is much easier to think of the founding fathers of the United States as deeply Christian, rather than deistic in their private beliefs and secular in their public commitments, as they are imagined to inhabit that primordial domain that also includes Jesus Christ himself.

All of this makes good poetic sense, just like the identity between my grandfather and George Washington, and just like the poetic history of the giants as described by Vico; it is useless to seek to defeat it by bombarding with facts someone who feels the poetry of it. I still cannot entirely disabuse myself of the identity I discerned early on between my mother's father and my country's founding father. Both of them emerged for me out of some incalculably distant primordial past, and the head on the US quarter remains to me something like an image from a family album. But I know to keep this to myself (until now anyway), and this is the principal difference between me and the politician who believes, or feels and therefore claims to believe, that English was the language of the apostles; or the creation scientist who believes, or feels and therefore claims to believe, that the inhabitants of the ancient Near East walked the earth—speaking English, of course—alongside dinosaurs.

Poetic history is good. Or, at least, it is such an essential part of the way human beings orient themselves in the world that it would be meaningless to call it bad. It can be edifying, revelatory, even a vehicle of understanding. This is what Matthew Arnold understood when he wrote in his 1852 poem "Empedocles on Etna," "He fables, yet speaks truth."[38] It is difficult to determine what explains the difference between my own private poetic history and the one that some politicians seek to impose on society as a whole. It does not seem that my myth about my grandfather could ever be anything more than a private quirk of my own development. Yet as with the difference between aviophobia and racism described in chapter 2, it may be that I am simply underestimating the potential for building a community among those people who believe that the founding father of our country is also, biologically or metaphysically, an ancestor. Similar beliefs, in fact, seem to be fairly common in quasi-mythological folk genealogies throughout the world. I could probably found a movement, if I really wanted to, organized around the idea that George Washington is the ancestor of all of my fellow Americans, and I could perhaps have him mingling with Jesus Christ millennia before his actual birth. If my movement worked at it, we could likely insert ourselves into the institutions of American government, and produce a few crackpot judges and other public officials who would argue that our beliefs should be enshrined into law and should constitute part of compulsory public education. But of course this is not going to happen. I have no impulse to turn my private poetic history, my dreamtime, into the collective mythos of a community, and from there into the hardened ideology of a modern administrative state.

Vico represents a hopeful tendency of early counter-Enlightenment thought, to the extent that he recognizes the ineliminability and the power of the poetic histories by which communities orient themselves, without for that reason failing to recognize the need for real facts about the past as the basis of his "new science." Thoroughly anti-Enlightenment, as opposed to merely counter-Enlightenment, is the judge who appeals to the Bible as the basis of his commitment to English-only laws in the United States, who wants, in other words, poetic history to be enshrined into the laws of a country whose legal system has historically been rooted in the protection of rights and freedoms, and not in enforcing conformity. To the extent that he gets his wish, we have a clear illustration of Adorno and Horkheimer's warning that Enlightenment threatens ever to degenerate into mythology. The danger of such degeneration can only be heightened by the new imperative to "make America great again," which is itself a four-word distillation of the very spirit of poetic history.

Enlightenment into Myth, Again

In recent years the defense of rationality has, for some, become mixed up with the project of defending a variety of political centrism. Some are convinced that humanity is perpetually balanced between opposite extremes of destructive action, and it is only centrism that can enable us to maintain this delicate balance. We are balanced, among other things, between backward-looking mythopoiesis and radiant utopian visions projected onto what is in fact an almost totally indeterminate future. Best, the centrists say, to just do what we can to navigate our way through the short term. Rationality thus comes to be exemplified in the virtues of prudence and humility. Many who oppose this middle path from both the left and the right, in turn, echo the wisdom of Melville's confidence man: "You are the moderate man, the invaluable understrapper of the wicked man," he announces to a potential customer who is uncertain as to whether to purchase a bottle of the protagonist's herbal potion. "You, the moderate man, may be used for wrong, but are useless for right."[39] This wisdom appears particularly compelling in the current political climate, and moderates have a difficult time avoiding, for long, the accusation of being useful idiots for sinister causes, of holding to a center that cannot hold. It is, however, important to recall, even or especially in such a climate, that the confidence man was, in uttering these words, attempting to pull off a con of his own, to play on a fellow human being's innate impulsiveness, to convince him that it is always better to do something than to do nothing, and, finally, to sell him a useless vial of herbs.

On the other hand, by choosing to do nothing, by supporting the status quo or the reigning order, one can contribute to gross injustice just as surely as if one were to join up for some bloody upheaval of the reigning order. The status quo is in any case an illusion, and to defend it at one point in time seldom has the same moral and political significance as defending it at a later point. This is the insight that underlies Tancredi Falconeri's observation about the fading Sicilian aristocracy in Giuseppe Tomasi di Lampedusa's 1958 novel *The Leopard*: "If we want things to stay as they are, things will have to change."[40] Not to see this, and to insist that things simply stay as they are, without changing, is to defend something different from the status quo; it is to defend an impossible version of the present based on a version of the past that only grows the more mythological, the further it recedes.

The mass slaughter of Tutsis by Hutus in Rwanda in 1994 was, surely, an outburst of irrationality; and irrational, too, is the everyday functioning of a bureaucracy, such as the notorious DMV, that allows its agents to exercise their gentle sadism behind the safe cover of rules, and of the way things are done and long have been done. Of course the Rwandan genocide, or any such moment of punctuated violence, is the culmination of a process that begins with intimidation, threats, pressure on the part of groups that may be operating within the constraints of the bureaucratic system, and even priding themselves on their respect for the rule of law—for example, the anti-immigrant demonstrators who celebrate the Second Amendment by openly carrying automatic weapons in close proximity to an Islamic community center.[41] Even though following rules and transgressing rules are in a sense opposite actions, the latter sort of action can evolve out of the former. Lawful application of heat can lead to chaotic boiling over. Patriotic defenders of the Constitution, or free-speech activists whose patent purpose is to lend legitimacy to a white-supremacist demonstration that threatens to spill over into violence, often continue to operate within a discursive range inherited from, and authorized by, Enlightenment rationalism.

In actual fact there are few people who represent a pure and consistent version of the latter. Many will talk of war and battle against the enemy, but when they are arrested, they will often fall back on legalistic demands for due process, and on an expectation that there is a system in place that recognizes that we are all equal before the law. Infamously, the Norwegian mass murderer and nationalist Anders Behring Breivik filed a petulant complaint in prison when the authorities declined to furnish him with the most up-to-date model of Nintendo PlayStation.[42] This is in the end only a more extreme expression of the basic incoherence at work wherever an extremist hides behind the hard-won triumphs of justice and fairness, enshrined into law and institutions, in order, quite simply, to get what he wants. Violence can be carried out not just in explosive rejection of rationality, but in devotion to it, and a violent life can also be a rational one. A vivid reminder of this might be discerned in Isidore of Seville's discussion of something seemingly as mundane as rational conjunctions, such as the Latin *ne*. These are so called, he writes, "from the reasoning [*ratio*] that someone uses in acting, as, 'How may I kill him *so that* [*ne*] I won't be recognized? By poison or blade?' "[43] One can be rational, in a strict sense of rationality, simply in making the proper choice of murder weapon.

No principle or ideal is so pristine as to not be subject to distortion, depending on who takes up its defense. Consider, for example, the rise and brief career in the limelight of Milo Yiannopoulos, who came to fame as the technology editor for Breitbart News, and became an icon of a certain sector of the alt-right, only to see his public following plummet after a comment about pedophilia. Although the niche he occupied placed him alongside sundry species of anti-Enlightenment ethnonationalists, white supremacists, enemies of democracy, and defenders of patriarchy, his ostensible cause was one that he inherited directly from the Enlightenment: free speech. A generation earlier, this was the issue that had galvanized the student movement at Berkeley, under the leadership of figures such as Mario Savio, who could, for their part, plausibly claim to descend directly from the philosophers of the Enlightenment to the extent that their other political commitments included, for example, racial and gender equality, opposition to nationalism, and international solidarity.[44]

And Yiannopoulos is hardly the only member of the new, mutated extreme right to think of himself, whether through willful self-delusion or simply an honest lack of self-understanding, as a descendant of the Enlightenment. The degradation of the ideal of free speech that Yiannopoulos evidences, an ideal that had once been a cornerstone of classical liberalism, offers us a vivid case study of the decay of enlightenment into mythology. From an ideal that had been seen as vital for the survival of both public honesty and, at an individual level, self-knowledge, free speech has been transformed into a cudgel by which to intimidate and antagonize other groups. The ideal became a caricature of itself, yet it has so far been hard for many to appreciate the totality and depth of this transformation, as it has generally been assumed that when anti-Enlightenment forces assert themselves in the public sphere, they will do so by announcing what it is they are against. We are less attuned to their strategy of appropriating and adapting for their own purposes the language of Enlightenment, and, in this language, emphasizing what it is they are for.

Many of the participants in the white-supremacist rally in Charlottesville, Virginia, on August 12, 2017, seem sincerely not to have understood that they were participating in a white supremacist rally, as they had been convinced that this was a rally for "equality"—more precisely, for ensuring the equality of white Americans in a political landscape where this is threatened by affirmative action, political correctness, and other such sinister forces. Certainly, some participants, such as Richard Spencer, explicitly called for the transformation of the United States into a white ethnostate, and many displayed Nazi symbols in full consciousness of what these were.[45] But the default rationalization for many involved was that they in fact wanted the same basic social goods for everyone, and were simply worried about not getting their fair share. Even Spencer claims not to be a white supremacist, but only a white nationalist, who is in reality seeking nothing more for white people than what people of color in turn rightly demand for their own communities: Spencer is, as he explains it, no more and no less "identitarian" than his political opponents.

This rationalization masquerading as rationality is packed into the mere three words of the now-familiar slogan of reaction: "All lives matter." On the surface this is a pristine expression of Enlightenment universalism and egalitarianism. It is also true, yet its truth alone cannot account for the majority of recent instances of its pragmatic usage. Recall in this connection the extensive discussion in chapter 1 of a number of ancient criticisms of logic, for example in Cicero, to the effect that even when perfectly sound and valid, logical arguments can still be deployed to gain the rhetorical upper hand, nor is there always a clear boundary between the honest work of the logician and the deceitful work of the rhetorician. The public force of the three-word phrase in question has most often been to deprive the more particular claim "Black lives matter" of its power, to change the subject away from the injustice and oppression black Americans face. And it is not only in the United States that we see this rhetorical move in operation. In France, over the past several years, the movement against same-sex marriage, spearheaded by the Catholic right, has come to be called *La Manif pour tous*, "the movement for everybody."[46] Whatever one thinks about the political aims of this movement, the *pour tous* is something of a rhetorical ruse. It is lifted from the common phrase *mariage pour tous*, "marriage for everybody" (that is, marriage for same-sex pairs as well), and adapted for a phrase in which its new meaning, should anyone be called on to explicitly state it, is that a society in which there is only other-sex marriage—and in which traditional family structures are preserved—is a society that is healthier and better *for everybody*. Thus the *pour tous* functions differently in *Manif pour tous* than in *mariage pour tous*: in the latter it is part of a demand for equal rights, based on the principle of universal equality; in the former it is part of an insistence on the preservation of a traditional inequality, based on the presumption that this inequality is better for society as a whole, and that this overall social good trumps individual rights.

And yet the organizers of the *Manif pour tous* understood that it would be useful to dress their movement for traditionalist inegalitarianism in a phrase that resonates with the spirit of Enlightenment egalitarianism. In both the American and the French cases, it is that curious quantifier "all" that allows the forces of counter-Enlightenment to disguise themselves as their opposite, much as creation science, to return to the topic of chapter 5, disguises itself as science. Here, too, it may be asked why those who disguise their movement in this way should bother at all, why they should willingly move to the playing field of their opponent, and subject themselves to home-team rules, where their own game is bound to be at its weakest.

Back in the United States, a critical moment seems to have been reached in 2017 in the debate over the place of free speech in society. In the Charlottesville incident in August of that year, one woman was killed and several people seriously injured when a young demonstrator drove his car into a crowd, in a scene that was very reminiscent of similar attacks by Islamist extremists in London, Nice, and Berlin. Trump responded by condemning the violence that he took to be occurring on "many sides," rather than doing what numerous Americans felt to be incumbent upon a person occupying his position: to denounce neo-Nazi provocations. Many other Americans, however, had come to believe that there is in fact a moral equivalence between extreme-right and extreme-left violence, and, furthermore, that the violence in Charlottesville was the result of extremism on both sides. Things would not have turned violent, many believed, if the left, particularly the activists involved in the Black Lives Matter movement, had not sought to prevent the participants in the Unite the Right demonstration from exercising their First Amendment rights. The American Civil Liberties Union, for its part, sought to ensure that the white nationalists be able to exercise these rights, thereby provoking the anger of many other organizations and commentators on the left. In earlier decades, many Americans had taken it for granted (in part because of a common conflation of "liberal" and "left" in US political debate) that there was no surer sign of a person's left-wing orientation than the ACLU membership card in her wallet. This had been a repeat joke on *All in the Family* and other barometers of US culture in the 1970s. And now the ACLU seemed suddenly to belong to another era.

What had changed? It may well be that in earlier generations, when the ACLU was defending the right of American Nazis to speak and to assemble, this support, and the abstract liberal principles behind it, were based on the presumption that whatever the Nazis were advocating could never in fact come to pass in such a successful liberal democracy as the United States. By 2017 this presumption no longer seemed reasonable: our understanding of the boundary between "mere speech" and speech that can bring about real, immediate harm had shifted. The fact that the marchers' views seemed to garner some sympathy at the highest level of officialdom, notwithstanding the president's minimal and ultimately unsuccessful attempts to follow protocol and to denounce "hate," was a sign of the real danger that one march may spawn further marches, and that these may quickly develop into organized militias or an extensive campaign of seditious terror. And like Breivik before them, who discovered in himself at least some appreciation for the rational system of official prison rules and regulations, the same activists who wished to see exactly such developments found it convenient and useful to draw in their own defense on the political philosophy enshrined in the First Amendment—the philosophy celebrated in the 1960s student movement, and mocked by the bigoted (but in the end good-hearted) Archie Bunker.

It was long presumed by many that there was something both politically more pragmatic and morally more virtuous in the American accommodation of political speech that is beyond the pale. The United States had enshrined into law and realized in practice an approach that was markedly different from that of most Western European democracies, notably France and Germany, in which the expression of Nazi sympathies, the supportive display of Nazi imagery, and the promotion of conspiracy theories denying the Holocaust were, and remain, illegal.

One reasonable objection to such prohibitions has been that no state official can be expected to be qualified in matters of semiotic interpretation, which is just what is required in order to distinguish a pro-Nazi display of a swastika from, say, a display in which the symbol is incorporated into a work, however mediocre, of "provocative" art. In the 1970s swastikas proliferated in the United States and Britain, not only among neo-Nazis, but also among outlaw bikers and punks who were seeking precisely to claim for themselves the most charged symbols floating around in the culture.[47] A symbol, as the punks and bikers seem to have understood, is nothing in itself, and it is for that reason a mistake to impose prohibitions.[48] And yet the European laws, while often curtailing freedom of expression in ways that would never have risen to the level of judicial attention in the United States, have often also done an effective job of curtailing right-wing radicalization. At the present moment Western European democracies seem at least slightly further from the precipice of fascism than the United States, though it would be difficult to make the case that the explanation for this current difference lies in the different limits placed on freedom of expression of extremist ideas in Europe as opposed to the United States. Rather, again, it is the hearing this expression gets at the top that seems to be responsible for the difference: the legitimation, by the highest powers in the land, of extremist ideas, and the consequent erosion of norms that kept these ideas, or so at least we believed, on the margins of society.

Symbols change, as the swastika did when it migrated from Nazi Germany into 1970s British and American counterculture—which had no essential far-right character and was much more often associated with the left—and from there to the websites of the alt-right in the lead-up to Trump's election. The evident irony in the alt-right's proliferation of potent and often bedazzling memes led many to conclude that the alt-right was not literally, directly promoting Nazism, but was, rather, somehow "playing" with it. They are devoted to Hitler in the same way that heavy metal in the 1980s was devoted to Satan, it was said.[49] Andrew Anglin, the founder of the overtly neo-Nazi website *The Daily Stormer*, averred that he drew much of his inspiration from frivolous, gossipy websites like *Gawker*, whose preferred mode of discourse was not hate, but "snark"—that is, chattiness and playful vituperation for its own sake. The white nationalist and anti-Semite Mike Peinovich, host of the podcast the *Daily Shoah*, acknowledges *Seinfeld* as one of his early influences: to the extent that that epoch-making sitcom was "about nothing" and rigorously depicted an amoral universe of self-interested pursuit of meaningless distraction—a universe in which no moral lessons were ever learned, and no episode ever concluded with hugs and reconciliation—it provided a template for the next generation's use of social media for "lulz." But lulz, in turn, were seized upon by some, including Anglin and Peinovich, for old-fashioned rabble-rousing.

The passage of time, and some needed historical perspective—as, for example, what should have been the obvious fact that the Ku Klux Klan, too, had originally introduced its ridiculous hoods and its talk of "wizards" and "dragons" as, in some sense, a joke[50]—have caused this initial judgment to appear as naive wishful thinking. And yet it is not the swastika itself that is the fixed reference point here, staying the same from one era to the other. The swastika had already been through remarkable transformations of context and of charge by the time it ended up in a meme on the armband of Pepe the Frog. No Nazi of the 1930s, certainly, would have been able to make any sense of this, nor recognize in the person who had created it a like-minded fellow. Again, one of the most remarkable transformations in the context of the symbol's display is that its spirit was borrowed from countercultural playfulness of earlier decades, generally more associated with the left. In the serious, nonplayful, articulation of defenses of this playfulness on the part of those involved, there was a common, widespread appeal to the unassailability of free speech—which, again, had also been most commonly associated with the left in the preceding decades, and had even been the rallying cry of much of the 1960s student movement.

By late 2016 there was a widespread public sentiment that "alt-right" was a deplorable euphemism, and that it would be better to call the people associated with this movement by their true name, "neo-Nazis," perhaps, or "white supremacists." But the term really did pick out a new cultural phenomenon, with the rise of the meme warfare that seems to have played a measurable role in Trump's election. The new generation of extreme-right activists had won for themselves the label of "alternative" with their sophisticated irony, their speed-of-light inventiveness, and their seeming commitment to no other objective than to *épater les bourgeois*. This had been an ethos much more strongly associated with the left, and by claiming the "alt-" distinction for themselves, the new extreme right effectively claimed its place as the vanguard of youth counterculture, even as its sensibilities placed it in a legacy whose earlier ancestors were icons of the left. Pepe the Frog owes more to Abbie Hoffman than to William F. Buckley; by certain measures Trump himself has more in common with, say, Wavy Gravy, than with Richard Nixon or Ronald Reagan. The Republican Party is now a *monde à rebours*, a topsy-turvy Dadaist-situationist stunt. As Angela Nagle has perceptively written, "Those who claim that the new right-wing sensibility online today is just more of the same old right, undeserving of attention or differentiation, are wrong . . . It has more in common with the 1968 left's slogan 'It is forbidden to forbid!' than it does with anything most recognize as part of any traditionalist right."[51]

At the present moment, we are witnessing what may turn out to be the complete breakdown of American democracy, for all its shortcomings and unfulfilled promise, with its hard-won and long-thought-out basis in constitutional law, as well as of the international liberal-democratic order that the United States, for better or worse, symbolically served to anchor. A form of insolent demagoguery is poised to replace the old brand, and this as an expression of the popular will of people who do not think of themselves as enemies of American political tradition, but who on the contrary have sought to restore the greatness of it, which they feel has been lost or degraded. This restoration movement has detached itself from the prevailing political tradition of the country that generated it, to the extent that it has embraced irrationalism as its motor and its method. It is a movement that gleefully rejects facts and arguments in favor of feeling, of passionate group identification and the titillating prospect of a fight: in a word, of irrationality.

But the right has no particular monopoly on unreason. As recently as the 1960s it was the left that was busy promoting its own trifecta of self-induced irrationality through sex, drugs, and rock and roll, while at the time conservatives were mostly the parent figures of the hippies, imposing on the younger generation their stifling rules. These rules, most agreed, were generally fairly sound when considered soberly, but the spirit of the revolution was to reject sobriety and judiciousness in search of extreme states and intense experiences, whatever their long-term effects may be. The tables have turned, and dramatically, since the dawn of the twenty-first century. Today it is often the right that is engaged in reckless stunts, while the left, typically, urges caution and hesitation, and top-down enforcement of this moral outlook. From electoral politics to informed-consent rules for campus dating, the left is nothing if not sober, while meanwhile the right has gone out on a bender. In 2016 it was at Trump rallies that we saw what anthropologists of religion call "effervescence," while supporters of Hillary Clinton meanwhile were congratulating themselves for their composure. The Democrats were fighting to preserve the status quo, while the popular sentiment driving the Republican Party was little more than a will to blow things up and to see what emerges from the rubble. The internet troll armies of the alt-right, a decisive force in the success of Trump's campaign, shared more in the spirit of explosive hijinks of Woodstock than they did with the Young Republicans' associations of old. Woodstock was an explosion of irrationality; so were the Nuremberg Rallies. Irrationality is in itself neither left nor right, nor good nor bad.

Why Democracy?

We have for the most part been proceeding in this book on the implicit understanding that democracy is the most rational political system, that the democratic society is the equivalent at the macroscale of the right-thinking rational individual at the microscale. But this is the sort of thing for which one must provide an argument, rather than simply assuming it. In recent years political scientists have taken seriously the possibility that there are other more rational systems that might be tried out, and that any a priori commitment to the superiority of democracy, without empirical data measuring how it fares compared to alternatives, is wholly ungrounded. One alternative system that has garnered a good deal of attention is lottocracy, in which capable citizens are chosen at random to serve in government, much as one would be chosen for jury duty.[52] In such an arrangement, political figures would be significantly less prone to the corruptions of power. The concern that they might be incompetent, in turn, hardly seems relevant in the present era: behind the veil of ignorance, many of us would find it rational to choose a random American citizen to serve as president, when the system that works through election rather than through lottery has proven so flawed as to propel into power a man with as many cognitive limitations and moral impairments as Trump. On these measures, Trump is significantly below average; therefore, it is proven that an electoral system carries with it the same risks as a lottery-based system, while also lacking some of its benefits.

In his book *Against Democracy*,[53] Jason Brennan makes a compelling case that at present the great majority of American voters are either "hobbits" or "hooligans"—that is, they are either "know-nothings" or ideologically committed to one side or the other of an issue for reasons they themselves do not understand, and fundamentally unable to articulate the opposing view in accurate terms, let alone to assess the arguments in favor of the opposing view. In Brennan's view, Americans are simply too ignorant to be entrusted with the responsibility of voting. His favored alternative is not lottocracy, but "epistocracy," in which mechanisms would be put in place to ensure that only people who have a certain level of political literacy, a competence in assessing arguments, statistics, and other social-science data, might be able to vote.

Brennan has thought of nearly all possible objections to his view, and has argued against them preemptively. His arguments are sometimes convincing, though he does not seem to be able to offer a plausible account of how, practically, the transition to such a system could be brought about in a way that does not advance the interests of those already in power, and who stand to gain from the further disenfranchisement of people who are already marginalized and estranged from the political process. Such people, as the history of IQ testing abundantly shows, very often find themselves in the social category of the unintelligent, of the epistemically inferior, but for reasons that have nothing to do with innate aptitude, and certainly not with a freely chosen social identity, but only with the economic and social obstacles to acquiring the sort of cultural capital that, in the end, being held to be intelligent is.

Nor are the only compelling objections to Brennan's argument of a simply practical nature. It is not just that it is unlikely that epistocratic government would work; we would also be giving up a great deal if we were to abandon the idea, inherited from the Enlightenment, that each individual has an inalienable right not to be dominated, and to participate in his or her own government. Rights of this sort, many have believed, are "trumps," on an earlier and more innocent connotation of this monosyllable, which has it that they *cannot* be traded, as if on a stock exchange, for something that promises to be more efficient. The warning against such a trade appears particularly compelling when we consider just how mercurial are our society's ever-shifting standards of excellence or accomplishment that might be interpreted as qualifying a given individual for inclusion within the epistocratic elite. At present, we already have an unelected and nonrepresentative epistocracy of sorts, but it is one made up almost entirely of grown men with the moral and intellectual depth of seventh-graders: the elite class of tech-industry nobles, namely, who often seem to have the power to plow right through or ignore existing laws and public institutions in order to achieve their own goals. They have managed to convince many people, including many politicians (witness Mark Zuckerberg's senate hearings in early 2018) that they know enough and are responsible enough to handle a significant proportion of the responsibilities many had once thought best left to the democratic process.

Herman Melville warned in 1857 that in a country where all the wolves have been killed off, the foxes will thrive. By the mid-nineteenth century European settlers in America no longer lived in constant fear for their lives, but they had a new existential worry to occupy them from birth to death: that of being taken for a ride by the frauds, charlatans, carnival barkers, hustlers, kayfabe illusionists, and confidence men who had rapidly populated the land. The metamorphic appearances of the confidence-man on Melville's Mississippi steamboat seem

smart, seem as though they might be good candidates for the epistocratic elite of their era. They seem worthy of confidence. But with their
ledgers embossed with the names of the Black Rapids Coal Company
or of the Seminole Widow and Orphan Asylum, which may or may not
be real, these characters anticipate nothing so much as the strange hybrid of philanthropy and self-serving ambition that we have learned to
expect from those who have come out on top in the most recent era of
American capitalism. It is naive in the extreme to believe that we can
plausibly separate out our judgment of "intelligence," of epistocratic
merit, from the general "big man" anthropology that has shaped American history, and that again and again conflates coming out on top with
"smarts."

The dream of conducting politics only in "adequate knowledge situations" has been around for a long time. For Leibniz, as we have already
seen, the locus of the specialized knowledge was to be not an elite
group of people, but rather machines, or at least formal processes that
could be either written out on paper or instantiated by data-processing
engines of some sort. For Brennan these will be human beings, but also
presumably aided by far more powerful engines than Leibniz ever
imagined. What prevented Leibniz's vision from taking hold is, first of
all, that even those with adequate political knowledge might not
choose to consistently make their choices on the basis of the knowledge, might reject the results their engines give them; and, second, that
the passions and fantasies of the know-nothings are going to continue
to complicate political matters, whether the political system is one in
which they have the right to vote notwithstanding their ignorance, or
whether they are deprived of this right. The know-nothings might become gate-crashers at any moment.

Brennan envisions a scenario in which the nonvoting majority
might pass its time going to sports events or to Applebee's. But this
does not seem to exhaust the range of what the masses do, or have ever
done, under any political arrangement. Even if the demand for political
participation might decrease when times are good, and even if we
might expect that a well-run epistocracy would ensure that things remain more or less good, the future is nonetheless simply too precarious,

for reasons often quite beyond human control, to permit us to expect that the nonepistocrats will be content to linger in their booth at Applebee's forever.

What the rise of the internet shows, with all of the disastrous consequences of the absence of democratic deliberation over how it is going to be used, is that such deliberation still holds out the best hope for ordering society in a rational way conducive to the greatest thriving of the most people. The internet was unleashed by self-appointed experts, who knew how to engineer, but had very little ability to reason about the social consequences of what they were doing. Many of them already think of themselves as epistocrats, of sorts, as sufficiently qualified to take over where failed democracy has left off. But the engineers have proven themselves no better able to make good decisions about how to order society than any Trump-voting denizen of Applebee's. Restoring the ideal of universal democratic participation, even only as an ideal, and restoring along with it rigorous civic education, remains the best hope for staving off—indeed reversing the rise of—both the illiberal populism of "real America" and the new technocratic anti-Enlightenment forces emerging out of Silicon Valley.

CHAPTER SEVEN

The Human Beast; or, the Internet

➤➤➤➤➤

An Escargotic Commotion

The old world, too, has its foxes, and long before the emergence of the internet as a technological reality, they were already there to sell people on the dream of it. In Paris in 1850, a young man, a former law student and radical candidate for the Constitutional Assembly by the name of Jules Allix, publishes in the feuilleton of *La Presse* a short article describing a new invention.[1] He is not himself the inventor, but is only speaking, he claims, on behalf of his associates, Monsieur Jacques Toussaint Benoît from Hérault near Montpellier, and a man identified only as "Monsieur Biat-Chrétien, the American" (later referred to simply as "Biat"). The discovery is of a "pasilalinic sympathetic compass" that will facilitate "universal and instantaneous communication of thought, at any distance whatever."

Allix dissimulates, stalls, takes an inordinate amount of time to tell us what this machine actually does. He moves through a survey of theological positions on magnetism. The distinguished men of Notre Dame, he tells us, are prepared to see this power of nature not as a trick or an illusion, but as the crowning mystery of God's creation, a constant announcement, in the seeking out of metal by metal, of divine wisdom and might. If we are prepared to admit gravity, why not other forces too? Why, for example, should we not admit the "galvano-magnetico-mineralo-animalo-adamical sympathy" that governs the pasilalinic sympathetic compass? Unlike the electrical telegraph, we are eventually told, the compass has no conductive wires, but only two unconnected and portable apparatuses, containing a voltaic pile, a wooden or metal wheel ringed with copper-sulfate-lined metal troughs. And, in each of these troughs, a snail.

A snail? Allix dwells in excessive detail on irrelevant points, and breezes right past relevant ones. He checks off shibboleths of the most recent science—Steinheil's advances in telegraphy in Munich, Matteucci's in Pisa—and he front-loads the technical terminology like *Star Trek*'s Captain Sulu explaining the impossible physics of hyperdrive. After long digression, however, we are offered a bare-bones description of how the machine is to work. He explains, first of all, the natural phenomenon, observable only in snails, of "sympathizing," which is to say of creating an indivisible bond through copulation:

> After the separation of the snails that have sympathized together, a sort of fluid is released between them, for which the earth is the conductor, which develops and unfolds, so to speak, like the nearly invisible thread of the spider or that of a silkworm, which one could unfold and elongate in an indefinite space without breaking it, but with this one difference, that the escargotic fluid is completely invisible and that it has as much speed in space as the electrical fluid, and that it would be by means of this fluid that the snails produce and communicate the commotion of which I have spoken.[2]

Why is this sympathy found only in snails? Allix does not say explicitly, though he does remind us that snails are hermaphrodites, "which is to say male and female at the same time."[3] We are perhaps invited here to recall the myth, or something like it, of the original androgyne, attributed to Socrates by Plato in the *Symposium*. In the beginning every human being had four arms and four legs, two heads, and two sets of genitals, and so every human being lacked nothing, and longed for nothing, and the body was in perfect communication with itself. To be male and female at once is to have it all; it appears that, at least in snails, this perfection is distilled into the sexual fluids, so that, once these are exchanged, each hermaphroditic snail now shares in the other's being completely.

But let us return to the mechanics of the thing. Each snail is matched with its corresponding snail, in the corresponding wooden box, with which it has previously sympathized, so to speak, and with which it, therefore, remains in perfect and instantaneous sympathetic contact.

Each pair of snails represents a single letter of the French alphabet, and when one of them is manipulated, it triggers an "escargotic commotion" that causes its partner snail to move. Successive manipulations of different snails in one box thus spell out words in the motions of the snails of the other box. Allix promises that with this device "all men will be able to correspond instantaneously with one another, at whatsoever distance they are placed, man to man, or several men simultaneously, at every corner of the world, and this without recourse to the conductive wires of electronic communication, but with the sole aid of what is basically a portable machine."[4] The machine will serve as the basis of a global system of instant wireless communication: an internet of snails.

Prior to this public appearance, our salesman and communard had been in hiding, following the 1848 "Days of June," a popular revolt in Paris in response to the closing of the National Workshops that had been set up after the previous February's revolution to provide training to the jobless.[5] He would be arrested one year later in connection with another uprising, and soon after would find his way into the company of the occultist and charlatan Jacques Toussaint Benoît, who had been cooking up a plan to gain sponsorship for the snail compass. He sought to interest the investor Hippolyte Triat, born Antoine Hypolitte Trilhac, who had recently founded the first modern athletic gymnasium in Paris.

On October 2, 1850, the experiment described by Allix in his article for *La Presse* was carried out in Benoît's Paris apartment. Messieurs Benoît, Allix, and Triat were all present, and if Allix's account is to be believed, Biat was there as well, at least in a modality that would later come to be known as "teleconferencing," from an undisclosed location in America. Allix was far more impressed than Triat. The prospective investor had been installed with one of the two compasses behind a curtain, with Allix and his own compass on the other side, while Benoît had set himself up between them to observe. It is not clear exactly what happened, but it appears that Benoît found a constant supply of pretexts for walking back and forth, on both sides of the curtain, influencing Triat's actions and gleaning hints and signs in a less than rigorously scientific way. Triat was indignant, and insisted that the experiment be tried out again. Benoît agreed, only to disappear into the night before Triat could have the satisfaction of exposing this dastardly fraud. A few years later, hiding from the authorities on the island of Jersey, Allix will become a footnote to the biography of Victor Hugo, when he will once again attempt to communicate by means of escargotic force, to the great amusement of the participants in Hugo's "talking table" séances.[6]

Allix's article in *La Presse* seems to have appeared at some point between the initial trial and Benoît's disappearance. He took on the task of drumming up public support with a dazzling display of salesmanship, erudition, and gumption. Perhaps most remarkable of all, in our present age of nanotechnology, was his promise that, although Benoît's first models of the machines were more than two meters high, eventually the public could expect to enjoy more convenient models, transformed into stylish furniture or even jewelry made of wood or metal or any material one wished, and would be found everywhere, from government offices to the tops of ladies' dressers, to the watch-chains around their waists. The original iteration had been built to accommodate snails representing every letter or character of every known writing system in the world, while future streamlined models, made for the larger public, would contain only a convenient twenty-five troughs, one for each letter of the French alphabet. And as each trough can be filled by any species of gastropod whatsoever, and as there are many species that are very small indeed, no larger than the head of a pin, soon, Allix assures us, there will be pasilalinic sympathetic compasses no larger than pocket watches, and ordinary men and women will carry them along as they go about their daily errands, from time to time sending off quick escargotic missives—texts, if you will—to their friends and loved ones down the street and around the world.

Allix promises that by means of the compass there will soon be "electronic newspapers, electronic mail,"[7] spreading across the entire world, as if by magic, at a minimal cost. There will not just be a "national press," in which the news is published in the *départements* at the same hour as in Paris, but readers will be able to browse "the English press, the German press, and that of all the countries of the world."[8] The activity of government, too, will be translated into the compass, and the walls of the parliament buildings "turned inside out," as invisible, dematerialized orators are "infinitely multiplied before an innumerably large audience"; their words will circulate "as rapidly as thought to all points in the world, thanks to the mysterious agent of the invisible sympathetic fluid, bringing with them not only the passion that drives the orator, but also the beating of his heart and the least vibrations of his soul!"[9] Allix quickly reels himself back in, reassumes his scientific composure: "I must remember," he says, "that I am not to give in to enthusiasm."[10]

The Modern Shiva

There are many important lessons we might draw from the true story of this great nineteenth-century confidence man. One is that we, too, are not to give in to enthusiasm, or, to use the synonym preferred by Kant in his lampooning of Swedenborg (see chapter 3), we are not to give in to spirit-seeing, to hastily concluding that the information we glean through our senses, increasingly mediated by technology, is the evidence of any new transcendence of our basic plight as human beings. Another lesson is, surely, that there is a long prehistory of the internet, which we would do well to understand if we wish to adequately understand the present moment. The preexistence of a technology as aspiration, as fantasy, in the absence of technical feasibility, reveals continuity where presentists prefer to think of new technologies as so transformative as to "change everything." According to his report, two of the first words that Allix caused to be transmitted through his internet of snails, between Europe and America, were *LUMIÈRE DIVINE*: "divine light." The real internet, however, the one built up from fiber-optic cables rather than escargotic fluid, has been much more successful at trafficking darkness and confusion.

The definitive transformation of the internet, from vehicle of light to vehicle of darkness, may be dated to 2016. That is the year in which the major social-media companies began slowly and belatedly to acknowledge how underequipped they were to handle the enormous new responsibilities for the preservation of democracy and of civil society that they had unwittingly been handed. That is the year, too, that a new sort of "hybrid warfare" waged largely through the internet came into public consciousness as a new reality and a growing problem. Russian spy agencies had by now got in on the playful fun of dark and sinister meme making. Part of Russia's intervention in the US election included placing ads on Facebook that spanned the political spectrum: some were in support of Black Lives Matter against police brutality; others supported "Blue Lives Matter," defending the bravery of police officers who put themselves in harm's way. Some were in support of crackdowns on illegal immigration, while others promoted LGBT rights, including one meme that invited social-media users to color in a muscular-hunk version of Bernie Sanders at the beach.[11]

What exactly was the strategy here? Some people have taken this willingness to play all sides as evidence that the Russian regime could not have been straightforwardly pro-Trump. But it seems to miss the point to suggest that that regime's responsibility in Trump's victory must have had anything straightforward about it at all, or that its support of Trump must have been in the same spirit as the support expressed by a misguided but nevertheless sincere American voter. The purpose of the Russian operation was to sow disorder and to weaken the American political establishment, and its agents understood that supporting left causes at the same time as they supported Trump was the best way to do this. In this Russia was following the exact strategy already worked out during the Greek crisis, in which its agents supported both the far-left Syriza Party and the neo-Nazi Golden Dawn.[12] They did not want the Republicans to triumph as an end in itself; they wanted chaos to triumph, and here they clearly succeeded. Unlike misguided American voters, they understood that Trump is not in any meaningful sense a Republican, but rather an agent of chaos.

And so the Russian intelligence agents took to social media, or, more precisely, they paid young Russian college graduates to work for their cause by farming likes out of a troll farm in St. Petersburg. And soon enough Russian trolls were successfully goading Americans on Twitter and Facebook into debating, sharing, and liking content on all manner of distractious hot-button issues. At least one social-media user by the name of Jenna Abrams turned out not to exist at all, but to have been invented as a false identity for one or several Russian trolls.[13] Before being exposed she had succeeded in riling Americans into engaging with her on the meaning of the Confederate flag; on Rachel Dolezal, the white American woman who had been outed after some years of living her life as an African American; and on "manspreading," the recently concocted transgression of men on public transportation who do not hold their legs sufficiently close together.

Social pressure, largely generated by social media, had by 2015 pushed New York City to make sitting with your legs too far apart an arrest-worthy offense, and that same year the Police Reform Organizing Project reported that at least two unidentified Latino men, with other outstanding warrants, had been arrested on the pretext of having manspread, after midnight, in a presumably fairly empty subway car.[14] This application of the force of law in the name of a newly emerging social norm was problematic in the extreme. Yet in social media, any acknowledgment of anything that looks like an objective dilemma is more or less impossible—as, for example, that there might be a conflict between the imperative to eliminate patriarchy as manifested in the microaggressions of male fellow citizens, on the one hand, and, on the other, the imperative to combat police persecution of marginalized communities. Acknowledgment of the complexities of reality is impossible, as social-media algorithms funnel our views into binarily opposed options, rather than inducing us to reflect and to doubt, or to "like" in a qualified way. And so the social-media-based left came down decisively in favor of wiping manspreading from the face of the earth, and doing its best not to see the downside of this campaign.

A society that spends its time talking about manspreading cannot be doing well. Jenna Abrams's role in keeping that particular conversation going was part of a broader effort to ensure that public discourse not improve, at least long enough to whisk into office a new American president who is himself the personification of this sickness, whose own orally produced speech sounds, in style and grammar and syntax, more or less echo his textual interventions in social media. The intelligence operation did not require any ingenious back-channel maneuvering, or any intelligence at all of the sort that we have traditionally expected spy agencies to excel in. In order to do their part in making a social-media celebrity the president of the United States (note, there is no claim here that the role of such efforts was the exclusive cause of his victory; it is yet another lamentable feature of social-media debate that complex events must have monocausal explanations), foreign intelligence operatives had only to get into the spirit of social media itself, to master the English lingo, to become fluent in meme making, and in general to adopt and promote the norms of discourse that in any case had already triumphed on social media in the United States. Russian intelligence agents did not invent manspreading—on the Moscow metro, in fact, a man is much more likely to be confronted for the opposite transgression of crossing his legs, which is perceived as feminine (I should know: I myself have been assaulted in Moscow for this very thing). But they did understand how to seize on this American invention and use it for the further corrosion of public discourse.

Nor, of course, did Russian intelligence come up with the new economy of likes, but this did not prevent its agents from incentivizing the work of its trolls by measuring their success in this new quasi-currency. As one troll told an interviewer about their work, "You should always write that sodomy is a sin, and that will bring you a couple dozen 'likes.'" This economy was devised in the United States (the inventor of the like button, Justin Rosenstein, born in 1983, has deleted his own Facebook account in part out of concerns about its addictive power).[15] But unlike the attempts in the 1990s of American economists and others to export economic expertise to a system that did not wish to receive it, like-seeking, though of course only in its early stages, appears ideally poised to take over the world.

It is particularly well suited to regimes, and to those sectors of society that serve them, that are intent on fostering chaos, precisely because, where likes are being sought, the goal of tolerance and understanding has almost certainly already been abandoned. In online discourse, to cite a well-known critic, "measured speech is punished by not getting clicked on, invisible Facebook and Google algorithms steer you towards content you agree with, and nonconforming voices stay silent for fear of being flamed or trolled or unfriended."[16] To certain holdouts from the old world, these punishments might seem to have to do only with such relatively unserious matters as our circles of friends and our self-esteem. But the emerging reality—a reality the trolls know how to exploit—is one in which what gets liked, and what gets flamed or trolled, is not just a concern that we have in our personal lives and that we leave behind when we think about political and economic matters. What gets liked or clicked or trolled, rather, is now, suddenly, at the very heart of politics and economics.

The internet is destroying everything. In the aftermath of its Shiva-like arrival, the rest of the world, all that was here before, can easily appear as a ruin. It has destroyed or is in the process of destroying long-familiar objects: televisions, newspapers, musical instruments, clocks, books. It is also destroying institutions: stores, universities, banks, movie theaters, democracy. On the plus side, some findings indicate that it is even bringing down teen-pregnancy rates, at least in the United Kingdom.[17] The Hindu god just invoked in comparison, often given the epithet "the destroyer," is not for that reason an entirely negative force. It is good and natural to raze the old, to slough off what is no longer vital or useful, as hunter-gatherer cultures understood already in deep pre-history when they mastered the practice of controlled burning. Fire, in fact, seems like the most suitable comparison in the prior history of technology: when our hominid ancestors learned to use it at least 400,000 years ago, the suite of changes they initiated was immense.[18] It brought cooking and heating, and it also brought countless deaths and immeasurable environmental destruction. It made us what we are, and the internet is already in the course of making us what we will be.

If we think the current transformations are unjust, or excessive, this cannot be because they constitute a break from the general course of human history since the Paleolithic. It is, rather, because they are a suddenly punctuated jerk (to invoke once again the language of Stephen Jay Gould) in the same direction in which we were already creeping—a change that has taken place without any collective decision having been made about it, in an era in which we had not long before come to believe that great transformations require, and deserve, collective rational deliberation, followed by a vote, followed by citizen oversight. The fact that there has never been any question of such a procedure for determining the way the internet is to be incorporated into our lives is in itself a clear indication of how much more powerful it is than liberal democracy. The internet trumps liberal democracy, as fire surely burned right through the myths and practices of hominid groups that had previously got by without it.

This in turn helps to explain why, even though it was still being heralded just a decade ago as the bringer of a new liberal-democratic utopia in the very near future, when Twitter was still winning awards for its role in bringing the Arab Spring,[19] it nevertheless could reveal itself to be doing exactly the opposite in such a short period of time. After all, its destructiveness has consisted largely in amplifying the very powers that had long been taken to be the bedrock of liberal democracy—most notably free speech. Billions of people now have a sort of free speech, in the sense that they have the power to say more or less whatever they think they want to say, and generally to get at least a few likes for it.

But they have this power in a new and mutated form, where it is disconnected from any obviously binding standard of truth, or any expectation that it will be deployed for the purpose of sincere communication, that computers, in sum, will be used in anything like the spirit Leibniz had in mind with his irenic-rationalist hortation "Let us compute!" The new free speech is free, moreover, only in that it seems to flow directly from the desire of the speaker (or writer, or tweeter). Once it is released, however, it is channeled by secret algorithms (on which, again, we have made no collective decision and in relation to which we have no oversight) along pathways where it is practically guaranteed not to bring any more light, human or divine, to anyone regarding the subject of interest. It will serve only to reinforce group solidarity in an online community, or to accost and attack an outsider to that group, usually by means of ad hominems, and in total ignorance of the past few millennia's hard-won effort to lay down rules for the avoidance of fallacies in our reasoning and communicating.

Online discourse feels free, to the extent that it is pleasing to the individual who puts it out there, but it is more or less always channeled either down the path of like-seeking, or down the path of trolling. This pseudofreedom affords authoritarian leaders the appearance of at least a vestigial concern to protect the core values of liberal democracy. As long as individual citizens continue to believe that democratic citizenship has attained its full realization in an unending online argument about manspreading, the autocrats, as they say, have won.

Nor is it the case that within a bubble, that is, within an algorithmically generated imagined community, all is peaceful and stable. Bubbles are fragile, and soap gets in your mouth. This is particularly so when other members of the community are constantly seeking to wash out the mouths of those whose speech they deem insufficiently pure. This dynamic seems to be intrinsic to left-wing debate online, to the so-called call-out culture that reigns there. As the critic Mark Fisher wrote, this culture is "driven by a priest's desire to excommunicate and condemn, an academic-pedant's desire to be the first to be seen to spot a mistake, and a hipster's desire to be one of the in-crowd."[20] Thus, to return to the issue of manspreading, it is not just that so many people are exhausting themselves arguing with Russian trolls pretending to be American conservatives who think it is a man's right and an anatomical necessity that he spread his legs as widely as he wishes. They are also exhausting themselves—and needlessly and destructively hardening themselves where obviously some flexibility is in order—to the extent that they are perpetually seeking out and condemning any recognition, however hesitant, that sometimes legitimate desiderata are mutually exclusive.

When unorthodox views are essayed online, the enforcers of the relevant orthodox community are ready to pounce, and to make the doubter know she or he is not in the in-crowd. This may be a small punishment, compared to public stocks or flogging, but it adds up to real-world effects. It is not the Cultural Revolution, but that does not mean that its spirit is not fundamentally Maoist. The fact that Maoism can thrive at a substate level, and have real political consequences, even in a world that is governed by right-wing populism, is a significant lesson, and one Mao himself surely could not have predicted. We are in a peculiar predicament, in which what are effectively purges are taking place at a substate level, in the name of a nominally left-wing ideal of redistributive justice, while at the helm of state, meanwhile, we have in the United States some ill-defined species of right-wing populism. This is an unusual state of affairs, and one might suspect that the substate actors leading the purges are acting on behalf of the state in a way that they themselves do not understand.

Observations of this sort are, however, for the most part met with denial. When Jonathan Haidt argued that the right wing in political power and the left wing on campus are two manifestations of the same threat, he was mocked on Twitter by Jeet Heer of the *New Republic*: " 'The Weimar Republic faced two threats: the Nazi Party and the musical theories of T. W. Adorno'. You see how silly this sounds?"[21] Without wishing to support the entirety of Haidt's argument, we may at least say with confidence that reactions such as Heer's are disingenuous in the extreme. There were also Nazi music theorists who, by themselves, did no real harm; conversely, music theory is not the only thing Marxism was being used to mobilize in the 1930s in Europe. There were also show trials, summary executions, ethnic cleansings. Nor is the boundary between theory and political injustice so clear. Adorno did no harm, but Maxim Gorky certainly did: he managed to scrape through the insanity of the Stalinist purges by vomiting up just the right spew of socialist-realist platitudes, and by looking the other way when his old friend and protégé Isaak Babel was hauled off and shot for his inability to talk the same talk (see chapter 4). And today, online, it is typically the most cutthroat and unflinching personalities who thrive, the Robespierres and the Berias. Virtually no one whose public reputation was built up entirely in social media can be said to be noteworthy rather than notorious. It is an ugly dystopia and has utterly failed to deliver on its promised goods.

We may well be at an early point in the history of the internet analogous to the moment when, after just having seized a lightning-struck branch and used it to keep warm for a night, an entire hominid encampment was burned down to ash. The warmth felt good initially, and then it didn't feel good anymore. After that first night's tragedy, human beings could of course have had no idea of all that was to come, all the violence and innovation, all the warmth and death. The great difference is that between the mastery of fire and the rise of the internet human beings came to aspire to a form of collective decision making, based on reason, and the internet seems now to be playing a central role in the rapid decline of that aspiration, even though until very recently it was hoped that the internet would strengthen and build up democratic institutions rather than weaken them.

Nothing Human Is Alien

Since the end of World War II, and the reckoning with their violent potentials that liberal democracies, not least the Federal Republic of Germany, have had to undertake, a particular anthropological model of the human being has come to predominate in much popular wisdom. According to this model most of us are neither fundamentally evil nor fundamentally good; rather, in order to maintain our goodness, we depend upon circumstances in which we are not invited, pressured, or encouraged to do evil things. This insight is a corollary of Hannah Arendt's perhaps overcited thesis concerning the "banality of evil": those who carry out evil deeds in social circumstances that make these deeds possible are doing so not monstrously, but banally.[22] The functionary who signs off on papers that will assuredly send people to the death camps is operating, often, under the illusion that this is just normal procedure, for if it were not, how could there be such clean and correct forms awaiting signature?

In a comparative ethological perspective as well, human violence is banal. A recent study shows that our species is fairly average among other primates with respect to its murderousness, though primates as a category are far more violent than other mammals.[23] Killing members of our own kind appears to be part of our behavioral repertoire as a species, for reasons that long precede us. This does not mean we should accept it, as some have supposed in setting up a false incompatibility between evolutionary explanations of human beings on the one hand, and aspirations to social improvement on the other. But it does help us to identify the depth of the problem: our violence is not a result of some recent degradation of social circumstances, but part of who we are.

There are also many cases in which "ordinary" people find themselves in circumstances they experience as extreme, unlike the Nazi functionary who experiences his job as routine, and who enter into a phase in which the usual moral rules that have previously shaped their lives are suspended or reversed. The examples are seared into our childhood imaginations, in stories we read and stories we invent. Consider, for example, Melville's description of drawing lots in a life-boat, to determine who will be eaten and who will get to eat, in his remarkable 1855 novella *Benito Cereno*, or any number of accounts, veridical or fictional, of wartime atrocities. There is nothing banal about devouring your slaughtered mate after hundreds of days drifting at sea, but you might just do it anyway.

Both the everyday evil of Nazi Germany and the exceptional transgressions of the shipwrecked are species, however, of the rather generic wisdom offered by the evil Noah Cross in the 1975 film *Chinatown*: "You see, Mr. Gittes, most people never have to face the fact that at the right time and right place, they're capable of anything." Cross, again, is evil: what he himself was capable of, and what he is here admitting to Jack Nicholson's character, the detective Jake Gittes, is that he has raped his daughter.

Surely we are not all capable of *that*. Or are we? Not all of us have daughters, and some of us are ourselves daughters who might be fending off rapist fathers, so if we are "all" capable of it, this capability is something rather more abstract than simply being among our present immediate options. Roman Polanski, himself a child rapist, was likely thinking in part of what he knew himself to be capable of, in a narrow and factual sense, when he approved this line of dialogue. But Cross's insight should not be simply waved off by upright watchers whose first inclination is to reply, "Speak for yourself!" It is, after all, a variation of Terence's famous adage *Humani nihil a me alienum puto* (Nothing human is alien to me).[24] We usually take this as an expression of the Roman playwright's liberality of spirit (in fact it is a character in one of his plays, and not Terence himself who says it), his unwillingness to condemn other human beings for being different or unfamiliar to him. But child rape and incest are human too, in the straightforward sense that there are, in reality, human beings who have committed such transgressions. So child rape and incest are not alien to Terence. Does this mean that he has committed them, or is likely to commit them? No, not necessarily, but only that he in fact has the resources within him, as a human being, to imagine his way into the inner life of someone who has—that he is not of a different nature or species from the child rapist; the two do not exist across some great ontological divide from one another.

The insight is not just Polanskian and Terentian. It is also deeply, fundamentally Christian. In this latter version it is articulated as "original sin." Why is it that, according to traditional Christian theology, an infant who has not yet had the chance to do much of anything at all is nonetheless held to be a sinner? Because it is a human being, and nothing human is alien to it. Augustine wondered in his *Confessions* whether he, as a baby, was not already putting his sinfulness on display with his unrestrained displays of desire for the breast, and with his petulant, self-absorbed tantrums when his desires were not satisfied. This behavior is, certainly, a sign of what is to come in the life of an adult sinner, but even if it were not manifested, even if the infant were, as they say, perfectly angelic, it would still be a sinner, simply in virtue of its participation in the human essence. From a Christian point of view, this is good news and bad news: it is a heavy burden to come into the world with all of the sins of all of our fellow humans attached to us, but it also shifts the criteria, radically, that determine warrant for love. Since we all have original sin, it makes no sense to deem an exceptionally well-behaved boy or girl somehow more worthy of love, or of eternal salvation, than any other. From a humanist point of view, it is likewise both good news and bad news: we can, through the insight that nothing human is alien to us, cultivate liberality of spirit, learn not to judge too swiftly, find ourselves motivated to defend political egalitarianism. At the same time the insight forces us to recognize that the horrible crimes we read about online are committed not by monsters of a different species, but by people more or less like us.

In neither its Christian nor its humanist iteration does the insight enjoy much popularity today, and least of all on the internet. In the dispensations of supposed justice that occur online, verdicts are as total as they are swift. Twitter outrage and other forms of online mobbing typically occur with no attempt at all to probe into the mind-set of one's opponent. This mobbing is underlain by a social ontology that subdivides humanity into fundamentally discrete kinds, where whatever is characteristic of another kind of human being is by definition alien, and where there is virtually no recognition of any broader genus of humanity in which the apparent alienness of another subgroup of human beings is resolved. We cannot write, or think, or imagine, or know anything at all across the chasms that separate us by race, gender, sexual orientation, and other common variables—and this notwithstanding the ostensible commitment, within this new mentality, to intersectionality, to the idea that we may be many things at once. Only certain variables can intersect, the thinking goes, while others are contrary or contradictory, and so mutually exclude one another.

This is a dismal state of affairs, and from even a slight distance it is self-evidently a symptom, within the online self-identified left, of the same historical moment that has propelled Trump into power. This is not to resort to the sort of facetious excuse making that we heard from Trump himself after the neo-Nazi violence in Charlottesville, in which he sought to blame "both sides." It is only to seek to diagnose the current political moment in the United States in a way that does not take the individual actors and interest groups as if they were on entirely separate causal trajectories, but rather sees them as, so to speak, adapting to the same ecosystem. And that ecosystem—with the perpetual forgetfulness of the mass media, lurching always from one outrage to another, with no cumulative lessons ever learned, with the identitarian mobs on social media exacting swift justice on perceived enemies who are in truth their brothers and sisters—is greatly polluted.

More Gender Trouble

Nowhere is this pollution more evident than in recent online conversation around gender. Here, many of the claims that are circulating might be most appropriately compared not with creation science, as discussed in chapter 5, but with flat-earth theory, in view of their extreme departure not only from prevailing causal theories of how the world got to be the way it is, but also from the most basic and immediately evident facts of human existence.

As of August 2018, Judith Butler, who has for decades stood atop the hierarchy of academic feminist theory, finds herself on the unpopular side of a sexual-harassment scandal involving one of her peers, and it may be that the process of her displacement, and of the succession of a new generation of theorists, has begun. However, up until just one month ago or so, as I write this, her word could still be cited in some circles as absolute authority, and few were made uneasy by this sort of argumentum ad auctoritatem. Consider, for example, this, from a recent online "syllabus": "[Judith] Butler proves that the distinction between sex and gender does not hold. A sexed body cannot signal itself as different sexually without cultural gender categories, and the idea that sex comes before cultural factors (which are believed to be only overlaid on top of sex), is disproven in this book. Gender is performance, there's no solid universal gender basis beneath these always creative performances. There is no concrete sexed body without constructed human categories to interpret it."[25]

But what happens when we move, as empirical science is prepared to do, from the question of human sex to the question of sex in the broader world of animals and plants? We know, for example, that the male of some species of anglerfish (e.g., *Haplophryne mollis*) is several times smaller and vastly weaker than its female counterpart. In order to mate, the only option it has is to bite into the side of the female's body, to pass its seminal material into her bloodstream, and then slowly to wither away, eventually becoming a tiny appendage of its polyandrous spouse.

Now, is there anything constructed about this? Anglerfish sexual dimorphism is extreme, but it is not different in principle from that of mammals. And if we insist that anglerfish reproduction is just a natural fact, while human sex and sex difference are constructed, then we are more or less explicitly claiming that human beings are not animals alongside others, but that their essence is nonnatural in origin. This is a fundamentally conservative stance to take, and Butlerites share it with traditional Christian theology, among other currents of thought. Butlerism buys its sex constructionism by means of a deepened commitment to species exceptionalism—and at a terrible exchange rate.

The "syllabus" says that Butler has *proven* that the distinction between sex and gender does not hold, while gender is constructed. Therefore, sex is constructed. But again, does this include ape sex, anglerfish sex, and so forth, or only human sex? And if only human sex, does it follow that human beings are not part of the same natural order that includes apes and anglerfish? None of these questions are meant to suggest that sexual dimorphism in the animal world is simple, obvious, or universal. We know there is tremendous variety out there, and this variety is also sometimes invoked by neo-Butlerites as biological evidence for the constructedness of human sexual binarism. But invoking this evidence, they only complicate matters. If it is true that a number of species of lizards can switch from sexual reproduction to asexual parthenogenesis in the absence of suitable mates, then there is at least some natural fact about lizards and sex. But the neo-Butlerite claim is that there is no natural fact about humans and sex ("there is no concrete sexed body"). What is the difference between humans and lizards that justifies this distinction?

Orangutans show not so much a high degree of sexual dimorphism between males and females of the species as a dimorphism between males: some mature males get "flanges," that strange condition that makes their faces into enormous discs, while others remain as they all had looked in adolescence, which is also the way female orangutans look across the life cycle. Look at a flanged male orangutan and try to insist there is something performative about *that*.

In the history of hominid evolution, dimorphism is clearly diminishing. Males of the *Australopithecus* genus were on average around 50 percent larger than females. In modern *Homo sapiens*, the disparity is closer to 15 percent. That is still not insignificant. (It is, for one thing, enough to yield the physical difference that gets translated into social reality as patriarchy.) A moderately well-trained physical anthropologist can look at the pelvis of a human skeleton and tell you fairly accurately whether it belonged to a man or a woman. The pelvis, like the living male orangutan's flanges, is a plain giveaway. Let us grant that *all* of the social and symbolic dimensions of womanhood that have been assigned to bearers of the one sort of pelvis throughout history have been completely and utterly arbitrary. It cannot follow from this that the perception of an anatomical difference so deep as to often be evident in the skeleton is nothing more than an illusion.

Perhaps in contemporary reflection on sex and gender there is a dim awareness of the past few million years of evolution, of the progress we have made from 50 percent to 15 percent, and a sense that this trend toward nondimorphism can be hastened by collective political will. Perhaps it can be. Still, flat denial of dimorphism is an expression of how one would like things to be, not a description of how things are. And when dimorphism is finally reduced to 0 percent, and reproduction is taken care of by technicians in laboratories, and patriarchy is banished to the past, the claim that there is now no sex difference will still be a factual claim about certain entities in nature (entities that have arrived in their present condition by a combination of evolution and technocultural innovation).

Imagine that our species had developed in such a way that males were not on average 15 percent larger than females, but, like the *Lamprologus callipterus* species of fish, sixty times or so larger. Suppose that nonetheless we managed to develop into a technologically complex, liberal-democratic society that put a high premium on individual thriving, on freedom and equality. Suppose that within that society a school of thought and a political movement emerged that held that, even though men are sixty times larger than women, both sexes nonetheless have the same basic neural equipment to thrive, to the extent that their physical dimensions permit, in more or less the same way.

But suppose then another school of thought emerged, which said that this first one did not go far enough, and insisted that men are not actually sixty times larger than women, and that it is only a result of ideological indoctrination that we have believed this up until now. "But my mate can fit only a single tip of an antenna into our home," some traditionalist woman might protest, "while I can swim around inside freely. He keeps accidentally eating me and having to spit me back out because I'm too small for him to detect, while when I'm with him he literally obstructs everything else from my field of vision. I think he's gaining weight—at this point it takes me more than a day just to circumnavigate him. Surely I'm not imagining *that*." And then of course she would be mobbed on Twitter for these heresies.

The thought experiment starts to founder when we note that such a species would never have "homes," and almost certainly not monogamous mates either, while our species in turn would never have developed into a complex, liberal-democratic, egalitarian society, or at least have tried to do so, if males had been, or had remained, sixty times larger than females. Culture, with the innovative technological workarounds that it has come up with to break the stranglehold of the sexual division of labor, and all the other ways it has been able to some degree to assure that biology, for men and women alike, is not destiny, has been the principal motor of our motion toward nondimorphism over the past few million years. Behind a veil of ignorance, you could surely know in advance that a species in which the males are sixty times larger than the females is not a species with automated payroll systems, cosmetic surgery, Twitter, or its own version of Judith Butler.

Again, it is likely that some dim awareness that this is the direction culture is pushing quite unsurprisingly leads some to suppose that culture must be pushed in turn, and we must eradicate whatever similarities remain to the *L. callipterus*. This is an understandable desire, but one also feels the need to warn against undue rashness. Biology may not be exclusive destiny, but it does dictate the terms under which the will is free to do its work. Will is not exclusive destiny either, and you are setting yourself up for ideological extremism, followed by disappointment, if you pretend that it is.

The reason for dwelling on these biological parameters of the world we share with orangutans and anglerfish is precisely that in social-media communication today, perhaps in part because of the way it disembodies our ideas, there are strong indications that many now reject the idea that biology imposes any limits at all upon the exercise of our will. There is a significant presence on social media of people agitating for a general moratorium on all references to "female reproductive anatomy," maintaining that there is simply no such thing as "female biology": their argument is that trans women do not have this anatomy and this biology, while some men, trans men, do have it. Men give birth too, this group tells us, and it is an entirely arbitrary piece of ideological baggage from our backward past that causes some to continue to believe that there is any special connection whatsoever, biological or conceptual, between femaleness and parturition. I contend that this is an extreme position to hold, a radicalization of reasonable demands for equality that has crossed over into the effervescence of unreason, where the ruling principle is to make increasingly implausible truth claims, and to denounce as enemies everyone who is unable to affirm them. A belief has overtaken this discursive community, moreover, according to which one must affirm all of its theoretical commitments concerning the nature of gender identity, if one wishes to avoid the accusation of exterminationism, of wishing for the elimination of trans people. This is the very definition of illiberalism: to believe that disagreeing with another person's theoretical commitments, while affirming and defending their right to exist and to hold these commitments, is insufficient. For this community, radicalized online but increasingly present in real institutions, nothing short of full acceptance of their theoretical claims is acceptable.

By dividing the world into "cis" and "trans"—allowing all sorts of gradations within the latter based on self-reporting alone, while seeing the former as an essential property of the people it supposedly describes—this new way of thinking has traded one binarism for another. "Cis-" is a prefix we previously knew from geography: for example, Cisjordania, also known as the West Bank, was an area on "this side" of the Jordan River. But in recent years it has come to refer primarily to people who are on "this side" of the gender identity into which they were born, rather than having crossed over, as when one fords a river, into what appears to be another sovereign land. To call a person "cis" is to hold that that person just is what she or he is, unambiguously, settledly. But if we are hoping to establish a way of looking at human variety that favors continuity and fluidity, how does it help matters to simply shift the fundamental rift from that between "male" and "female" to that between "cis" and "trans"? There is an irresolvable tension between the insistence, on the one hand, upon the illegitimacy of binary thinking, and, on the other, the equally strong insistence that an individual's identity as, say, a cis man, is plainly and simply a matter of straightforward fact.

In March 2018 a blog post on the website of the American Philosophical Association audaciously complained that attendees at a recent APA conference had failed in large numbers to wear stickers stating their "preferred pronouns," even though these had been made available to them.[26] It was noted that most of the people who declined were "cis" males, while in the same post it was also insisted that one cannot tell simply from looking at a person what their gender identity is. But this is a blatant contradiction. If you cannot know a person's gender identity by looking at them, then how can you, from a visual scan of a conference room, tell the gender of the people who are being uncooperative with the effort to announce preferred pronouns? A contradiction this glaring seems nothing short of intentional: as in religious mystery cults (about which, see chapter 1), the willingness to embrace the contradiction can function as a shibboleth of insider status; and the willingness to question it marks one off, sharply, as an outsider and an enemy. It is this sort of radical goats-and-sheep bifurcation that the algorithms of social media—which have now made the leap and come to determine the tone and tenor of such fora as the blog of the American Philosophical Association—have stoked and amplified over the past years.

It is not the question of transgender identity that interests me in particular here. This is only a particularly vivid example of a general feature of the current environment, which disinvites us from thinking about what it is like to be another sort of human being. This is particularly regrettable in the case of transgender identity, since on at least one plausible interpretation, which reaches back to the original semantics of the prefix "trans-," to be transgender is precisely to have a *transcendent* experience of gender, to be able to know the experience of a different kind of people from the ones you were initially expected to spend your life identifying with. It is just this sort of transcendent experience that some radical feminists deny, and one might find it a missed opportunity that contemporary progressive thought has failed to fully embrace the account of what is happening when one changes one's social identity from "man" to "woman," or vice versa, as a variety of transcendence.

When Walt Whitman engages in a course of introspection, he discovers not only that he is a woman, a saurian, a plant, but that he also contains within him the entire geological history of the earth. "I find I incorporate gneiss, coal, long-threaded moss," writes the poet.[27] The illiberal, discussion-closing accusation of transphobia is often accompanied by a claim that anyone who views matters differently from the enforcers of the new orthodoxy is in no position to speak, because such dissenters have not mastered and cited "the relevant literature" of the "experts" in the scholarly study of transgender identity and experience. But one might with far more justice insist that they themselves are in no position to speak, as they do not seem for their part to have read Ovid, Saxo, or Whitman, say, well enough to have absorbed certain crucial lessons. Nor have they studied the oral folk traditions of the world that offer rich insight into the continuity human beings experience between the identity assigned to them at birth and the many other sorts of entity with which, in a narrow empirical sense, they are nonidentical.

For most of human history, in most cultures, in fact, it was perfectly meaningful and comprehensible to believe and to say things like "I partake of the essence of bear"[28] or "I am a jaguar."[29] For many people in many places and times, claims of transspecies identity have given shape and meaning to social reality. There is an ample literature on such claims, produced both in the past two hundred years or so of

Western anthropological scholarship, as well as in the past few millennia of world literary traditions. Yet no one in the new scholarly protection racket surrounding the discussion of what it is to be trans ever takes an interest in the possibility of this sort of identity, or appears even to be aware of it. It is hard nonetheless in the light of it to see casuistic distinctions between, say, claims of transracial identity on the one hand, of the sort that the "white" Rachel Dolezal attempted to pull off in claiming to be "black," and claims of transgender identity on the other, as anything more than a particular culture's efforts in a particular narrow time slice to work out problems that are much broader than that culture knows, and that are worked out *very* differently elsewhere.

In 2017, among countless other cases of internet mobbing, the philosopher Rebecca Tuvel was excoriated for daring to publish an article that explored some of the ways in which Dolezal's experience of her identity is perhaps similar to that of a transgender person.[30] As Lewis R. Gordon would brilliantly sum up her argument, Tuvel is not seeking to show that either transgenderism (as she calls it) or transracialism is more or less legitimate than the other. Rather, she is "stating that one commitment, without a uniquely differentiating premise available, entails commitment to the other."[31] The reason for the infuriated reaction to her argument, in Gordon's view, is simple: in order to continue denying this entailment, one must be operating in bad faith. Tuvel, he observes, "did something indecent from a bad faith perspective. She called it out."[32] But of course no one would dare make an explicit charge of "indecency," and so other crimes had to be trumped up. A key charge against Tuvel, as one could have predicted, was that she had failed to cite the relevant literature. But this was fatuous nonsense. None of the experts within the narrow community of scholars Tuvel was faulted for ignoring had themselves cited more than the tiniest fraction of potentially relevant literature for making sense of what is going on when a human being claims kinship, identity, or affiliation with a being held by others to be of a distinct nature.

If there is some sense in which we contain all of the diversity of nature within us, then surely also we contain all of the diverse possibilities of human gender or "race." Or consider the example of beardedness. There are people, most of whom identify as men, for whom having a beard is a deep, central, ineliminable feature of their identity. For them to suddenly appear clean-shaven would be, for those who know them, nearly as revolutionary as if they were to change gender identity. The significance of the beard may be wrapped up with their religious commitments, or the beard may have grown over its many decades into a sort of visible excrescence, an *explicatio* or unfolding, of what we take to be the condition of that person's inner life: the outward sign of learnedness, piety, world renunciation, or some other deep value I have not imagined. A beard is a powerful natural symbol, again, in Mary Douglas's sense,[33] and in some cases it is far more than simply a "fashion choice." We might think the bearded/unbearded dichotomy is less important than the male/female or the cis/trans dichotomy, but this may simply be because we value different things, or we fail to notice certain other things.

I am clean-shaven, but it seems to me there is an obvious sense in which I have a beard "in me," not just that I would be bearded soon enough if I stopped shaving—"for this goodly beard, should we not by generous anticipation give the man-child, even in his cradle, credit?" asks Melville's confidence man[34]—but that the world of the bearded person is not inaccessible to me. I do not think that this is just because I have the right hormonal profile to grow a beard, either. Every human being has the experience of hair growth, and most have the experience of hair removal. Hirsuteness belongs to the human essence, or at least it is, like the ability to laugh, what the medieval logicians would have called a property *quarto modo* of humanity: something that belongs to each human, even if it is not part of our essence, as that distinction is deserved for reason alone. There is only a difference of degree from here, and perhaps not a very large one, to suppose that I have another gender "in me": that the experience of the world through another gender identity is not foreign to me, even if it is not now, or perhaps has never been, part of my public presentation of myself, part of my "performance." In order to be consistently inclusive, one should be prepared to recognize as trans those who feel themselves to be at odds with their assigned gender, but are too busy pursuing other things to bother to modify their appearance and behavior in order to perceptibly approximate what they feel their true gender to be. This would expand the notion to include very many of us, and all the better.

The prevailing identity-based commitments of a prominent sector of social-media communicants presupposes a strict and narrow empiricism, according to which each of us can speak only from within our actual daily reality; if you are not a member of a group, then what it is like to be a member of that group is strictly unthinkable. But one thing this misses is the way identities contain other identities, not by intersection so much as by *emboîtement* or enfolding, as my clean-shavenness contains beardedness. I know disability too, not because of any particular marked feature of my social identity, but because I am living out my life in a mortal corruptible body that is constantly threatening to unravel, and will assuredly do so one day in the not-too-distant future. Disability is the way of all flesh. I contain it within me. I would be prepared to say, with Whitman, that I contain a lot more besides, from the entire evolutionary history of life and even, beyond that, to the stuff of geology and cosmology. But we do not need to go nearly that far in order to accept Terence's much more modest claim that we each contain—which is to say that we find familiar, or nonalien—everything that is human.

I do not know whether it is rational, or indeed the height of unreason, to make claims such as these. It is certainly inadvisable. It will be read, by those who are invested in the views I have described, as an imperious taking for myself of what is not mine, and it will be noted that the presumption of a right to do this is typical of people who match my public profile in terms of gender, race, class, and so on. But what I am attempting to do is to reach back in history, and to find genetic strands for this presumption in places where the narrow identitarians of today would not expect to find them. There is, to be sure, the danger of a sort of raving excess in the discovery that one, so to speak, contains multitudes, of which perhaps Whitman himself was guilty, and raving of this sort can hardly be rational. Yet if we restrict ourselves to the human sphere, Whitmanian multitudinousness does share with rationalism at least the connected aspiration to universality. This universalism is present in many ancient traditions, far preceding the Enlightenment. It is there in the cosmopolitan dimensions of the Gospels, in Christ's insistence upon the universal applicability of his good news, and the senselessness of restricting any true religious faith to a single nation or ethnicity.

Correlative to this sort of universalism is the idea that one is misunderstanding what is at stake, philosophically, spiritually, or existentially, in the question "Who am I?" if the only answers one is able to come up with are of the sort "I am a Jew," "I am a Roman," "I am a white working-class American," "I am a trans woman." It is only ignorant, or arrogant, or puffed-up people (to use the language of St. Paul) who mistake the variables of their social identities for features of their souls.

This is what Emily Dickinson understands when she insists that she is nobody, and that to proclaim who you are, in any usual sense, is only the croaking of a baselessly prideful frog (see chapter 8). The universalism that says, "I know what it is like to be you, for we, humans, are not so different in the end," continues the rationalist project as well, to the extent that it is reason, or the inherence of a rational immortal soul, that has most often served as the bedrock nature in which sundry variations can occur: bearded, female, thin, paraplegic, and so forth. The presumption that we do have within us the power to know the other has often been used to deny real distinctions, and to deprive people with whom commonality is being claimed of something that they value. And yet, unless the authors of the Gospels, and Terence, and Alexander Pope, and Emily Dickinson simply did not know what they were talking about, we must suppose that the presumption has a significant amount of truth to it. Since it is impossible to eradicate truth, we are well advised not to seek to deny the presumption, but rather to remain cautious to avoid its misapplication.

An Age of Extremes

At present, the preoccupation with identity that has taken over social media and much of academia, as well as the ever-growing gray area between these two spheres of public life, is demanding of us, in ever more strident terms, that we remain within the ever-shrinking boundaries of our narrow public identities, and that we acknowledge no community, no shared life, with those with whom we are not deemed to intersect sufficiently closely. This is the collapse of civil society into sundry units resembling nothing so much as the steppe-combing clans; or, in the more commonly invoked comparison, the internet is currently moving through its "Wild West" phase.

We are familiar with those intellectuals of the twentieth century who were willfully blind to the crimes of totalitarianism. Many denied the existence of the gulag in their own era, and were so committed to the righteousness of the 1789 storming of the Bastille that they have difficulty facing up to the excesses of the Reign of Terror between 1791 and 1794. Sartre even went so far as to claim that the only real failure is that Robespierre did not get a chance to spill even more blood—that if he had, the goals of the Revolution would have been fulfilled and enshrined for the ages.[35]

It is true that the no-platformers, who seek to block the speaking engagements of people with whom they disagree politically, and social-media mobbers of various stripes, are not state agents, and they are operating in a world in which those with "real power," the regimes in control of states, pose vastly more threat to transgender people than student activists can pose to Germaine Greer. But Robespierre also did not operate on behalf of the state, until he did, and if we oppose authoritarianism only after it has taken the reins of state power, surely we are failing to understand how it succeeds in doing this in the first place. One might well have been dismayed by the Moscow purges of 1938 without being opposed to workers' control of the means of production. Just so, to be concerned as we watch people being mobbed, ostracized, losing their jobs and livelihoods, for a poorly worded tweet about, say, the innateness of gender inequality, does not mean that we must support, or even give an inch to, gender inequality.

These conclusions seem almost too commonplace and moderate to warrant explicit statement. Yet, as Margaret Atwood has recently commented, surveying many of the recent developments considered here, "in times of extremes, extremists win, . . . and the moderates in the middle are annihilated."[36] The polarization and radicalization that have been exacerbated in the past few years by Trumpism and by social media have created a landscape in which bland and commonplace statements have difficulty gaining any foothold in public discourse, even if they are perfectly true. It may be more important than ever to make them, then, and to keep repeating them, if not in tweets, where we know in advance that they will go unloved at best and brutally punished at worst, then perhaps in books—where their fate is unknown as we write them, and to write them at all feels something less like the clamoring and jockeying of public debate, and more like an act of faith.

CHAPTER EIGHT

Explosions; or, Jokes and Lies

➤➤➤➤➤

Into Nothing

As suggested already in chapter 1, a joke might be understood as a distortion or perversion of ordinary logical reasoning with the intention of inducing an agreeable, if also often malicious, sense of surprise. As such, jokes are like little morsels of condensed irrationality. If, again, a logical argument gives us, in its conclusion, the gradual confirmation that a robust expectation is in fact something, a joke gives us in its punch line, to cite Kant's ingenious formulation, the sudden transformation of a strained expectation into nothing.

Jokes are, at their best, truth revealing, yet they also share something with lies and deceit. Like sophisms, they seem to be perversions or, so to speak, curdlings of logical argumentation. Sophisms and jokes aim at the truth, but do so by flirting with mendacity. This is dangerous business. Yet jokes are also a shibboleth of intelligence, of the sort of freedom and playfulness of spirit that we often associate with societies or cultures that are organized on sound, healthy, rational principles. It is where unreason is most fully enshrined into social institutions, notably law and policing, that jokes are most rigorously suppressed. By contrast, figures who are most iconically associated with the Enlightenment, notably Voltaire, are praised, rightly or wrongly, for their embodiment of humor. We might be inclined to suppose that humor itself is irrational, and that Enlightened societies accommodate it rather as a matter of principle, as a healthy and manageable "release valve" for what strictly speaking is a residue of unenlightenedness, of irrational cruelty and carnivalesque chaos. But Voltaire is not cracking his jokes simply in order to get them out of his system. They are central to his persona and to his project, and the place of humor in the history of Enlightenment cannot be relegated simply to a formal tolerance as a matter of principle.

We have seen in recent years a growing intolerance of offensive humor broadly construed, and a growing readiness to denounce humorous publications and entertainments that had previously been seen as beacons of the Enlightenment commitment to freedom. The tenuous bond between the liberal center left and the illiberal far left has often appeared ready to unravel entirely upon the snag of humor and its public expression. Where has reason gone in all of this? Is it with the old-guard jokesters, who enjoy making clever little digs at the jihadists and the bishops? Or is it with the stern new left, prepared to tell us, purse-lippedly, that whatever is offensive is ipso facto not funny?

One senses one is losing one's grip on the subject. While they have served as extremely potent fuel for the rise of irrationalism as a political force in the Western world over the past few years—particularly in the form of memes, as discussed in the previous chapter—at the same time jokes have long been held, and continue to be held, as central to the form of life envisioned by the Enlightenment, as the supreme expression of freedom and individual self-expression, in contrast with rigid piety and conformism.

Charlie Hebdo and After

The question of the limits of humor in a healthy society was thrust into the center of public debate in Europe and the United States in 2015, after a group of humble caricaturists in France were murdered for their work. That year I myself engaged in an extended and diffuse jeremiad, arguing to whomever I could get to listen that humor is the highest expression of freedom and the thing most to be defended in society. The tirade culminated in my delivery of the annual Pierre Bayle Lecture in Rotterdam, in November of that year, titled "The Gravity of Satire."[1] I had been invited to speak in the same forum that had hosted such defenders of freedom as Adam Michnik and Léon Poliakov, and I chose to focus on humor. This turn of events gave me new impetus and motivation to begin writing on humor as a serious philosophical and political problem.

At the time, my view of the semantics and ethics of humor, a view I had taken to calling my "gelastics" (from the Greek *gelos*, "laughter"), was roughly the following. I cited and insisted upon the august genealogy of *Charlie Hebdo*, invoking the venerable tradition of French satire, going back to Alfred Jarry, Honoré Daumier, and of course Voltaire. It is a mistake to assess the purpose and function of satire, I argued, in strictly political terms, as a lowly but necessary part of the functioning of a free society. Critics of *Charlie Hebdo* from the left and the right, ranging from Jean-Marie Le Pen to the dissident members of the PEN American Center writers' organization, did just this. Le Pen called it an "anarchist rag" and stopped just short of thanking the Kouachi brothers for murdering its most prominent contributors.[2] Critics on the left, in turn, were often unable or unwilling to distinguish its cartoons from racist propaganda, the overt intention of which was, they held, to drum up hatred of an enemy group in preparation for war or pogroms.[3]

In 2015, when I came out in defense of *Charlie Hebdo*, I did so not just in defense of its formal right to exist, but in defense of its content and its spirit. I maintained at the time that the only adequate defense is the one that considers satire from a distanced perspective, and that seeks to understand it as a rhetorical mode with special rules governing it, rules that are different from those that govern straightforward political speech. A Nazi propaganda cartoon that depicts Jews as rats is not satire. It has a straightforward purpose: to dehumanize Jews in the minds of readers. Satire, by contrast, takes up the voice of its intended target, in order to reveal the inherent moral baseness or logical incoherence of this voice. It might say "Jews are rats," but when it does, its target is not Jews, but rather those who would nonsatirically say such a thing. Satire is thus a sort of ventriloquy, and as such it is inevitably in constant danger of being misinterpreted. Critics of satire will often complain that it has "gone too far," but what they really ought to say in such instances is that it has done its job too well, and has discomforted the critics themselves in its ability to reproduce satirically language that originates in straight-faced literalness.

It may be that there is no other way for satirists to proceed than to perpetually court condemnation. Perhaps they should simply accept that society will heap its scorn on them, as if *they* were the earnest evil ones, just as the jester in Andrei Tarkovsky's 1966 film *Andrei Rublev* is abused and debased by the local prince's men for the simple fact that he lives in order to make people laugh—which is to say, to remind people of the absurdity of human social life and the illusion of power it grants, for example, to local princes. But this does not mean that we as analysts and critics should aspire to join in the abuse. We should rather seek to understand how this particular category of speech functions: it says what it means by saying the opposite of what it means, and, by lying, exposes the lies on which society is built.

One of the lies, or at least conceits, on which society is built, is, as Mary Douglas has brilliantly shown, the one that conceals the functions of the body. By holding in expulsions and ejaculations, not just of fluids and gases, but also of certain words, we become properly social beings; to let these demons out is precisely to challenge and to threaten the social order. In this way vulgarity becomes one of the most powerful weapons in the satirist's arsenal, and also one of the elements of satire that makes it easiest for polite society to distance itself from the lowly work of the satirist, even while weakly affirming satire's formal right to exist. Thus, in the weeks after the *Charlie Hebdo* attacks, did we often hear prim liberals insisting that, while they are of course against extrajudicial assassination, vulgar cartoons are "just not their cup of tea." But the vulgarity is not gratuitous; it is essential. As already mentioned in chapter 3, when Aristophanes has his fictional version of Socrates deny the existence of celestial divinities by comparing the thunder of the clouds to farting, he is not just telling "fart jokes" for their own sake; he is, rather, undermining the reigning vision of the order of nature, which perceives divine intention in great and lofty things, by instead accounting for this order in the same terms as lowly and undignified things. This is, in Douglas's sense, the intrusion of the body where it does not belong, and it is dangerous indeed.

The right to intrude in this way is undoubtedly an important formal freedom, gained in the West with the rise of liberalism's commitment to liberty of expression and of the press. *Charlie Hebdo* emerges directly out of the period that saw some of the final obstacles to these liberties falling away, with the decline of laws against vulgarity and sacrilege in France and other democracies in the latter half of the twentieth century. Yet many left intellectuals today (in contrast with the 1960s) tend to see vulgarity as at best a formal freedom to be tolerated, rather than a dangerous force to be tapped into. They have ceded vulgarity to the alt-right, which has not been slow in using it to construct unprecedentedly powerful stink bombs. Meanwhile Eliot Weinberger, writing in the *London Review of Books*, scoffs that *Charlie Hebdo* is nothing but a bastion of "frat-boy humour."[4] As if France had "frat-boys," and as if vulgarity were not also central to the aesthetic and moral vision of Cervantes, Boccaccio, and Rabelais.

All good humor that is cruel is also self-cruel, and always remains aware of the fact that whatever is being said of the other loops back, at least potentially, upon oneself. To laugh at, say, the unattractiveness or illness of others, or to laugh at it wisely, is, it might be suggested, to do so in a way that recognizes that the person who is laughing may just as easily take the place of the joke's butt. It is thus to recognize our shared humanity, and indeed an equality that is so total as to amount to interchangeability. Just before the death of the French rock-and-roll icon Johnny Hallyday, a *Charlie Hebdo* cover showed him in a hospital bed, hooked up to various machines that were making "bzz" and "bip" sounds. The headline suggested that the old rocker had unexpectedly made a late-career turn to techno. It is extremely cruel to make fun of someone who is dying. But is it so hard to imagine one of Hallyday's own loved ones visiting him in the hospital and making the same joke in his presence? Is it so hard to imagine Hallyday himself making it? And are we really expected to suppose that the cartoonist has no awareness that he himself could end up in a similar predicament soon enough? Reconsidered in this way, the joke now almost seems sweet, loving, the heavy stuff of life and death being processed among intimates. I laughed when I saw the cover at a newsstand, and then spent the next several days thinking about it, and feeling far more sympathy for the French adoration of Johnny Hallyday than I ever had previously. I had always found him mediocre, repulsive even, and yet it was a supposedly cruel joke that first caused me to see him in a different light.

It is this element of self-reflexivity that makes the dialogues some years ago between Donald Trump and the "shock jock" radio host Howard Stern so remarkable.[5] Both often boasted of their sexual rapaciousness and their contempt for ordinary people and ordinary morality. But Stern cut his big talk with running asides on his own ridiculousness, on the vanity of these pursuits, on his tragic awareness of where it is all headed. Trump knew only one register. He wanted to impress Stern, to convince him that he is no less a bad boy than his host. It was painful to listen to him, and it is part of Stern's comic genius that he knew how to inflict this pain on us, the listeners, by playing on Trump's infantile perception, or hope, that he and Stern are creatures of the same nature.

The comic mode is one in which our humanity can be most fully expressed, by playful use of the imagination, and by its twin tools of vulgarity and cruelty, in the aim of capturing, expressing, and somewhat relishing our common plight as human beings. It is also inherently dangerous, inherently unstable, always threatening to "go too far." When it does go too far, the common reaction from those who are offended is that the humorist had been doing something he should not have been doing at all—telling a joke about a certain subject—rather than that he was doing something perfectly worthy and legitimate in itself, but that he did it poorly, that he misfired. The offended parties pretend to want, or imagine that they in fact really want, a world in which jokes of the same species as the one that misfired are simply never told. But they do not grasp or acknowledge quite how much of human inventiveness and playfulness would have to be purged in order for this to happen. They do not grasp or acknowledge that there really is no settled, stable, acceptable future scenario in which we have purged any inclination to say things that might hurt others, and yet are perfectly at peace with this strange new quiet. If they think they are imagining such a scenario, this is only by fastidiously avoiding the specifics.

The unquiet, precarious balance between offensiveness on the one hand, and dreary self-censorship or oppressive community or state censorship on the other hand, of course looks a good deal like the precarious balance we have discerned in other chapters, on at least apparently unrelated matters. One must, for example, try to allow the faculty of the imagination to thrive, without lurching into hallucinatory madness, and also without allowing fear of madness to become an impediment to imagination's full flourishing. And one must strive to allow social disorder—carnival, revelry, mosh pits, the American radio genre known as "morning zoo"—to have its place, without permitting the erosion of ordinary civility. And one must strive to allow the fantasies and myths of communities to find their expression, without becoming enshrined into official ideology and leveraged for the oppression or extermination of nonmembers of those communities.

These, in broad outline, were my views in 2015. The events of the following year, however, forced me to reconsider many of my most basic convictions. In 2016, I, a latecomer and a normie (that is, an outsider to the various internet subcultures that generate memes, and that would surely mock any attempt at defining this term), was finally made to understand the new political force of humor, when I came upon the meme stashes of the alt-right. They scared me. Nor could I ignore the evident fact of their evolutionary lineage: they were not of an entirely different genus from the expressions of ribald, offensive, and playful humor I myself had spent much effort defending: *Charlie Hebdo*, Howard Stern; even *Seinfeld,* as already mentioned, would soon be implicated, as an early influence on the white nationalist and anti-Semite mememonger Mike Peinovich. Perhaps the scolds were right: there is no safe release valve for nihilism, for cruel delight, no space for these in society that will not soon enough be filled up by sheer evil. By August of 2016 I was scouring the dirtiest parts of the internet trying to understand Pepe the Frog—whom Hillary Clinton had called out that same month, to the delight of Pepe's supporters, as the mascot and avatar of the alt-right—and knowing, in my heart, as I witnessed the ebullience of his followers, that Donald Trump was going to win this cursèd election.

As Emily Nussbaum observed in the *New Yorker*, Trump's victory was in no small measure the victory of jokes. "Like Trump's statements," Nussbaum wrote of the armies of online "shit-posters," "their quasi-comical memeing and name-calling was so destabilizing, flipping between serious and silly, that it warped the boundaries of discourse."[6] Nussbaum cites Chuck Johnson, a troll who has been banned from Twitter: "We memed a President into existence."[7] With his election, for the first time in my life I found myself echoing the scolds I used to despise, who would conflate offensiveness and unfunniness every time they judged of something, "That's not funny!" It turned out they were right: the enormous, singular joke of our epoch was not funny. Trump's victory amounted to a conquest of reality by satire, and so by forces that naturally and fittingly ought to be confined to the playing fields of the human imagination. Trump was a joke, in other words, but to the extent that he was now being taken as something else, as "president," he was truly, literally, not funny.

The liberal humor industry that had sprung up purportedly to counter and combat this new regime seemed, moreover, fundamentally unsuited to the task: palliative rather than combative, part of the smoothly functioning machine rather than a wrench thrown in to disrupt it. Durable authoritarian regimes have always carved out a space for jesters. Nazi Germany had Tran and Helle, a comedy duo whose mild political satire enabled them to squeak through with official acceptance for much of the regime's duration, while also managing to convince admirers, and perhaps themselves, that this approval was not incompatible with true subversion. In retrospect, it is not hard to see that their comedy sketches were hardly what was needed in that historical moment. By contrast, as Rudolph Herzog comments in his *Foreign Policy* article "Laughing All the Way to Autocracy," "It is hard to imagine Claus von Stauffenberg, the one-eyed war veteran [and would-be assassin of Hitler], ever cracking trivial jokes."[8]

But still, I continued to tell myself even after Trump's election, the playing field of the imagination is infinite, and this is an advantage it will always have over the finite bounds of reality, including political reality, however dreary this may become. Even though humor forces us back into our heavy bodies—and even though, therefore, we can never mistake a gelastic experience for an aesthetic one—nevertheless in the gelastic mode too we experience a variety of freedom. When this freedom is the only sort available, as in the thriving Soviet circulation of underground *anekdoty* that gave us Rabinovich and so many other delightful characters (Soviet census-taker: "Does Rabinovich live here?" Rabinovich: "You call *this* living?"), it is merely palliative. It should not for this reason be condemned, but we must nonetheless do what we can to hold on, by political means, to a form of freedom more concrete than palliation.

It will always be a difficult matter, based on a million subtle contextual facts, to determine when humor merely functions as autocracy's built-in pressure valve, and when it is the dynamite autocracy fears. One and the same comedy sketch might devolve from confrontation into palliation if it is drawn out too long, and the regime finds a way to adapt to or even co-opt it. There are no easy rules for determining which role humor is playing in society at any given time. Jokes are, in the end, entirely dependent on context. ("Finally, something warm," legend has Winston Churchill saying when he was brought a glass of champagne after a meal.) Jokes can even degenerate into nonjokes, as circumstances change, or indeed bold and revolutionary humor can become normalized to the point where it helps to maintain tyranny rather than challenge it.

The balance to strike, then, is one in which we do not take the palliative humor of the late-night talk shows for political resistance, but in which we also do not underestimate the potential political power of a humorist's voice that cannot be bent to the purposes of the regime. Stephen Colbert is no Isaak Babel, and we may be sure that he is in no danger of being rubbed out. By the same token, in the darkest moments of our political present, we may find more power for political liberation in going back to *The Odessa Tales* than the late-night talkers can ever offer.

Pseudologia Generalis

That Donald Trump is a liar is a proven fact, like sexual dimorphism in anglerfish or the orbit of the earth around the sun. But are we really dealing here with a case of morally culpable mendacity, or is there something about his cognition that compels him to lie, distort, and fantasize without, generally, realizing it? For the Greeks this would be a distinction without any real difference: they did not punish wrongdoers only on the condition that the wrongdoers could have done otherwise; they punished based on the nature of the act itself, not on an interpretation of the moral condition of the actor. But we are different, and we generally want to know whether misdeeds are done with *mens rea*, a guilty mind, or, rather, committed by someone who is so deficient or impaired as to be unable to be judged truly guilty at all. Living permanently in a fantasy world of one's own making, not sharing in the common world, yet not being aware of the distinction, may itself exculpate a person such as Trump from the morally far more charged accusation of lying.

In a letter to the *New York Times* of March 2017, the prominent psychiatrists Judith L. Herman and Robert Jay Lifton described Trump's "repeated failure to distinguish between reality and fantasy, and his outbursts of rage when his fantasies are contradicted."[9] They predicted that "faced with crisis, President Trump will lack the judgment to respond rationally."[10] The physicians were only expressing what was by then common wisdom, but the statement was significant nonetheless for its rupture with a long-standing prohibition among American psychiatrists against venturing clinical diagnoses, from afar and in public, of political figures. Diagnosis of political enemies, of course, has a long and disgraceful history. But in these extreme circumstances some clinicians believed they found themselves forced to weigh the danger of repeating such past crimes against what they had come to think of as a duty to warn.

Political warnings—that this candidate does not have America's interests at heart, that he has no intention of making America great again—had not done the trick, and so some perceived the need to move to the level of expert diagnosis, and to present as scientific fact the case for the unfitness of a president, a case that has been repeatedly dismissed when it is made not as scientific fact but as political opinion.

Those who are aware of the history of psychiatry, and of science in general, will understand that this movement to the level of purported fact is in truth only pursuit of the same public-discursive end at a different register. It is a continued push in defense of an opinion, in a culture that takes opinions as private possessions to be cherished, rather than to be weighed against other opinions and perhaps traded in. To complicate matters, however, this is a culture that values the facts that others might deliver to us even less than it values their opinions, and so Lifton and Herman are paying to deliver their case in what is in effect a deflated currency—the currency of scientific expertise, which will in any case be rejected as mere political partisanship by those who are not inclined to believe what they have to say. Our political opinions are not having any effect on those on the other side, say the exasperated opponents of Trumpism. So let us move to the level of scientific fact, they say, only to discover that their opponents are having none of that either.

Unlike, say, dreaming or fiction writing, to lie is to do something of incontestable negative moral import—though, as we have seen, even dreaming and fiction writing are often judged to be at least morally questionable. If one is not fully conscious of the fact that one is lying, then the act seems to descend back into that shady but not plainly morally culpable realm of standard-run irrationality, as when one claims falsely that dinosaurs and human beings walked the earth together. Conscious lying is, or almost always is, a short-term solution to a problem that will fail in the long run to solve that problem, and that will likely generate new problems of its own. As in the satisfaction of other short-term desires, to get away with lying will likely provoke in the liar a mixture of satisfaction and regret, and it is likely, as well, that the latter sentiment will outlive the former. Folk wisdom about wicked webs confirms these general observations.

And yet, other folk wisdom tells us that it is good to deny to the SS that we are hiding Jews in our attic, and it is good to affirm to our elderly aunt that we appreciate her Jell-O recipe. These lies, if they are successful, do not entail regret; on the contrary the regret comes only if they are disbelieved by their hearers. But which other people are in relations to us sufficiently analogous to that of the Nazi soldiers or of our aunt to warrant our lying to them? This is a question that obviously can have no easy answer, and so we are left each with our own complex interpersonal ties, to determine for ourselves the moral valence of dishonesty. Kant was an exceptional philosopher in his insistence that no one ever has a right to lie, under any circumstances, even those I have just adduced as examples. This commitment was grounded in his deontological ethics, an ethics that squarely rejects utilitarian considerations of the consequences of our deeds, and focuses entirely on the moral character of the deeds themselves. Utilitarians would say, of course, that the moral quality of an act cannot even begin to be measured without consideration of the effects it brings about. But if you assume at the outset that the two moments, act and effect, are distinct, then the blanket rejection of a right to lie in some circumstances becomes more comprehensible.

"Determination is negation," Spinoza writes in a 1674 letter to his friend Jarig Jelles, an idea that would later be taken up by Hegel.[11] To specify what a thing is, is also, necessarily, to deny infinitely many attributes of it, to exclude infinitely many other possibilities. To affirm that a shirt is red is to deny that it is blue. Some properties can inhere in the same subject together, of course; to affirm of a shirt that it is red is not, obviously, to deny that it is long sleeved. Much ordinary reasoning consists in determining whether two or more properties are opposed, like "red" and "blue," or merely different, like "red" and "long sleeved." I can recall being small and responding to the banal claim of credulous adults that "you can be whatever you want to be" that, well, I would like to be a brain surgeon *and* an astronaut *and* an Olympic athlete . . . Obviously, the adults were not including conjunctive career paths under their idea of "whatever." We might be able to conjoin at most two remarkable careers within a single lifetime, but for the most part to determine what it is that one wants to be is to exclude the possibility of becoming something else. We ordinarily take it as a sign of maturity when a person comes to terms with this inevitable exclusion and allows herself to just be one thing, while perhaps granting to one's earlier hopes the etiolated status of "hobbies." But even the fact that we must demote in this way the things to which we had once hoped to devote our lives, simply in order to respectably engage with them at all, serves as a constant reminder that Spinoza's dictum was not just about our descriptions of ordinary things like shirts—it also applies directly to our own lives.

The dictum may be adapted to make sense of the philosophical complexities of lying. In legal contexts we are sometimes asked to tell "the truth, the whole truth, and nothing but the truth." To tell something other than the truth is straightforwardly to lie, and so the meaning of the last element of this three-part phrase is obvious enough. But can one tell the whole truth? And is it possible to tell both the truth and the whole truth together? Or is there already something about the determinations one makes as to what one is going to say that excludes the possibility of saying an infinite number of other things—things that are not, for their part, lies, but that are nonetheless implicitly negated in the course of our determinations? Every act of telling, whether providing testimony on the witness stand or spinning out a story by the campfire, is an act of sculpting, of choices made as to what to include, and what to leave out.

There are both pragmatic and moral choices that tell us where to chip, what to include and what to leave out. If we wish to explain to the jury that we were in the bathroom when a crime occurred in the kitchen, we will not go into unnecessary detail about the condition of our bowels. Simple discretion prevents us from telling the whole truth. We will also avoid what has been called "truth dumping,"[12] for more serious moral reasons. Honest criticism of another passes over from being morally edifying to being simply cruel if it goes on for too long, even when the points of criticism that might be made after a given cutoff point are not of a different character, or any less accurate or true, than the ones that preceded it. And similarly for truth and history. The truth about the Vietnam War, and our duty to tell the truth, surely involves, for example, an up-frontness and sobriety about the My Lai massacre.

But what level of graphic detail must we reach in the name of honesty? And after what point does the detail become gratuitous, even transforming from what was initially intended into its very opposite, an invitation to revel in the horrible spectacle? In 2017 it became very common, one might say fashionable, to share video images of policy brutality against black American men on social media. Most who did this were proceeding in a spirit of honesty, of telling "the whole truth" about racism in America. As often happens in social media—where earnest "hot takes" are followed by a wave of contrarian attempts to shame those who arrived on the scene first—there was soon enough a sharp reaction to this practice. Some felt that, particularly when done by white Americans, sharing such footage revived, however unintentionally, the atrocious old practice of making and selling postcards on the occasion of lynchings, with the dumb grinning faces of white yokels posing in front of the dead black man's body.

How then do we tell the whole truth? How do we face up honestly to racism or to war crimes without crossing over into base titillation, not to mention serving the propaganda efforts of forces that assuredly could not care less about truly fighting against the social problem the aspiring truth-tellers are seeking to keep in the public eye, for example the chaos-promoting bots that, while agreeing that black lives matter, insisted no less fervently that blue lives matter too? It seems, again, that telling the moral truth necessarily means *not* telling the whole truth, but rather crafting a compelling account of the truth—where this is derived from one's moral sensibility rather than imagined to be a simple reportage upon the facts—that leaves quite a bit out, that involves far more exclusions than positive determinations.

I want, for example, to make the case, before a group of doubters, that racism in America is a grave problem. The case I am able to make will be one that hits just the right register, that responds to the subtle hints about what they as listeners are prepared to hear. The case I am able to make will also be determined in no small measure by who I am, what my own racial identity is perceived to be, what my own interest in establishing this case is perceived to be, and so on. It is by no means every context in which the most gruesome and atrocious images or descriptions of lynchings will be the most effective vehicle of truth. Yet it is true that racism is a grave problem in America, and it is true that countless lynchings have occurred and continue to occur. But the most effective way to impart this truth may well be to abandon the expectation that one must always tell the whole truth.

The whole truth would be an infinite concatenation of mostly irrelevant facts, with an occasional dose of, in textspeak, "TMI," too much information—when, for example, you ruin the case you were making against factory farming by going into such detail about how painful de-beaking is for chickens that your listener simply shuts you out and struggles to think about something else. So we do not tell the whole truth; we tell carefully crafted stories, and we do this even when our moral purpose is to tell the truth. It is for this reason, perhaps, that "story" and "history" are identical words in most European languages, and that until recently history writing was unproblematically thought of as a variety of storytelling. This commonality of ends remained unproblematic, in fact, until Rankean positivism came to dominate in academic history (see chapter 6), and the impossible ideal of giving an account of things "as they actually were," and doing so exhaustively, came to dominate as the exclusive desideratum of the historical discipline. But this simply cannot be done. To acknowledge as much, however, is not to give up on the truth, but only to acknowledge that the aspiration to the truth is a moral aspiration, and not a cognitive or evidential task of simple enumeration.

In the preface to the 1999 edition of her book *Lying*, Sissela Bok cites a few cases in which people plainly speak falsehoods, but just as plainly do not intend deceit, as, for example, when Alzheimer's patients engage in "confabulation": spinning out stories that are entirely disconnected from reality, but in a way that seems grounded in some real part of their characters, to reflect some real aspect of their inner lives.[13] She also mentions those who are diagnosed with the condition of *Pseudologia fantastica*, which is, she says, to lying what kleptomania is to stealing.[14] Pseudologues spin so many falsehoods about their own lives that they no longer seem cognitively able to separate truth from falsehood.

Bok believes, however, that it is possible to distinguish the true liars (among whom she places pseudologues, but not Alzheimer's patients) from those who do not intend to deceive, and she is interested in her investigation only in true liars.[15] But it may be more appropriate to envision a continuum on which there is no clear boundary separating the people who enjoy telling tales from the pathological deceivers. In other words, there may be no clear boundary between fiction and lies, and the morally charged dimensions of the writing of literature, of spinning out worlds, may indeed—as Cervantes understood but we seem to have forgotten—be worthy of investigation together with more mundane and more obviously reprehensible instances of lying.

Something akin to nontruthfulness of this sort, playfully spinning out worlds that we know not to exist, seems to be centrally, ineliminably involved in our individual developmental histories, in the way we forge our own characters through a mixture of aspiration and pretending. If you are not yet the sort of person you would like to be, as no one ever is at the outset, then part of the path to getting there seems to involve behaving, deceptively, as if you already were there. "Fake it till you make it" is the formula to which folk wisdom reduces this insight. Of course the deception is not fooling anyone, and yet it is tolerated or even encouraged, often by elders who have already made it, because they understand that it is a necessary part of the process of maturation.

Life is imitation, and therefore not really the thing it is pretending to be, for as long as it is aspiration. Once it arrives at the goal, it is authentically what it is, and can no longer be otherwise, but when this happens it comes to seem, if fully honest, also something like a living death. Life is in the pretending. Or, to anticipate an idea developed more fully in the following chapter, our experience of life is something like that of a cargo cult, worshipping and duplicating the scarcely understood, mysterious cargo that has been dropped in our midst, or into whose midst we ourselves have been dropped—until one day we do understand it. Then the charm disappears, and we find ourselves removed from the cult that worships the cargo, and now, from here on out, placed in some dreary night watchman's job, overseeing the cargo for minimum wage. The high school football players at their homecoming put on ties, and it is obvious to anyone who wears a tie as a central feature of his daily identity that these boys are not *really* wearing ties, but have only appended a foreign element to their ordinary high school attire, to their ordinary high school selves. They put on the tie in order to give the appearance, on a special day, of being more important than they are, and to this extent the tie is a lie.

Children play at getting married, struggling to master the concept of marriage by acting out the few elements of it they understand, and fantasizing about the parts they can only vaguely limn. Many in their teens and twenties continue to play in this way in their dating lives, imitating in certain respects, to the extent that it is pleasurable, the ideal form of the monogamous couple, but without the deep lifelong commitment or the eternal promises. And then at the end of this process many find themselves actually, literally married, and they find, often to their surprise, that they have traded in that spirit of play for what we often hear described as "hard work."

And Trump plays at being president, in the way that a child might who is impressed with the evident bigness of the idea of that office, but who is not cognitively or emotionally ready to appreciate all that it involves. Most American presidents surely had childish fantasies at some point about that position, but they were aged and ripened by the work of getting there, and by the time they arrived they have seemed, for the most part, to grasp that it is a real-world responsibility—that it is "hard work" and not simply a matter of the rest of the world accommodating itself so that they can continue to play within a sort of full-immersion fantasy.

In this respect Trump's presidency is a lie, and one that occurs far past the age where the lying can be rationalized as make-believe, as play. This dimension of mendacity is combined with his propensity to confabulation, to saying things that simply and verifiably are not true, even though these things often seem to be sincerely felt by him.

Whether the confabulations have as their etiology something like what Bok describes in Alzheimer's patients, or whether rather it is a case of *Pseudologia fantastica* not connected to any cognitive or neural degeneration, is a matter of speculation at present. But that he is a liar, and that his presidency is a lie, is certain to any honest onlooker.

Trump's mendacity is a venomous species of a genus that also includes kinds that are beneficial and necessary to our human lives. Lying is continuous with fantasy, with storytelling, with the free play of the imagination, while these in turn are the capacities that make us human and that make our lives worthwhile. Trump is eminently human, and his presence might be appreciated at a family reunion, an old uncle installed on the couch, full of passably funny, offensive quips that cause his younger, more with-it relations to roll their eyes and laugh knowingly. But that is not where Trump has ended up.

The structural irrationality that allowed Trump to end up where he never should have ended up, is one that in part channels the irrationality of individual members of society, brought together by irrational ideology, by fantasies that make sense only for as long as they are not submitted to rational scrutiny. But he ended up there in part, also, as a result of a poorly designed system, by disorder in the way things are set up: gerrymandered voting districts that have no plausible justification in the language of democracy; an electoral college that trumps popular will; and mass media that make it effectively impossible for the low-information voter to apprehend what the relevant political issues in the campaign are. This long-developing failure of the media in turn metastasized with the surge of social media as a factor in political campaigns, and the inability of the directors of the new social-media companies to recognize their new role and to assume the responsibility that they had stumbled into, to assure the survival of deliberative democracy in the era of digital hyperconnectedness. Instead, they allowed secret algorithms to produce, in individual newsfeeds, the appearance of a custom-made fantasy world, one that strangely mirrors at the microlevel of the individual citizen the fantasy world inhabited by the president. In this respect, the irrationality is externalized, into the systems of information flow and of the social processing of individual actions such as voting, rather than being internal to our individual minds (see chapter 2 for an extensive discussion of this distinction).

It is not that in order for deliberative democracy to function, a "liberal" American needs to be exposed to, and to engage with, the fringe ideas that have taken over the mainstream of the Republican Party. Rather, it is in large part the prior absence of reciprocal exposure and engagement that has caused fringe ideas to appear legitimate at all. I am certainly not going to engage, on its merits, with the idea that Democrats have been running a pedophilia ring in a Washington, DC, pizza restaurant, or with the QAnon conspiracy theory that has more recently bubbled up out of the darkest corners of 4chan. I will not take these ideas seriously, and in this refusal I do not believe that I am in any way failing to do my part to maintain or revive a healthy deliberative democracy. The structural irrationality, the failure of the algorithms to ensure serious political debate, has contributed to a situation in which the ideas that inform the political camps, that give life to the objectives of political communities, are no longer worth discussing; they can be addressed only as symptoms of a vastly larger problem.

Croaking

Donald Trump has a sense of himself: in fact he appears to be a pure bundle of unfettered will and assertion. But this is not the ennobling sense that is sometimes said to have accompanied "the discovery of the self" in ancient Greek thought, or again in Renaissance authors such as Michel de Montaigne. It is rather the sense of self that Emily Dickinson so wisely rejects in one of her most celebrated poems (already referenced above, but worth citing more fully here):

I'm Nobody! Who are you?
Are you – Nobody – too?
Then there's a pair of us!
Don't tell! they'd advertise – you know!

How dreary to be somebody!
How public, like a frog
To tell your name the livelong day
To an admiring bog.[16]

The name in the case at hand is what has been aptly described as a Dickensian characternym, accurately epitomizing the character to whom it is attached.[17] To "trump," in card games, has come to mean "to have a better hand," but this in turn is rooted in a deeper, older meaning, still expressed by the French cognate *tromper*, which can mean, variously, "to pull one over on one's adversary," or, simply, "to deceive." During the 2017 French elections, a common slogan on placards was *Ne vous "trumpez" pas*, which is to say, "Do not fool yourselves" (by voting for the extreme-right candidate Marine Le Pen), but also, thanks to the phrase's slight and intentional misspelling, "Don't 'Trump' yourselves." The fact that this usurper's very name spelled out so unambiguously what he was up to should have set off alarm bells. Yet liberal Americans, who like all Americans are generally indifferent to etymology conceived as the science of truth—for this is the etymology of "etymology"—preferred the utterly toothless mockery they thought they would be able to extract from his ancestral German surname, Drumpf. But what is wrong with Drumpf? It is a perfectly average German name. And meanwhile here was this reality-TV actor turned politician, screaming his real name to his bog: his real name literally meant "to deceive," and no one cared. And he was elected.

St. Paul wrote in the First Letter to the Corinthians that "knowledge puffs up, but love builds up" (1 Corinthians 8:1). Trump lacks both knowledge and love, and what he is inflated with, one suspects, is something much more like that miasmatic air by which the bullfrog asserts its existence in the middle of the bog. Paul's letter, however, brings us back to something fundamental that has been central to our concerns: even if we are filled with knowledge of a sort, including knowledge of who we happen to think we are (white working-class Americans, Jews, Romans, people who put "PhD" after their names), we are only in fact inflating ourselves, out of the same sort of crude pride of which even a frog is capable, when we put this knowledge, or this semblance of self-knowledge, on display, and this inflation would occur in just the same way even if we didn't have knowledge at all.

The book of Psalms tells us, "All men are liars" (Psalm 116:11) or, more profoundly, as it is rendered in some translations, "Every man is a lie." This sounds extreme, but if we supplement it with the insights of Dickinson and St. Paul together, we get a richer sense of what is at issue: to the extent that we take our status as "somebody"—our individual distinctions, the knowledge we have gained, the titles we have in some sense earned, the approval ratings we receive on television or in office—we are mistaken about who we are, and whence we derive our value, and our proclamations about ourselves amount to mere croaking. Our value is derived, rather, from our recognition that we are "nobody," or at least nobody in particular. In other words, whatever it is that is true of us, that gives us a share of the truth, is something we share equally with everybody, and thus we are in every respect that matters perfectly interchangeable with our neighbor. This recognition is in turn the basis of what St. Paul has in mind by "love."

And yet can we not at least strive to know things, and speak them, in the name of truth? Or is *all* knowing and speaking mere puffing and croaking? In a stunningly desolate poem of 1968, responding to the brutal termination of the Prague Spring by Soviet forces and their servants in Czechoslovakia, W. H. Auden introduces the figure of the Ogre:

> The Ogre does what ogres can,
> Deeds quite impossible for Man,
> But one prize is beyond his reach:
> The Ogre cannot master Speech.
>
> About a subjugated plain,
> Among the desperate and slain,
> The Ogre stalks with hands on hips,
> While drivel gushes from his lips.[18]

"Speech," in the elevated sense in which the poet intends it here, might properly be read as a translation of *logos*, a term introduced at the beginning of chapter 1. Gustáv Husák, the secretary of the Czechoslovak Communist Party in the period of "Normalization" following the Prague Spring, was in some sense of course able to speak. Trump can still speak too, though his syntax and syllables are ever diminishing.

But neither can speak truth, and in the sense of "Speech" that Auden is evoking, this is as much as to say that they cannot speak at all. "The Word," to return to the New Testament rendering of *logos*, is necessarily true, or else it is not what it claims to be. To put this another way, human reason as articulated in "Speech" reflects the real order of the world, or it is not what it claims to be, but rather drivel. And the only way in which drivel can be passed off as Speech is by subjugation, whether with tanks, massive disinformation and de-education of the populace, or some combination of these two.

Since we have brought together such a motley crew of thinkers and nonthinkers, it is worth noting that St. Paul, like Donald Trump, is in his way an anti-intellectual. But his rejection of knowledge in the First Letter to the Corinthians is precisely not a rejection of truth. It is, rather, motivated by the idea that worldly knowledge is an impediment to apprehension of the only sort of truth that ultimately matters, a transcendental truth about God's love and the possibility of sharing in it. Thus the "knowledge" (γνῶσις) that Paul rejects could not be said to share in *logos*. In Platonic terms, this so-called knowledge would not be knowledge at all, but mere opinion.

Knowledge of trivial, worldly things, even when "true" in a strict sense, is nonetheless, on a certain understanding, when put on display for vain or venal reasons, a lie. And this in turn is how a man can be, in himself, as the Psalms put it, "a lie," even if he sometimes tells the truth. Studies show that Trump at least sometimes tells the factual truth, but not in any way that flows from truthfulness of character or provides any evidence that he is anything other than a lie. Facts may be mixed into drivel without changing its character, just as fresh vegetables may be sprinkled into bog water without making it soup.

To fail to "master Speech," in the sense in which Auden understands it, is not simply to be functionally illiterate or relatively inarticulate. It is to be unable to speak the truth, which is to say, to speak in a way that accords with the order of things. This order has since antiquity often been identified as *logos*, and the failure to harmonize one's speech with it has been held to be the very definition of "irrationality." Such irrationality is as much a moral matter as a cognitive one.

CHAPTER NINE

The Impossible Syllogism; or, Death

➤➤➤➤➤

"In the long run we are all dead"

Already in chapter 1, we called into question the idea that rationality involves determinations made by individual actors in the aim of improving their own individual lot: the idea that it is rational, for example, to seek one's own long-term economic well-being and good health. This has been the default model of rationality in most research in economics and is the cornerstone of so-called rational-choice theory. While John Maynard Keynes did observe that "in the long run we are all dead,"[1] thus acknowledging that there is a limit to how far into the future we might project our hope or expectation for improving our own individual plight, for the most part the economic model of the individual actor has tended to envision him or her (generally him) as being of infinite duration, as not standing before the horizon of his own finitude.

Although in the most recent epoch many Anglophone philosophers have taken their cue from economists in these matters, other philosophers, since antiquity, have generally been more prepared to see mortality as a fundamental condition or horizon of human existence, and thus as of the utmost importance for understanding what a human being is. If we were not mortal, many philosophers have thought, we would not be human at all. A human being is the mortal rational animal—which would perhaps be the most common formulation of the definition of the species, were it not for the fact that it is redundant, since all animals, being composed of fragile organic bodies that must eventually come apart, are by definition mortal. To try to take stock of human rationality without considering the way human life is conditioned by death is to skirt the subject at hand. Philosophy, as Socrates understood, and Montaigne after him, is nothing other than a preparation for death.

Socrates's original insight concerned not just death, but the aging that leads to it, and was grounded in the awareness that earthly acquisitions, distinctions, and attachments grow increasingly ridiculous as one ages. The measure of the ridiculousness is proportional to the propinquity of death. What is the pleasure of being a high-status old man, having medals pinned on you every other day, being decorated, as Perry Anderson said of the elderly Jürgen Habermas, like some sunken Brezhnevite general?[2] Such honors can easily seem more like sad consolations in the face of decline, demonstrations of the paradoxical law of the human life span, according to which rewards come only at a point when it is either unhelpful or unseemly to accept them. When they are, on occasion, bestowed on the young, as sometimes happens in the music and entertainment industries, the kids seem not to know what to do with them. It is as if they have been handed chunks of uranium, and one worries for their futures. By contrast, an old person who has achieved any sort of wisdom cannot relish them; if she or he accepts them, this can only be with a keen sense of embarrassment. Who, then, benefits from accolades, if not the young, and not the old?

Surely in our striving to accomplish things, to make a name for ourselves in a field, we are naturally striving for the sort of achievement that culminates in recognition of some sort? Surely our own awareness of the horizon of death should not cause us to abandon all outwardly focused projects or maneuvering for social distinction as mere vanity? After all, if it were simply for the love of the thing itself, we could write novels and then simply leave them in a desk drawer, or we could philosophize in a cave rather than publishing books and giving lectures. But in that case we would not just have fewer awards pinned on us; others would also have fewer books in their lives, less to think about. How can embarrassment be the appropriate response to recognition for legitimate contributions?

Some have sought a way out of this dilemma through public refusal of their awards, such as the economist Thomas Piketty, who turned down membership in the French Legion of Honor in 2015,[3] or the surviving members of the Sex Pistols, who in 2006 turned down membership in the Rock & Roll Hall of Fame in a suitably vulgar memo they dashed off to that distinguished academy.[4] Yet it is clear enough that the occasion to make this public refusal is its own reward, and that those who get a chance to do it delight in it as much as others might delight in having someone even more elderly than they are fasten a pin to their chest. If Piketty and Johnny Rotten manage to make their public display of defiance without the embarrassment they would have faced at the official awards ceremony, this is perhaps only another form of self-deception, as their inversion of the awards ceremony through public refusal is itself no less a self-celebration and a self-inflation. Better what then? To be offered no awards at all? But that is the fate only of those who do consistently mediocre work, and surely *that* cannot be one's goal at the outset.

The horizon of death, in any case, transforms what we consider desirable, and transforms the significance of transformation itself. There is, again, no human being who in his or her essence matches the abstract economic model of the rational agent, an agent generally taken to be ageless, or generically at the prime of life. Yet one must always consider the stage on life's way at which an actor finds him- or herself. This is something that modern academic disciplines—whether philosophy, economics, or the various "me-search" departments that now occupy significant portions of the humanities wings of universities—have largely failed to do. We have been analyzing human diversity to no end over the past several decades, but the sort of diversity of human experience that emerges from the fact that we are all of different ages, that there *are* stages on life's way, has been largely neglected.[5] Many have fought for desegregation of country clubs and for integrated classrooms and equal opportunities for women in college athletics. But no one has even thought to insist that, say, an octogenarian should have the right to enroll in first grade. The case has been made (not without tremendous controversy) for a transracialism grounded in the same reasons as transgender identity, but almost no one has attempted to justify "transgenerationalism," where, say, an elderly person who claims to feel "young at heart" begins to insist that others validate this inward sense of who she is by treating her in every way as if she were young. When a thirty-three-year-old woman was exposed as having falsified her identity to join a high school cheerleading team, the condemnation was swift and universal, and few people considered the jail sentence she received as too harsh.[6] She was only fifteen years older than her oldest teammates, a span of time that can seem a mere blink of an eye, and yet that was enough to create the perception of a difference of essence: a high school student is a different species of creature from an adult. I know that now, in my midforties, I am not welcome in most nightclubs frequented by twenty-somethings, and I have no recourse at all to appeal this injustice. We can change, by free choice, the definition of marriage so as to be indifferent to the genders of the two members involved, but with a few narrow exceptions we are not able to change the definition of "adoption" to include a pairing in which the adoptive parent is younger than the adoptive child.

There is a tremendous disparity, in short, between the small amount of interest we pay to age as a factor in defining our diverse roles in society, on the one hand, and the vast amount we pay to gender, ethnicity, sexual orientation, and other vectors of identity on the other.[7] Age is different from these others, but in a way that should make it more interesting, and not less: for the most part, though of course with many exceptions, a person will remain in the same gender identity, ethnic identity, and sexual orientation over the course of a life, while all of us, of necessity, pass through several different ages. There is some sort of solidarity in generations, and elderly people in many societies come together to form an organized political block, such as the American Association of Retired Persons in the United States. But retired persons were not born that way, and when they dream, they often find themselves inhabiting earlier phases of their lives: phases that continue to constitute their current identity.

Aging is strange, and singular, and like the death in which it culminates it constitutes a basic parameter of human existence. No model of human agency or rationality that neglects it will tell us much at all about either of these. It is because we are going to die, and because the horizon of death shapes our experience as we age, that we come to prefer what economic models tell us we cannot possibly prefer. We come to prefer, typically, some good other than our own: that of our children, for example, or of our community. Such a preference is most typical of those who have matured enough to understand that no matter how well things are going for them right now, this constant improvement in one's own lot cannot possibly last forever. Given this basic limit, it comes to seem rational to many to stop looking to maximize their own good, and instead to figure out a way to make a graceful, or perhaps glorious, exit. Our paragon of rationality, Socrates, did just this when he spoke the truth about himself at his trial, and refused to make any persuasive case in his own defense, since "it is not hard, men, to escape death, but it is much harder to escape villainy. For it runs faster than death."[8] It would be villainous, Socrates thinks, to lament and supplicate, as if in so doing he, a seventy-year-old man, might thereby become immortal.

Was Socrates being irrational? My own father justified his smoking habit, until the very end, with this favorite line: "I don't want another five years in my eighties. I want another five years in my thirties." Was *he* being irrational? It is perhaps irrational to desire something that is strictly impossible, to go back in time, but this was not his point. His point was rather closer to that of Socrates: we are all going to die, and this brute fact inevitably conditions our choices, and influences what it is to be rational in a way that the most simple models of human agency, those that are most often deployed in economics and rational-choice theory, fail to comprehend.

Radical Choices

If there were one domain of culture especially devoted to enabling us to see our true plight, as mortal beings whom no rational calculus will save, we might expect it to be found in the therapy industry. There is of course a small tradition of existential psychotherapy that presumably attempts to take stock of our mortality as a central conditioner of our happiness; and there is a recent trend of "philosophical," though decidedly nonexistential, therapy, which seems to draw from Socrates the valuable lesson that to philosophize is to prepare to die, but also seems to spend most of its energy on training clients to think critically about the choices available to them, and then to make the best choices.[9] Most therapy, in fact, tends to presuppose that there is a right course of action, and that the therapist, in his or her expertise, is in a position to help you find it.

What we often experience in these interactions is in fact a sort of witness leading, where the patient faces an apparent dilemma, but has a clear implicit preference, rational or irrational, for one of its two horns, while the therapist simply helps the patient to come to grips with this preference. Thus if someone goes to a therapist with the clear conviction that her marriage is rotten to the core, but also expresses some vestigial love for her husband and some fear of taking the leap into a new, single life, then the therapist will likely seek to emphasize the importance in life of asserting yourself, of breaking off on your own to pursue your destiny, and so on. If the emphasis at the outset is the reverse, where the patient stresses how much she loves her husband and how troubled she is by some recent signs of crisis and of doubt as to the future of the marriage, the therapist will likely seek to emphasize the importance of sticking things out, of taking commitments seriously, and so on. By contrast, a person might at some point in her life encounter an objective dilemma, a situation in which there is no single right solution to her quandary as to how to proceed, but only radically free choice between two incomparable conceptions of the good. Such a case is generally beyond the therapist's conception of her professional responsibilities.

And if an aggrieved member of a couple turns to her friends to spell out her grievances, we may predict in advance that they will find that the other member of the couple is indeed to blame, and that their distressed friend, who has just divulged her grievances to them, is a beacon of lucidity, rationality, and righteousness. Little does it matter that the same scenario might be playing out at the very same moment, elsewhere in town, with the other member of the couple and his friends. There is little room, in this case as in the case of the therapist, to explore the possibility that no right path exists, that there is no formula for correct action such that, if followed, happiness will ensue. Therapy, whether offered by professionals or by well-meaning friends, seldom entertains true existential dilemmas, in which the agent understands at the outset that whatever choice is made, it is not a choice that is going to be dictated by reason. It is a choice that might become right in the making of it and in one's subsequent commitment to it, but it is not a choice that can be said to be right in any absolute or a priori way.

It is just this sort of dilemmas that have been of central interest to philosophers such as Kierkegaard, who featured prominently in chapter 5, and who spent some years belaboring the question not of separation or of divorce, but rather of getting married in the first place, only, ultimately, to decide against it in favor of a more severe, ascetic form of life in which a spouse, in this case the long-suffering *frøken* Regine Olsen, could have no place.[10] His life was, we may discern in retrospect, likely significantly shortened by this decision. Living alone, isolated, he had some good years of intense productivity and of ingenious insight into the human condition, and then he died at the age of forty-two. His work, today, may offer a sort of consolation, but not of the therapeutic variety. It will not tell you how to live, or reassure you that you have made the right decisions. There are no right decisions, but only radical choices. The radical choice you might end up making, in turn, might be one that leads to a swifter decline, or that disadvantages you in all sorts of ways that would make the choice appear decisively wrong by the standards laid out in rational-choice theory, or by your solicitous therapist. But this cannot be an argument against that radical choice, any more than wealth and fame in the wake of the opposite choice might be confirmation that it was in fact the right one. Kierkegaard removes himself, and the reader who is prepared to follow him, from this sort of calculus altogether.

In very recent years some Anglophone analytic philosophers have attempted to take on existential choices somewhat similar to those that Kierkegaard scrutinized so profoundly—choices that cannot be assessed in terms of some calculus of expected outcomes, but that are such that the good or the bad consequences of them are so foreign to one's life at the time the choice is made as to make a before-and-after comparison of the different stages of life impossible. These are choices that send us down a path of what has been called "transformative experience."[11] It may be, however, that those who have contributed to this literature grant too much authority to the rational-choice approach they are ostensibly aiming to move beyond. The preferred example in this literature is the decision to have children, and it is generally taken for granted among these authors, as among other members of their social caste, that having children *is* a decision, rather than something imposed by circumstances or coercive family members.[12] If I do have children, the reasoning goes, I will be so transformed by this experience that what is good for me-with-children simply cannot be placed in comparison with what is good for me unreproduced.

So, then, should I have children? Not surprisingly, analytic existentialism is also domesticated existentialism. Whereas Kierkegaard ultimately chose an ascetic form of life, of which he had already had significant firsthand experience at the time of his radical choice, it seems a foregone conclusion in the recent analytic scholarship on the topic of transformative choices that it is indeed right to make them— that we should fill our lives with a few children at least, as well as with a "partner" who takes equal responsibility in raising them, a generous selection of educational wooden toys, and so forth. As far as I know, all the parents who have contributed to this body of literature are delighted with the choice they made, and seem to want others in their community to know it.

Youth and Risk

Socrates, at the age of seventy, found his loyalty to truth, and to making the right inferences from what he knew, more worthy of his attachment than a few more years of life would have been. Around the same age my father found smoking worthy in the same way. Socrates's commitment is rational, for how could a commitment to reason be anything other than rational? My father's commitment seems less rational. But why? It is substantially the same as Socrates's: a commitment to something other than one's own continued self-preservation, in light of awareness of one's own inevitable eventual demise. It seems in my father's case that the object to which the mortal human attaches himself causes us to revert to the abstract economic model of rationality: what is rational is what maximizes one's own self-interest, and there is no greater failure to do this than to hasten your own death by smoking. Why we revert in this way on some occasions and not others seems to depend on the way in which we value, or fail to value, the particular thing, or gesture, or ideal, in the name of which we choose to die—given, again, that we are going to die anyway. In truth most such ideals or life choices are plotted somewhere between truth and pleasure, between reason and hedonism.

One common exit strategy, often depicted heroically in stories and movies, is to die for the next generation. An older person is in fact expected, as a matter of protocol, to step forward as a volunteer for death, when volunteers are called for, as when, say, there are limited spots in the lifeboat and numerous young people with potentially bright futures upon the sinking ship. In wars the reverse typically occurs: young people are expected to die for old people. Many who do so attempt to convince themselves of the rationality of this arrangement, not because they would not otherwise have had long prosperous lives ahead of them, but because a long prosperous life is not worth living if it is at the expense of the glory, or even just the continued survival, of the nation. This is a romantic ideal, and one that is also at odds with the abstract economic model of rationality as maximization of self-interest.

Of course it might in fact be an expression of rationality to defend the homeland, if the alternative is brutal occupation. But war seldom, perhaps never, presents such a clear dichotomy. An individual soldier's contribution to a war, particularly a distant foreign war, cannot be measured and shown to constitute the small effort that made the difference between winning and losing. Nor can it be shown to be the effort that made or preserved the proper conditions within the homeland for what would have been, had he or she returned from war, a long and prosperous life. Nonetheless, the romantic ideal that motivates self-sacrifice for the nation is often inadequately translated into the terms of a rational calculus: "If you value your freedom, thank a soldier." This formulation cannot stand up to scrutiny, especially if it is understood to mean that any individual soldier is all that stands between me and unfreedom. But it is interesting that the translation is even attempted. In his dedicatory epistle in the *Meditations* to the faculty of theology at the Sorbonne, Descartes assured its members that he was only trying to rationally argue for the truth of religion for the sake of those who lack the ungrounded but infinite faith of theologians and other true believers. So too, it seems, the bumper stickers and T-shirts admonishing us to thank soldiers seek to articulate for the faithless a defense, in cost-benefit terms, of the martial form of life.

In *Wolf Hall*, Hilary Mantel's popular fictional retelling of the life of Thomas Cromwell, the aged Cromwell looks back on his life as a young soldier—fighting, as most soldiers in the sixteenth century did, not for his own nation, but as a foreign mercenary—and reflects on what he thought about on the battlefield as he faced death. What a waste it would be, he had thought, to die now, when there is so much more to do. Youth, generally, is itself a long violent throe, and to be thrown from there into mortal violence, without the calm industriousness of later years, would seem far more pointless than never to have existed at all. Was the experience of war worth it, though, given that he did not die? Some might suppose—quite apart from any defense of the homeland, which, again, was not the reason Cromwell went to war, nor, surely, the reason why the majority of young men have found themselves on battlefields throughout history—that if one survives the risk, and is not too damaged by the trauma, one's later character may be fortified by the years of soldierdom.

Youth, for deeply ingrained primatological reasons, seems to bear a special relationship to risk: driving too fast, having multiple sex partners, brawling, dueling, in general testing out the limits of one's own freedom. When life is most valuable, and most full of potential, it is also made most precarious through such trials. Going to war may simply be a further addition to this list. All of these behaviors are irrational from the point of view of short-term individual self-interest. But they may appear different when we zoom out and take stock of the whole life at once, in which early risks help to give shape and meaning to a life that, if it had been foreshortened by any of them, could easily have turned out to be meaningless. If we zoom out even further, to the level of the species, and of its history, the reason of unreasonable risks at a certain stage of life comes even more clearly into focus, as a selective force.

But let us not move to that level, not here. What is important for now is the fact on which we all presumably agree, that some risk in life is compatible with the human good. If the goal in pursuit of which the risk is taken is central to one's self-conception, then even if the risk is very high, one still might deem that it is worth it. Here we encounter widely varying ideas of what sort of risk one might rationally take, since we have such widely different goals constituting our individual self-conceptions. When in 2017 Alex Honnold climbed Yosemite's El Capitan slope without ropes, the risk of death was indeed very high, but the prospect of a long life in which Honnold had not climbed El Capitan was too far from his conception of his own life to prevail against the risk.[13] From the outside, for those attached to a form of life that requires no such great risk, Honnold's decision could easily have seemed like the height of irrationality. For those whose life centrally involves seeing to the well-being of young Honnold himself, such as Honnold's mother, the decision may seem hurtful and unconscionable (evidently he avoided telling her in advance about his plan to make the climb).[14]

There is no fixed standard in relation to which we may weigh the suitability of this sort of endeavor, as there is no fixed and uniform conception of what would or would not constitute a life worth living. And although Honnold's incredible accomplishment tends to elicit praise and awe (now that he has succeeded at it, anyway), while other forms of youthful recklessness—that of the speeders, the brawlers, the mercenaries, the duelists—generally elicit condemnation, all may be plotted within a range of attempts, again, to feel out the limits of freedom. These attempts, too, make sense only in light of the fact that our freedom is bounded by mortality, and if Honnold risked only a bump on his head, like Wile E. Coyote whenever he falls from a cliff, his feat would be of little interest. The exercise of freedom always happens in the shadow of death.

Such feelings-out, in turn, are different—at least with respect to the self-understanding of those who make them—from the risks and self-sacrifice of the patriot, who goes to war not to edify himself or in pursuit of individual life goals, but because he believes his individual self-interest must be subordinated to the interests of the nation. But the patriot resembles the mercenary, or the cliff-climber, at least in that he prefers the high risk of imminent death over a likely long life that, had he not taken the risk that presents itself, would not be worth living. He does not seem to be much like the brawler or the speeder, however, who are testing out the limits of their freedom without much thought of any future, whether one worth living or not.

The relationship between freedom and rationality is complicated, and well beyond the scope of our interests in this chapter. It will suffice to note only that irrationality often involves, in part, a failure or a refusal to think of oneself objectively, and thus to think of one's own plight as determined by the same forces that would govern others in a similar situation. The refusal here can sometimes be laudable, as when one rushes into battle knowing one has next to no chance of surviving, and is subsequently, and postmortem, deemed "brave." What it takes to rush like that is a capacity to suspend any consideration of the objective probability of a desired outcome. Typically the assessment of such an action, by surviving onlookers, will be a matter of perspective. While some will say the soldier was brave, others will say he was foolhardy, that he gave up his life out of a misguided impulse, but would have done better to stay behind in the foxhole and wait for a moment, or for another day, when his fighting skills could have been more usefully deployed.

But those on both sides will agree on one thing: that what lifted the soldier out of the foxhole was not his faculty of reason, but rather something deeper, something we share with the animals, which the Greeks called *thumos* and which is sometimes translated as "spiritedness." It is a faculty that moves the body without any need for deliberation. It is something like what propels us when we are driven by desire, when we dive into a mosh pit or into bed with someone we don't quite trust. It is something to which we are more prone when we are drunk, or enraged, or enlivened by the solidarity and community of a chanting crowd.

These manifestations of irrationality, it should be clear, are, as the saying goes, beyond good and evil. Life would be unlivable if they were suppressed entirely. But to what precise extent should they be tolerated or, perhaps, encouraged? It will do no good to say flatly that they should be tolerated "in a reasonable balance" or "in moderation." For the ideal of moderation is one that is derived from reason, and it is manifestly unfair to allow reason to determine what share it should itself have in human life in a competition between it and unreason. So if we can neither eliminate unreason, nor decide on a precise amount of it that will be ideal for human thriving, we will probably just have to accept that this will always remain a matter of contention, that human beings will always be failing or declining to act on the basis of rational calculation of expected outcomes, and that onlookers, critics, and gossipers will always disagree as to whether their actions are worthy of blame or praise.

The speeder and the duelist and the others seem guilty of no failure to correctly infer from what they already know, in order to make decisions that maximize their own interests. Rather, in these cases there is a rejection of the conception of life that it must be a maximization of one's own individual long-term interests in order to be a life worth living. This rejection may be based on the belief, right or wrong, that one simply has no long-term interests, or none that would justify avoiding current risks or self-destructive behavior. It might be irrational to proceed in this way, but as Socrates already showed us, it is also irrational to pretend you are going to live forever. Between this latter form of irrationality, at the one extreme, and impulsive, reckless self-destruction at the other, there is an infinitely vast gray area, with infinitely many possible courses of action that may be deemed rational by one person and irrational by another. All of this uncertainty, and this perpetual balance between two extremes of irrationality, are a direct implication of the fact that we are mortal, that we feel ourselves to be making all of our decisions, to quote Nabokov, between two eternities of darkness.[15]

The Impossible Syllogism

Irrationality is not, generally, simple ignorance. If you do not have the relevant information, then you cannot rightly be faulted for not making the correct inferences. Irrationality must rather be, then, some sort of failure to process in the best way information one does already have.

It is, however, difficult to say, often, whether a given failure results from innocently not knowing, or rather from a culpable failure to bring into play what one does know. What we might call "Kansas irrationality," after Thomas Frank's popular 2004 book *What's the Matter with Kansas?* is a case in point.[16] If such a species of irrationality exists in the most strongly imputed form, then average Kansas voters would have to be knowingly making choices that subvert their own interests. Yet how often in the past few years have we heard the special pleading for voters of this sort, whether from Kansas, the Rust Belt, or any other stereotyped red landscapes of Trump's America, that they are not to be blamed, that they are simply the victims of a manipulative mass media, of a failed public-education system, but not themselves the agents? And if they do not know they are voting against their own interests, then how can they be held to be irrational?

Between the one extreme of action in total ignorance, and the other extreme of knowing what the best thing to do is while instead doing the opposite, there is an enormous middle ground, in which a person may well be in the paradoxical state of knowing without knowing, of knowing something "deep down" but refusing to acknowledge it. For example, a person may know deep down that single-payer health care is rationally preferable, at least according to a model of rationality as the maximization of one's own interests. That same person may also know that she would be personally significantly disadvantaged by the loss of insurance, yet nonetheless she may shut out those considerations in order to defend the argument that such a health system would amount to a loss of freedom, would be tantamount to authoritarianism, or, worse, a plot of sinister global forces.

In the vernacular English I recall from my adolescent social circles, one often heard the accusation, leveled from one friend to another, "You ain't trying to hear me!" The strange syntax reveals a complex state on the part of the accused, something like the species of irrationality I am attempting to describe. It is not that one does not know or hear, and not even that one is *trying not* to know or hear, but something subtly different from this latter possibility: one is *not trying* to know or hear. One is declining to do the necessary work, to pay the necessary attention. And making the right inferences does take work. The failure to do that work is sometimes both morally blameworthy and cognitively irrational at once.

There is a long tradition in philosophy, associated most closely with Socrates, which has it that *all* intellectual failure is moral failure, and vice versa: to act immorally is to act from an intellectually unsound judgment, and, conversely, to err is to have failed, in a morally blameworthy way, to seek out the knowledge that would have enabled one to avoid error.[17] As Miles Burnyeat sums up, "always the greatest obstacle to intellectual and moral progress with Socrates is people's unwillingness to confront their own ignorance."[18] This is not to say that someone who fails to answer a question correctly on *Jeopardy* should be punished, since, for one thing, memorization of trivia of that sort is too, well, trivial, to really count as the work of the intellect at all. We fail in a moral-cum-intellectual way, rather, when we show ourselves unwilling to make the right inferences from what we know.

On a certain understanding of how political commitments are forged and maintained, moreover, we all always know enough, at least concerning the key issues open to public debate in our era, to make the right inferences. It is not that the rejection of the single-payer model by the Trump voter is a simple consequence of having failed to read this or that study by some insurance analyst showing that it would in fact be more economical for the individual citizen and more conducive to long-term health. It is not on the basis of particular facts of this sort that a person decides to reject single-payer health insurance. By the same token, there is also likely no new information that will convince him to change his mind. The rejection plays out at the level of group affiliation and hostility to out-group interests. It is irrational, but it is not ignorant.

Among the rationalizations for their opposition to what they see as socialized health care, Republican voters, when pressed on whether they themselves are adequately insured, have been known to deny that they personally need health care, since good health runs in their family. As mentioned already, others at Tea Party protests in the middle of the Obama era were heard to recommend alternative treatments, such as those practiced by Native Americans and ancient Chinese tradition, as a means of getting by without health insurance. These are bold statements. The second of them is not just antisocialist, but rigorously antimodern: it does not simply reject a socialized system of paying for medical care; it rejects medical care itself as it has come to be understood over the past several centuries. It implicitly denies that the supposed advances in scientific research in the modern period have really brought about any improvement in human health and well-being.

The former claim, that one has no need of health insurance in view of the fact that one is in any case healthy, is even bolder: it asserts a freedom that is not shaped by mortality, a total freedom that is not limited by the body and its eventual, inevitable breakdown. It fails to appreciate that "health" is not an essential property of any living body. No body, no family, is essentially healthy, any more than a day is essentially sunny or the sea is essentially calm. It can be glorious, in the moments in which we are relishing our good health, or the beautiful weather, to imagine that this is just how things are. But it is also infantile, for the mature apprehension of these goods is always permeated by an awareness of their fleeting character. The protester who insists she does not need health insurance, because she is essentially and permanently healthy, is, then, either stunted and delusional in regard to her true condition, or disingenuous. Or perhaps there is a third possibility: that these two states are not dichotomous, but rather represent the two ends of a spectrum with several points in between. The boundary between self-delusion and delusion of others, in other words, may not be perfectly clear. The protester might simply not want to have to face up to a hard truth, either in her speaking or in her thinking, that she is like others in respect of her bodily existence, and therefore is subverting her own interests in seeking to shut down a system that would provide her with health insurance.

Her protest, like that of other members of the Tea Party movement, is ostensibly in defense of freedom: freedom from a variety of forced collectivization. We have already, perhaps too swiftly, judged her denial of her own precarious condition as a variety of moral failure. Yet if it is motivated by a romantic impulse, of the same sort that sends soldiers off to war for the nation, rather than by simple delusion, then perhaps we will find ourselves compelled to take back that judgment. Delusion is the freedom exercised by those who believe falsely that they have broken away from the collectivity and have managed to defy the determinations into which we are born, as members of a particular social class, community, or biological species. The romantic who embraces death, by contrast, or a path toward quicker death, does so with a lucid understanding of what is at stake, but believes that throwing away her life for the sake of some attachment of community, or some vision of the good, is preferable to some other compromise that would extend her individual life but would also attach her to a collective form of life that she finds alien. The ugly iteration of this romantic vision is by now too familiar. It says, in essence, "How can I accept health insurance if it comes from a black president?" The "soft" iteration—soft in the same way that Herder's nationalism was soft while Hitler's was "hard"—says, "Why are suited bureaucrats far away trying to tell us how to live, to discourage us from eating fried foods and drinking corn syrup, taking away the things we love and the things that bring us together in love?"

Significantly, the protester's demand for recognition of her individual freedom from the big government and the society it claims to hold together, a society that includes ethnic minorities and coastal elites with whom she does not identify, is at the same time a demand for recognition of the community with which she does identify, the struggling white working class, or however she may conceive it. The constraints that this community places on its members, in turn, with respect to speech, clothing, and comportment, are to a great extent incompatible with full individual freedom, and would seem particularly unworthy of an individual so exceptional as to not even be subject to bodily demise. The protester's expression of her individual freedom is at the same time an expression of a desire to be absorbed into a community in which her individuality is dissolved altogether, as the soldier's individuality is dissolved into his nation when he falls on the battlefield, or when he flies his fighter plane into an enemy battleship (perhaps reciting the romantic poetry of Hölderlin in his last seconds, as we know at least some Japanese kamikaze pilots did).[19] So the Obamacare protester is a romantic after all: a delusional romantic.

But could it really happen that an adult human being should fail to grasp his own mortality? In his 1886 novella *The Death of Ivan Ilyich*, Lev Tolstoy depicts a bourgeois man who has led a thoroughly unexamined life, until in his prime he comes down with a fatal illness. On his deathbed he recalls the well-known syllogism he had been taught in school, which has it that all men are mortal; that Caius is a man; and, therefore, that Caius is mortal. Ivan Ilyich, a dying man, realizes that even as a child he had understood all the terms of the inference, and he had understood that the inference was valid, yet, somehow, he had failed to notice that he could substitute his own name for that of Caius, and that this could have prepared him, early on, for the misfortune that would eventually arrive:

> In the depth of his heart he knew he was dying, but not only was he not accustomed to the thought, he simply did not and could not grasp it.
>
> The syllogism he had learnt from Kiesewetter's *Logic*: "Caius is a man, men are mortal, therefore Caius is mortal," had always seemed to him correct as applied to Caius, but certainly not as applied to himself. That Caius—man in the abstract—was mortal, was perfectly correct, but he was not Caius, not an abstract man, but a creature quite, quite separate from all others. He had been little Vanya, with a mama and a papa, with Mitya and Volodya, with the toys, a coachman and a nurse, afterwards with Katenka and with all the joys, griefs, and delights of childhood, boyhood, and youth.[20]

For most of his life, Ivan Ilyich did not know something he knew. He could not bring himself to make the proper inferences given the facts he already possessed in order, then, to lead the best sort of life possible: one that acknowledges death, is not afraid of it, and that frees one to construct one's projects in recognition of it. Tolstoy had seen this failure as principally a trait of the bourgeoisie, of members of that class which, in nineteenth-century Russia, was supposed by the intellectuals to cling to a self-image forged from trivial things, from social niceties, from the selection of wallpaper motifs and similar distractions. In more recent years, cultural historians such as Peter Gay[21] and economic historians such as Deirdre McCloskey[22] have offered, in very different ways, compelling, even loving, accounts of the integrity and internal depth of the lives of the bourgeois classes that emerged across Europe in the eighteenth and nineteenth centuries. One does not have to agree with them on all points in order to see that perhaps Tolstoy is being a bit hard on his own Ivan Ilyich, and perhaps, moreover, that this character's denial of death had to do not so much with his class affiliation as with, quite simply, a deeply human difficulty in coming to terms with our own impending individual nonexistence.

We have seen the denial of death, more recently, in members of the disenfranchised working class in America, or those who had fallen through the corroded bottom layer of what in the United States is called, not the bourgeoisie (for fear, presumably, of an awakening class consciousness among the proletariat), but rather the "middle class." An inauthentic life, a life spent in self-delusion about death, is, then, evidently not one that is restricted to any particular social class. It seems intrinsically to be a result neither of privilege nor of desperation. It can remain a private failure, as seems to have been the case for Tolstoy's protagonist, or it can become public and can affect, or infect, a political movement. Ivan Ilyich's failure to carry out the syllogism seems to have harmed no one but himself. Those who wished during the Tea Party protests to be freed of their Obamacare, and who were willing to deprive others of it along with them, are considerably more threatening to the general social good, just as anti-vaxxers are to crowd immunity. This species of irrationality is sometimes private, sometimes public, and the same irrational beliefs that in one context may quietly be taken to one's grave without any social consequences, may in another social context be the seed from which a social climate of unreason and self-destructive politics grows.

Even now, as I write this, I am not certain I have fully grasped the force of the old syllogism about mortality. I too understand that all men are mortal, and I understand that Caius is a man. I understand what all this means . . . for Caius. I assume that Caius, moreover, is long dead. But what all this has to do with me, exactly, is something that I seem, somehow, to know and not know at once. If full rationality requires me to fully come to terms with my own coming death and to act in accordance with this fact, then I fear full rationality remains, for now, quite out of reach. I can write a book about, among other things, the irrationality of a life spent in refusal to acknowledge one's own mortality. Yet I cannot acknowledge my own mortality, not fully. I cannot substitute my own name into the syllogism. In moments of great pride, often pride born of panic, I find myself especially prone to thinking about myself as immortal, and about my vain and trivial endeavors as all-important. I find myself alternating between this inflated attitude and its opposite; as William Butler Yeats wrote, "the day's vanity" is "the night's remorse."[23] I am not so different from the woman who denies she will be needing health insurance, and I am not so different from Ivan Ilyich.

Ivan Ilyich, having failed to think his way through to something more authentic, makes do with a vision of life constituted by bourgeois comforts and simple, ultimately meaningless pleasures. For Tolstoy, what a more authentic life would look like, though this vision lies beyond the scope of the novella itself, is one that is charged with spiritual depth and structured by a sort of pacifistic, nondenominational Christianity, of the sort Tolstoy himself practiced. At the end of the nineteenth century it was more common, however, to see, as the suitable form of life for those who have abandoned bourgeois complacency, not quiescent spirituality, but rather bold, transgressive action. Thus Charles Baudelaire evokes the thirst for "an oasis of horror in a desert of boredom."[24] Such a vision of a meaningful life would in turn inspire many in the twentieth century who saw in war and violence the only salvation from self-deluding complacency. Pankaj Mishra has portrayed in detail the case of Gabriele D'Annunzio, the Italian aristocrat, poet, and fighter pilot who briefly occupied the town of Fiume in 1919, proclaiming himself *il Duce*, a title that would of course later be associated with Benito Mussolini. "He invented the stiff-armed salute," Mishra relates, "which the Nazis later adopted, and designed a black uniform with pirate skull and crossbones, among other things; he talked obsessively of martyrdom, sacrifice and death."[25]

The turn toward violent transgression as a solution to the inadequacy of a life spent in small comforts and denial of death is generally understood as an expression of irrationalism. It is a romantic, counter-Enlightenment tendency, and has likely been a significant impediment to the construction of a just and equal global society over the course of the twentieth century. It remains one today, in the era of Trump and of recrudescent nationalism in Turkey, India, and elsewhere. And yet it gets at least something right, something that we fault Ivan Ilyich for failing to see, and that we, seemingly rightly, see in him as irrational. D'Annunzio looked death in the face, while Ivan Ilyich turned away in fear. D'Annunzio recognized the basic condition of human life. Is this not rational? Is this not what Socrates, the paragon of reason, also did when he accepted his own death sentence?

"Do not take others out with you," might be a fitting corollary to the imperative that we recognize death as the horizon of human life, and that we live our lives accordingly not in the worship of small comforts, but in preparation for life's end. The Stoics for their part acknowledged that suicide might often be a rational and fitting decision, and that there is no absolute bad in it.[26] But they were not so keen on defending murder. How exactly we get from the imperative to recognize our own mortality (as Tolstoy and Socrates argue we must) to the justification or even celebration of bringing about the premature mortality of others (as Baudelaire, D'Annunzio, and so many others have at least flirted with defending) is a difficult question. It is one that is at the heart of the problem of the relationship between irrationality as a shortcoming of an individual mental faculty, on the one hand, and as a political or social phenomenon of masses in motion on the other.

Tie Me Up

Irrationality, we have seen, is often inadequately treated as if it were merely an intellectual failure: a failure to make the right inferences from known facts. If this were all it is, it would not be terribly interesting. People would make inferential mistakes, and if they were to verbalize these mistakes, others would kindly correct them, and that would be that. Things get more complicated when we consider irrationality as a complex of judgment and action. In fact, when we turn our attention to action, we see that much of what is commonly deemed irrational is not based on incorrect inferences at all, is not based so much on a failure to know what we know, as it is on a failure to want what we want.

Many of the irrational things people do are in fact done with full, perspicuous knowledge of their irrationality. Smoking is the classic and most familiar example of this. How many smokers have we heard say, as they light up, that they really should not be doing what they are doing, that they in fact would prefer not to be doing it? This sort of irrationality is commonly called "akratic," from the Greek *akrasia*, ordinarily translated as "weakness of will." It does not involve an incorrect inference from known facts, but rather an action that in no way follows from the correct inference one has made.

We cannot simply assume at the outset that smoking is irrational. A smoker may have gone through a rigorous cost-benefit analysis and chosen to risk the future costs of smoking in order to derive the pleasure now—perhaps not only the pleasure of the nicotine in the bloodstream, but also the more abstract pleasure of being a smoker, of having a social identity as someone who lives for "the now," or of someone who is, quite simply and undeniably, cool. Or he may be persuaded by the reflection on mortality that yields up a popular bit of folk wisdom: that we ought to "find the thing we love and let it kill us slowly." This is the wisdom behind an old Soviet joke about smoking. In the USSR there was an ad campaign against smoking, denouncing it as "slow death." A man looks at the ad, says to himself, "That's all right, I'm in no big hurry," and lights up. The joke, if it must be explained, is that the man reads the ad as advising against smoking only because it is an *ineffective* means of suicide. It takes too long, whereas if you really want to commit suicide you'll take care of it swiftly. The man, for all his misunderstanding, seems to have a fairly rational disposition with regard to smoking and mortality: life, even in the shadow of death, is not so bad; one might as well do what one enjoys, as long as this does not hasten death *too* much.

Often, by contrast, a person relates to smoking, or some similar activity, very differently, as something she would very much like not to do, but that she does anyway. How, now, is such a predicament even possible? In a pair of groundbreaking books, the analytic Marxist and rational-choice theorist Jon Elster masterfully analyzed some of the central features of practical irrationality. In 1979's *Ulysses and the Sirens*, he focused on the curious phenomenon whereby individual people freely choose their own constraints, on the expectation that they will in the future behave irrationally, in contradiction with what their present selves would want.[27] They are like the hero of Homer's tale, who arranges to be bound to the mast of his ship by his mates, in order not to give in to the temptation of the Sirens' call. In the follow-up work, 1983's *Sour Grapes*, Elster takes on Jean de La Fontaine's rendering of the traditional fable about a fox who, finding that the most delicious grapes are out of reach, determines that he does not want them anyway, as they are "trop verts . . . et faits pour des goujats" (too green, . . . and suitable for suckers).[28]

Thus in the one work we are confronted with the problem of people who know how they would act in the absence of constraints, and so act preemptively so as not to act; in the other work, we encounter the problem of people who find themselves, already, under constraints, and accordingly modify their preferences to the point where they believe they would not act differently even if they were not under these constraints. This latter sort of behavior does not strike me as obviously irrational. It involves at least initial self-deceit, but only for the purpose of accommodating reality, and not of denying reality. At least one rationalist philosopher, Leibniz, would in fact hold that whatever reality has in store really is, by definition, the best, and moreover that reality cannot be otherwise. If we do not experience it as the best, this is only because we are unwisely unable to appreciate it from the perspective of the entire rational order of the world.

The grapes that are out of my reach might in fact be, in view of their intrinsic properties, the best, and it might in fact be dishonest to myself if I try to convince myself that they are not the best. But it does not follow that either the world, or my own individual life, would be better if I had the grapes; only children and stunted adults believe that life itself improves with the acquisition of sweet morsels and delightful toys. It is good to be able to do the sort of work on oneself that results in a perspective on life that recognizes the nonnecessity of the grapes to my thriving, not to mention to the goodness of the world. There might be a problem for moral philosophy about the resort to dishonesty toward oneself—that is, convincing oneself that the intrinsic properties of the out-of-reach grapes are not as good as they are—and it might in fact be better to come to a state of indifference toward the grapes by honest means. But it still does not seem to be irrationality that is in play here.

In the case of Ulysses, by contrast, we are dealing not with someone who strives to not want what he cannot have, but rather someone who arranges to not have what he wants, and moreover is initially in a position to have. How are we to understand this strange scenario? In fact, it is not at all hard to understand. The perfect fluidity of Homer's ingenious tale requires, in fact, that we recognize what Ulysses is doing, and that we see ourselves in him: as when we, say, ask our friends in advance to hide our cigarettes on a night of anticipated heavy drinking. The difficulty in understanding, rather, sets in only when we begin to analyze what is happening, when we spell out explicitly the peculiar fact about human beings that they can both want and not want the same thing.

This condition has often been discussed in the literature as the opposition between first-order and second-order desires. My first-order desire is for a cigarette; my second-order desire is to lead a long, healthy life. Ulysses's first-order desire is to rush forthwith toward the Sirens;

his second-order desire is simply to live until tomorrow. One might argue that there is really no problem here, either, that me-at-present and me-in-the-future are sufficiently different that they can want different things, have different interests, have different courses of action that are good for them. There might be some perplexities here about the metaphysics of time and of personal identity over time, but nothing inherently irrational in the recognition of the differences between these two different people sharing the same memories and the same body (along, perhaps, with infinitely many other individuals, each enduring for only a tiny sliver of time). There might be practical problems that arise for political philosophy: for example, whether people should be allowed to make contracts with themselves, such that, if they fail to follow through with a plan or a course of conduct, they consent, now, to their future self being punished.[29] But again, these problems do not seem to have to do preeminently with irrationality.

Just as Ivan Ilyich knows something he does not know, Ulysses wants something he does not want. Ivan Ilyich irrationally thinks that he is not going to die—or, more precisely, does not think that he is going to die—and this belief is irrational precisely because, in fact, he knows perfectly well he is going to die. He *can* perform the syllogism that begins "All men are mortal," and replace the name of Caius with his own, but he declines to do so. Ulysses in turn knows that he wants what he does not want, and there is no sense in which he does not know that he has this bit of knowledge. He therefore takes the necessary steps to avoid getting this thing that he wants and does not want. On a certain understanding, his approach is consummately rational, even as the very coexistence within him of first- and second-order desires testifies to his irrational nature. His rationality is a matter of developing an effective means of managing his irrationality. Well done, Ulysses.

Cargo Cults

"Sour grapes," as we have seen, is the phenomenon whereby we come to believe that what we are constrained to have is better than what we cannot have. La Fontaine's fable, and Elster's engagement with it, are in fact rather different from what we ordinarily understand by this phrase today. Someone who experiences "sour grapes," in common parlance, is imagined as having a face puckered with acid resentment, as positively stewing at the thought that things might be better for others elsewhere. La Fontaine's fox, by contrast, is at ease, in a state of what the Stoics called "ataraxia," or equanimity, convinced, now, that things are best just where he himself is and nowhere else. The fox might indeed appear to be a paragon of rationality, in contrast with the person who lives according to that other interpretation of "sour grapes" that we have just considered: the one who believes, to invoke another folk saying, that the grass is always greener on the other side of the fence.

The oscillation between these two interpretations, in fact—between the belief that things are just fine as they are here at home, and the belief that we must expand our efforts ever further in order to bring sweeter fruit back to where we live—would seem to offer a fairly comprehensive summary of modern European history, and of the paired, and apparently opposite, motions of blood-and-soil nationalism, on the one hand, and imperialist expansion on the other.

The expansion of Europeans throughout the world since the beginning of the modern period, certainly, whether for commerce, war, or colonization, has seldom been constrained by the perception that this or that fruit is inaccessible. Indeed what we see is perhaps a different species of irrationality altogether: not one wherein existing desires are curtailed in view of limitations, but rather wherein limitations are overcome for the purpose of creating new desires. This is, in sum, the argument of many historians of exploration and trade, notably Sidney Mintz, in his influential 1985 work *Sweetness and Power: The Place of Sugar in Modern History*.[30] Early modern globalization was not, as we might imagine, driven by a dire need among Europeans to go out and find absolutely essential goods of which there had previously been a short supply. Rather, it was driven in no small part by a search for luxury goods: spices, silk, coffee, tobacco, sugar, and many other commodities Europeans naturally did not know they needed until they knew they existed.

The Romans did just fine without intensive production of cane sugar; honey and fruit-based ingredients were quite enough to sweeten their foods. But Europeans have been seeking out new desires since long before they had acquired any self-conception as Europeans. In the tenth century the pagan Scandinavians made deep inroads into eastern Europe, and ultimately into central Asia and the Middle East, in order to trade their furs and soapstone for exotic luxuries.[31] In crafting the funeral masks of pharaohs, the ancient Egyptians used lapis lazuli, a precious stone that had to be brought all the way from Afghanistan.[32] There is in fact substantial evidence of long-distance transmission of status-conferring luxury commodities as early as the Upper Paleolithic.[33] For as long as we have been human, we have not been content to take just what we need from our immediate surroundings, but have traveled far, or relied on others who have traveled far, in search of things we did not know we needed until we got there. We do not, of course, need these things in the sense that we would perish, as individuals, without them. But human cultures seem to need things they do not need, and would likely perish, as cultures, without them.

It is human to need what you do not need, just as it is human, evidently, to know what you do not know, and to want what you do not want.

Culture, in this sense, we might say, is irrational. It depends for its existence on the symbolic value of hard-won commodities that it could perfectly well do without in a material sense. In the current era, this symbolic value is often embodied not by imported goods brought from far-off lands, for there are no such lands any more, but rather by commodities that are manufactured with the explicit purpose of being sold as luxury goods, and often that are luxury goods only to the extent that they are packaged and marketed as such. Many food items are deemed to be high status, and consequently are more highly priced, for reasons that have nothing to do with their relative scarcity. To cite a well-known example from the anthropologist Marshall Sahlins, if we were to price the cuts of beef based on abundance, we could expect the tongue to be the most costly, whereas in fact in our culture it is deemed to be of little value and sold at a low cost.[34] We might pretend that this valuation has only to do with the bare gustatory properties of eating tongue as opposed to eating some other more choice cut of meat, but in fact it has everything to do with culture, with the way we carve things up according to our internally meaningful but externally arbitrary standards.

There is of course usually at least something about luxury items that makes them somewhat better, more desirable, and therefore rightly more difficult to acquire: a Lamborghini is truly better than a Chrysler K-Car, from an engineering point of view, and truly more pleasurable to drive. But to appeal to the intrinsic properties of high-valued objects in a culture is almost always only to scratch the surface. Many people now believe that refined cane sugar offers the least desirable means of sweetening food. They are returning to honey and fruit sweeteners, to ingredients that had been available in the old world since antiquity. What, then, were those centuries of forced plantation labor for, the millions dead and displaced, the obesity and diabetes, the tooth decay? What made the sweet but insipid and rather juvenile taste of cane sugar seem, for so long, to be worth such an incalculable toll? Has this not been the height of irrationality?

Again, if we call it irrational, then we must level this accusation not only against modern Europeans, but against humanity, since it is in the end only a further development of what human beings have been doing all along. But to say that it is irrational for human cultures to value things that are not, strictly speaking, necessary for them, seems rather severe, as the only alternative is the sort of bare "animal" existence that takes care of immediate needs and nothing more, a form of existence we *also* routinely disparage as irrational. Sugar and spice and silks are not in themselves necessary, but the culturally embedded satisfaction they are able to give seems to be essentially human and ineliminable.

Our taste for cane sugar, or for agave-syrup sugar substitute, or for Caspian caviar or Andean quinoa, is all very much conditioned by global economic and historical forces that are generally quite beyond the scope of our immediate perception of these foods' sensible properties. The failure to think beyond these immediate properties—to understand the commodities we consume as having a history, prior to our contact with them, that involved human labor and likely also human and also animal and environmental suffering—is a variety of irrationality that the Marxists call "false consciousness." This is, again, a failure to know what one knows. On some accounts, such as that offered by the pathbreaking French Marxist sociologist Pierre Bourdieu in his 1979 *Distinction: A Social Critique of the Judgment of Taste*,[35] perfect overcoming of false consciousness would involve the recognition that every preference we believe we have, as consumers of food, music, furniture, packaged vacations, and the like, is a pure expression of our class identity, while the intrinsic properties of these things, though they may be undeniably pleasant, are strictly irrelevant in the true and exhaustive account of why we seek them out.

Anthropologists have long been interested in what they have called "cargo cults."[36] The term gets its name from a cultural phenomenon first observed in New Guinea during World War II, in which indigenous Melanesians constructed, using available natural materials, semblances of the cargo that the British army delivered to its troops stationed there. The indigenous people went so far as to build duplicate runways, and, on them, they constructed what looked like airplanes, but were in fact elaborate life-sized wood sculptures simulating airplanes. These creations were not intended as decoys for any reasons having to do with wartime strategy, and in fact they served no practical purpose whatsoever. Or at least they served no purpose that outside observers could understand. They were, it was concluded, something like cult objects, symbols in a spontaneous new religious movement among "natives" who were thought to be naturally very impressed with the technological superiority of the British.

In fact it would not be out of line to suggest that the cargo cult is the general model of all culture. I was recently in a restaurant that had salt-and pepper-shakers in the image of anthropomorphic smartphones: they were smiling people, but they were pocket telecommunication devices, but they were condiment dispensers. What is the logic of this? Presumably the novelty and cutting-edge quality of smartphones gave them, in the early to mid-2010s, a sort of cultural prestige that could then be borrowed in the production of a number of other cultural artifacts, including ones like salt- and pepper-shakers that have been around for centuries, simply by giving these artifacts a resemblance to their new sleek descendant. But why then also give them human faces? To remind us, one imagines, as the New Guineans presumably already knew, that human-made objects share in the humanity of their makers.

It is, one may further suggest, this same cargo-cult phenomenon at work when we happen upon a "museum" in a remote village somewhere, housing no more than a few historical objects from the region, plus perhaps some laminated sheets of information or of old photographs that have been printed out from the internet. I have often felt, similarly, when I am visiting what is billed as an upscale restaurant in a small city in a distant, provincial corner of the world, that I am not so much visiting an upscale restaurant as I am visiting a simulation of what the local people think an upscale restaurant in some faraway capital city must be like. Sartre thought that *even* a Parisian waiter is in a sense imitating a Parisian waiter—that is, he artificially enacts in his gestures and behavior some ideal image he has of what it is that someone such as himself should be doing. He can even overdo it, and be, paradoxically, too much the person he is. This sort of imitation can only be more pronounced, and often more excessive, when one is not in Paris, but, say, in a restaurant with a French name, or a French-sounding name, in Nebraska or Transnistria. The ritual can all the more easily come to seem ridiculous out here on the geographical margins: Why must this waiter pour my water so ceremoniously? And when did he learn that coming with an enormous pepper mill directly to the table and offering to dispense a bit of it was something one does? Everything about upscale restaurants is absurd, but when it is rationalized by those involved by reference to the way things are done—correctly, perfectly, exaltedly—somewhere far away, then this seems to add a further layer of irrationality, as it groundlessly imagines that there *is* a reason for the way the activity is done elsewhere, and that we can attain to this reason simply by imitation.

One further example is perhaps in order. Friends from my hometown spent considerable time and energy debating, a few years back, the municipal government's intention to use public funds to acquire a sculpture made by Jeff Koons (or by his employees). More or less all who were in favor of its acquisition noted how valuable the presence of such a work could be for raising the city's profile. There was little or no discussion of the aesthetic value or meaning of the work in question; there was only an acknowledgment of what was already for them a given fact: that meaning had been created elsewhere. This meaning might be inscrutable, but here in our city we are not the ones charged with determining what it is, let alone with creating works that might be presented to the world as yet other material distillations of meaning. Here, in our city, meaning is imported ready-made from elsewhere, after which our city gains a place on the broader map of meaning, like a town that has been recently connected by a new rail line to the metropolis. Again, however irrational it may be to shell out for Jeff Koons in London or New York, there is an added layer of irrationality to do so in Sacramento, simply on the grounds that one knows it is what one does in London or New York.

But what *is* this action that so many of us want in on? What is the special power of the Koons sculpture or of the perfect wallpaper? What leads us to declare that we absolutely love kale or our Toyota Prius, or the way the waiter turns the crank on the pepper mill, or that we simply could not do without our annual restorative trip to the French Riviera? Combining the insights of Bourdieu and Tolstoy, we begin to discern that the particular form of not knowing what we in fact know that underlies such declarations has something to do—like Ivan Ilyich's preoccupation with his choice of wallpaper—with the difficulty of facing up to the fact that we are going to die. Bourdieu and Tolstoy both see the inability to meet this difficulty square on as a great failure to realize the full potential of a human life. Others, including Sahlins, tend to see this failure as itself ineliminably human, to see absorption in the preference of this cut of meat over that one, of this lapel pin or handshake over those of our peculiar neighbors, as part of the wonder of what it is to be a human being embedded in a human culture. How remarkable that we can be so captivated by such things as to forget that we are going to die! That is not a failure, but a victory!

Those who have wanted to jolt us out of this preoccupation with the trivialities of human culture, forcing us to face up to the fact of our death, have often been motivated by big plans for what we will do after our awakening, by a vision of a radically different, and often utopian, rearrangement of society. It is generally recognized that such a rearrangement will come at a high cost, even that lives will be lost, and that people must therefore be prepared to abandon their small comforts for the sake of something greater. Many, indeed, are willing to take up this trade, this exchange of wallpaper for a world-renouncing commune, or of consumer goods for jihad. Those who go in for this deal are correct in recognizing that they are going to die, and they conclude from this, rightly or wrongly, that they would do better to die *for* something. Others in turn look their own death in the face, and find that they despise the trivialities of death-denying daily life, but still do not wish to join up with anything particularly bold or self-transcending. They might wish only, as Krzysztof Kieślowski announced he was going to do when he retired from filmmaking, to sit in a dark room and smoke. This was in 1994; two years later, he was dead of a heart attack at the age of fifty-four.[37]

There is no way out of it: every response to the specter of mortality can be criticized for its irrationality. If we absorb ourselves in home decoration, we are failing to know something we in fact know; if we run off and join some glorious cause, we are failing to maximize our own individual interest; if we just sit alone and let the thing we love kill us slowly (or quickly), we are, so our friends and family tell us, failing to do everything we could have done to get the most out of life. When the brutally bitter, astoundingly honest and self-knowing Austrian writer Thomas Bernhard received the Austrian Literature Prize in 1968, he created a scandal with his acceptance speech, and succeeded in doing, through his acceptance, what Piketty and the (surviving) Sex Pistols had hoped to do through their refusal. His speech began, "There is nothing to praise, nothing to condemn, nothing to criticize, but it is all ridiculous [*lächerlich*]; it is all ridiculous, if you just think about death."[38]

In Loving Repetition

We have spoken on several occasions throughout this book of our "ordering" our lives, and we have identified the very concept of "order," as *kosmos*, as having a deep historical and conceptual connection to that of reason, as *logos*. Many have supposed that the universe itself is rational in view of the way in which it is ordered. Many have also thought that human life gains its reason in part from the way we order it, not from the things we believe, but rather from the things we do. For many people, this ordering takes the form of religious ritual, which, as we saw in chapter 4, the poet Les Murray has described, in reference to his own Catholic faith, as "loving repetition."

It may be that the shift in modern philosophy, and modern thought in general, to language as the locus of significance in human life has in turn caused repetition to appear, against Pina Bausch's claim (see, again, chapter 4), as "mere repetition." The philosopher Frits Staal, who immersed himself in Brahminic rituals for many decades, developed a theory of ritual as a system of "rules without meaning," which, he came to believe, is in fact more primordial than language in giving order and orientation, if not conceptual tools, to human existence.[39] Many who are raised in the Protestant world, and trained up to believe that the essence of religion is a personal relationship to God, are surprised when they travel to, say, southern Italy or to the Balkans, and encounter for the first time a conception of religion in which the rituals—the quick sign of the cross when passing a church on the street, the cycles of fasting and feasting, the ex-voto candles lit and the prayers muttered—are presumed to be sine qua non for the survival of religious belief. Some scoff when they encounter this, and insist that such religious people are not religious at all, but superstitious.

Tolstoy would unequivocally reject ritual-bound religion, arguing instead, famously, that "the Kingdom of God is within you," and therefore that true religiosity consists in recognition, via introspection, of the divine. But if Staal is correct, one hopes in vain to arrive at some pure core of religion through the abolition of its attendant rituals, as in fact the ritual is what defines religion as a sphere of human life. Seen from a different angle, in fact, one might suppose on the contrary that when we strip away the rituals, it is only a superstitious core of belief that remains: rituals themselves cannot be superstitious, since, as Staal notes, they have no meaning at all, while this is not at all the case for beliefs about transcendental powers or about life after death. Thus for Staal ritual is not simply the superstitious chaff we might hope to remove from the wheat of rationalized religion; it is the reason of religion itself, although in a deeper sense of "reason" than we ordinarily understand it, as order rather than conceptual articulation. It is ritual, some have felt, that holds the world together.

Having spent considerable time in the Balkans, I have learned that what early on looked to me like mindless superstitions surrounding death—the way Balkan cultures tend to the graves of their loved ones, have periodic feasts and rituals in commemoration of the dead, often culminating, seven years on, in a digging up and cleaning of the bones—are in fact a complex and effective sort of cultural processing. As one French demographer familiar with the funerary practices of the region has noted, in the Balkans death occupies a place at the center of communal life comparable to that occupied by sex in Western countries.[40] By placing death and the intervals of funerary ritual in the center of social life, these cultures have found a way of rendering comprehensible what is in itself irreducibly mysterious, and what is in fact no less mysterious in a culture such as my own, where we euphemistically "celebrate the life" of the ones we have loved and lost, without truly facing up to the full reality of their deaths, not least their ghoulish corpses and bones.

An e. e. cummings poem describes a love so intense that the beloved comes to be seen as "the wonder that's keeping the stars apart," that is, holding the stars in their place and preventing them from collapsing together. But in the absence of another person to embody that wonder, many have sought to modulate or process it through their own actions. Nor must one belong to a particular religion with prescribed rituals in order to come to the conclusion that it is ritual that holds the world together, that keeps the stars apart. Thus the protagonist of Andrei

Tarkovsky's 1986 film *The Sacrifice*, on the brink of a nuclear apocalypse, entertains the idea that if only he had dutifully done some deed each day, even if it were just flushing the toilet at the same time, perhaps the world could have held together: an absurd thought, of course, but one coming from somewhere deeper than fear and desperation. If reason is order, there is no more effective way to enact it in an individual human life than through repetition. Yet there is also nothing more apparently irrational, as Tolstoy, and indeed Martin Luther and most Protestant theologians since have believed, than to find oneself enslaved to the obsessive compulsions of religious ritual. Here, as often, we find that the very same thing can appear as the height of rationality, or as its opposite, depending only on the frame of our judgment.

It is all ridiculous, this choice between opposite expressions of irrationality, in the face of death, but we do the best we can, for as long as we can, to impose a share of order on it, by choosing nice new wallpaper, by respecting feast days and fast days, by honoring the ancestors according to the rhythms and intervals that they themselves devised; by aspiring to understand them better than they understood themselves, and so to honor them in ways they could not have imagined.[41]

Conclusion

>>>>>

Irrationality is ineliminable. We have no choice but to sleep at night, and so to lose our grip on the law of the excluded middle. When we wake, we cannot help but feel, whatever our society tells us to the contrary, that what we experience in our dream life has some share of truth, even if it is strictly speaking impossible. Nor can we help but throw ourselves into things that are in important respects really not good for us. The problem is a serious one. It is not just that we are not doing things quite right. Rather, we sense that if we were exclusively to do things that are good for us, this would in itself not be good for us. Because we are all going to die, and therefore we know that all expected rational utility of our actions will eventually be canceled out, life itself can easily appear intrinsically irrational, and all the more so when it is spent in zealous commitment to the enforcement of rationality.

The thesis of this book—that irrationality is as potentially harmful as it is humanly ineradicable, and that efforts to eradicate it are themselves supremely irrational—is far from new. You did not need to hear it from me. It has by now been perfectly obvious for at least a few millennia. The dual case, however, against mythologizing the past, and against delusions about our ability to impose a rational order on our future, always benefits from being made afresh, as evidently what has been perfectly obvious for a few millennia nonetheless keeps slipping back into that vast category of things we know but do not know.

>>>>>

There are a number of other works that have served in varying degrees and ways as models for the present one. The most obvious is Erasmus's

In Praise of Folly of 1511. For folly, or madness, is a species of irrationality. But what the great Dutch humanist praises and celebrates, we have sought here rather only to understand and, as necessary, to accommodate, in a spirit that is neither for nor against the condition in question. This has not been a contribution to what in German is helpfully called *Narrenliteratur*, the "literature of fools," celebrating human weakness through caricature and exaggeration. Indeed I have followed at least somewhat more closely in the spirit of Michel Foucault, in his 1961 *Madness and Civilization: History of Madness in the Age of Reason* (*Folie et déraison. Histoire de la folie à l'age classique*), for whom fools arise in the world more through society's imposition of this category than through their own foolish thoughts and actions. This book, moreover, like his, is a "history" in that it attempts to paint a broad picture of how the current world came to be as it is, while dispensing with rigorous chronology and any purported causal sequence of events (in French, again, "history" and "story" are the same word). But here too the author's focus is on a relatively narrow species of the broad genus that interests us, and his conclusions about madness's historical contingency are ultimately somewhat too far from the humanist affirmation of an innate foolishness in our species that cannot be analyzed away as a mere construction or contingency. There is also an echo of William Barrett's *Irrational Man: A Study in Existential Philosophy* of 1958, which for all its many virtues seems nonetheless far too contingent upon the concerns of its historical era, upon the midcentury mood that it breathes, to appear as having either much currency in the present moment, or much timeless insight to lift us out of the present moment. And there is surely a significant residue here, too, of Thomas Browne's delirious *Pseudodoxia epidemica* of 1646, in which the English author records, with prurient fascination, the "epidemic" of popular false beliefs of his revolutionary age. It is a great paradox of the present age that, even though the totality of all human learning is more accessible than ever before in history, indeed billions of us on earth can now easily access it with a special device we carry in our pockets, nonetheless false beliefs are as epidemic as ever.

Perhaps one more title is worth mentioning, but not without some preliminary explanation. In the writing of this book, mostly between 2016 and 2018, I quit drinking, I bought a Fitbit and a blood-pressure monitor, I closed my Facebook account (a plague on humanity worse than any drug), I finally committed to being fully honest with everyone in my life, and I got my long-sloppy finances in order. I pulled myself together, wised up: finally carried out the "impossible syllogism" and realized I've got only a finite amount of time to do everything I want to do. I got rational, in my limited and relative way. In this respect, I tell myself, I have followed in the path of Richard Klein, who finally and unexpectedly quit smoking in the course of writing his wonderful paean to that filthy habit, *Cigarettes Are Sublime* of 1993. The true self-help, it turns out, is not in the facile teachings of the self-help professionals and confidence men, but in thoroughly working through everything that is good, everything we love, in what we also hate and wish to be free of: all the delirium and delusion, the enthusiasms, excesses, manias, mythmaking, rhapsodies, stubbornness, and self-subversion that make human life, for good or ill, what it is.

ACKNOWLEDGMENTS

>>>>>>

This book emerged at the intersection of professional productivity and essayistic exploration, of enjoyable work and serious play, of reason and imagination. The conversations that fed into it were sometimes with colleagues and sometimes with old friends, sometimes with people who are a combination of both, with some of whom I've spent countless hours, and a few of whom I've never yet met in person. These include Noga Arikha, D. Graham Burnett, Emanuele Coccia, James Delbourgo, Philippe Descola, Jeff Dolven, Jerry Dworkin, Rodolfo Garau, Jessica Gordon-Roth, Geoffrey Gorham, Catherine Hansen, Philippe Huneman, Gideon Lewis-Kraus, Stephen Menn, Richard Moran, Yascha Mounk, Ohad Nachtomy, Steve Nadler, Sina Najafi, Paolo Pecere, S. Abbas Raza, Anne-Lise Rey, Jessica Riskin, Jerry Rothenberg, Adina Ruiu, Jesse Schaefer, Kieran Setiya, J. B. Shank, Jean-Jacques Szczeciniarz, and Charles T. Wolfe. Some of the conversations and encounters that influenced the final shape of this book happened long ago, notably with Jack Goody; with Daniel Rancour-Laferriere, who first taught me how to read a poem (it was Aleksandr Blok's "Двенадцать"); with Catherine Wilson, and with Richard Wollheim, both of whom showed me early on how it is possible to do philosophy with one's whole person. I am grateful to my agent, Andrew Stuart, for convincing me to take this topic on; and to my editor at Princeton, Rob Tempio, whose love of books and knowledge of how to craft them never cease to amaze me.

A significant portion of the first section of chapter 5 was previously published as "The Internet of Snails," *Cabinet Magazine* 58 (2016): 29–37. Part of the early portion of chapter 8 was previously published under the title "Punching Down," in *The Point Magazine* 14 (Autumn, 2017): 117–23.

Paris, August 2018

NOTES

➤➤➤➤➤

Preamble

1. Iamblichus, *Life of Pythagoras*, trans. Thomas Taylor (London, 1818), 65.

2. Pappus of Alexandria, *The Commentary of Pappus on Book X of Euclid's* Elements, ed. and trans. William Thomson (Cambridge, MA: Harvard University Press, 1930).

3. James Merrill, *The Changing Light at Sandover* (New York: Knopf, 1982), 55.

Introduction

1. Paul Hazard, *La crise de la conscience européenne, 1680–1715* (Paris: Fayard, 1961 [1935]), 117.

2. Theodor W. Adorno and Max Horkheimer, *Dialectic of Enlightenment*, trans. John Cumming (London: Verso, 1997 [1944]).

3. Pascal Bruckner, *The Temptation of Innocence: Living in the Age of Entitlement* (New York: Algora Publishing, 2007 [1995]), 19.

4. Zeev Sternhell, *Les anti-Lumières. Une tradition du XVIIIe siècle à la guerre froide* (Paris: Fayard, 2006), 17; published in English as *The Anti-Enlightenment Tradition*, trans. David Maisel (New Haven, CT: Yale University Press, 2009).

5. Pankaj Mishra, *Age of Anger: A History of the Present* (New York: Farrar, Straus and Giroux, 2017), 147.

6. Steven Pinker, *Enlightenment Now: Reason, Science, Humanism, and Progress* (New York: Penguin Random House, 2018).

7. Germaine de Staël, *De la littérature, considérée dans ses rapports avec les institutions sociales*, in *Oeuvres complètes de Madame de Staël, publiées par son fils*, vol. 4 (Brussels: Louis Hauman et Co., 1830), 360.

8. Paul Lewis, "'Our Minds Can Be Hijacked': The Tech Insiders Who Fear a Smartphone Dystopia," *Guardian*, October 6, 2017. https://www.theguardian.com/technology/2017/oct/05/smartphone-addiction-silicon-valley-dystopia.

9. See, e.g., Sam Kestenbaum, "Got Nazis? Milk Is New Symbol of Racial Purity for White Nationalists," *Forward*, February 13, 2017. https://forward.com/fast-forward/362986/got-nazis-milk-is-new-symbol-of-racial-purity-for-white-nationalists/.

10. Virginia Woolf, "The Lady in the Looking Glass: A Reflection," in *Virginia Woolf: Selected Short Stories*, ed. Sandra Kemp (London: Penguin Classics, 1993 [1929]), 78.

Chapter One. The Self-Devouring Octopus; or, Logic

1. See Justin E. H. Smith, *The Philosopher: A History in Six Types* (Princeton, NJ: Princeton University Press, 2016), chap. 3.

2. See Roger Bigelow Merriman, ed., *The Life and Letters of Thomas Cromwell: Letters from 1536* (Oxford: Clarendon Press, 1902).

3. See Walter J. Ong, *Ramus, Method, and the Decay of Dialogue: From the Art of Discourse to the Art of Reason* (Cambridge, MA: Harvard University Press, 1958).

4. Cited in ibid., 27.

5. See Stephen Jay Gould, "Nonoverlapping Magisteria," *Natural History* 106 (March 1996): 16–22.

6. Herman Melville, *The Confidence-Man: His Masquerade*, and *Billy Budd, Sailor* (London: Penguin, 2012 [1857]), 30.

7. Cicero, *Tusculan Disputations* 2.12.29.

8. Lucian of Samosata, *Thirty Conferences of the Dead: Diogenes and Pollux*, in *Lucian of Samosata*, trans. and ed. William Tooke, 2 vols. (London: Longman, Hurst, Rees, Orme, and Brown, 1820), 1:383–84.

9. Themistius, *Orations* 14, cited in Pierre Gassendi, *Syntagma philosophicum*, in *Opera Omnia in sex tomos divisa* (Lyon: Laurence Anisson and Jean-Baptiste Devenet, 1658), 1:88.

10. Aulus Gellius, *Attic Nights*, trans. J. C. Rolfe, Loeb Classical Library 212 (Cambridge, MA: Harvard University Press, 1927), 3:162, bk. 16, chap. 9.

11. Cicero, *Tusculan Disputations* 3.10.22, citing Plutarch, *De sollertia animalium*, Loeb Classical Library 12 (Cambridge, MA: Harvard University Press, 1957), 359.

12. Leibniz, *Projet d'un art d'inventer*, in Louis Couturat, *La logique de Leibniz, d'après des socuments inédits* (Paris: Félix Alcan, 1901), 176.

13. Gassendi, *Syntagma philosophicum*.

14. Anton Wilhelm Amo, *Tractatus de arte sobrie et accurate philosophandi* (Halle, 1738). This argument works more smoothly in Latin, where there are no indefinite articles and where "your" and "yours" are identical in form: "Haec capra est tua; haec capra est mater; ergo, haec capra est tua mater."

15. Immanuel Kant, *Kritik der Urtheilskraft* §54, AA 5, 332.

16. Ludwig Wittgenstein, *Tractatus Logico-Philosophicus*, trans. C. K. Ogden (London: Kegan Paul, Trench and Trübner, 1922). "But all propositions of logic say that same thing. That is, nothing" (5.4.3).

17. Martin Heidegger, *Logic: The Question of Truth*, trans. Thomas Sheehan (Bloomington: Indiana University Press, 2010), 10.

18. Gassendi, *Syntagma philosophicum*, Pars Prima: Logica, 80.

19. See in particular Robert Nozick, "Newcomb's Problem and Two Principles of Choice," in *Essays in Honor of Carl G. Hempel*, ed. Nicholas Rescher (Dordrecht: Reidel, 1969), 114–46; David H. Wolpert and Gregory Benford, "The Lesson of Newcomb's Paradox," *Synthese* 190, no. 9 (2013): 1637–46; Arif Ahmed, "Infallibility in the Newcomb Problem," *Erkenntnis* 80, no. 2 (2015): 261–73.

20. See André Vauchez, *Francis of Assisi: The Life and Afterlife of a Medieval Saint*, trans. Michael F. Cusato (New Haven, CT: Yale University Press, 2013).

21. See, e.g., Karigoudar Ishwaran, ed., *Ascetic Culture: Renunciation and Worldly Engagement*, International Studies in Sociology and Social Anthropology (Leiden: Brill, 1999).

22. See Jean-Jacques Rousseau, *Discours sur l'origine et les fondements de l'inégalité parmi les hommes* (Amsterdam: Marc Michel Rey, 1762), 122–24.

23. Aristotle, *Metaphysics*, ed. W. D. Ross, Oxford: Clarendon Press, 1924, 1074b33.

24. Porphyry, *Life of Plotinus*, in *The Essence of Plotinus: Extracts from the Six Enneads and Porphyry's* Life of Plotinus, ed. Grace H. Turnbull, trans. Stephen MacKenna (New York: Oxford University Press, 1934), 10.

25. Ibid.

26. On the strange history of the uptake of inscrutable French philosophy within American academia, see François Cusset, *French Theory. Foucault, Derrida, Deleuze et Cie et les mutations de la vie intellectuelle aux États-Unis* (Paris: La Découverte, 2005).

27. Perry Anderson, "Dégringolade," *London Review of Books* 26, no. 17 (September 2, 2004): 3–9.

28. I am drawing here mostly on my memory of a public lecture from Badiou, entitled "Les attributs de l'Absolu," delivered at the American University of Paris on June 17, 2015.

29. Leibniz to Foucher, 1692, in G. W. Leibniz, *Lettres et opuscules inédits de Leibniz*, ed. A. Foucher de Careil (Paris: Librairie Philosophique de Ladrange, 1854), 89. Cited in Jorge Luis Borges, "Pierre Menard autor del Quijote," in Jorge Luis Borges, *Cuentos completos* (Barcelona: Lumen, 2015), 110.

30. Barry Meier, "Inside a Secretive Group Where Women Are Branded," *New York Times*, October 17, 2017. https://www.nytimes.com/2017/10/17/nyregion/nxivm-women-branded-albany.html.

Chapter Two. "No-Brainers"; or, Reason in Nature

1. See John McDowell, *Mind and World* (Cambridge, MA: Harvard University Press, 1996 [1994]).

2. I owe this insight to D. Graham Burnett (in personal correspondence).

3. Les Murray, "The Meaning of Existence," in *Poems the Size of Photographs* (Sydney: Duffy & Snellgrove, 2002), 104.

4. Carlos Fraenkel, *Philosophical Religions from Plato to Spinoza: Reason, Religion, and Autonomy* (Cambridge: Cambridge University Press, 2012), 128.

5. Benedictus de Spinoza, *Theological-Political Treatise* 5.45, in *The Collected Works of Spinoza*, trans. and ed. Edwin Curley, vol. 2 (Princeton, NJ: Princeton University Press, 2016); Spinoza, *Ethics* 4, Proposition 68, Scholium, in *The Collected Works of Spinoza*, trans. and ed. Edwin Curley, vol. 1 (Princeton, NJ: Princeton University Press, 1986).

6. Peter Godfrey-Smith, *Other Minds: The Octopus, the Sea, and the Deep Origins of Consciousness* (New York: Farrar, Straus and Giroux, 2016).

7. For a helpful account of the distinction between these two phenomena—the detaching of the hectocotylus, or autotomy, and the eating of the arms, or autophagy—see B. U. Budelmann, "Autophagy in *Octopus*," *South African Journal of Marine Science* 20, no. 1 (1998): 101–8.

8. Godfrey-Smith, *Other Minds*, 76.

9. Girolamo Rorario, *Hieronymi Rorarii ⋯ gati pontificii, Quod animalia bruta ratione utantur melius homine*, libri duo (Amsterdam: Apud Joannem Ravesteinium, 1654 [1555]).

10. René Descartes, *Méditations*, in *Oeuvres de Descartes*, ed. Charles Adam and Paul Tannery (Paris: Léopold Cerf, 1904) [hereafter "AT"], 9:48.

11. Jean-Paul Sartre, *Being and Nothingness: A Phenomenological Essay on Ontology*, trans. Hazel Barnes (New York: Washington Square Press, 1956 [1943]), 785.

12. Pierre Bayle, *Dictionnaire historique et critique*, 3rd ed., vol. 3 (Rotterdam, 1715 [1697]).

13. Ibid., 441.

14. Ibid.

15. Dennis Des Chene, "'Animal' as Category: Bayle's 'Rorarius,'" in *The Problem of Animal Generation in Early Modern Philosophy*, ed. Justin E. H. Smith (Cambridge University Press, 2006), 215–34, 219.

16. Francisco Suárez, *De anima* 1c5n02, in *Opera omnia*, ed. Charles Berton (Paris: Apud Ludovicum Vivès, 1889), 3:500. Cited in Des Chene, "'Animal' as Category: Bayle's 'Rorarius.'"

17. Francisco Suárez, *Disputationes metaphysicae* 23.10.14, in *Opera omnia*, vol. 24.

18. Emanuele Coccia, *La vie des plantes. Une métaphysique du mélange* (Paris: Bibliothèque Rivages, 2016), 137.

19. Ibid., 133.

20. Eduardo Kohn, *How Forests Think: Toward an Anthropology beyond the Human* (Berkeley: University of California Press, 2013).

21. See Richard Marshall, "Why You Don't Need Brain Surgery to Change Logic" (interview with Hartry Field), *3:AM Magazine*, May 3, 2018. http://www.3ammagazine.com/3am/why-you-dont-need-brain-surgery-to-change-logic/.

22. Isidore of Seville, *Etymologies*, trans. and ed. Stephen A. Barney, W. J. Lewis, J. A Beach, and Oliver Berghof (Cambridge: Cambridge University Press, 2006), 81.

23. Hugo Mercier and Dan Sperber, *The Enigma of Reason* (Cambridge, MA: Harvard University Press, 2017).

24. Ibid., 7.

25. Descartes, AT, 6:2; cited in Mercier and Sperber, *The Enigma of Reason*, 16.

26. Mercier and Sperber, *The Enigma of Reason*, 203.

27. Ibid.

28. For a summary of this research, see Justin E. H. Smith, *Nature, Human Nature, and Human Difference: Race in Early Modern Philosophy* (Princeton, NJ: Princeton University Press, 2015), chap. 1.

29. Edouard Machery and Luc Faucher, "Why Do We Think Racially? Culture, Evolution and Cognition," in *Categorization in Cognitive Science*, ed. Henri Cohen and Claire Lefebvre (Amsterdam: Elsevier, 2005), 1009–33.

30. See Sam Frank, "Come with Us If You Want to Live," *Harper's Magazine*, January 2015, 26–36. As Gideon Lewis-Kraus convincingly explains, this tendency in Silicon Valley culture is only one among many, even if it has received considerable, and somewhat sensationalist, press coverage. The prevailing political culture there remains a sort of passive liberalism that aligns fairly closely with the center of the Democratic Party, and that presupposes, without altogether too much reflection, that technological growth and innovation are on balance good for democracy (from personal conversation).

31. Peter Thiel, "The Education of a Libertarian," *Cato Unbound: A Journal of Debate*, April 13, 2009. https://www.cato-unbound.org/2009/04/13/peter-thiel/education-libertarian.

32. http://www.imitatio.org/about-imitatio/.

33. http://www.imitatio.org/team/.

34. http://rationality.org/workshops/upcoming.

35. http://lesswrong.com/lw/ouc/project_hufflepuff_planting_the_flag/.

36. Ibid.

37. Jean-Paul Sartre, *No Exit, and Three Other Plays* (New York: Vintage Books, 1955 [1944]), 47.

Chapter Three. The Sleep of Reason; or, Dreams

1. "Relation de ce qui s'est passé de plus remarquable . . . ès années 1670 et 1671, envoyé au Reverend Père Jean Pinette, Provincial de la Province De France," in *Relations des Jésuites, contenant ce qui s'est passé de plus remarquable dans les missions des pères de la Compagnie de Jésus dans la Nouvelle France* (Quebec City: Augustin Côté, 1858), 3:22.

2. Bruce Trigger, *The Children of Aataentsic: A History of the Huron People to 1660* (Montreal: McGill-Queens University Press, 1987), 504.

3. Aristotle, *On Prophecy in Sleep*, in *On the Soul. Parva Naturalia. On Breath*, trans. W. S. Hett, Loeb Classical Library 288 (Cambridge, MA: Harvard University Press, 1957), 462b13–14, 375.

4. Ibid., 1.462b20–22, 375.

5. Johannes Kepler, *Somnium: The Dream, or, Posthumous Works on Lunar Astronomy*, trans. Edward Rosen (Mineola, NY: Dover Publications, 1967).

6. Sor Juana Inés de la Cruz, *Obras completas*, vol. 1, *Lírica personal*, ed. Alfonso Méndez Plancarte (Mexico City: Fondo de Cultura Económica, 1951).

7. Denis Diderot, *Le rêve de d'Alembert*, in *Oeuvres complètes de Diderot*, vol. 2, ed. Assézat Tourneux (Paris: Garnier Frères, 1875).

8. Gaston Bachelard, *La terre et les rêveries du repos* (Paris: José Corti, 1948), 11.

9. Ibid.

10. Saxo Grammaticus, *The First Nine Books of the Danish History of Saxo Grammaticus*, trans. Oliver Elton (London: David Nutt, 1894), 26.

11. Ibid.

12. See Jack Goody, *The Logic of Writing and the Organization of Society* (Cambridge: Cambridge University Press, 1986).

13. Jacob and Wilhelm Grimm, *Kinder- und Hausmärchen* (Göttingen, 1812).

14. A. N. Afanas'ev, *Narodnye russkie rasskazy A. N. Afanas'eva*, 2nd ed., 4 vols. (Moscow: K. Soldatenkov, 1873).

15. Elias Lönnrot, *Kalevala* (Helsinki: J. C. Frenckellin ja Poika, 1835).

16. Kant, *Träume eines Geistersehers, erläutert durch Träume der Metaphysik*, in *Immanuel Kants gesammelte Schriften*, ed. Prussian Academy of Sciences (Berlin, 1902) [hereafter "AA"], 2:317.

17. Ibid., 315.

18. Ibid., 349.

19. G. W. Leibniz, "The Body-Machine in Leibniz's Early Medical and Physiological Writings: A Selection of Texts with Commentary," ed. and trans. Justin E. H. Smith, *Leibniz Review* 27 (2007): 141–79.

20. Mary Douglas, *Natural Symbols: Explorations in Cosmology* (London: Barrie & Rockliff, 1970).

21. G. W. Leibniz, *Directiones ad rem medicam pertinentes*, appendix 1 to Justin E. H. Smith, *Divine Machines: Leibniz and the Sciences of Life* (Princeton, NJ: Princeton University Press, 2011), 286.

22. Woolf, *Selected Short Stories*, 58.

23. Julian Jaynes, *The Origin of Consciousness in the Breakdown of the Bicameral Mind* (Boston: Houghton Mifflin, 1976), 75.

24. Ibid., 73–74.

25. Ibid., 82.

26. See in particular G.E.R. Lloyd, *The Ideals of Inquiry: An Ancient History* (Oxford: Oxford University Press, 2014).

27. Walter J. Ong, *Orality and Literacy: The Technologizing of the Word* (London: Taylor & Francis, 2002 [1982]).

28. James C. Scott, *Against the Grain: A Deep History of the Earliest States* (New Haven, CT: Yale University Press, 2017).

29. E. R. Dodds, *The Greeks and the Irrational* (Berkeley: University of California Press, 1951), 105.

30. Ibid., 106.

31. Ibid., 107.

32. Ibid.

33. Ibid.

34. Ibid.

35. Ibid., 108–9.

36. See Aristotle, *On Dreams* 3, 461b5–8; cited in Dodds, *The Greeks and the Irrational*, 115.

37. Dodds, *The Greeks and the Irrational*, 112.

38. Ibid.

39. Ibid.

40. See W.V.O. Quine, "Two Dogmas of Empiricism" (1951), in W.V.O. Quine, *From a Logical Point of View* (Cambridge, MA: Harvard University Press, 1953), 20–46.

41. Sigmund Freud, *The Interpretation of Dreams*, trans. A. A. Brill (London: Wordsworth Classics, 1997 [1899]), 278–79.

42. Ibid., 183. The translator claims to have inserted this example himself, since Freud's own example "cannot be translated." It is not clear, however, whether this example is one that Freud initially heard from a patient, or whether it has simply been made up.

43. Ibid., 184.

44. Vladimir Nabokov, "Conclusive Evidence," *New Yorker*, December 28, 1998–January 4, 1999, 124–33, 133. See also Leland de la Durantaye, "Vladimir Nabokov and Sigmund Freud, or a Particular Problem," *American Imago* 62, no. 1 (2005): 59–73.

45. Vladimir Nabokov, *Speak, Memory: An Autobiography Revisited* (New York: Vintage International, 1989 [1951]), 20.

Chapter Four. Dreams into Things; or, Art

1. David Hume, *Treatise of Human Nature*, ed. L. A. Selby-Bigge, rev. P. H. Nidditch (Oxford: Clarendon Press, 1975 [1739–40]), T II.3.3 415.

2. Maxim Gorky, cited in Karen Petrone, *The Great War in Russian Memory* (Bloomington: Indiana University Press, 2011), 122. I have been unable to locate an original Russian source for this quotation, oft cited in English.

3. A. A. Zhdanov, "Report on the Journals *Zvezda* and *Leningrad*, 1947," in *On Literature, Music, and Philosophy* (New York: Lawrence and Wishart, 1950), 19–35.

4. Mikhail Zoshchenko, *Prikliucheniia obez'iany* (Moscow: Eksmo, 2017 [1945]).

5. Zhdanov, "Report on the Journals *Zvezda* and *Leningrad*, 1947."

6. Jorge Luis Borges, "Tlön, Uqbar, Orbis Tertius," in Borges, *Cuentos completos*, 105.

7. I recall first reading this observation in something written by Arthur C. Danto but am unable to locate it, or anything similar, when I go back through his work.

8. Baruch Spinoza, *Treatise on the Emendation of the Intellect*, in *The Collected Works of Spinoza*, ed. and trans. Edwin Curley, vol. 1 (Princeton, NJ: Princeton University Press, 1985).

9. Descartes, *Méditations*, AT, 58: "Que s'il est question de considerer un Pentagone, il est bien vray que ie puis concevoir sa figure, aussi bien que celle d'un Chiliogone, sans le secours de l'imagination."

10. Blaise Pascal, *Pensées de Blaise Pascal*, ed. J.-M.-F. Frantin, 3rd ed. (Paris: Lagny, 1870), chap. 4, article 3, 70.

11. Ibid.

12. Cicero, *Tusculan Disputations*, trans. J. E. King, Loeb Classical Library 141 (Cambridge, MA: Harvard University Press, 1927), 3.1.2.

13. Descartes, *Discourse on Method*, AT, 6:1–2.

14. Descartes, *Rules*, AT, 10:373.

15. Kant, *Critique of the Faculty of Judgment* §46, AA, 5:308.

16. Antoine Galland, *Les mille et une nuits, contes arabes traduits en François, par M. Galland*, 12 vols. (Paris: La Veuve Claude Barbin, 1704–6 [vols. 1–7]; Paris: Claude Barbin, 1709 [vol. 8]; Paris: Florentin Delaulne, 1712 [vols. 9, 10]; Lyon: Briasson, 1717 [vols. 11, 12]). See also Marina Warner, *Stranger Magic: Charmed States and the Arabian Nights* (Cambridge, MA: Harvard University Press, 2012).

17. Kant, *Kritik der Urtheilskraft* §46, AA, 5:307.

18. Ibid., 309.

19. Mary MacLane, *I Await the Devil's Coming* (1902), in *Human Days: A Mary MacLane Reader* (Austin, TX: Petrarca Press, 2014), 77.

20. Descartes, AT, 10:219; see also *Discourse* pt. 4, AT, 6:139; *Principles of Philosophy*, pt. 1, art. 37, AT, 8:205.

21. Dodds, *The Greeks and the Irrational*.

22. See Arthur C. Danto, *The Transfiguration of the Commonplace: A Philosophy of Art* (Cambridge, MA: Harvard University Press, 1981).

23. Dodds, *The Greeks and the Irrational*, 1.

24. Anna Kisselgoff, "Pina Bausch Dance: Key Is Emotion," *New York Times*, October 4, 1985. http://www.nytimes.com/1985/10/04/arts/pina-bausch-dance-key-is-emotion .html?pagewanted=all.

25. See Nelson Goodman, *Languages of Art: An Approach to a Theory of Symbols*, Indianapolis, IN: The Bobbs-Merrill Company, 1968.

26. Kieran Cashell, *Aftershock: The Ethics of Contemporary Transgressive Art* (London: I. B. Tauris, 2009), 1; cited in Angela Nagle, *Kill All Normies: Online Culture Wars from 4chan and Tumblr to Trump and the Alt-Right* (Winchester, UK: Zero Books, 2017), 28.

27. See Danielle Spera, *Hermann Nitsch: Leben und Arbeit* (Vienna: Brandstätter, 2005).

28. Christopher Smart, *The Poetical Works of Christopher Smart*, vol. 1, *Jubilate Agno*, ed. Karina Williamson (Oxford: Clarendon Press, 1980), 89.

29. Louis Riel, "Dissertation on Monads," trans. Justin E. H. Smith, *Cabinet Magazine* 49 (2013): 26–27, 26.

30. See Karl Popper, "Philosophy of Science: A Personal Report," in *British Philosophy in Mid-Century*, ed. C. A. Mace (Crows Nest, NSW: Allen and Unwin, 1951), 155–91.

31. Larry Laudan, "The Demise of the Demarcation Problem," in *Physics, Philosophy and Psychoanalysis*, ed. R. S. Cohen and Larry Laudan (Dordrecht: Reidel, 1983), 111–27.

32. See Massimo Pigliucci, "The Demarcation Problem: A (Belated) Response to Laudan," in *Philosophy of Pseudoscience: Reconsidering the Demarcation Problem*, ed. Massimo Pigliucci and Maarten Boudry (Chicago: University of Chicago Press, 2013), 9–28.

33. Hazard, *La crise de la conscience européenne, 1680–1715*, pt. 2, chap. 1.

34. See Richard Yeo, *Defining Science: William Whewell, Natural Knowledge, and Public Debate in Early Victorian Britain* (Cambridge: Cambridge University Press, 1993).

35. See Bertrand Lemoine, "L'entreprise Eiffel," *Histoire, économie et société* 14, no. 2 (1995): 273–85.

36. Jules Verne, *De la terre à la lune. Trajet direct en 97 heures 20 minutes* (Paris: Bibliothèque d'éducation et de récréation, 1872 [1865]).

37. Friedrich Nietzsche, *Die fröhliche Wissenschaft* 2.84, in *Philosophische Werke in sechs Bänden* (Hamburg: Felix Meiner Verlag, 2013), 5:95.

38. Charles Baudelaire, *Les petits tronçons du serpent. Pensées choisies et précédées d'une introduction* (Paris: Sansot, 1918), 26.

39. See Matthew Arnold, *Culture and Anarchy: An Essay in Political and Social Criticism* (London: Smith, Elder and Co., 1869).

40. Johann Wolfgang von Goethe, *Maximen und Reflexionen*, no. 863, in *Werke*, vol. 12 (Hamburg: Deutscher Taschenbuch Verlag, 1953), 487.

Chapter Five. "I believe because it is absurd"; or, Pseudoscience

1. G. W. Leibniz, *Die philosophischen Schriften von G. W. Leibniz*, ed. C. I. Gerhardt (Berlin, 1849–60), 3:562.

2. Theodor W. Adorno, *The Stars Down to Earth, and Other Essays on the Irrational in Culture*, ed. Stephen Crook (London: Routledge, 1994).

3. Amanda Hess, "How Astrology Took Over the Internet," *New York Times*, January 1, 2018. https://www.nytimes.com/2018/01/01/arts/how-astrology-took-over-the-internet.html?hp&action=click&pgtype=Homepage&clickSource=story-heading&module=second-column-region&region=top-news&WT.nav=top-news&_r=0.

4. Jim Lindgren, "The Six Political Groups Least Likely to Believe That Astrology Is Scientific," *Washington Post*, February 20, 2014.

5. See "The Tea Party & the Circus—Final Healthcare Reform Protest," particularly 5:18–5:54, published on YouTube March 18, 2010. https://www.youtube.com/watch?v=pilG7PCV448&t=26s.

6. M. Dacke et al., "Dung Beetles Use the Milky Way for Orientation," *Current Biology* 23 (2013): 298–300.

7. Cited in Kendrick Frazier, "Science and Reason, Foibles and Fallacies, and Doomsdays," *Skeptical Inquirer* 22, no. 6 (1998): 6.

8. Kathy Niakan, "Using CRISPR/Cas9-Mediated Genome Editing to Investigate Mechanisms of Lineage Specification in Human Embryos," paper delivered at the conference "Les natures en questions," Collège de France, October 20, 2017.

9. On the notion of Promethean ambition and its significance to the history of science, see William R. Newman, *Promethean Ambitions: Alchemy and the Quest to Perfect Nature*, Chicago: University of Chicago Press, 2004.

10. Paul Feyerabend, "How to Defend Society against Science," *Radical Philosophy* 11, no. 1 (Summer 1975): 3–9.

11. On Lysenko and Lysenkoism, see Dominique Lecourt, *Lyssenko. Histoire réelle d'une 'science prolétarienne'* (Paris: Presses Universitaires de France, 1995 [1976]).

12. For a critical study of the museum, and its place in American society and history, see Susan L. Trollinger and William Vance Trollinger, Jr., *Righting America at the Creation Museum* (Baltimore: Johns Hopkins University Press, 2016).

13. For a summary statement of his views, see Ken Ham, *Six Days: The Age of the Earth and the Decline of the Church* (Green Forest, AR: Master Books, 2013).

14. For an example of a scientific, evolutionist account of such a process, see D. C. Garcia-Bellido and D. H. Collins, "Moulting Arthropod Caught in the Act," *Nature* 429, no. 40 (May 6, 2004): 6987. For a pseudoscientific, creationist account of the very same process, see David Catchpoole, "Moulting Arthropod Fossilized in a Flash!" *Creation* 27, no. 2 (March 2005): 45. Exclamation points are generally not typical punctuation in scientific publications, and may serve as a rough shibboleth for distinguishing them from their pseudoscientific imitations.

15. Harun Yahya, *Atlas of Creation* (Istanbul: Global Kitap, 2006); translation of Harun Yahya, *Yaratılış Atlası* (Istanbul: Global Kitap, 2006).

16. Richard Dawkins, "Venomous Snakes, Slippery Eels and Harun Yahya," website of the Richard Dawkins Foundation, accessed 2006 (since removed). The relevant image of the fishing lure is found on p. 244 of the *Atlas of Creation*.

17. In fact Tertullian's version was rather different, namely: "Prorsus credibile est, quia ineptum est," that is, "It is altogether credible, because it is absurd." See *Tertullian's*

Treatise on the Incarnation, ed. and trans. Ernest Evans (Eugene, OR: Wipf and Stock, 1956), 18.

18. For a particularly compelling recent account of the mendacity of the Trump regime, and of the cultural and political developments that fostered it, see Michiko Kakutani, *The Death of Truth: Notes on Falsehood in the Age of Trump* (New York: Tim Duggan Books, 2018).

19. See Harry G. Frankfurt, *On Bullshit* (Princeton, NJ: Princeton University Press, 2005).

20. G.E.R. Lloyd, *Aristotle: The Growth and Structure of His Thought* (London: Cambridge University Press, 1968), 162.

21. See Joseph Lehman, "A Brief Explanation of the Overton Window," Mackinac Center for Public Policy. http://www.mackinac.org/OvertonWindow#Explanation.

22. Nabokov, *Speak, Memory*, 125.

23. For a further development of these reflections, see Justin E. H. Smith, "The Art of Molting," *RES: Anthropology and Aesthetics* 67/68 (2016/17): 1–9.

24. Nadja Durbach, *Bodily Matters: The Anti-Vaccination Movement in England, 1853–1907* (Durham, NC: Duke University Press, 2005).

25. Donald J. Trump (@realdonaldtrump), Tweet dated March 28, 2014. https://twitter.com/realDonaldTrump/status/449525268529815552.

26. Alain Fischer, "La médecine face à la nature, un combat acceptable?" Colloquium paper delivered at "Les Natures en questions: Colloque de rentrée 2017–18," Collège de France, Paris, October 20, 2017.

27. Tom Nichols, *The Death of Expertise: The Campaign against Knowledge and Why It Matters* (New York: Oxford University Press, 2017), 5.

28. Ibid.

29. Richard Hofstadter, "The Paranoid Style in American Politics," *Harper's Magazine*, November 1964, 74–86.

30. Martin Heidegger, *Being and Time: A Translation of* Sein und Zeit, trans. Joan Stambaugh (Albany: SUNY Press, 1996 [1953]), 96.

31. Ibid.

32. See Margaret Wertheim, *Physics on the Fringe: Smoke Rings, Circlons, and Alternative Theories of Everything* (New York: Bloomsbury, 2011).

33. See Ron Suskind, "Faith, Certainty, and the Presidency of George W. Bush," *New York Times Magazine*, October 17, 2004. It is now widely believed that Suskind's source for this quotation was Karl Rove, though Rove denies it.

Chapter Six. Enlightenment; or, Myth

1. Eliot A. Cohen, "Two Wounded Warriors," *Atlantic*, October 22, 2017. https://www.theatlantic.com/politics/archive/2017/10/two-wounded-warriors/543612/.

2. This is an opportune moment to remind the reader that "or" has at least two basic meanings, each represented by its own word in many other languages, including Latin: *sive* is the "or" of alternative ways of saying the same thing, while *seu* is pure disjunction, forcing you to choose one or the other of two very different things.

3. See Jonathan I. Israel, *Radical Enlightenment: Philosophy and the Making of Modernity, 1650–1750* (Oxford: Oxford University Press, 2002); *Enlightenment Contested: Philosophy, Modernity, and the Emancipation of Man, 1670–1752* (Oxford: Oxford University Press, 2006); *Democratic Enlightenment: Philosophy, Revolution, and Human Rights, 1750–1790* (Oxford: Oxford University Press, 2013).

4. See in particular Nick Nesbitt, *Universal Emancipation: The Haitian Revolution and the Radical Enlightenment* (Charlottesville: University of Virginia Press, 2008).

5. See René Girard, "Mimesis and Violence: Perspectives in Cultural Criticism," *Berkshire Review* 14 (1979): 9–19.

6. Mishra, *Age of Anger*, 98.

7. Hazard, *La crise de la conscience européenne*, 117–18.

8. Ibid., 118.

9. Ibid., 126.

10. Ibid.

11. Franklin Perkins, *Leibniz and China: A Commerce of Light* (Cambridge: Cambridge University Press, 2005).

12. See Marc Fumaroli, *Quand l'Europe parlait français* (Paris: Éditions de Fallois, 2001).

13. J. G. Herder, "An die Deutschen," in *Johann Gottfried von Herder's sämmtliche Werke*, vol. 14 (Tübingen: In der J. G. Cotta'schen Buchhandlung, 1815), 174.

14. See Holger Nowak et al., *Lexikon zur Schlacht bei Jena und Auerstedt 1806. Personen, Ereignisse, Begriffe* (Jena: Städtische Museen, 2006).

15. G.W.F. Hegel, *Hegel: The Letters*, ed. and trans. Clark Butler and Christiane Seiler (Bloomington: Indiana University Press, 1984), 114; see also David P. Jordan, "Entr'acte: A Sighting in Jena," in *Napoleon and the Revolution* (New York: Palgrave Macmillan, 2012), 112–24.

16. Hegel, *The Letters*, 114.

17. Klaus Brinkbäumer, Julia Amalia Heyer, and Britta Sandberg, "Interview with Emmanuel Macron: 'We Need to Develop Political Heroism,'" *Der Spiegel Online*, October 13, 2017. http://www.spiegel.de/international/europe/interview-with-french-president-emmanuel-macron-a-1172745.html.

18. Ibid.

19. Ibid.

20. See Jean-François Lyotard, *The Postmodern Condition: A Report on Knowledge* (Manchester: Manchester University Press, 1979).

21. Brinkbäumer, Heyer, and Sandberg, "Interview with Emmanuel Macron."

22. "Trump Praises Macron, Considers July 4 Military Parade Like One He Saw in Paris," *Reuters*, September 18, 2017. https://www.reuters.com/article/us-usa-trump-macron/trump-praises-macron-considers-july-4-military-parade-like-one-he-saw-in-paris-idUSKCN1BT2GX.

23. Evidently the phrase "surrender monkeys" has its origins, as an insult for the French, in a 1995 episode of *The Simpsons*. It appears to have first been elongated by Jonah Goldberg, "Cheese-Eating Surrender Monkeys from Hell," *National Review Online*, April 16, 1999.

https://web.archive.org/web/20150130235956/ http://www.nationalreview.com/articles /204434/cheese-eating-surrender-monkeys-hell/jonah-goldberg.

24. See Justin E. H. Smith, "The Ibis and the Crocodile: Napoleon's Egyptian Campaign and Evolutionary Theory in France, 1801–1835," *Republic of Letters* 6, no. 1 (March 2018): 1–20.

25. On the origins of Right Hegelianism, see Michael H. Hoffheimer, *Eduard Gans and the Hegelian Philosophy of Law* (Dordrecht: Kluwer, 1995).

26. See in particular Franz Boas, *Race, Language, and Culture* (Chicago: University of Chicago Press, 1940).

27. Giambattista Vico, *The New Science of Giambattista Vico*, unabridged translation of the third edition (1744) with the addition of "Practic of the New Science," ed. and trans. Thomas Goddard Bergin and Max Harold Fisch (Ithaca, NY: Cornell University Press, 1948).

28. See Michel Pastoureau, *L'ours. Histoire d'un roi déchu* (Paris: Éditions du Seuil, 2007).

29. Vico, *The New Science*, 118.

30. Ibid.

31. See Leopold von Ranke, *Geschichte der romanischen und germanischen Völker von 1494 bis 1514*, 3rd ed. (Leipzig: Verlag von Duncker & Humblot, 1885 [1824]).

32. See in particular Frances Yates, *Giordano Bruno and the Hermetic Tradition* (London: Routledge, 1964).

33. See in particular D. P. Walker, *The Ancient Theology* (Ithaca, NY: Cornell University Press, 1972), esp. 1–21. Walker cites the well-known line of the second-century Platonist Numenius of Apamea "What is Plato but Moses talking Attic Greek?" This view would become widespread in the Italian Renaissance, notably in the work of Marsilio Ficino.

34. See Athanasius Kircher, *China monumentis* (Amsterdam: Apud Jacobum à Meurs, 1667 [repr. Frankfurt: Minerva, 1966].

35. See Giuliano Gliozzi, *Adamo e il nuovo mondo. La nascità dell'antropologia come ideologia coloniale: della genealogie bibliche alle teorie razziale (1500–1700)* (Florence: Franco-Angeli, 1977).

36. See, for example, Roxanne Dunbar-Ortiz, *An Indigenous Peoples' History of the United States* (Boston: Beacon Press, 2015).

37. These rumors, while plausible, are generally either unconfirmed or appear to involve speakers who were themselves trying to make a joke. The earliest known occurrence dates back to a *New York Times* article of 1881, in which a simple farmer is reported to have asked, "What's wrong with the good old King James version? That was good enough for St. Paul, and it's good enough for me" ("Preaching on the Bible; Pulpit Opinions of the New Version," *New York Times*, May 23, 1881, 8). More recently, a meme created in early 2014 falsely attributed to the Republican congresswoman Michele Bachmann the claim that "If English was good enough for Jesus when he wrote the Bible it should be good enough for Coke," purportedly replying to a multilingual Coca-Cola advertisement. See W. Gardner Selby, "Michele Bachmann Didn't Say Bible Written in English," *Politifact*, December 23, 2014. http://www.politifact .com/texas/article/2014/dec/23/michele-bachmann-didnt-say-bible-written-english/.

38. Matthew Arnold, "Empedocles on Etna: A Dramatic Poem," in *The Oxford Authors: Matthew Arnold*, ed. Miriam Farris Allott and Robert Henry Super (Oxford: Oxford University Press, 1986), 98.

39. Melville, *The Confidence-Man*, 135.

40. Giuseppe Tomasi di Lampedusa, *The Leopard*, trans. Archibald Colquhoun (London: Collins Harvill Press, 1960), 40.

41. Molly Jackson, "Are Open Carry Protesters Fueling Fear outside a Texas Mosque?" *Christian Science Monitor*, November 22, 2015. https://www.csmonitor.com/USA/USA-Up date/2015/1122/Are-open-carry-protesters-fueling-fear-outside-a-Texas-mosque.

42. "En prison, Breivik se dit 'torturé' et réclame une Playstation 3," *Le Monde* with Agence France Presse, February 14, 2014. http://www.lemonde.fr/europe/article/2014/02/14 /en-prison-breivik-se-dit-torture-et-reclame-une-playstation-3_4366976_3214.html.

43. Isidore of Seville, *Etymologies* 1.12, 46.

44. See Robert Cohen, *Freedom's Orator: Mario Savio and the Radical Legacy of the 1960s* (New York: Oxford University Press, 2009).

45. For a comprehensive account of the relevant events and actors in the Charlottesville rally, see Joe Heim, "Recounting a Day of Rage, Hate, Violence, and Death," *Washington Post*, August 14, 2017. https://www.washingtonpost.com/graphics/2017/local/charlottesville -timeline/?utm_term=.a083a7b926fd.

46. See, e.g., Gaëlle Dupont, "Pour La Manif pour tous, 'c'est le moment de se faire entendre,'" *Le Monde*, October 15, 2016. http://www.lemonde.fr/famille-vie-privee/article/2016/10/15/pour -la-manif-pour-tous-c-est-le-moment-de-se-faire-entendre_5014280_1654468.html.

47. See especially Steven Heller, *The Swastika: Symbol beyond Redemption?* (New York: Allworth Press, 2000).

48. For an excellent survey of this literature, see Keith Allan and Kate Burridge, *Forbidden Words: Taboo and the Censoring of Language* (Cambridge: Cambridge University Press, 2006).

49. This particular claim was made by Allum Bokhari and Milo Yiannopoulos in their notorious post, "An Establishment Conservative's Guide to the Alt-Right," *Breitbart News*, March 29, 2016. http://www.breitbart.com/tech/2016/03/29/an-establishment-conservatives -guide-to-the-alt-right/.

50. See in particular Linda Gordon, *The Second Coming of the KKK: The Ku Klux Klan of the 1920s and the American Political Tradition* (New York: W. W. Norton, 2017).

51. Nagle, *Kill All Normies*.

52. See in particular Alexander A. Guerrero, "Against Elections: The Lottocratic Alternative," *Philosophy & Public Affairs* 42, no. 2 (2014): 135–78.

53. Jason Brennan, *Against Democracy* (Princeton, NJ: Princeton University Press, 2016).

Chapter Seven. The Human Beast; or, the Internet

1. The text, dated October 17, 1850, is published anonymously in *La Presse*, in two parts, on October 25 and 26, 1850, under the title "Communication universelle et instantanée de la pensée, à quelque distance que ce soit, à l'aide d'un appareil portatif appelé Boussole pasi-lalinique sympathique." The Biblothèque nationale de France has made available a digital archive of the newspaper. The relevant issues may be found at http://gallica.bnf.fr/ark: /12148/bpt6k475317s and http://gallica.bnf.fr/ark:/12148/bpt6k4753185.

2. Allix, "Communication universelle." October 25, 1850.

3. Ibid.

4. Ibid.

5. The secondary literature on Allix is small, but a biography may be pieced together from various sources, notably J. Clère, *Les hommes de la Commune*, 5th ed. (Paris: Dentu, 1872); Charles Chincholle, *Les survivants de la Commune* (Paris: Boulanger, 1885). For an earlier version of the present account of Jules Allix and his escargotic machine, see Justin E. H. Smith, "The Internet of Snails," *Cabinet Magazine* 58 (2016): 29–37.

6. See Gustave Simon, *Chez Victor Hugo. Procès-verbaux des tables tournantes de Jersey* (Paris: Louis Conard, 1923), particularly the séance of September 3, 1854.

7. Allix, "La communication universelle," October 26, 1850.

8. Ibid.

9. Ibid.

10. Ibid.

11. See Masha Gessen, "Russian Interference in the 2016 Election: A Cacophony, Not a Conspiracy," *New Yorker*, November 3, 2017. https://www.newyorker.com/news/our-colum nists/russian-interference-in-the-2016-election-a-cacophony-not-a-conspiracy.

12. On the Greek far left's ties to Russia, see, e.g., Sam Jones, Kerin Hope, and Courtney Weaver, "Alarm Bells Ring over Syriza's Russian Links," *Financial Times*, January 28, 2015. https://www.ft.com/content/a87747de-a713-11e4-b6bd-00144feab7de. On the Greek far right's ties to Russia, see Hannah Gais, "How Putin Is Making Greece's Nazi Problem Worse," *Business Insider*, March 26, 2015. http://www.businessinsider.com/putin-is-making -greeces-nazi-problem-worse-2015-3?IR=T.

13. See Summer Meza, "Jenna Abrams, Alt-Right Hero on Twitter, Was Really a Russian Troll Who Tricked Republicans and Celebrities," *Newsweek*, November 3, 2017. http://www .newsweek.com/jenna-abrams-fake-russian-troll-account-700801.

14. See Nathan Tempey, "Cops Arrest Subway Riders for 'Manspreading.'" *Gothamist*, May 28, 2015. http://gothamist.com/2015/05/28/manspreading_crackdown.php.

15. Lewis, "'Our Minds Can Be Hijacked'" (see introduction, n8).

16. Jonathan Franzen, "Is It Too Late to Save the World?" *Guardian*, November 4, 2017. https://www.theguardian.com/books/2017/nov/04/jonathan-franzen-too-late-to-save -world-donald-trump-environment.

17. See John Bingham, "How Teenage Pregnancy Collapsed after Birth of Social Media," *Telegraph*, March 9, 2016. http://www.telegraph.co.uk/news/health/news/12189376/How -teenage-pregnancy-collapsed-after-birth-of-social-media.html.

18. See Scott, *Against the Grain*, chap. 1.

19. For a comprehensive appraisal of the role of Twitter and other social media in the Egyptian and Tunisian revolutions, and connected events in the Middle East between 2009 and 2012, see Philip N. Howard and Muzammil M. Hussain, *Democracy's Fourth Wave? Digital Media and the Arab Spring* (Oxford: Oxford University Press, 2013). For the current best account of the prospects and limits of social media in political protest, see Zeynep Tufekci, *Twitter and Tear Gas: The Power and Fragility of Networked Protest* (New Haven, CT: Yale University Press, 2017). See also David Patrikarakos, *War in 140 Characters:*

How Social Media Is Reshaping Conflict in the Twenty-First Century (New York, Basic Books, 2017).

20. Mark Fisher, "Exiting the Vampire Castle," *North Star*, November 22, 2013. https://www.opendemocracy.net/ourkingdom/mark-fisher/exiting-vampire-castle.

21. Jeet Heer (@heerjeet), Tweet dated December 20, 2017. https://twitter.com/heerjeet/status/943496646515556352?lang=en. Heer is responding here to Jonathan Haidt, "The Age of Outrage: What the Current Political Climate Is Doing to Our Country and Our Universities," *City Journal*, December 17, 2017. https://www.city-journal.org/html/age-outrage-15608.html.

22. Hannah Arendt, *Eichmann in Jerusalem: A Report on the Banality of Evil* (New York: Viking Press, 1963).

23. José María Gómez, Miguel Verdú, Adela González-Megías, and Marcos Méndez, "The Phylogenetic Roots of Human Lethal Violence," *Nature* 538 (October 13, 2016): 233–37.

24. Terence, *Heautontimouremos: The Self-Tormentor*, in *The Comedies of Terence*, ed. and trans. Henry Thomas Riley (New York: Harper and Brothers, 1859), 139.

25. See "Syllabus on Sex and Gender Differences: How to Disprove Sexist Science," at librarycard.org, August 14, 2017. http://librarycard.org/2017/08/14/syllabus-sex-gender-differences-disprove-sexist-science/.

26. Hannah Trees, "Normalizing Pronoun-Sharing at Philosophy Conferences," *Blog of the APA*, March 20, 2018. https://blog.apaonline.org/2018/03/20/normalizing-the-use-of-preferred-pronouns-at-philosophy-conferences/.

27. Walt Whitman, *Leaves of Grass—1860*, "Proto-Leaf," in *Walt Whitman: Selected Poems, 1855–1892*, ed. Gary Schmidgall (New York: Stonewall Inn Editions, 1999), 50.

28. See Pastoureau, *L'Ours. Histoire d'un roi déchu*.

29. For an account of the animistic ontology in which such a claim might make sense, see in particular Philippe Descola, *Par-delà nature et culture* (Paris: Gallimard, 2005).

30. Rebecca Tuvel, "In Defense of Transracialism," *Hypatia: A Journal of Feminist Philosophy* 32, no. 2 (2017): 263–78.

31. Lewis R. Gordon, "Thinking Through Rejections and Defenses of Transracialism," *Philosophy Today* 62, no. 1 (Winter 2018): 11–19, 12.

32. Ibid., 12.

33. See chapter 3, n20.

34. Melville, *The Confidence-Man*, 146.

35. Jean-Paul Sartre, interview with *Actuel*, February 28, 1973. "Les révolutionnaires de 1793 n'ont probablement pas assez tué."

36. Margaret Atwood, "Am I a Bad Feminist?" *Globe and Mail*, January 14, 2018. https://www.theglobeandmail.com/opinion/am-i-a-bad-feminist/article37591823/.

Chapter Eight. Explosions; or, Jokes and Lies

1. Justin E. H. Smith, "The Gravity of Satire: Offense and Violence after the Paris Attacks," the Pierre Bayle Lecture, Pierre Bayle Foundation, Rotterdam, The Netherlands, November 27, 2015.

2. This statement first appeared in an interview Le Pen *père* gave to the Russian newspaper *Komsomol'skaya Pravda* in early 2015. See Dar'ia Aslamova, "Zhan-Mari le Pen—'KP': Nam nuzhna edinaia Evropa ot Parizha do Vladivostoka," *Komsomol'skaya Pravda*, January 15, 2015. https://www.kp.ru/daily/26329.4/3212604/.

3. See, most disconcertingly, the many dispatches on the topic from *Jacobin Magazine* from 2015 to 2017, for example, Manus McGrogan, "Charlie Hebdo: The Poverty of Satire," *Jacobin Magazine*, January 7, 2017. https://www.jacobinmag.com/2017/01/charlie-hebdo -satire-islamophobia-laicite-terrorism-free-speech/.

4. Eliot Weinberger, "Charlie, encore une fois . . . ," *LRB blog*, April 28, 2015. https://www .lrb.co.uk/blog/2015/04/28/eliot-weinberger/charlie-encore-une-fois/.

5. For a comprehensive, keyword-searchable archive, see "Donald Trump: The Howard Stern Interviews, 1993–2015," *Factbase*. https://factba.se/topic/howard-stern-interviews.

6. Emily Nussbaum, "How Jokes Won the Election," *New Yorker*, January 23, 2017. https:// www.newyorker.com/magazine/2017/01/23/how-jokes-won-the-election.

7. Cited in ibid.

8. Rudolph Herzog, "Laughing All the Way to Autocracy," *Foreign Policy*, February 8, 2017. http://foreignpolicy.com/2017/02/08/laughing-all-the-way-to-autocracy -jokes-trump-dictatorship/.

9. Judith L. Herman and Robert Jay Lifton, Letter to the Editor, *New York Times*, March 8, 2017. https://www.nytimes.com/2017/03/08/opinion/protect-us-from-this-dangerous- president-2-psychiatrists-say.html.

10. Ibid.

11. Benedictus de Spinoza, *Opera*, ed. Carl Gebhardt (Heidelberg: Carl Winter Verlag, 1925), Letter 50, 4, 240, 6–15. For a comprehensive treatment of Spinoza's use of this phrase, and of Hegel's subsequent appropriation of it, see Yitzhak Y. Melamed, " 'Omnis determinatio est negatio'—Determination, Negation, and Self-Negation in Spinoza, Kant, and Hegel," in *Spinoza and German Idealism*, ed. Eckart Förster and Yitzhak Y. Melamed (Cambridge: Cambridge University Press, 2012), 175–96.

12. The term was coined by the psychiatrist Will Gaylin but given its limited popularity by Sissela Bok, in the preface to the third edition of *Lying: Moral Choice in Public and Private Life* (New York: Vintage Books, 1999 [1978]).

13. Ibid.

14. Ibid.

15. Ibid.

16. Emily Dickinson, "I'm Nobody! Who are you?" *The Poems of Emily Dickinson*, ed. Ralph W. Franklin (Cambridge, MA: Belknap Press of Harvard University Press, 1998), no. 260.

17. See Tom Bissell, "Who's Laughing Now? The Tragicomedy of Donald Trump on *Saturday Night Live*," *Harper's Magazine*, October 2017. https://harpers.org/archive/2017/10 /whos-laughing-now/2/.

18. W. H. Auden, "August 1968," in *Collected Poems* (New York: Faber, 2007), 804.

Chapter Nine. The Impossible Syllogism; or, Death

1. John Maynard Keynes, *A Tract on Monetary Reform* (1923), in *The Collected Writings of John Maynard Keynes*, vol. 4, ed. Donald Moggridge (London: Macmillan, 1981), 65.

2. Perry Anderson, "After the Event," *New Left Review* 73 (January–February 2012): 49–61, 51.

3. "Thomas Piketty refuse la Légion d'honneur," *Le Monde*, January 1, 2015. http://www.lemonde.fr/culture/article/2015/01/01/l-economiste-thomas-piketty-refuse-la-legion-d-honneur_4548309_3246.html.

4. David Sprague, "Sex Pistols Flip Off Hall of Fame," *Rolling Stone*, February 24, 2006. http://www.rollingstone.com/music/news/sex-pistols-flip-off-hall-of-fame-20060224.

5. Simone de Beauvoir made a strong case for thinking of aging as a central problem of the analysis of human existence, in her 1970 work *La Vieillesse* (translated as *The Coming of Age*). This work has been studied with subtlety and insight by Penelope Deutscher, in her *The Philosophy of Simone de Beauvoir: Ambiguity, Conversion, Resistance* (Cambridge: Cambridge University Press, 2008).

6. Jeff Maysh, "Why One Woman Pretended to Be a High-School Cheerleader," *Atlantic*, July 6, 2016. https://www.theatlantic.com/health/archive/2016/07/wendy-brown/486152/.

7. One notable exception to this generalization in recent Anglophone philosophy is Kieran Setiya's sharp and profound *Midlife: A Philosophical Guide* (Princeton, NJ: Princeton University Press, 2016). It is telling, however, that an accomplished philosopher such as Setiya who takes this topic on does so somewhat in the spirit of an interruption of his ordinary work, in order to venture into "self-help."

8. Plato, *Apology* 39a–b.

9. See in particular Lou Marinoff, *Therapy for the Sane: How Philosophy Can Change Your Life* (Argo-Navis, 2013).

10. See Søren Kierkegaard, *Either/Or: A Fragment of Life*, trans. Alastair Hannay (New York: Penguin, 1992 [1843]).

11. See L. A. Paul, *Transformative Experience* (New York: Oxford University Press, 2014).

12. The locus classicus for philosophical reflection on childbearing and child rearing as transformative experience is L. A. Paul, "What You Can't Expect When You're Expecting," *Res Philosophica* 92, no. 2 (2015): 1–23. As far as I know it is Eric Schliesser who, in a series of blog posts in 2014 and 2015, dubbed the new reflection on transformative experience in Anglophone philosophy "analytical existentialism."

13. See Tom McCarthy, "The Edge of Reason: The World's Boldest Climb and the Man Who Conquered It," *Guardian*, September 10, 2017. https://www.theguardian.com/sport/2017/sep/10/climbing-el-capitan-alex-honnold-yosemite.

14. Mike McPhate, "California Today: An 'Incomprehensible' Climb in Yosemite," *New York Times*, June 6, 2017. https://www.nytimes.com/2017/06/06/us/california-today-alex-honnold-el-capitan-climb.html.

15. Nabokov, *Speak, Memory*, 19.

16. Thomas Frank, *What's the Matter with Kansas? How Conservatives Won the Heart of America* (New York: Henry Holt and Co., 2004).

17. See in particular Plato, *Protagoras* 345c4–e6.

18. M. F. Burnyeat, "Socratic Midwifery, Platonic Inspiration," in *Explorations in Ancient and Modern Philosophy*, vol. 2 (Cambridge: Cambridge University Press, 2012), 21–35, 33.

19. For some of their stories, see Emiko Ohnuki-Tierney, *Kamikaze, Cherry Blossoms, and Nationalisms: The Militarization of Aesthetics in Japanese History* (Chicago: University of Chicago Press, 2002).

20. L. N. Tolstoy, *Smert' Ivana Il'icha* (Saint Petersburg, 1886), chap. 6.

21. See Peter Gay, *The Bourgeois Experience: Victoria to Freud*, 5 vols. (New York: Oxford University Press, 1984–98).

22. See in particular Deirdre McCloskey, *Bourgeois Equality: How Ideas, Not Capital or Institutions, Enriched the World* (Chicago: University of Chicago Press, 2016).

23. William Butler Yeats, "The Choice," in *The Winding Stair and Other Poems* (New York: Macmillan and Co., 1933), 39.

24. Charles Baudelaire, "Un voyage," in *Les fleurs du mal* (Boston: David R. Godine, 1983), 334.

25. Mishra, *Age of Anger*, 1.

26. See Epictetus, *Discourses* 2.6.17–19.

27. Jon Elster, *Ulysses and the Sirens: Studies in Rationality and Irrationality* (Cambridge: Cambridge University Press, 1979).

28. Jon Elster, *Sour Grapes: Studies in the Subversion of Rationality* (Cambridge: Cambridge University Press, 1983), 109, citing La Fontaine, *Fables* 30, 11.

29. It remains in any case a fundamental premise of contract law that one may not form a contract with oneself. See Charles Fried, *Contract as Promise: A Theory of Contractual Obligation* (New York: Oxford University Press, 2015 [1981]), chap. 4.

30. Sidney W. Mintz, *Sweetness and Power: The Place of Sugar in Modern History* (New York: Penguin Books, 1985).

31. See Anders Winroth, *The Conversion of Scandinavia: Vikings, Merchants, and Missionaries in the Remaking of Northern Europe* (New Haven, CT: Yale University Press, 2012).

32. See Yusuf Majidzadeh, "Lapis Lazuli and the Great Khorasan Road," *Paléorient* 8, no. 1 (1982): 59–69.

33. See Rahul Oka and Chapurukha M. Kusimba, "The Archaeology of Trading Systems, Part 1: Towards a New Trade Synthesis," *Journal of Archaeological Research* 16 (2008): 339–95.

34. Marshall Sahlins, "La Pensée Bourgeoise: Western Society as Culture," in *Culture and Practical Reason* (Chicago: University of Chicago Press, 1976), 166–204.

35. Pierre Bourdieu, *La distinction. Critique sociale du jugement* (Paris: Les Éditions de Minuit, 1979).

36. For an early account of this phenomenon, see Peter Worley, *The Trumpet Shall Sound: A Study of 'Cargo Cults' in Melanesia* (New York: Schocken Books, 1957). For a more critical treatment, arguing that the very idea of the cargo cult resulted, from the beginning, from a Western perspective that centers economic commodities in social life, see Lamont Lindstrom, *Cargo Cult: Strange Stories of Desire from Melanesia and Beyond* (Honolulu: University of Hawai'i Press, 1993). The prevailing view in current anthropology follows Lindstrom in

most respects, though the term "cargo cult" continues to be adapted and used freely beyond the narrow context of Melanesian ethnography in which it was first developed, not least by the Nigerian novelist Chinua Achebe, in describing the mentality of the leaders of developing nations in Africa. See Achebe, *The Trouble with Nigeria* (Oxford: Heinemann, 1983), 9.

37. See Derek Malcolm, "Krzysztof Kieslowski—Obituary," *Guardian*, March 14, 1996. https://www.theguardian.com/film/2011/nov/09/krzysztof-kieslowski-obituary.

38. See Thomas Bernhard, *Es ist alles lächerlich. Acht philosophische Mauerhaken* (Frankfurt: Suhrkamp, 2008).

39. Frits Staal, *Ritual and Mantras: Rules without Meaning* (New York: Peter Lang, 1990).

40. This insight comes from Christophe Z. Guilmoto (in personal conversation).

41. Anthropologists, in contrast with philosophers, economists, and other social scientists and humanists, have been particularly insightful as to the importance of the category of "ancestors" for the ordering of human social reality. See in particular Jack Goody, *Death, Property and the Ancestors: A Study of the Mortuary Customs of the Lodagaa of West Africa* (London: Tavistock, 1959).

BIBLIOGRAPHY

▶▶▶▶▶

Print Sources

AA. See under Kant.

Achebe, Chinua. *The Trouble with Nigeria*. Oxford: Heinemann, 1983.

Adorno, Theodor W. *The Stars Down to Earth, and Other Essays on the Irrational in Culture*. Edited by Stephen Crook. London: Routledge, 1994.

Adorno, Theodor W., and Max Horkheimer. *Dialectic of Enlightenment*. Translated by John Cumming. London: Verso, 1997 [1944].

Afanas'ev, A. N. *Narodnye russkie rasskazy A. N. Afanas'eva*. 2nd ed. 4 vols. Moscow: K. Soldatenkov, 1873.

Ahmed, Arif. "Infallibility in the Newcomb Problem." *Erkenntnis* 80, no. 2 (2015): 261–73.

Allan, Keith, and Kate Burridge. *Forbidden Words: Taboo and the Censoring of Language*. Cambridge: Cambridge University Press, 2006.

Allix, Jules. "Communication universelle et instantanée de la pensée, à quelque distance que ce soit, à l'aide d'un appareil portatif appelé Boussole pasilalinique sympathique." *La Presse*, October 25 and 26, 1850.

Amo, Anton Wilhelm. *Tractatus de arte sobrie et accurate philosophandi*. Halle, 1738.

Anderson, Perry. "After the Event." *New Left Review* 73 (January–February 2012): 49–61.

———. "Dégringolade." *London Review of Books* 26, no. 17 (September 2, 2004): 3–9.

Arendt, Hannah. *Eichmann in Jerusalem: A Report on the Banality of Evil*. New York: Viking Press, 1963.

Aristotle. *Metaphysics*. Edited by W. D. Ross. Oxford: Clarendon Press, 1924.

Aristotle, *On Prophecy in Sleep*. In *On the Soul. Parva Naturalia. On Breath*, translated by W. S. Hett. Loeb Classical Library 288. Cambridge, MA: Harvard University Press, 1957.

Arnold, Matthew. *Culture and Anarchy: An Essay in Political and Social Criticism*. London: Smith, Elder and Co., 1869.

———. *The Oxford Authors: Matthew Arnold*. Edited by Miriam Farris Allott and Robert Henry Super. Oxford: Oxford University Press, 1986.

AT. *See under* Descartes.

Auden, W. H. *Collected Poems*. New York: Faber, 2007.

Augustine. *The Confessions of Saint Augustine*. Edited and translated by Frank J. Sheed. London: Sheed & Ward, 1944.

Bachelard, Gaston. *La terre et les rêveries du repos*. Paris: José Corti, 1948.

Barrett, William. *Irrational Man: A Study in Existential Philosophy*. New York: Doubleday, 1958.

Baudelaire, Charles. *Les fleurs du mal*. Boston: David R. Godine, 1983.

———. *Les petits tronçons du serpent. Pensées choisies et précédées d'une introduction*. Paris: Sansot, 1918.

Bayle, Pierre. *Dictionnaire historique et critique*. 3rd ed. Vol. 3. Rotterdam, 1715 [1697].

Bernhard, Thomas. *Es ist alles lächerlich. Acht philosophische Mauerhaken*. Frankfurt: Suhrkamp, 2008.

Boas, Franz. *Race, Language, and Culture*. Chicago: University of Chicago Press, 1940.

Bok, Sissela. *Lying: Moral Choice in Public and Private Life*. 3rd ed. New York: Vintage Books, 1999 [1978].

Borges, Jorge Luis. *Cuentos completos*. Barcelona: Lumen, 2015.

Bourdieu, Pierre. *La distinction. Critique sociale du jugement*. Paris: Les Éditions de Minuit, 1979.

Brennan, Jason. *Against Democracy*. Princeton, NJ: Princeton University Press, 2016.

Brie, Michael. *Die witzige Dienstklasse. Der politische Witz im späten Staatssozialismus*. Berlin: Karl Dietz Verlag, 2004.

Browne, Thomas. *Pseudodoxia Epidemica; or, Enquiries into very many Received Tenents, and commonly Presumed Truths*. London, 1648.

Bruckner, Pascal. *The Temptation of Innocence: Living in the Age of Entitlement*. New York: Algora Publishing, 2007 [1995].

Budelmann, B. U. "Autophagy in *Octopus*." *South African Journal of Marine Science* 20, no. 1 (1998): 101–8.

Burnyeat, M. F. *Explorations in Ancient and Modern Philosophy*. Vol. 2. Cambridge: Cambridge University Press, 2012.

Cashell, Kieran. *Aftershock: The Ethics of Contemporary Transgressive Art*. London: I. B. Tauris, 2009.

Catchpoole, David. "Moulting Arthropod Fossilized in a Flash!" *Creation* 27, no. 2 (March 2005): 45.

Cervantes, Miguel de. *Don Quijote de la Mancha*. Edited by John Jay Allen. 27th ed. Madrid: Ediciones Cátedra, 2008. English edition: *Don Quixote*. Translated by Edith Grossman. New York: Harper Collins, 2003.

Chincholle, Charles. *Les survivants de la Commune*. Paris: Boulanger, 1885.

Cicero. *Tusculan Disputations*. Translated by J. E. King. Loeb Classical Library 141. Cambridge, MA: Harvard University Press, 1927.

Clère, Jules. *Les hommes de la Commune*. 5th ed. Paris: Dentu, 1872.

Coccia, Emanuele. *La vie des plantes. Une métaphysique du mélange*. Paris: Bibliothèque Rivages, 2016.

Cohen, Robert. *Freedom's Orator: Mario Savio and the Radical Legacy of the 1960s*. New York: Oxford University Press, 2009.

Couturat, Louis. *La logique de Leibniz, d'après des documents inédits*. Paris: Félix Alcan, 1901.

Cusset, François. *French Theory. Foucault, Derrida, Deleuze et Cie et les mutations de la vie inellectuelle aux États-Unis*. Paris: La Découverte, 2005.

Cyrano de Bergerac, Savinien. *Les états et empires de la Lune*. Paris, 1665.

Dacke, M., et al. "Dung Beetles Use the Milky Way for Orientation." *Current Biology* 23 (2013): 298–300.

Danto, Arthur C. *The Transfiguration of the Commonplace: A Philosophy of Art*. Cambridge, MA: Harvard University Press, 1981.

Descartes, René. *Oeuvres de Descartes*. Edited by Charles Adam and Paul Tannery. 13 vols. Paris: Léopold Cerf, 1897–1913. [AT]

Des Chene, Dennis. "'Animal' as Category: Bayle's 'Rorarius.'" In *The Problem of Animal Generation in Early Modern Philosophy*, edited by Justin E. H. Smith, 215–34. Cambridge University Press, 2006.

Descola, Philippe. *Par-delà nature et culture*. Paris: Gallimard, 2005.

Deutscher, Penelope. *The Philosophy of Simone de Beauvoir: Ambiguity, Conversion, Resistance*. Cambridge: Cambridge University Press, 2008.

Dickinson, Emily. *The Poems of Emily Dickinson*. Edited by Ralph W. Franklin. Cambridge, MA: Belknap Press of Harvard University Press, 1998.

Diderot, Denis. *Le rêve de d'Alembert*. In *Oeuvres complètes de Diderot*, edited by Assézat Tourneux, vol. 2. Paris: Garnier Frères, 1875.

Dodds, E. R. *The Greeks and the Irrational*. Berkeley: University of California Press, 1951.

Dougherty, Tom, Sophie Horowitz, and Paulina Sliwa. "Expecting the Unexpected." *Res Philosophica* 92, no. 2 (April 2015): 301–21.

Douglas, Mary. *Natural Symbols: Explorations in Cosmology*. London: Barrie & Rockliff, 1970.

Dunbar-Ortiz, Roxanne. *An Indigenous Peoples' History of the United States*. Boston: Beacon Press, 2015.

Durantaye, Leland de la. "Vladimir Nabokov and Sigmund Freud, or a Particular Problem." *American Imago* 62, no. 1 (2005): 59–73.

Durbach, Nadja. *Bodily Matters: The Anti-Vaccination Movement in England, 1853–1907*. Durham, NC: Duke University Press, 2005.

Elster, Jon. *Sour Grapes: Studies in the Subversion of Rationality*. Cambridge: Cambridge University Press, 1983.

———. *Ulysses and the Sirens: Studies in Rationality and Irrationality*. Cambridge: Cambridge University Press, 1979.

Erasmus, Desiderius. *The Praise of Folly*. Translated by John Wilson. London, 1668.

Feyerabend, Paul. "How to Defend Society against Science." *Radical Philosophy* 11, no. 1 (Summer 1975): 3–9.

Fischer, Alain. "La médecine face à la nature, un combat acceptable?" Colloquium paper delivered at "Les Natures en questions: Colloque de rentrée 2017–18," Collège de France, Paris, October 20, 2017.

Foucault, Michel. *Madness and Civilization: A History of Insanity in the Age of Reason*. New York: Vintage Books, 1988 [1961].

Fraenkel, Carlos. *Philosophical Religions from Plato to Spinoza: Reason, Religion, and Autonomy*. Cambridge: Cambridge University Press, 2012.

Frank, Sam. "Come with Us If You Want to Live." *Harper's Magazine*, January 2015, 26–36.

Frank, Thomas. *What's the Matter with Kansas? How Conservatives Won the Heart of America*. New York: Henry Holt and Co., 2004.

Frankfurt, Harry G. *On Bullshit*. Princeton, NJ: Princeton University Press, 2005.

Frazier, Kendrick. "Science and Reason, Foibles and Fallacies, and Doomsdays." *Skeptical Inquirer* 22, no. 6 (1998): 6.

Freud, Sigmund. *The Interpretation of Dreams*. Translated by A. A. Brill. London: Wordsworth Classics, 1997 [1899].

Fried, Charles. *Contract as Promise: A Theory of Contractual Obligation*. New York: Oxford University Press, 2015 [1981].

Fumaroli, Marc. *Quand l'Europe parlait français*. Paris: Éditions de Fallois, 2001.

Galland, Antoine. *Les mille et une nuits, contes arabes traduits en François, par M. Galland*. 12 vols. Paris: La Veuve Claude Barbin, 1704–6 (vols. 1–7); Paris: Claude Barbin, 1709 (vol. 8); Paris: Florentin Delaulne, 1712 (vols. 9, 10); Lyon: Briasson, 1717 (vols. 11, 12).

Garcia-Bellido, D. C., and D. H. Collins. "Moulting Arthropod Caught in the Act." *Nature* 429, no. 40 (May 6, 2004): 6987.

Gassendi, Pierre. *Syntagma philosophicum*. In *Opera omnia in sex tomos divisa*. Lyon: Laurence Anisson and Jean-Baptiste Devenet, 1658.

Gay, Peter. *The Bourgeois Experience: Victoria to Freud*. 5 vols. New York: Oxford University Press, 1984–98.

Gellius, Aulus. *Attic Nights*. Vol. 3. Translated by J. C. Rolfe. Loeb Classical Library 212. Cambridge, MA: Harvard University Press, 1927.

Girard, René. "Mimesis and Violence: Perspectives in Cultural Criticism." *Berkshire Review* 14 (1979): 9–19.

Gliozzi, Giuliano. *Adamo e il nuovo mondo. La nascità dell'antropologia come ideologia coloniale: della genealogie bibliche alle teorie razziale (1500–1700)*. Florence: FrancoAngeli, 1977.

Godfrey-Smith, Peter. *Other Minds: The Octopus, the Sea, and the Deep Origins of Consciousness*. New York: Farrar, Straus and Giroux, 2016.

Goethe, Johann Wolfgang von. *Werke*. Vol. 12. Hamburg: Deutscher Taschenbuch Verlag, 1953.

Gómez, José María, Miguel Verdú, Adela González-Megías, and Marcos Méndez. "The Phylogenetic Roots of Human Lethal Violence." *Nature* 538 (October 13, 2016): 233–37.

Goodman, Nelson. *Languages of Art: An Approach to a Theory of Symbols*. Indianapolis, IN: The Bobbs-Merrill Company, 1968.

Goody, Jack. *Death, Property and the Ancestors: A Study of the Mortuary Customs of the Lodagaa of West Africa*. London: Tavistock, 1959.

———. *The Logic of Writing and the Organization of Society*. Cambridge: Cambridge University Press, 1986.

Gordon, Lewis R. "Thinking Through Rejections and Defenses of Transracialism." *Philosophy Today* 62, no. 1 (Winter 2018): 11–19.

Gordon, Linda. *The Second Coming of the KKK: The Ku Klux Klan of the 1920s and the American Political Tradition*. New York: W. W. Norton, 2017.

Gould, Stephen Jay. "Nonoverlapping Magisteria." *Natural History* 106 (March 1996): 16–22.

Grimm, Jacob and Wilhelm. *Kinder- und Hausmärchen*. Göttingen, 1812.

Guerrero, Alexander A. "Against Elections: The Lottocratic Alternative." *Philosophy & Public Affairs* 42, no. 2 (2014): 135–78.

Ham, Ken. *Six Days: The Age of the Earth and the Decline of the Church*. Green Forest, AR: Master Books, 2013.

Hazard, Paul. *La crise de la conscience européenne, 1680–1715*. Paris: Fayard, 1961 [1935].

Hegel, G.W.F. *Hegel: The Letters*. Edited and translated by Clark Butler and Christiane Seiler. Bloomington: Indiana University Press, 1984.

Heidegger, Martin. *Being and Time: A Translation of* Sein und Zeit. Translated by Joan Stambaugh. Albany: SUNY Press, 1996 [1953].

———. *Logic: The Question of Truth.* Translated by Thomas Sheehan, Bloomington: Indiana University Press, 2010.

Heller, Steven. *The Swastika: Symbol beyond Redemption?* New York: Allworth Press, 2000.

Herder, J. G. *Johann Gottfried von Herder's sämmtliche Werke.* Vol. 14. Tübingen: In der J. G. Cotta'schen Buchhandlung, 1815.

Hoffheimer, Michael H. *Eduard Gans and the Hegelian Philosophy of Law.* Dordrecht: Kluwer, 1995.

Hofstadter, Richard. "The Paranoid Style in American Politics." *Harper's Magazine,* November 1964, 74–86.

Holt, Jim. *Stop Me If You've Heard This: A History and Philosophy of Jokes.* New York: W. W. Norton, 2008.

Howard, Philip N., and Muzammil M. Hussain. *Democracy's Fourth Wave? Digital Media and the Arab Spring.* Oxford: Oxford University Press, 2013.

Hume, David. *Treatise of Human Nature.* Edited by L. A. Selby-Bigge. Revised by P. H. Nidditch. Oxford: Clarendon Press, 1975 [1739–40].

Iamblichus. *Life of Pythagoras.* Translated by Thomas Taylor. London, 1818.

Ishwaran, Karigoudar, ed. *Ascetic Culture: Renunciation and Worldly Engagement.* International Studies in Sociology and Social Anthropology. Leiden: Brill, 1999.

Isidore of Seville, *Etymologies.* Translated and edited by Stephen A. Barney, W. J. Lewis, J. A Beach, and Oliver Berghof. Cambridge: Cambridge University Press, 2006.

Israel, Jonathan I. *Democratic Enlightenment: Philosophy, Revolution, and Human Rights, 1750–1790.* Oxford: Oxford University Press, 2013.

———. *Enlightenment Contested: Philosophy, Modernity, and the Emancipation of Man, 1670–1752.* Oxford: Oxford University Press, 2006.

———. *Radical Enlightenment: Philosophy and the Making of Modernity, 1650–1750.* Oxford: Oxford University Press, 2002.

Jaynes, Julian. *The Origin of Consciousness in the Breakdown of the Bicameral Mind.* Boston: Houghton Mifflin, 1976.

Jordan, David P. *Napoleon and the Revolution.* New York: Palgrave Macmillan, 2012.

Sor Juana Inés de la Cruz. *Obras completas.* Vol. 1, *Lírica personal.* Edited by Alfonso Méndez Plancarte. Mexico City: Fondo de Cultura Económica, 1951.

Kakutani, Michiko. *The Death of Truth: Notes on Falsehood in the Age of Trump.* New York: Tim Duggan Books, 2018.

Kant, Immanuel. *Immanuel Kants gesammelte Schriften.* Edited by the Prussian Academy of Sciences. Berlin, 1902. [AA].

Kepler, Johannes. *Somnium: The Dream, or, Posthumous Works on Lunar Astronomy.* Translated by Edward Rosen. Mineola, NY: Dover Publications, 1967.

Keynes, John Maynard. *The Collected Writings of John Maynard Keynes.* Edited by Donald Moggridge. Vol. 4. London, 1981.

Kierkegaard, Søren. *Either/Or: A Fragment of Life.* Translated by Alastair Hannay. New York: Penguin, 1992 [1843].

Kircher, Athanasius. *China monumentis*. Amsterdam: Apud Jacobum à Meurs, 1667. Reprint, Frankfurt: Minerva, 1966.

Klein, Richard. *Cigarettes Are Sublime*. Durham: Duke University Press, 1993.

Kohn, Eduardo. *How Forests Think: Toward an Anthropology beyond the Human*. Berkeley: University of California Press, 2013.

Laudan, Larry. "The Demise of the Demarcation Problem." In *Physics, Philosophy and Psychoanalysis*, edited by R. S. Cohen and Larry Laudan, 111–27. Dordrecht: Reidel, 1983.

Lecourt, Dominique. *Lyssenko. Histoire réelle d'une 'science prolétarienne.'* Paris: Presses Universitaires de France, 1995 [1976].

Leibniz, G. W. "The Body-Machine in Leibniz's Early Medical and Physiological Writings: A Selection of Texts with Commentary." Edited and translated by Justin E. H. Smith. *Leibniz Review* 27 (2007): 141–79.

———. *Directiones ad rem medicam pertinentes*. Appendix 1 to Justin E. H. Smith, *Divine Machines: Leibniz and the Sciences of Life*, 286. Princeton, NJ: Princeton University Press, 2011.

———. *Lettres et opuscules inédits de Leibniz*. Edited by A. Foucher de Careil. Paris: Libraire Philosophique de Ladrange, 1854.

———. *Die philosophischen Schriften von G. W. Leibniz*. Edited by C. I. Gerhardt. 7 vols. Berlin, 1849–60.

Lemoine, Bertrand. "L'entreprise Eiffel." *Histoire, économie et société* 14, no. 2 (1995): 273–85.

Lindgren, Jim. "The Six Political Groups Least Likely to Believe That Astrology Is Scientific." *Washington Post*, February 20, 2014.

Lindstrom, Lamont. *Cargo Cult: Strange Stories of Desire from Melanesia and Beyond*. Honolulu: University of Hawai'i Press, 1993.

Lloyd, G.E.R. *Aristotle: The Growth and Structure of His Thought*. London: Cambridge University Press, 1968.

———. *The Ideals of Inquiry: An Ancient History*. Oxford: Oxford University Press, 2014.

Lönnrot, Elias. *Kalevala*. Helsinki: J. C. Frenckellin ja Poika, 1835.

Lucian of Samosata. *Lucian's True History*. Translated by Francis Hickes. London: A. H. Bullen, 1902.

———. *Thirty Conferences of the Dead: Diogenes and Pollux*. In *Lucian of Samosata*, translated and edited by William Tooke. 2 vols. London: Longman, Hurst, Rees, Orme, and Brown, 1820.

Lyotard, Jean-François. *The Postmodern Condition: A Report on Knowledge*. Manchester: Manchester University Press, 1979.

Machery, Edouard, and Luc Faucher. "Why Do We Think Racially? Culture, Evolution and Cognition." In *Categorization in Cognitive Science*, edited by Henri Cohen and Claire Lefebvre. Amsterdam: Elsevier, 2005.

MacLane, Mary. *I Await the Devil's Coming* (1902). In *Human Days: A Mary MacLane Reader*. Austin, TX: Petrarca Press, 2014.

Majidzadeh, Yusuf. "Lapis Lazuli and the Great Khorasan Road." *Paléorient*, 8, no. 1 (1982): 59–69.

Marinoff, Lou. *Therapy for the Sane: How Philosophy Can Change Your Life*. Argo-Navis, 2013.

McCloskey, Deirdre. *Bourgeois Equality: How Ideas, Not Capital or Institutions, Enriched the World*. Chicago: University of Chicago Press, 2016.

McDowell, John. *Mind and World*. Cambridge, MA: Harvard University Press, 1996 [1994].

Melamed, Yitzhak Y. "'Omnis determinatio est negatio'—Determination, Negation, and Self-Negation in Spinoza, Kant, and Hegel." In *Spinoza and German Idealism*, edited by Eckart Förster and Yitzhak Y. Melamed, 175–96. Cambridge: Cambridge University Press, 2012.

Melville, Herman. *The Confidence-Man: His Masquerade*, and *Billy Budd, Sailor*. London: Penguin, 2012 [1857].

Mercier, Hugo, and Dan Sperber. *The Enigma of Reason*. Cambridge, MA: Harvard University Press, 2017.

Merrill, James. *The Changing Light at Sandover*. New York: Knopf, 1982.

Merriman, Roger Bigelow, ed. *The Life and Letters of Thomas Cromwell: Letters from 1536*. Oxford: Clarendon Press, 1902.

Mintz, Sidney. *Sweetness and Power: The Place of Sugar in Modern History*. New York: Penguin Books, 1985.

Mishra, Pankaj. *Age of Anger: A History of the Present*. New York: Farrar, Straus and Giroux, 2017.

Murray, Les. *Poems the Size of Photographs*. Sydney: Duffy & Snellgrove, 2002.

Nabokov, Vladimir. "Conclusive Evidence." *New Yorker*, December 28, 1998–January 4, 1999, 124–33.

———. *Speak, Memory: An Autobiography Revisited*. New York: Vintage International, 1989 [1951].

Nagle, Angela. *Kill All Normies: Online Culture Wars from 4chan and Tumblr to Trump and the Alt-Right*. Winchester, UK: Zero Books, 2017.

Nesbitt, Nick. *Universal Emancipation: The Haitian Revolution and the Radical Enlightenment*. Charlottesville: University of Virginia Press, 2008.

Newman, William R. *Promethean Ambitions: Alchemy and the Quest to Perfect Nature*. Chicago: University of Chicago Press, 2004.

Niakan, Kathy. "Using CRISPR/Cas9-Mediated Genome Editing to Investigate Mechanisms of Lineage Specification in Human Embryos." Paper delivered at the conference "Les natures en questions," Collège de France, October 20, 2017.

Nichols, Tom. *The Death of Expertise: The Campaign against Knowledge and Why It Matters*. New York: Oxford University Press, 2017.

Nietzsche, Friedrich. *Philosophische Werke in sechs Bänden*. Hamburg: Felix Meiner Verlag, 2013.

Nowak, Holger, et al. *Lexikon zur Schlacht bei Jena und Auerstedt 1806. Personen, Ereignisse, Begriffe*. Jena: Städtische Museen, 2006.

Nozick, Robert. "Newcomb's Problem and Two Principles of Choice." In *Essays in Honor of Carl G. Hempel*, edited by Nicholas Rescher, 114–46. Dordrecht: Reidel, 1969.

Ohnuki-Tierney, Emiko. *Kamikaze, Cherry Blossoms, and Nationalisms: The Militarization of Aesthetics in Japanese History*. Chicago: University of Chicago Press, 2002.

Oka, Rahul, and Chapurukha M. Kusimba. "The Archaeology of Trading Systems, Part 1: Towards a New Trade Synthesis." *Journal of Archaeological Research* 16 (2008): 339–95.

Ong, Walter J. *Orality and Literacy: The Technologizing of the Word*. London: Taylor & Francis, 2002 [1982].

———. *Ramus, Method, and the Decay of Dialogue: From the Art of Discourse to the Art of Reason*. Cambridge, MA: Harvard University Press, 1958.

Pappus of Alexandria. *The Commentary of Pappus on Book X of Euclid's* Elements. Edited and translated by William Thomson. Cambridge, MA: Harvard University Press, 1930.

Pascal, Blaise. *Pensées de Blaise Pascal.* Edited by J.-M.-F. Frantin. 3rd ed. Paris: Lagny, 1870.

Pastoureau, Michel. *L'ours. Histoire d'un roi déchu.* Paris: Éditions du Seuil, 2007.

Patrikarakos, David. *War in 140 Characters: How Social Media Is Reshaping Conflict in the Twenty-First Century.* New York, Basic Books, 2017.

Paul, L. A. *Transformative Experience.* New York: Oxford University Press, 2014.

———. "What You Can't Expect When You're Expecting." *Res Philosophica* 92, no. 2 (2015): 1–23.

Perkins, Franklin. *Leibniz and China: A Commerce of Light.* Cambridge: Cambridge University Press, 2005.

Petrone, Karen. *The Great War in Russian Memory.* Bloomington: Indiana University Press, 2011.

Pigliucci, Massimo, and Maarten Boudry, eds. *Philosophy of Pseudoscience: Reconsidering the Demarcation Problem.* Chicago: University of Chicago Press, 2013.

Pinker, Steven. *Enlightenment Now: Reason, Science, Humanism, and Progress.* New York: Penguin Random House, 2018.

Plutarch. *De sollertia animalium.* Loeb Classical Library 12. Cambridge, MA: Harvard University Press, 1957.

Popper, Karl. "Philosophy of Science: A Personal Report." In *British Philosophy in Mid-Century,* edited by C. A. Mace, 155–91. Crows Nest, NSW: Allen and Unwin, 1951.

Porphyry. *Life of Plotinus.* In *The Essence of Plotinus: Extracts from the Six Enneads and Porphyry's* Life of Plotinus, edited by Grace H. Turnbull, translated by Stephen MacKenna. New York: Oxford University Press, 1934.

"Preaching on the Bible; Pulpit Opinions of the New Version." *New York Times,* May 23, 1881, 8.

Quine, W.V.O. "Two Dogmas of Empiricism" (1951). In W.V.O. Quine, *From a Logical Point of View,* 20–46. Cambridge, MA: Harvard University Press, 1953.

Ranke, Leopold von. *Geschichte der romanischen und germanischen Völker von 1494 bis 1514.* 3rd ed. Leipzig: Verlag von Duncker & Humblot, 1885 [1824].

"Relation de ce qui s'est passé de plus remarquable ... ès années 1670 et 1671, envoyé au Reverend Père Jean Pinette, Provincial de la Province De France." In *Relations des Jésuites, contenant ce qui s'est passé de plus remarquable dans les missions des pères de la Compagnie de Jésus dans la Nouvelle France,* vol. 3. Quebec City: Augustin Côté, 1858.

Riel, Louis. "Dissertation on Monads." Translated by Justin E. H. Smith. *Cabinet Magazine* 49 (2013): 26–27.

Rorario, Girolamo. *Hieronymi Rorarii ex legati pontificii, Quod animalia bruta ratione utantur melius homine.* Libri duo. Amsterdam: Apud Joannem Ravesteinium, 1654 [1555].

Rousseau, Jean-Jacques. *Discours sur l'origine et les fondements de l'inégalité parmi les hommes.* Amsterdam: Marc Michel Rey, 1762.

Sahlins, Marshall. "La Pensée Bourgeoise: Western Society as Culture." In *Culture and Practical Reason,* 166–204. Chicago: University of Chicago Press, 1976.

Sartre, Jean-Paul. *Being and Nothingness: A Phenomenological Essay on Ontology.* Translated by Hazel Barnes. New York: Washington Square Press, 1956 [1943].

———. Interview with *Actuel,* February 28, 1973.

———. *No Exit, and Three Other Plays*. New York: Vintage Books, 1955 [1944].

Saxo Grammaticus. *The First Nine Books of the Danish History of Saxo Grammaticus*. Translated by Oliver Elton. London: David Nutt, 1894.

Scott, James C. *Against the Grain: A Deep History of the Earliest States*. New Haven, CT: Yale University Press, 2017.

Setiya, Kieran. *Midlife: A Philosophical Guide*. Princeton, NJ: Princeton University Press, 2018.

Simon, Gustave. *Chez Victor Hugo. Procès-verbaux des tables tournantes de Jersey*. Paris: Louis Conard, 1923.

Smart, Christopher. *The Poetical Works of Christopher Smart*. Vol. 1, *Jubilate Agno*. Edited by Karina Williamson. Oxford: Clarendon Press, 1980.

Smith, Justin E. H. "The Art of Molting." *RES: Anthropology and Aesthetics* 67/68 (2016/17): 1–9.

———. "The Gravity of Satire: Offense and Violence after the Paris Attacks." The Pierre Bayle Lecture, Pierre Bayle Foundation, Rotterdam, The Netherlands, November 27, 2015.

———. "The Ibis and the Crocodile: Napoleon's Egyptian Campaign and Evolutionary Theory in France, 1801–1835." *Republic of Letters* 6, no. 1 (March 2018): 1–20.

———. "The Internet of Snails." *Cabinet Magazine* 58 (2016): 29–37.

———. *Nature, Human Nature, and Human Difference: Race in Early Modern Philosophy*. Princeton, NJ: Princeton University Press, 2015.

———. *The Philosopher: A History in Six Types*. Princeton, NJ: Princeton University Press, 2016.

Spera, Danielle. *Hermann Nitsch: Leben und Arbeit*. Vienna: Brandstätter, 2005.

Spinoza, Benedictus de. *The Collected Works of Spinoza*. Translated and edited by Edwin Curley. Princeton, NJ: Princeton University Press, 1985 (vol. 1), 2016 (vol. 2).

———. *Opera*. Edited by Carl Gebhardt. Heidelberg: Carl Winter Verlag, 1925.

Staal, Frits. *Ritual and Mantras: Rules without Meaning*. New York: Peter Lang, 1990.

Staël, Germaine de. *De la littérature, considérée dans ses rapports avec les institutions sociales*. In *Oeuvres complètes de Madame de Staël, publiées par son fils*, vol. 4. Brussels: Louis Hauman et Co., 1830.

Sternhell, Zeev. *Les anti-Lumières. Une tradition du XVIIIe siècle à la guerre froide*. Paris: Fayard, 2006. English edition: *The Anti-Enlightenment Tradition*. Translated by David Maisel. New Haven, CT: Yale University Press, 2009.

Suárez, Francisco. *Opera omnia*. Edited by Charles Berton. 28 vols. Paris: Apud Ludovicum Vivès, 1856–78.

Suskind, Ron. "Faith, Certainty, and the Presidency of George W. Bush." *New York Times Magazine*, October 17, 2004.

Terence. *Heautontimouremos: The Self-Tormentor*. In *The Comedies of Terence*, edited and translated by Henry Thomas Riley, 139. New York: Harper and Brothers, 1859.

Tertullian. *Tertullian's Treatise on the Incarnation*. Edited and translated by Ernest Evans. Eugene, OR: Wipf and Stock, 1956.

Tolstoy, L. N. *Smert' Ivana Il'icha*. Saint Petersburg, 1886.

Trigger, Bruce. *The Children of Aataentsic: A History of the Huron People to 1660*. Montreal: McGill-Queens University Press, 1987.

Trollinger, Susan L., and William Vance Trollinger, Jr. *Righting America at the Creation Museum*. Baltimore: Johns Hopkins University Press, 2016.

Tufekci, Zeynep. *Twitter and Tear Gas: The Power and Fragility of Networked Protest*. New Haven, CT: Yale University Press, 2017.

Tuvel, Rebecca. "In Defense of Transracialism." *Hypatia: A Journal of Feminist Philosophy* 32, no. 2 (2017): 263–78.

Vauchez, André. *Francis of Assisi: The Life and Afterlife of a Medieval Saint*. Translated by Michael F. Cusato. New Haven, CT: Yale University Press, 2013.

Verne, Jules. *De la terre à la lune. Trajet direct en 97 heures 20 minutes*. Paris: Bibliothèque d'éducation et de récréation, 1872 [1865].

Vico, Giambattista. *The New Science of Giambattista Vico*. Unabridged translation of the third edition (1744) with the addition of "Practic of the New Science." Edited and translated by Thomas Goddard Bergin and Max Harold Fisch. Ithaca, NY: Cornell University Press, 1948.

Walker, D. P. *The Ancient Theology*. Ithaca, NY: Cornell University Press, 1972.

Warner, Marina. *Stranger Magic: Charmed States and the Arabian Nights*. Cambridge, MA: Harvard University Press, 2012.

Wertheim, Margaret. *Physics on the Fringe: Smoke Rings, Circlons, and Alternative Theories of Everything*. New York: Bloomsbury, 2011.

Whitman, Walt. *Walt Whitman: Selected Poems, 1855–1892*. Edited by Gary Schmidgall. New York: Stonewall Inn Editions, 1999.

Winroth, Anders. *The Conversion of Scandinavia: Vikings, Merchants, and Missionaries in the Remaking of Northern Europe*. New Haven, CT: Yale University Press, 2012.

Wittgenstein, Ludwig. *Tractatus Logico-Philosophicus*. Translated by C. K. Ogden, London: Kegan Paul, Trench and Trübner, 1922.

Wolpert, David H., and Gregory Benford. "The Lesson of Newcomb's Paradox." *Synthese* 190, no. 9 (2013): 1637–46.

Woolf, Virginia. *Virginia Woolf: Selected Short Stories*. Edited by Sandra Kemp. London: Penguin Classics, 1993 [1929].

Worley, Peter. *The Trumpet Shall Sound: A Study of 'Cargo Cults' in Melanesia*. New York: Schocken Books, 1957.

Yahya, Harun. *Atlas of Creation*. Istanbul: Global Kitap, 2006. Translation of Harun Yahya, *Yaratılış Atlası*. Istanbul: Global Kitap, 2006.

Yates, Frances. *Giordano Bruno and the Hermetic Tradition*. London: Routledge, 1964.

Yeats, William Butler. *The Winding Stair and Other Poems*. New York: Macmillan and Co., 1933.

Yeo, Richard. *Defining Science: William Whewell, Natural Knowledge, and Public Debate in Early Victorian Britain*. Cambridge: Cambridge University Press, 1993.

Zhdanov, A. A. *On Literature, Music, and Philosophy*. New York: Lawrence and Wishart, 1950.

Zoshchenko, Mikhail. *Prikliucheniia obez'iany*. Moscow: Eksmo, 2017 [1945].

Online Resources

For the complete URL, please see endnotes.

Aslamova, Dar'ia. "Zhan-Mari le Pen—'KP': Nam nuzhna edinaia Evropa ot Parizha do Vladivostoka." *Komsomol'skaya Pravda*, January 15, 2015.

Atwood, Margaret. "Am I a Bad Feminist?" *Globe and Mail*, January 14, 2018.

Bingham, John. "How Teenage Pregnancy Collapsed after Birth of Social Media." *Telegraph*, March 9, 2016.

Bissell, Tom. "Who's Laughing Now? The Tragicomedy of Donald Trump on *Saturday Night Live*." *Harper's Magazine*, October 2017.

Bokhari, Allum, and Milo Yiannopoulos. "An Establishment Conservative's Guide to the Alt-Right." *Breitbart News*, March 29, 2016.

Brinkbäumer, Klaus, Julia Amalia Heyer, and Britta Sandberg. "Interview with Emmanuel Macron: 'We Need to Develop Political Heroism.'" *Der Spiegel Online*, October 13, 2017.

Cohen, Eliot A. "Two Wounded Warriors." *Atlantic*, October 22, 2017.

Dawkins, Richard. "Venomous Snakes, Slippery Eels and Harun Yahya." Website of the Richard Dawkins Foundation, accessed 2006 (since removed).

"Donald Trump: The Howard Stern Interviews, 1993–2015." *Factbase*.

Dupont, Gaëlle. "Pour La Manif pour tous, 'c'est le moment de se faire entendre.'" *Le Monde*, October 15, 2016.

"En prison, Breivik se dit 'torturé' et réclame une Playstation 3." *Le Monde* with Agence France Presse, February 14, 2014.

Fisher, Mark. "Exiting the Vampire Castle." *North Star*, November 22, 2013.

Franzen, Jonathan. "Is It Too Late to Save the World?" *Guardian*, November 4, 2017.

Gais, Hannah. "How Putin Is Making Greece's Nazi Problem Worse." *Business Insider*, March 26, 2015.

Gessen, Masha. "Russian Interference in the 2016 Election: A Cacophony, Not a Conspiracy." *New Yorker*, November 3, 2017.

Goldberg, Jonah. "Cheese-Eating Surrender Monkeys from Hell." *National Review Online*, April 16, 1999.

Haidt, Jonathan. "The Age of Outrage: What the Current Political Climate Is Doing to Our Country and Our Universities." *City Journal*, December 17, 2017.

Heer, Jeet (@heerjeet), Tweet dated December 20, 2017.

Heim, Joe. "Recounting a Day of Rage, Hate, Violence, and Death." *Washington Post*, August 14, 2017.

Herman, Judith L., and Robert Jay Lifton. Letter to the Editor. *New York Times*, March 8, 2017.

Herzog, Rudolph. "Laughing All the Way to Autocracy." *Foreign Policy*, February 8, 2017.

Hess, Amanda. "How Astrology Took Over the Internet." *New York Times*, January 1, 2018.

Jackson, Molly. "Are Open Carry Protesters Fueling Fear outside a Texas Mosque?" *Christian Science Monitor*, November 22, 2015.

Jones, Sam, Kerin Hope, and Courtney Weaver. "Alarm Bells Ring over Syriza's Russian Links." *Financial Times*, January 28, 2015.

Kestenbaum, Sam. "Got Nazis? Milk Is New Symbol of Racial Purity for White Nationalists." *Forward*, February 13, 2017.

Kisselgoff, Anna. "Pina Bausch Dance: Key Is Emotion." *New York Times*, October 4, 1985.

Lehman, Joseph. "A Brief Explanation of the Overton Window." Mackinac Center for Public Policy.

Lewis, Paul. "'Our Minds Can Be Hijacked': The Tech Insiders Who Fear a Smartphone Dystopia." *Guardian*, October 6, 2017.

Malcolm, Derek. "Krzysztof Kieslowski—Obituary." *Guardian*, March 14, 1996.

Marshall, Francesca. "PC Criticised for Warning 'Feminine Care' Supermarket Signs Are Sexist." *Telegraph*, August 13, 2017.

Marshall, Richard. "Why You Don't Need Brain Surgery to Change Logic" (interview with Hartry Field). *3:AM Magazine*, May 3, 2018.

Maysh, Jeff. "Why One Woman Pretended to Be a High-School Cheerleader." *Atlantic*, July 6, 2016.

McCarthy, Tom. "The Edge of Reason: The World's Boldest Climb and the Man Who Conquered It." *Guardian*, September 10, 2017.

McGrogan, Manus. "Charlie Hebdo: The Poverty of Satire." *Jacobin Magazine*, January 7, 2017.

McPhate, Mike. "California Today: An 'Incomprehensible' Climb in Yosemite." *New York Times*, June 6, 2017.

Meier, Barry. "Inside a Secretive Group Where Women Are Branded." *New York Times*, October 17, 2017.

Meza, Summer. "Jenna Abrams, Alt-Right Hero on Twitter, Was Really a Russian Troll Who Tricked Republicans and Celebrities." *Newsweek*, November 3, 2017.

Nussbaum, Emily. "How Jokes Won the Election." *New Yorker*, January 23, 2017.

Selby, W. Gardner. "Michele Bachmann Didn't Say Bible Written in English." *Politifact*, December 23, 2014.

Sprague, David. "Sex Pistols Flip Off Hall of Fame." *Rolling Stone*, February 24, 2006.

"Syllabus on Sex and Gender Differences: How to Disprove Sexist Science." At librarycard.org, August 14, 2017.

"The Tea Party & the Circus—Final Healthcare Reform Protest," particularly 5:18–5:54, published on YouTube March 18, 2010.

Tempey, Nathan. "Cops Arrest Subway Riders for 'Manspreading.'" *Gothamist*, May 28, 2015.

Thiel, Peter. "The Education of a Libertarian." *Cato Unbound: A Journal of Debate*, April 13, 2009.

"Thomas Piketty refuse la Légion d'honneur." *Le Monde*, January 1, 2015.

Trees, Hannah. "Normalizing Pronoun-Sharing at Philosophy Conferences." *Blog of the APA*, March 20, 2018.

Trump, Donald J. (@realdonaldtrump). Tweet dated March 28, 2014.

"Trump Praises Macron, Considers July 4 Military Parade Like One He Saw in Paris." *Reuters*, September 18, 2017.

Weinberger, Eliot. "Charlie, encore une fois . . ." *LRB blog*, April 28, 2015.

INDEX

➤➤➤➤➤